FAIRY TAIL

52

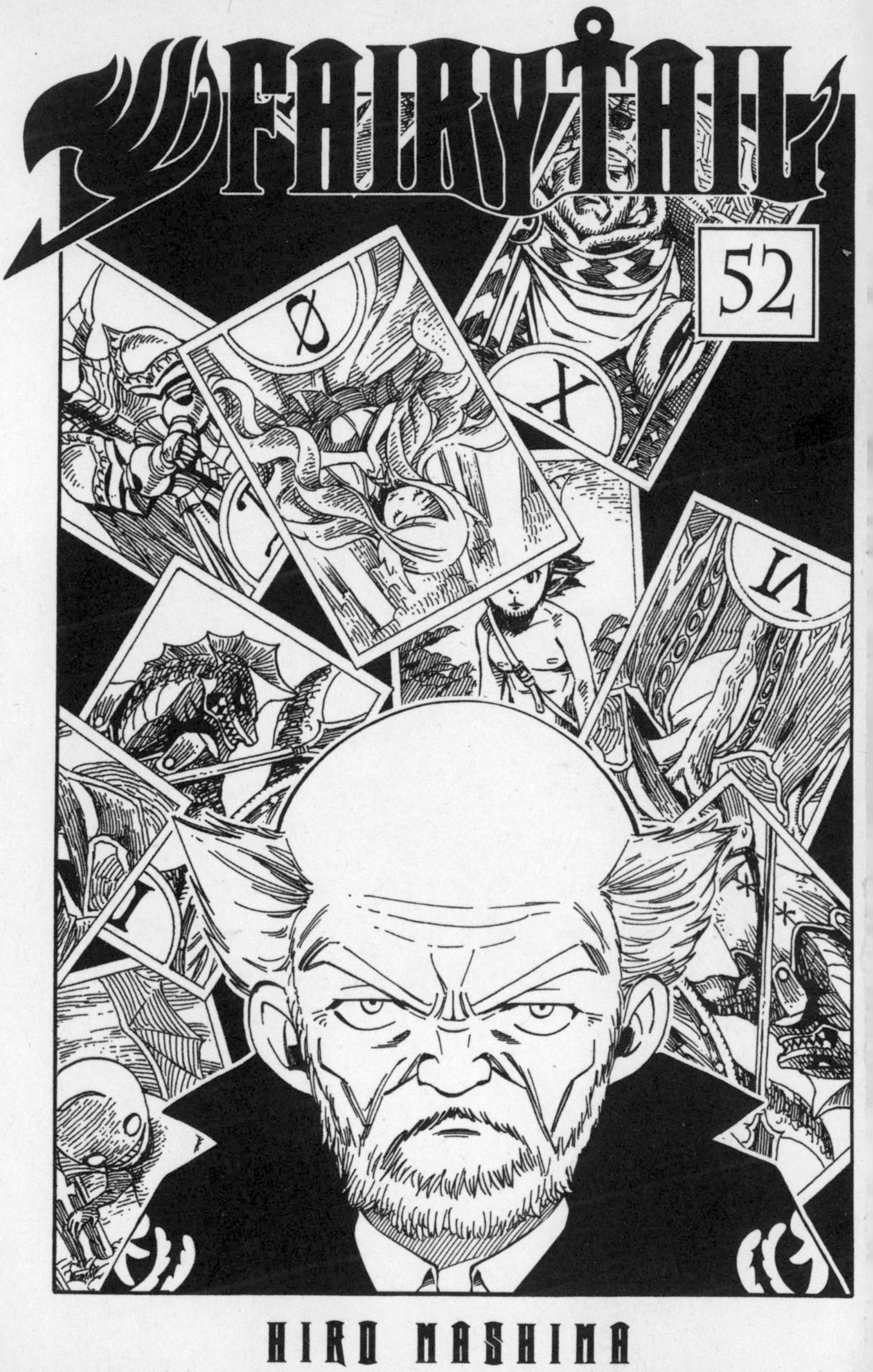

HIRO MASHIMA

FAIRYTAIL 52 CONTENTS

FAIRY TAIL

フェアリーテイル

Chapter 439: The Albareth Empire

Elma

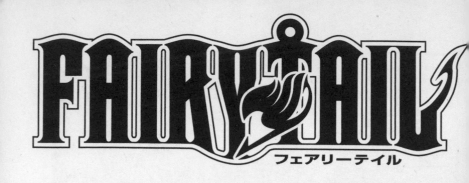

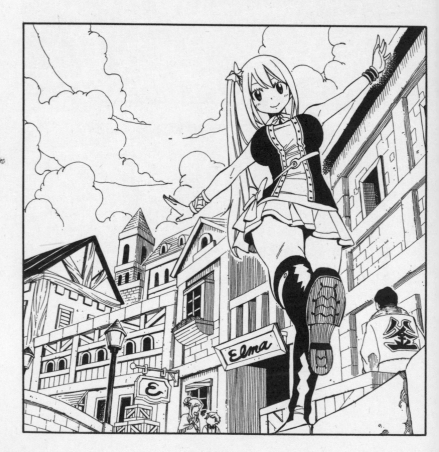

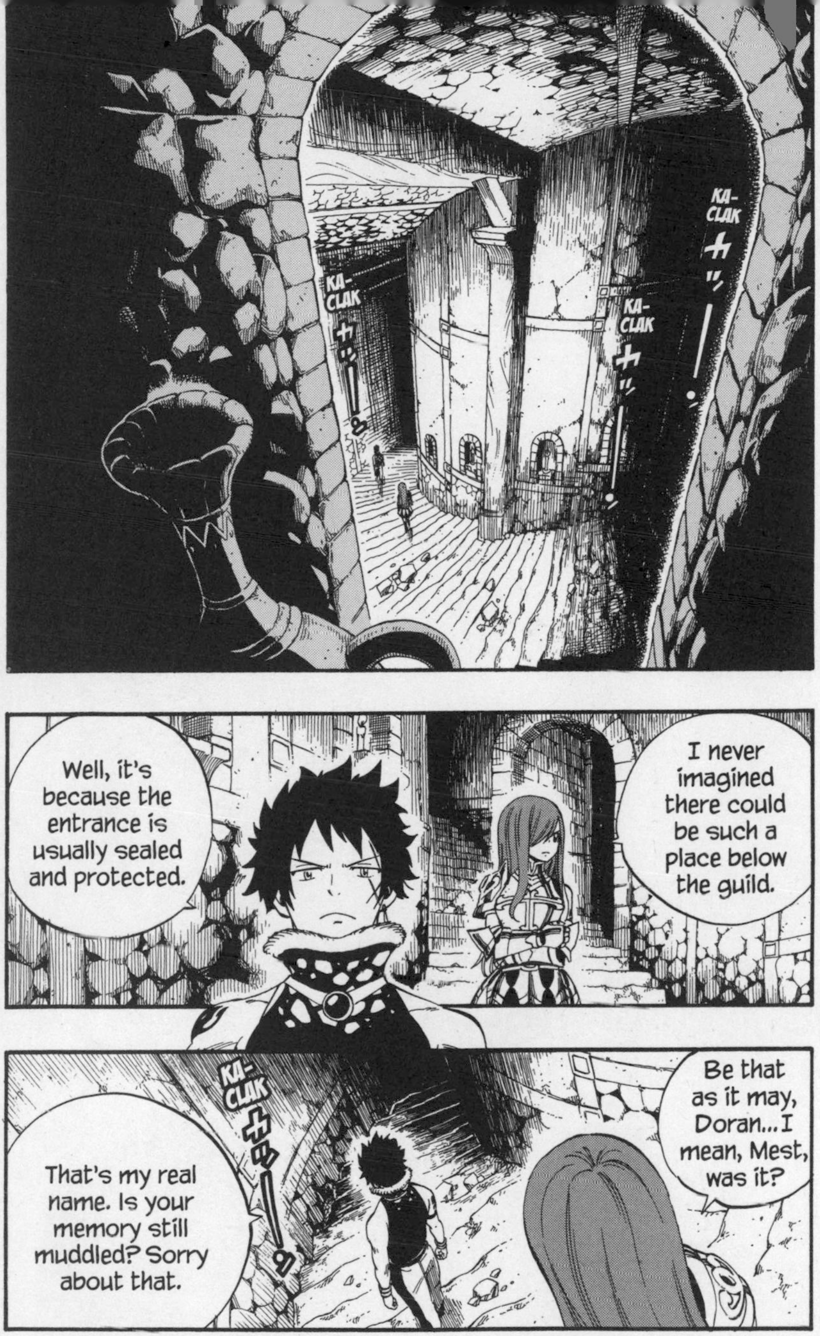
KA-CLAK
KA-CLAK
KA-CLAK
I never imagined there could be such a place below the guild.
Well, it's because the entrance is usually sealed and protected.
Be that as it may, Doran...I mean, Mest, was it?
KA-CLAK
That's my real name. Is your memory still muddled? Sorry about that.

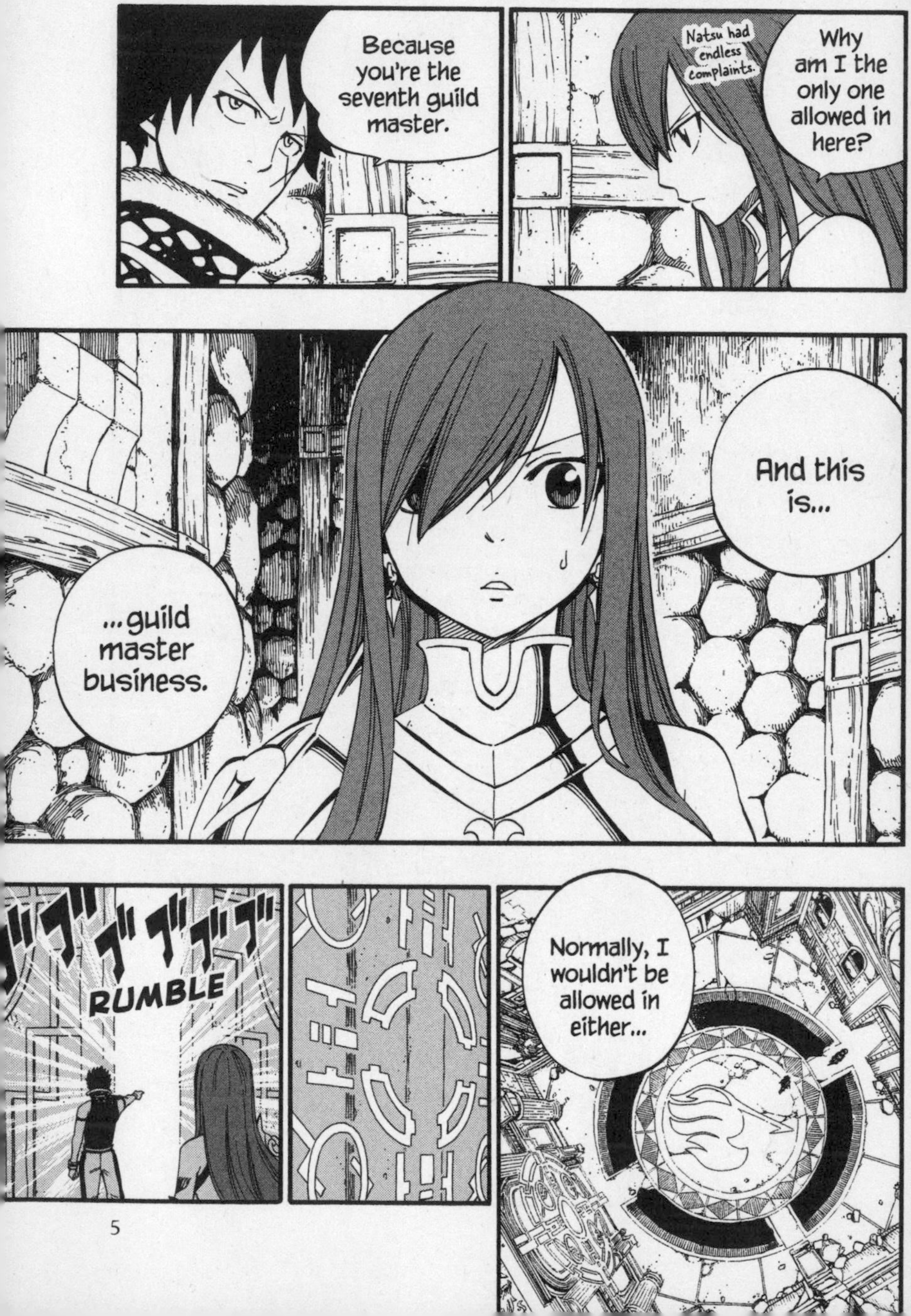
Why am I the only one allowed in here?
Natsu had endless complaints.
Because you're the seventh guild master.
And this is...
...guild master business.
Normally, I wouldn't be allowed in either...
RUMBLE

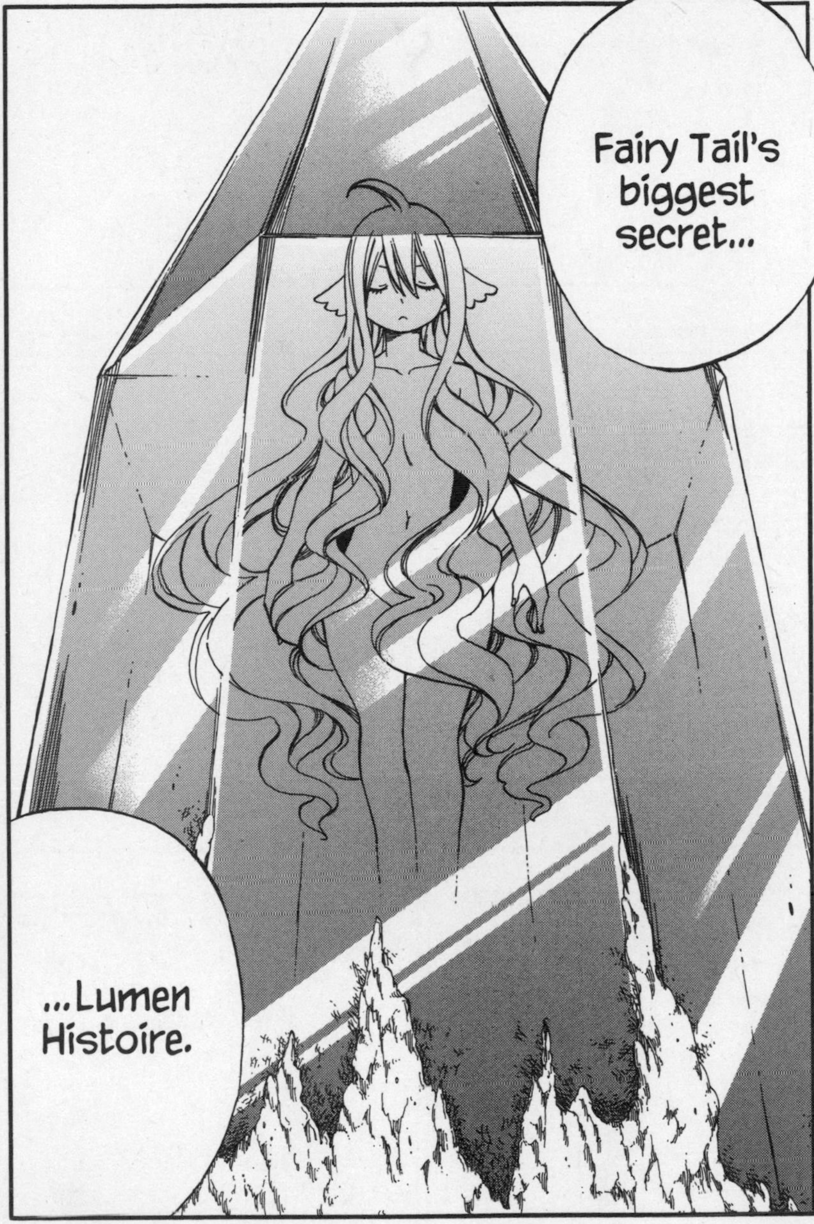
Fairy Tail's biggest secret...
...Lumen Histoire.

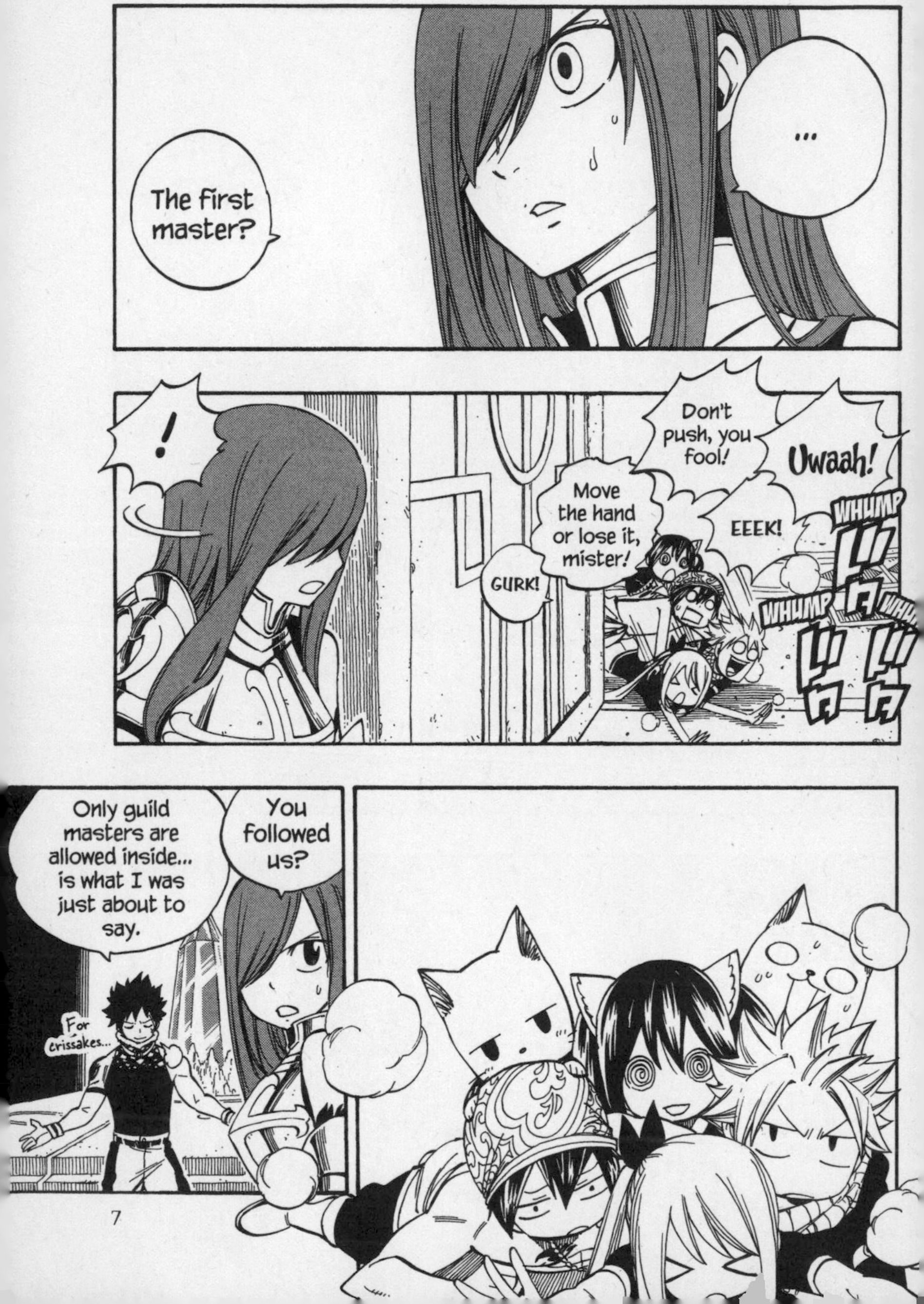
...
The first master?
Uwaah!
Don't push, you fool!
EEEK!
Move the hand or lose it, mister!
GURK!
WHUMP
WHUMP
WHUMP
!
You followed us?
Only guild masters are allowed inside... is what I was just about to say.
For crissakes...

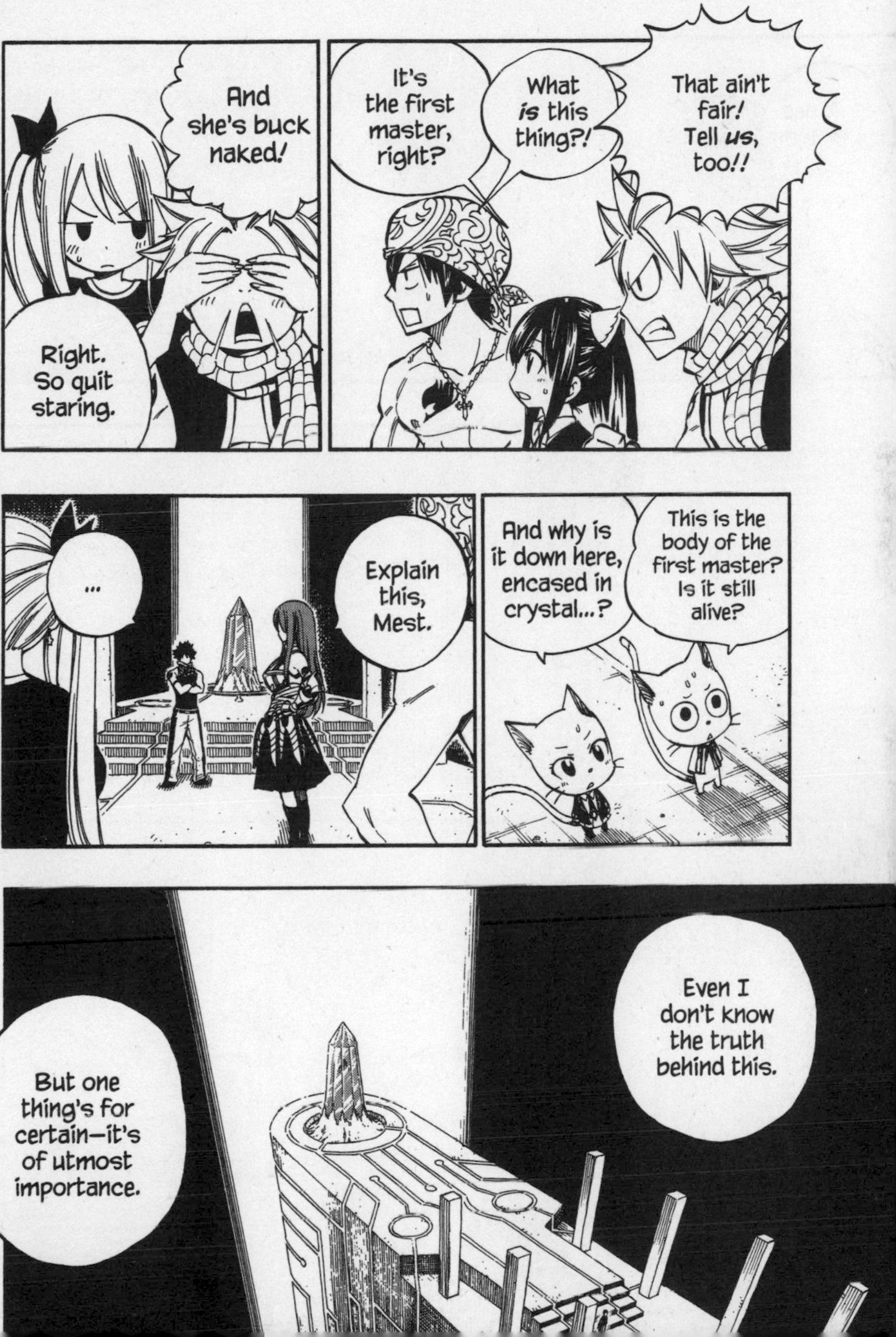
That ain't fair! Tell *us*, too!!
What *is* this thing?!
It's the first master, right?
And she's buck naked!
Right. So quit staring.
This is the body of the first master? Is it still alive?
And why is it down here, encased in crystal...?
Explain this, Mest.
...
Even I don't know the truth behind this.
But one thing's for certain—it's of utmost importance.

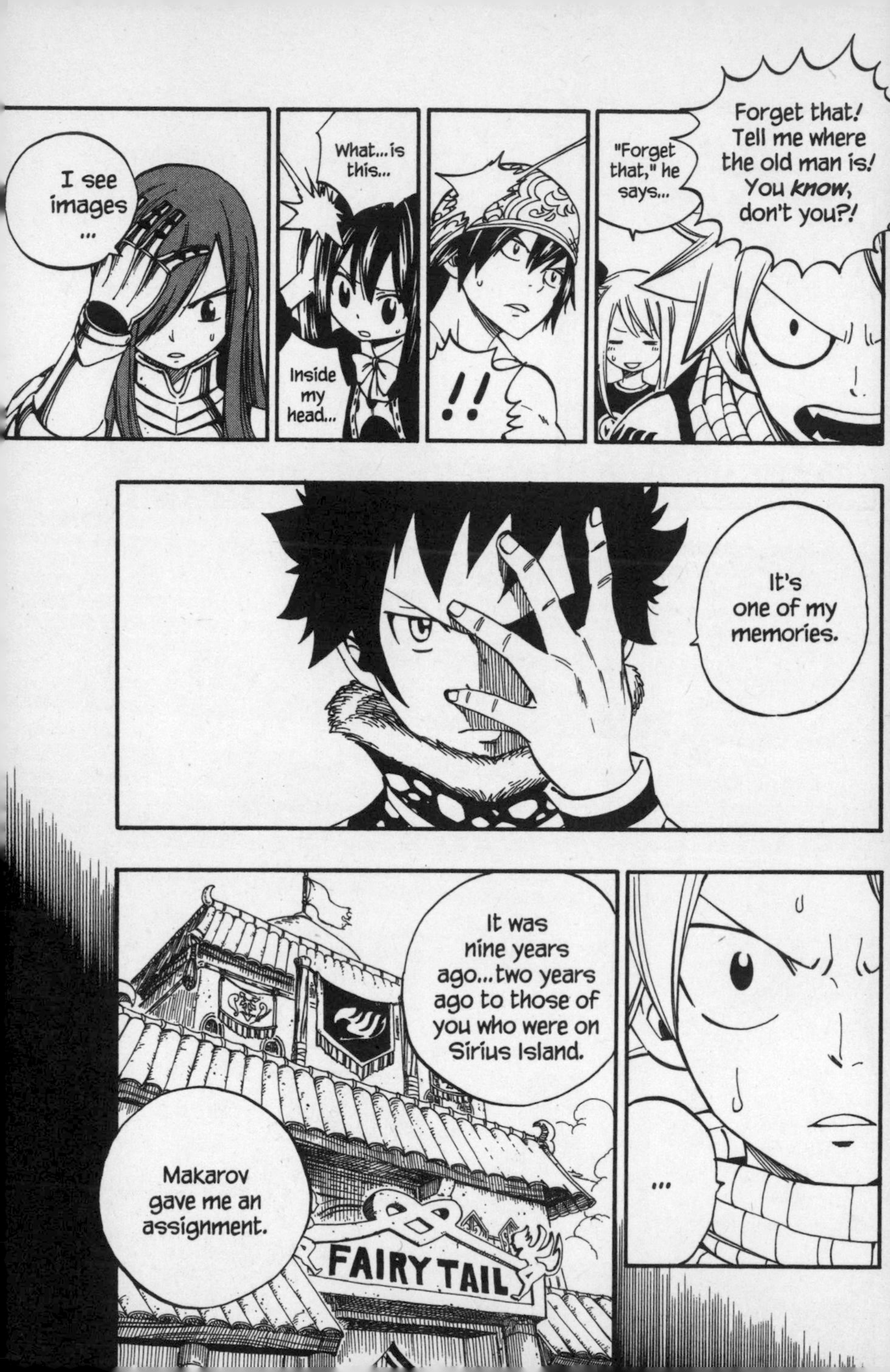
Forget that! Tell me where the old man is! You *know*, don't you?!
"Forget that," he says...
!!
What...is this...
Inside my head...
I see images ...
It's one of my memories.
...
It was nine years ago...two years ago to those of you who were on Sirius Island.
Makarov gave me an assignment.
FAIRY TAIL

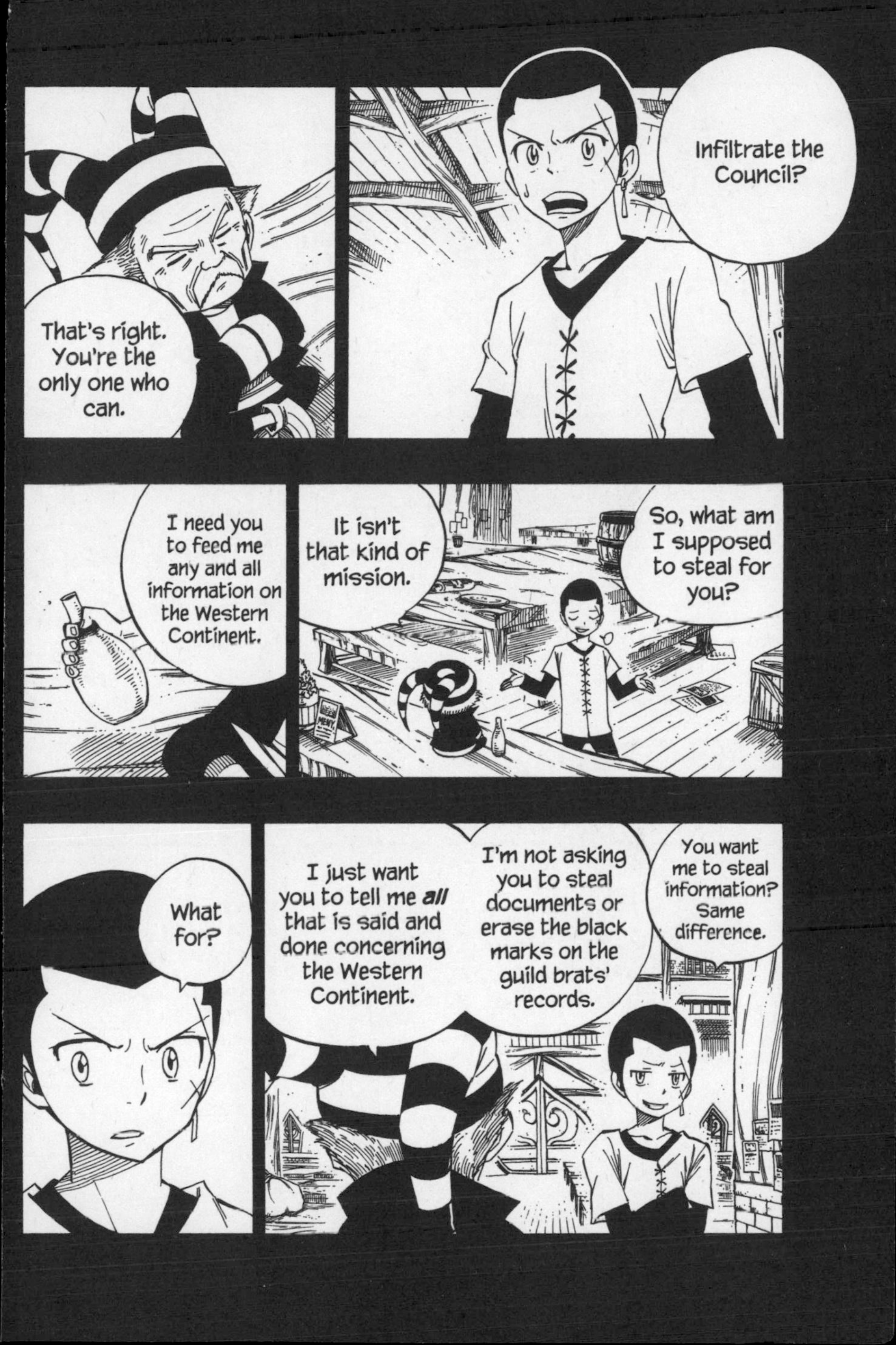
Infiltrate the Council?
That's right. You're the only one who can.
So, what am I supposed to steal for you?
It isn't that kind of mission.
I need you to feed me any and all information on the Western Continent.
You want me to steal information? Same difference.
I'm not asking you to steal documents or erase the black marks on the guild brats' records.
I just want you to tell me *all* that is said and done concerning the Western Continent.
What for?

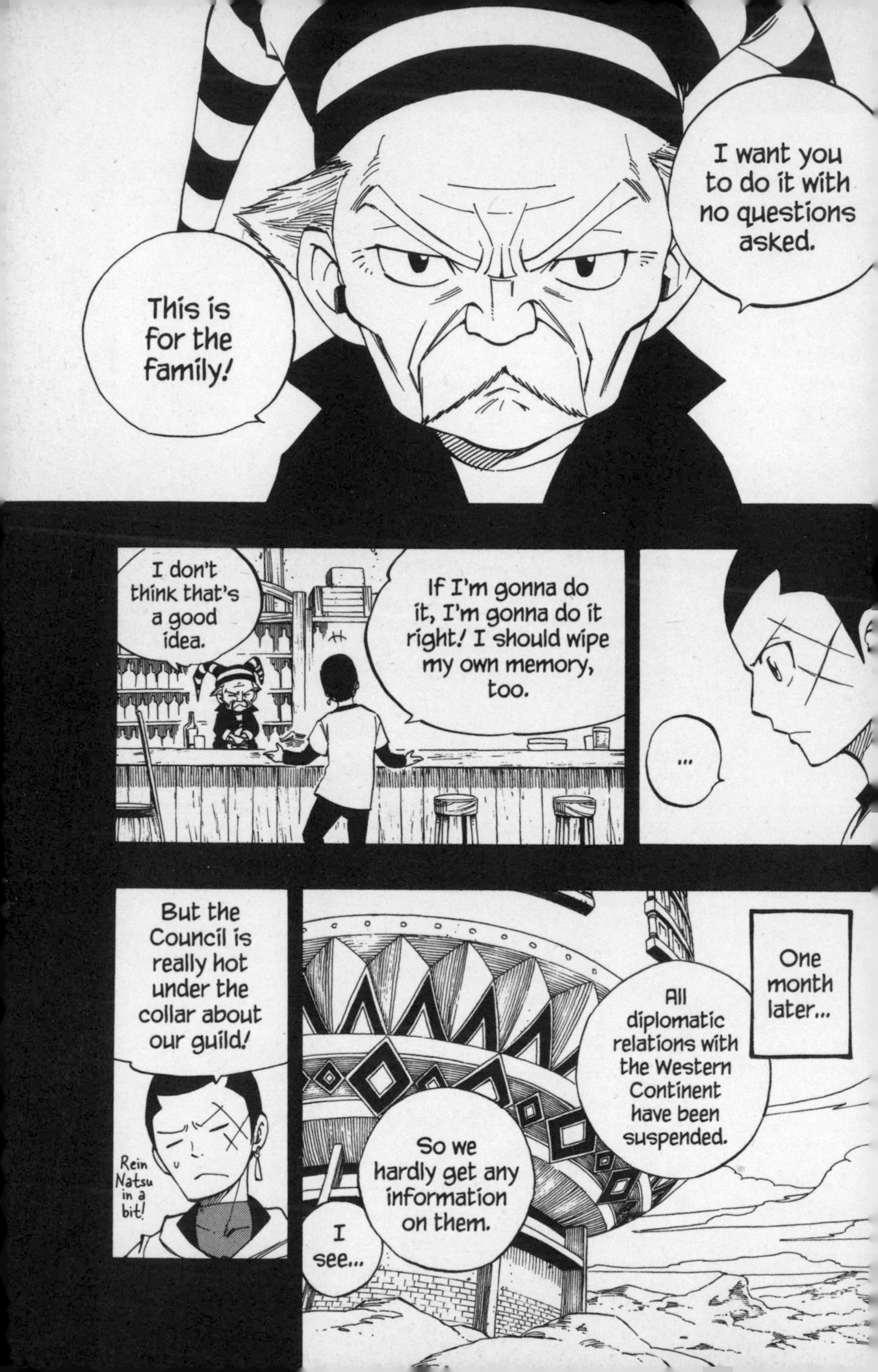
I want you to do it with no questions asked.
This is for the family!
...
If I'm gonna do it, I'm gonna do it right! I should wipe my own memory, too.
I don't think that's a good idea.
One month later...
All diplomatic relations with the Western Continent have been suspended.
So we hardly get any information on them.
I see...
But the Council is really hot under the collar about our guild!
Rein Natsu in a bit!

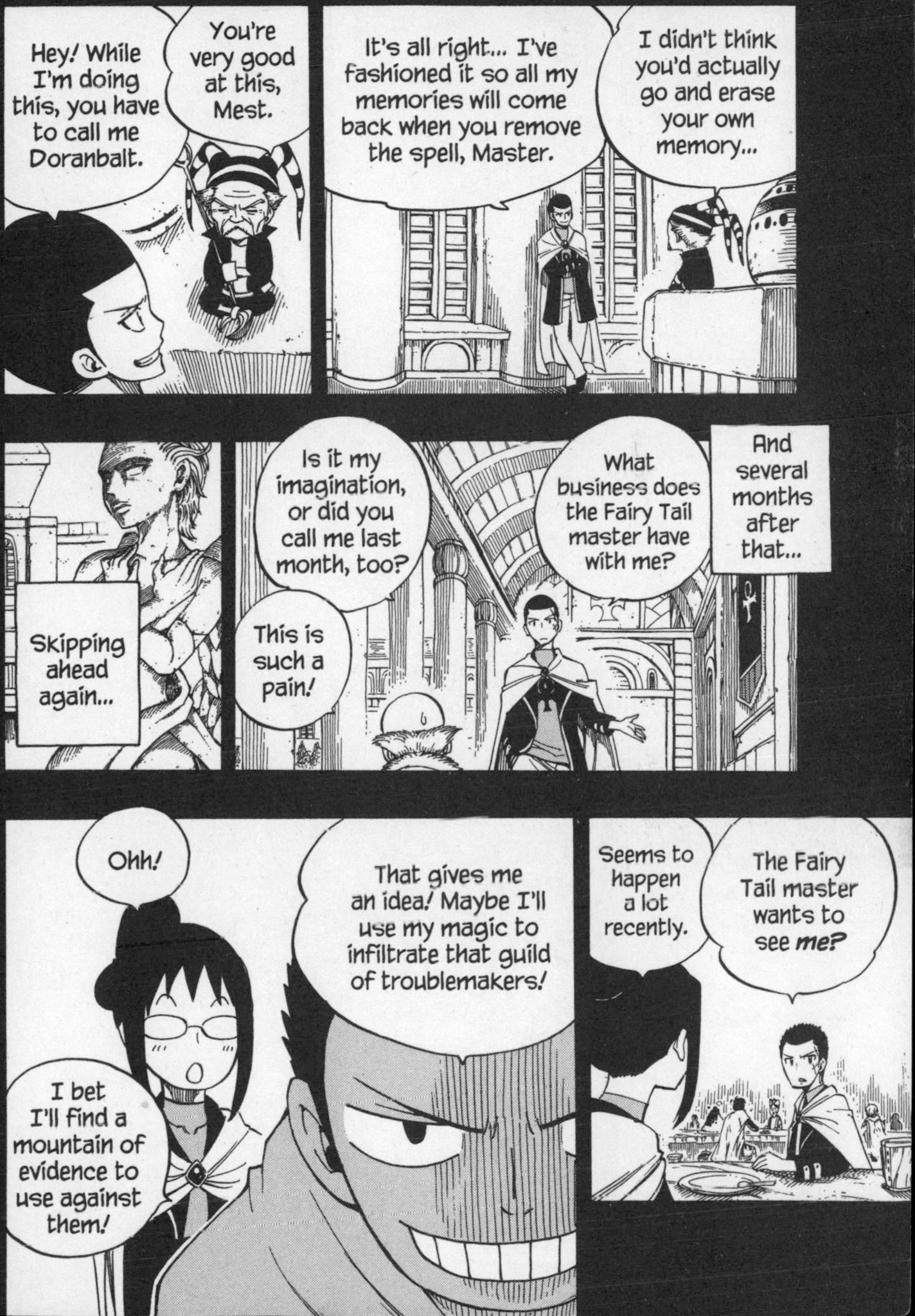
I didn't think you'd actually go and erase your own memory...
It's all right... I've fashioned it so all my memories will come back when you remove the spell, Master.
You're very good at this, Mest.
Hey! While I'm doing this, you have to call me Doranbalt.
And several months after that...
What business does the Fairy Tail master have with me?
Is it my imagination, or did you call me last month, too?
This is such a pain!
Skipping ahead again...
The Fairy Tail master wants to see *me?*
Seems to happen a lot recently.
That gives me an idea! Maybe I'll use my magic to infiltrate that guild of troublemakers!
Ohh!
I bet I'll find a mountain of evidence to use against them!

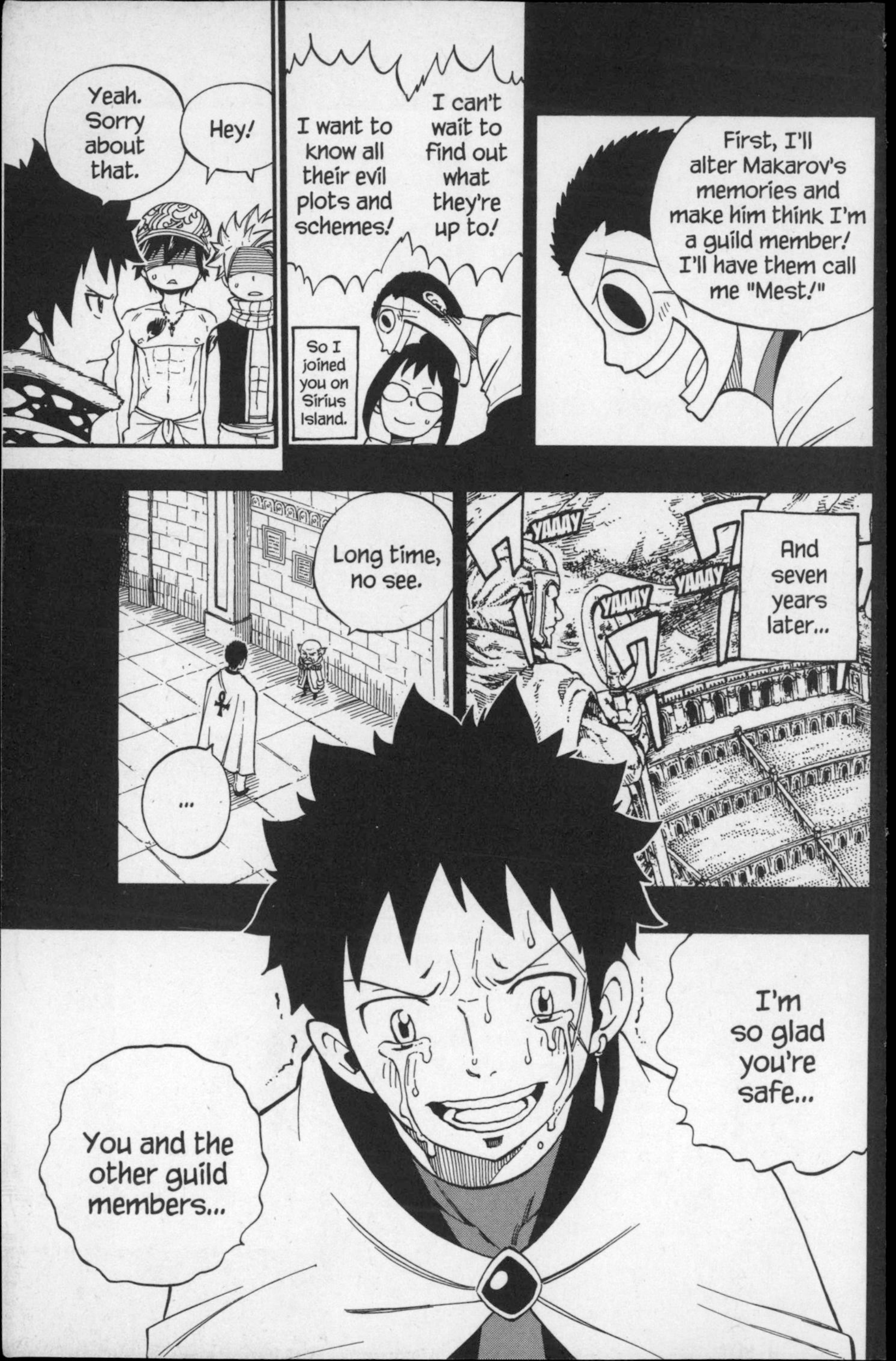
First, I'll alter Makarov's memories and make him think I'm a guild member! I'll have them call me "Mest!"
I can't wait to find out what they're up to!
I want to know all their evil plots and schemes!
So I joined you on Sirius Island.
Hey!
Yeah. Sorry about that.
And seven years later...
YAAAY
YAAAY
YAAAY
Long time, no see.
...
I'm so glad you're safe...
You and the other guild members...

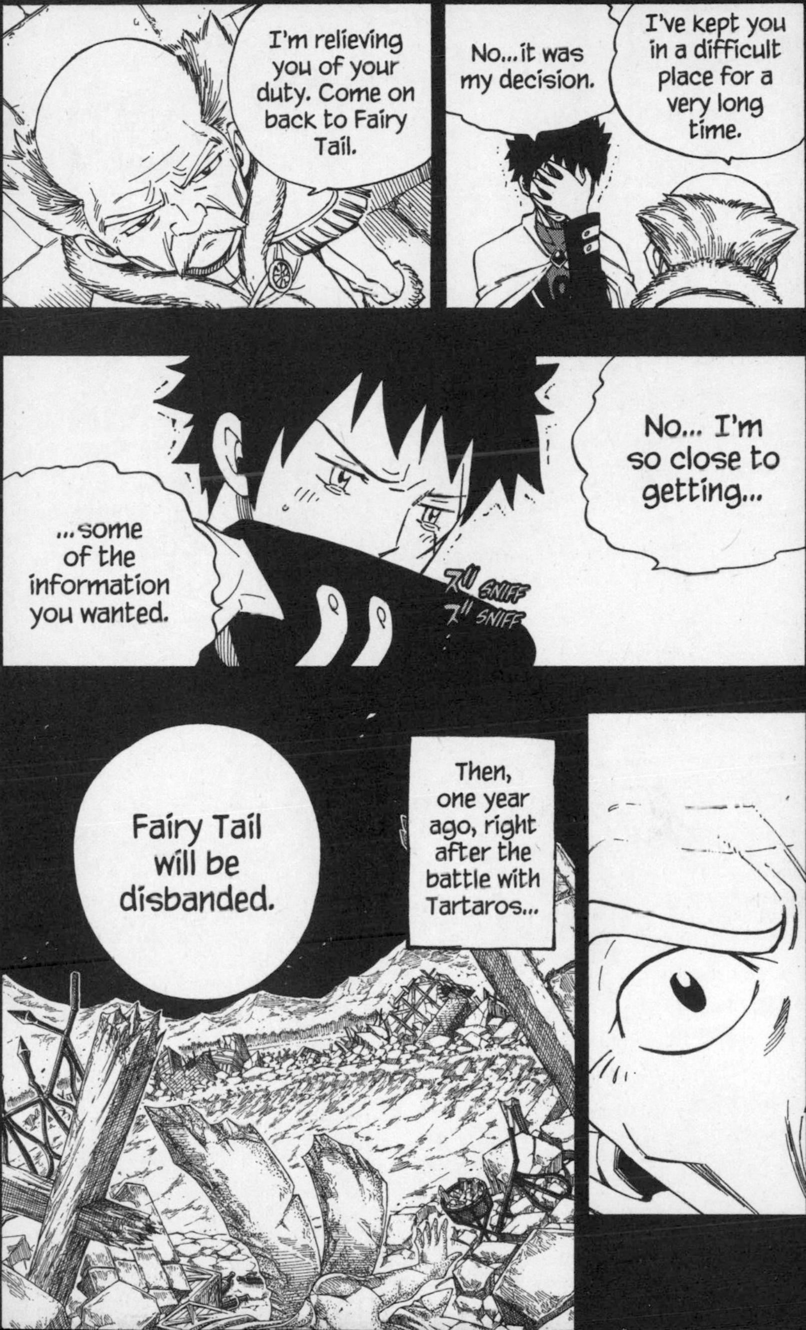
I've kept you in a difficult place for a very long time.
No...it was my decision.
I'm relieving you of your duty. Come on back to Fairy Tail.
No... I'm so close to getting...
...some of the information you wanted.
SNIFF
SNIFF
Then, one year ago, right after the battle with Tartaros...
Fairy Tail will be disbanded.

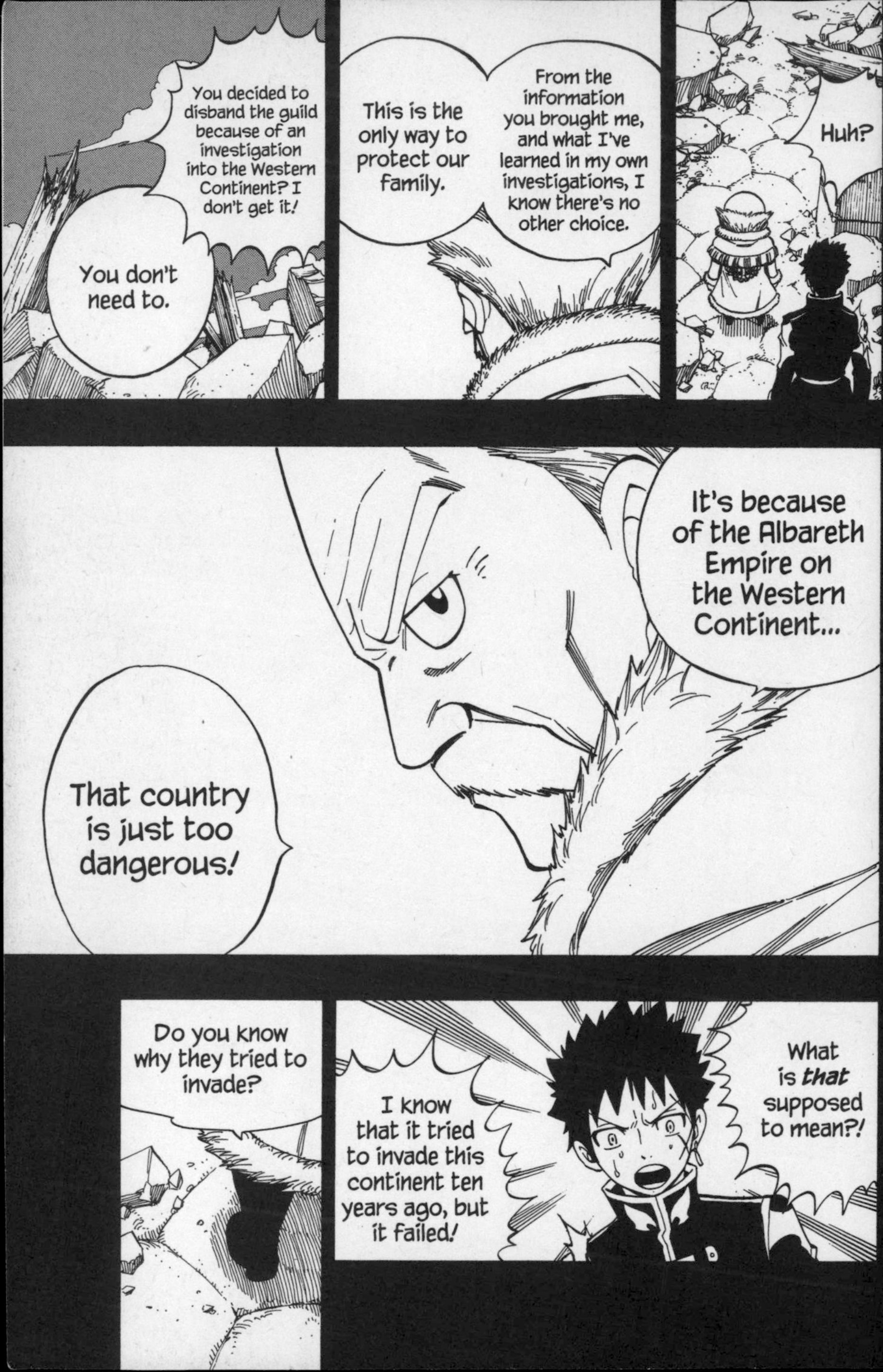
Huh?
From the information you brought me, and what I've learned in my own investigations, I know there's no other choice.
This is the only way to protect our family.
You decided to disband the guild because of an investigation into the Western Continent? I don't get it!
You don't need to.
It's because of the Albareth Empire on the Western Continent...
That country is just too dangerous!
What is *that* supposed to mean?!
I know that it tried to invade this continent ten years ago, but it failed!
Do you know why they tried to invade?

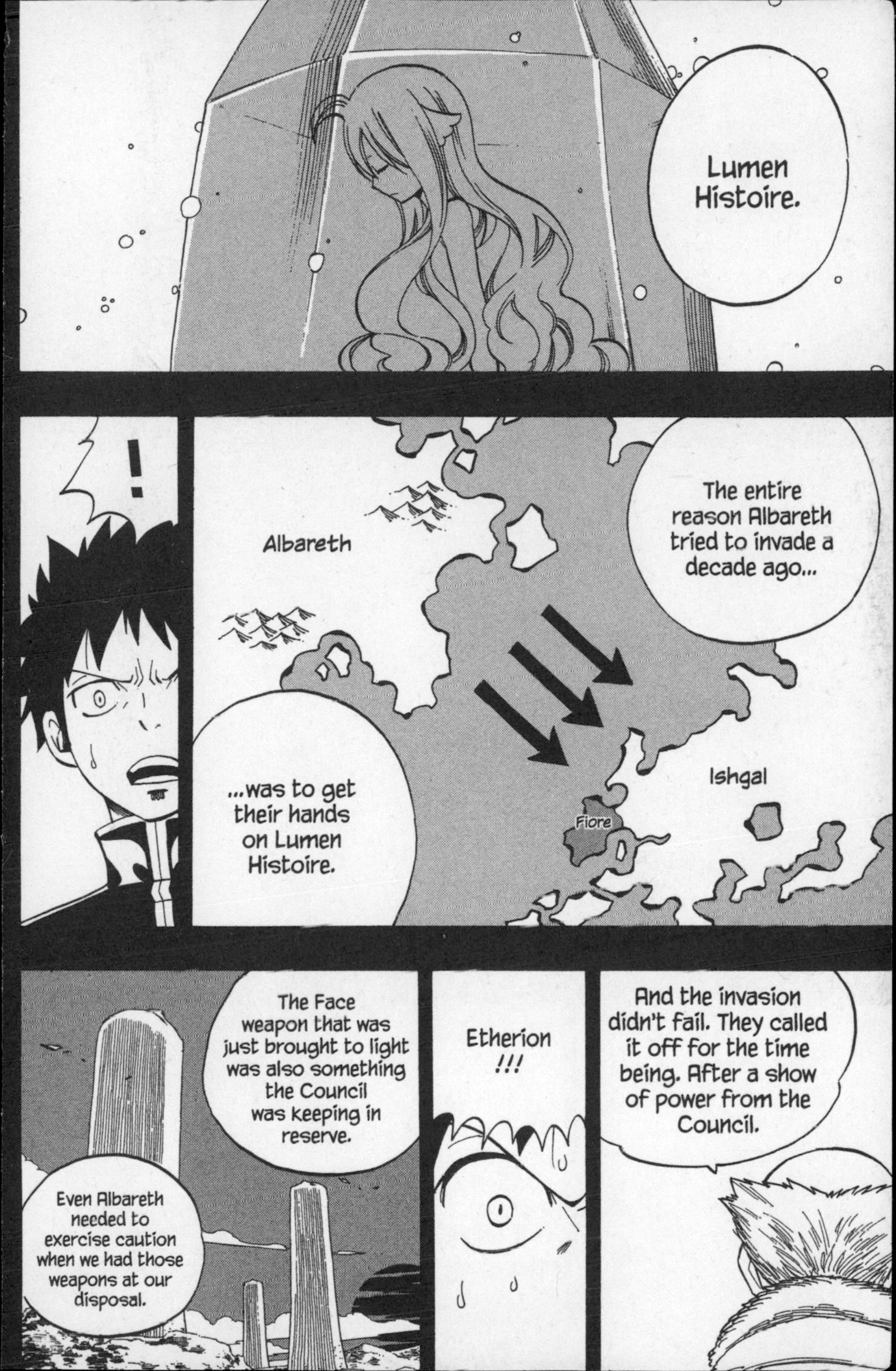
Lumen Histoire.
The entire reason Albareth tried to invade a decade ago...
Albareth
Ishgal
Fiore
...was to get their hands on Lumen Histoire.
!
And the invasion didn't fail. They called it off for the time being. After a show of power from the Council.
Etherion !!!
The Face weapon that was just brought to light was also something the Council was keeping in reserve.
Even Albareth needed to exercise caution when we had those weapons at our disposal.

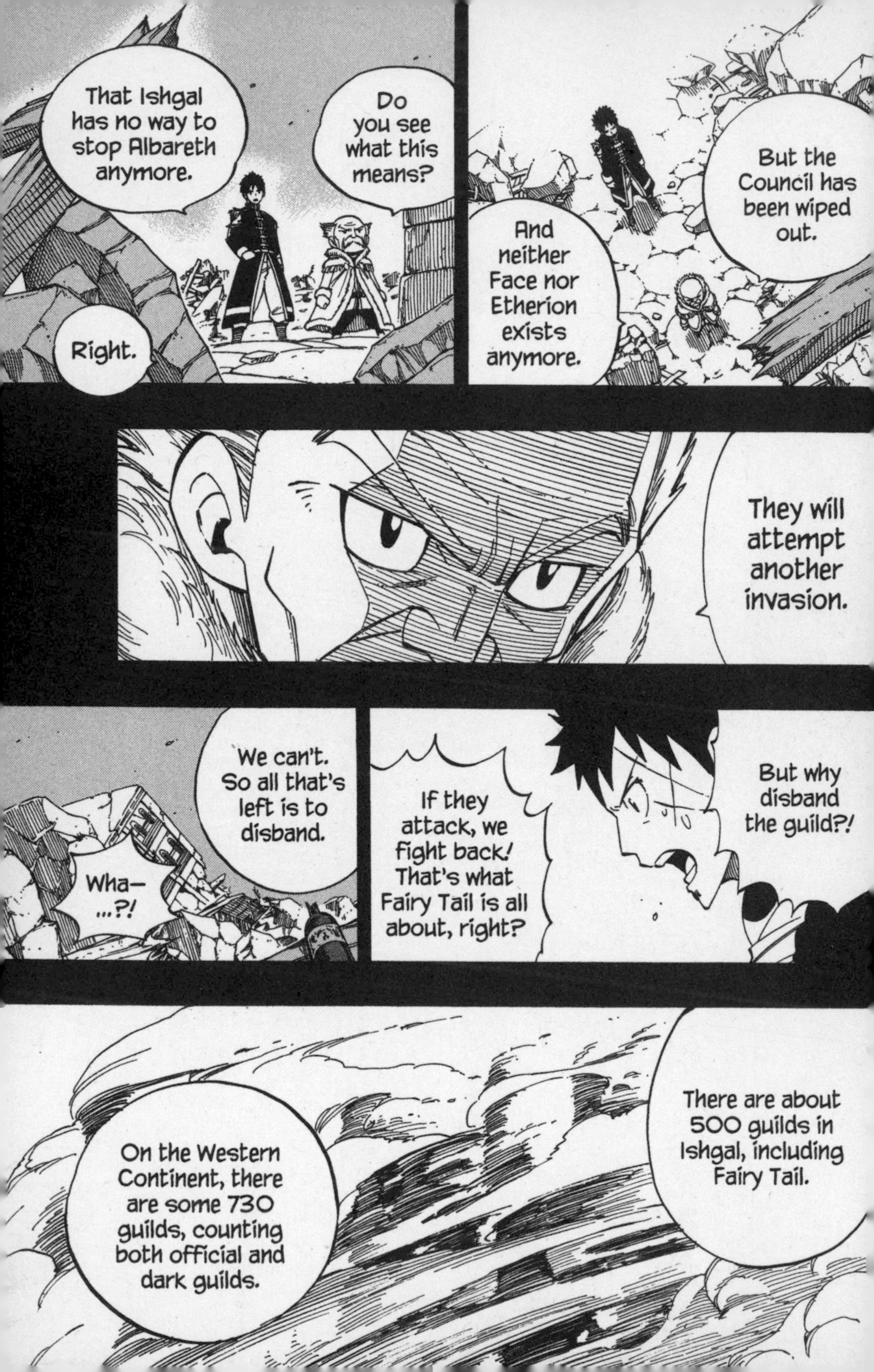
But the Council has been wiped out.
And neither Face nor Etherion exists anymore.
Do you see what this means?
That Ishgal has no way to stop Albareth anymore.
Right.
They will attempt another invasion.
But why disband the guild?!
If they attack, we fight back! That's what Fairy Tail is all about, right?
We can't. So all that's left is to disband.
Wha— ...?!
There are about 500 guilds in Ishgal, including Fairy Tail.
On the Western Continent, there are some 730 guilds, counting both official and dark guilds.

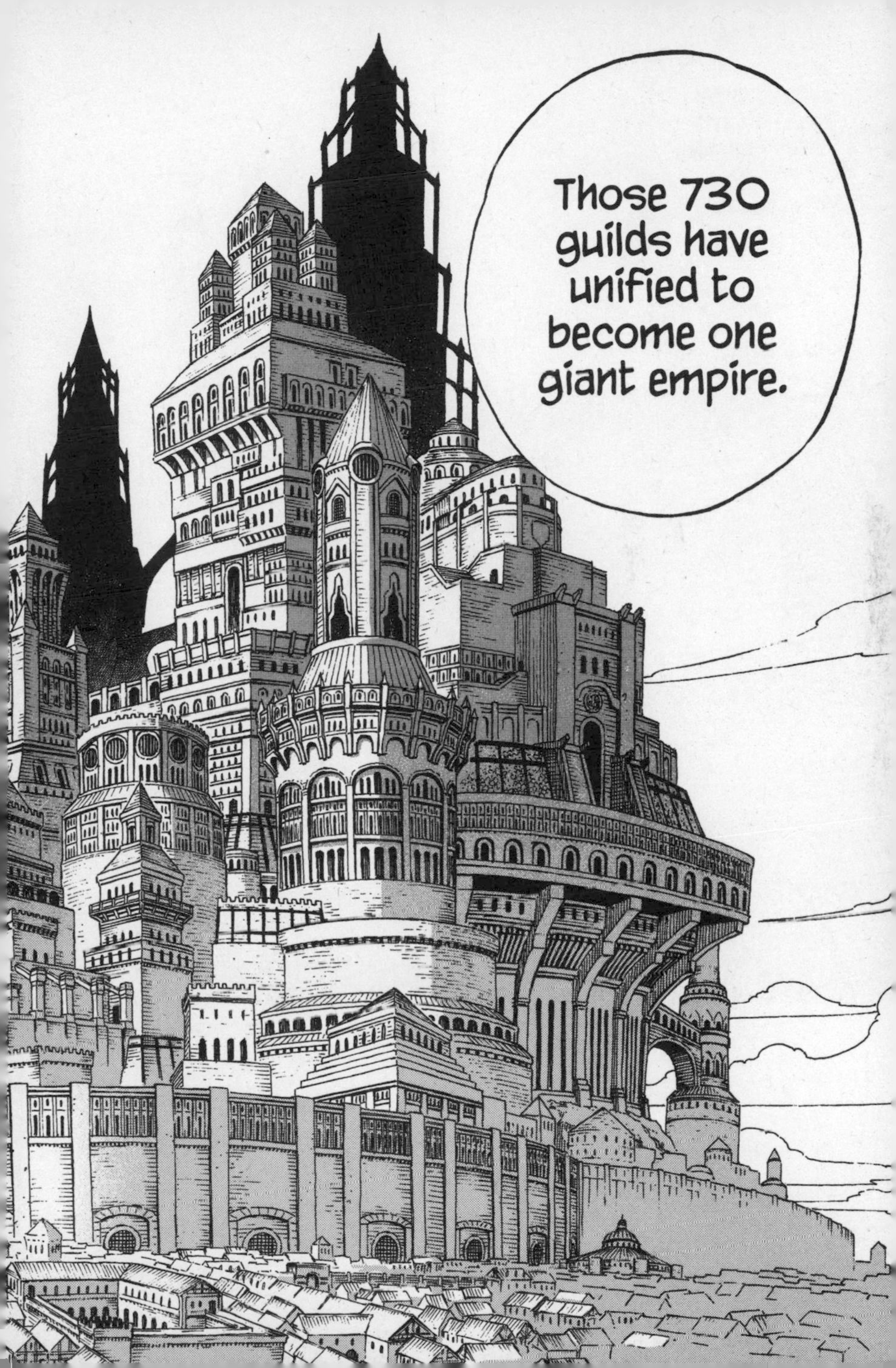
Those 730 guilds have unified to become one giant empire.

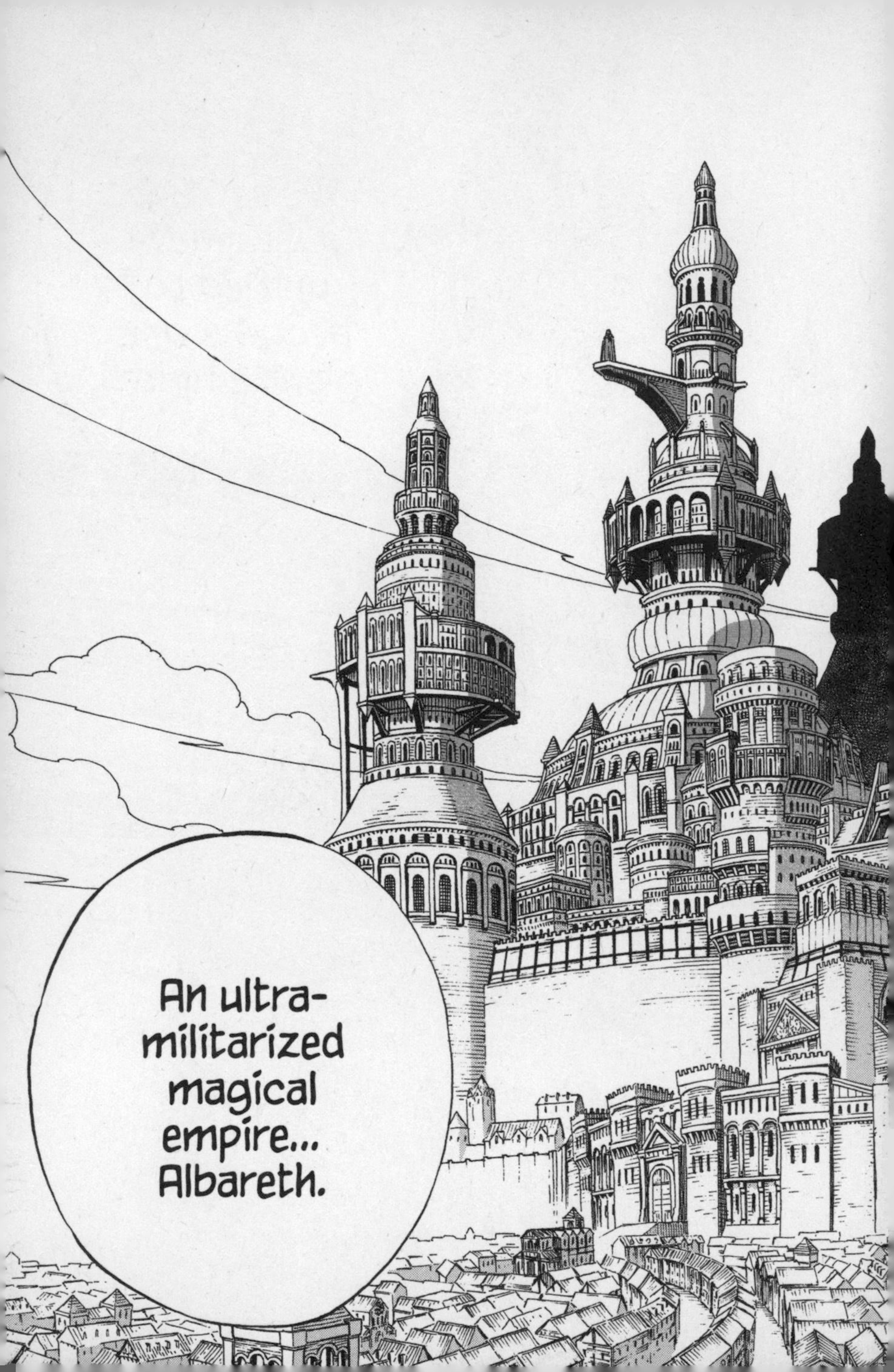
An ultra-militarized magical empire... Albareth.

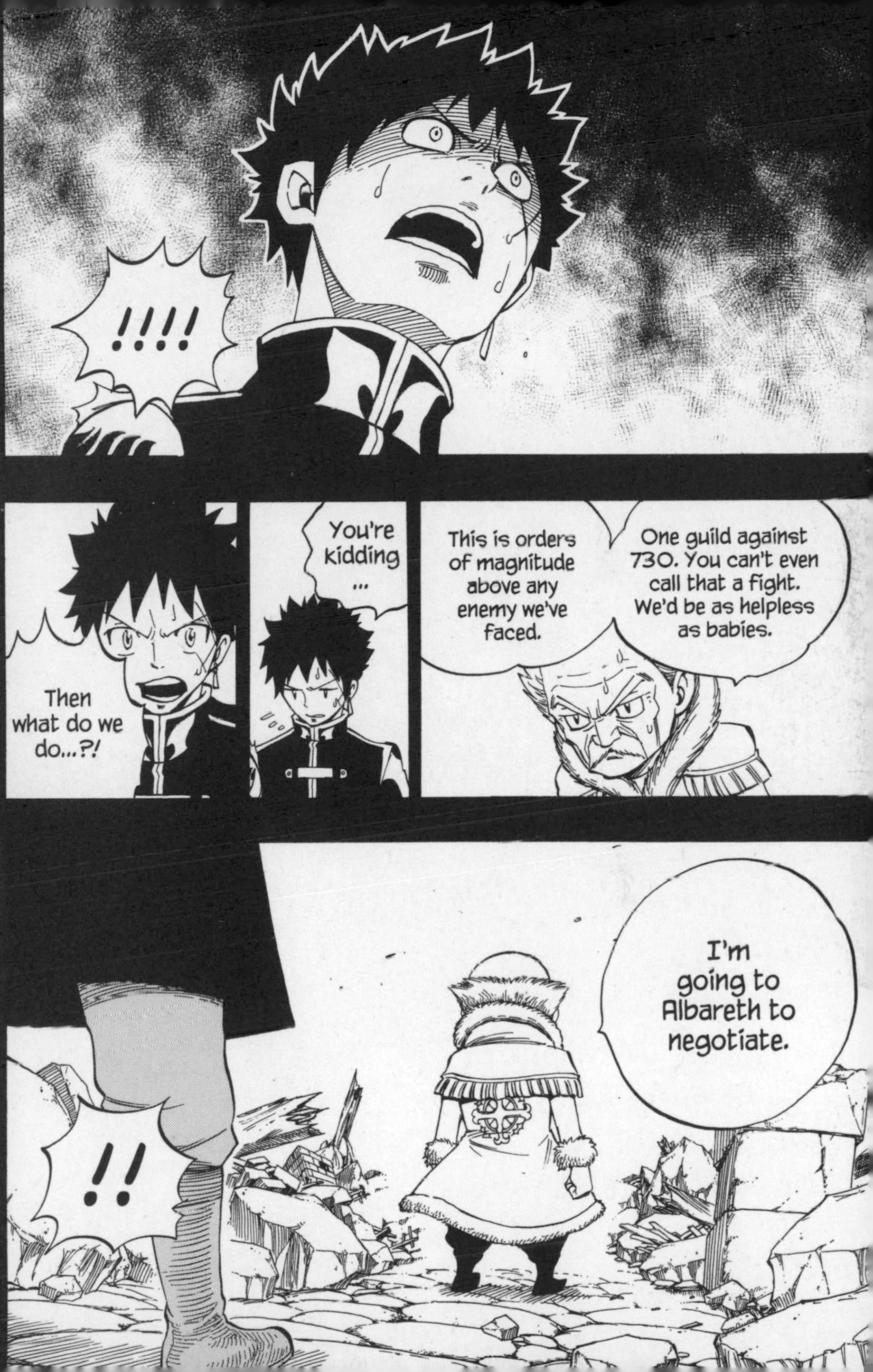
!!!!
One guild against 730. You can't even call that a fight. We'd be as helpless as babies.
This is orders of magnitude above any enemy we've faced.
You're kidding ...
Then what do we do...?!
I'm going to Albareth to negotiate.
!!

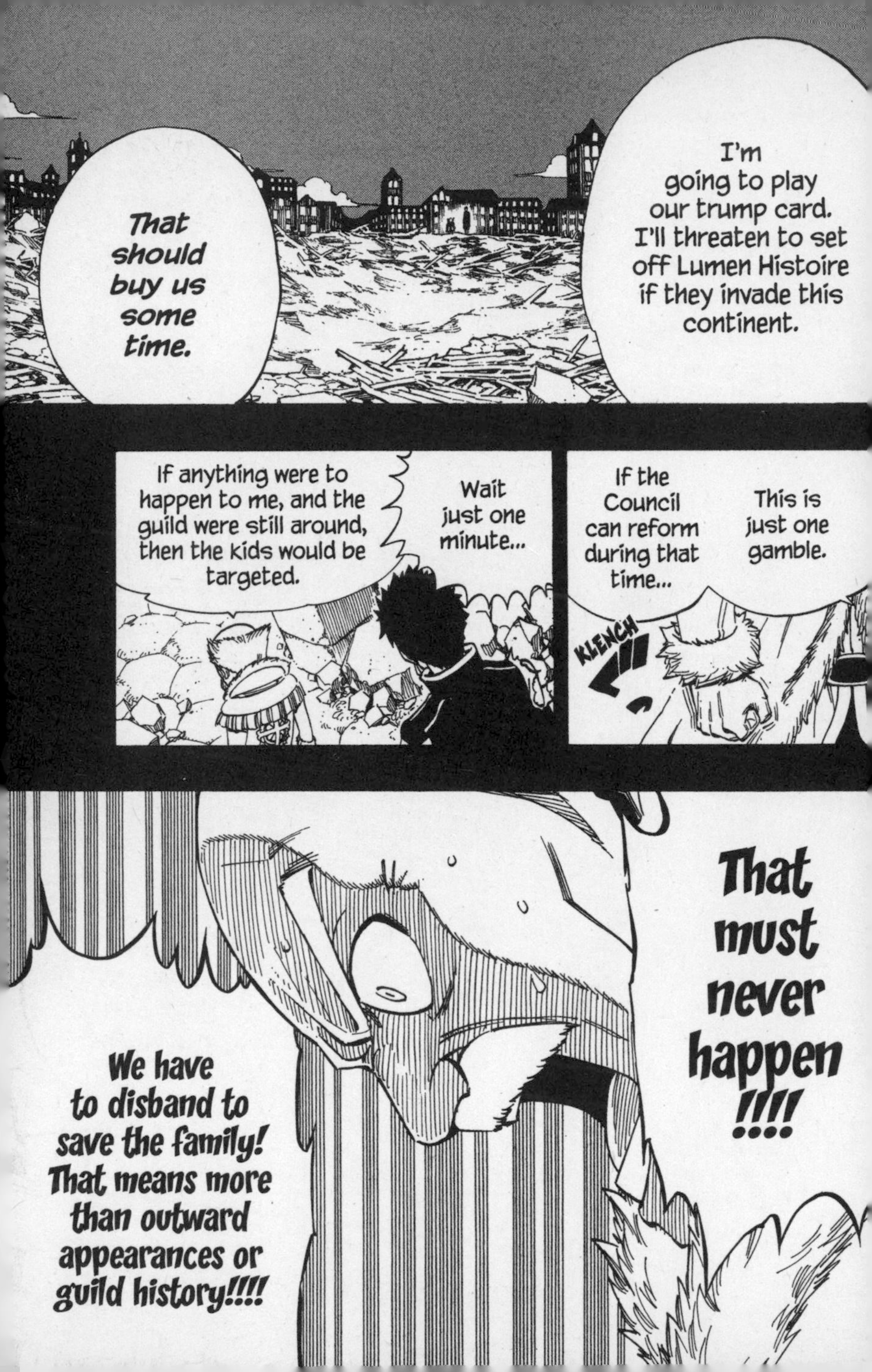
I'm going to play our trump card. I'll threaten to set off Lumen Histoire if they invade this continent.
That should buy us some time.
This is just one gamble.
If the Council can reform during that time...
KLENCH
Wait just one minute...
If anything were to happen to me, and the guild were still around, then the kids would be targeted.
That must never happen!!!!
We have to disband to save the family! That means more than outward appearances or guild history!!!!

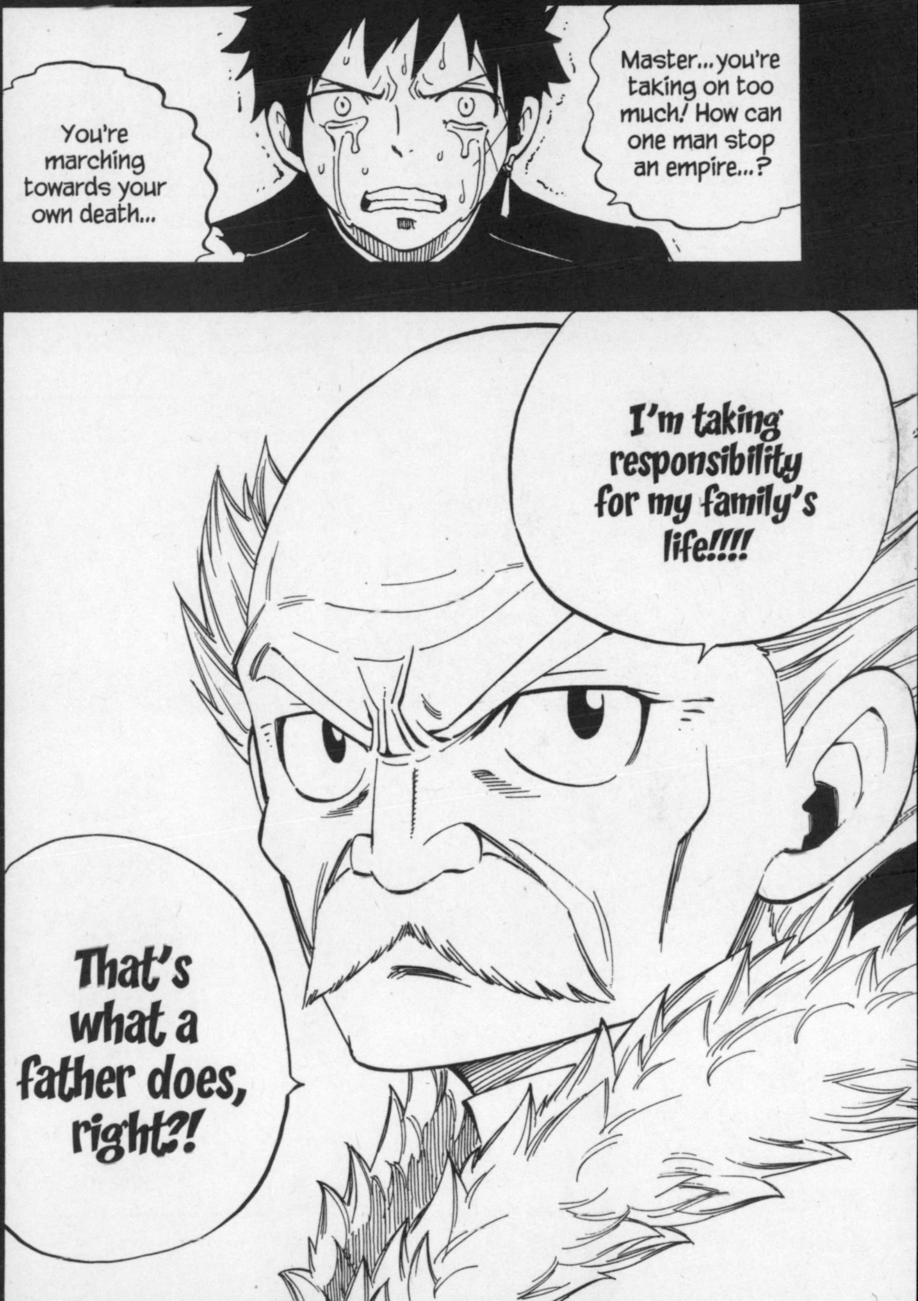
Master...you're taking on too much! How can one man stop an empire...?
You're marching towards your own death...
I'm taking responsibility for my family's life!!!!
That's what a father does, right?!

FAIRY TAIL

フェアリーテイル

Chapter 440: God Serena

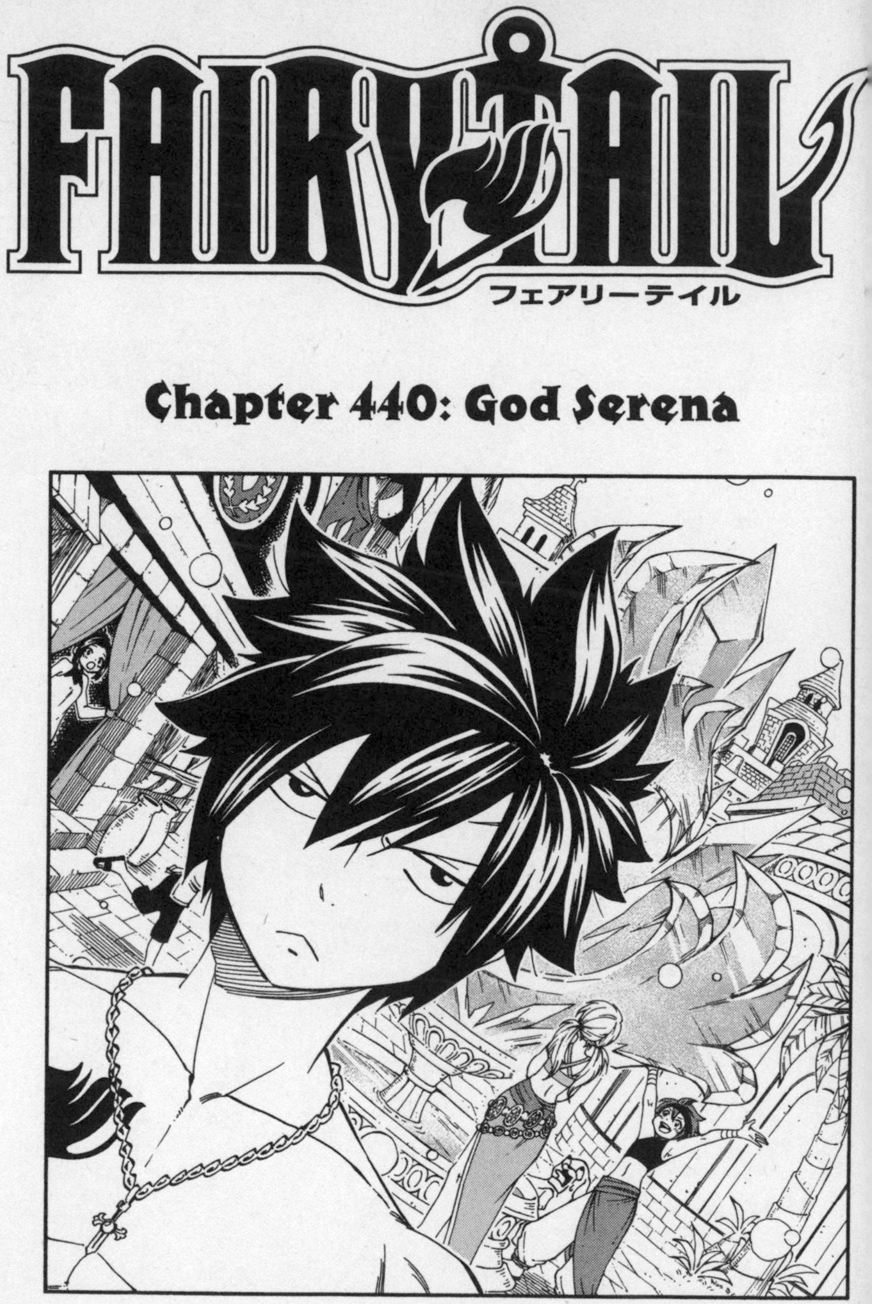

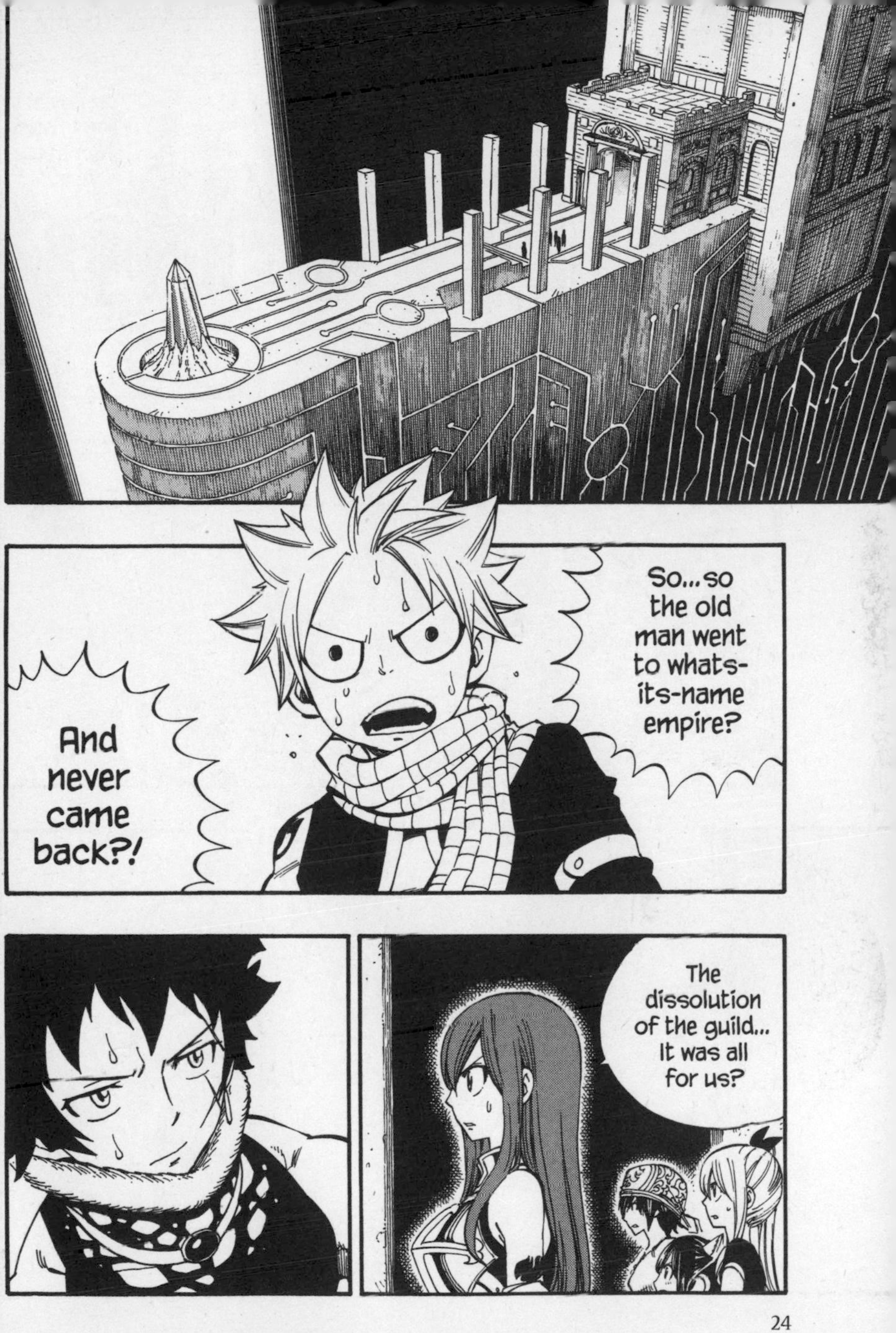
So... so the old man went to whats-its-name empire?
And never came back?!
The dissolution of the guild... It was all for us?

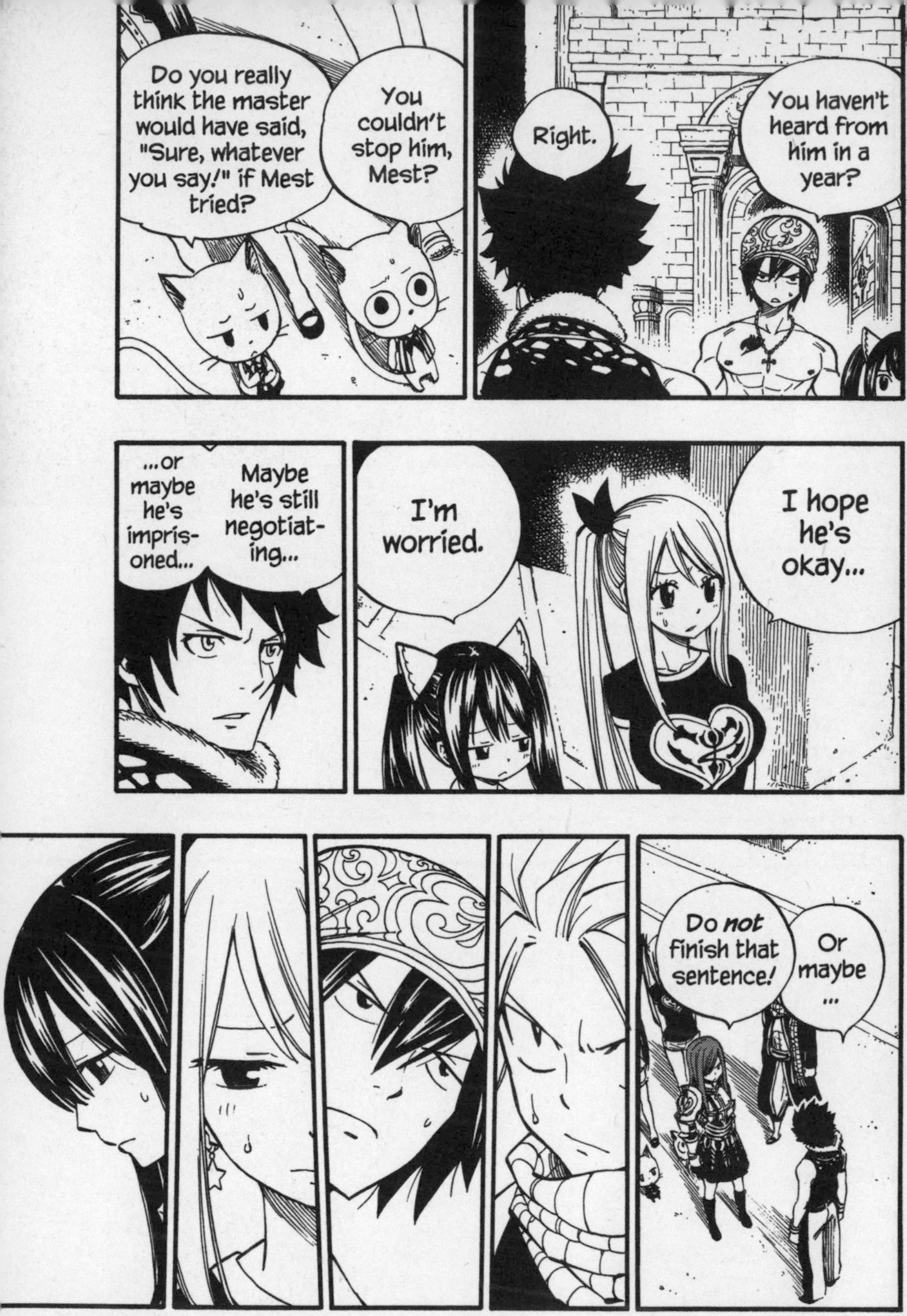
You haven't heard from him in a year?
Right.
You couldn't stop him, Mest?
Do you really think the master would have said, "Sure, whatever you say!" if Mest tried?
I hope he's okay...
I'm worried.
Maybe he's still negotiat-ing...
...or maybe he's impris-oned...
Or maybe ...
Do **not** finish that sentence!

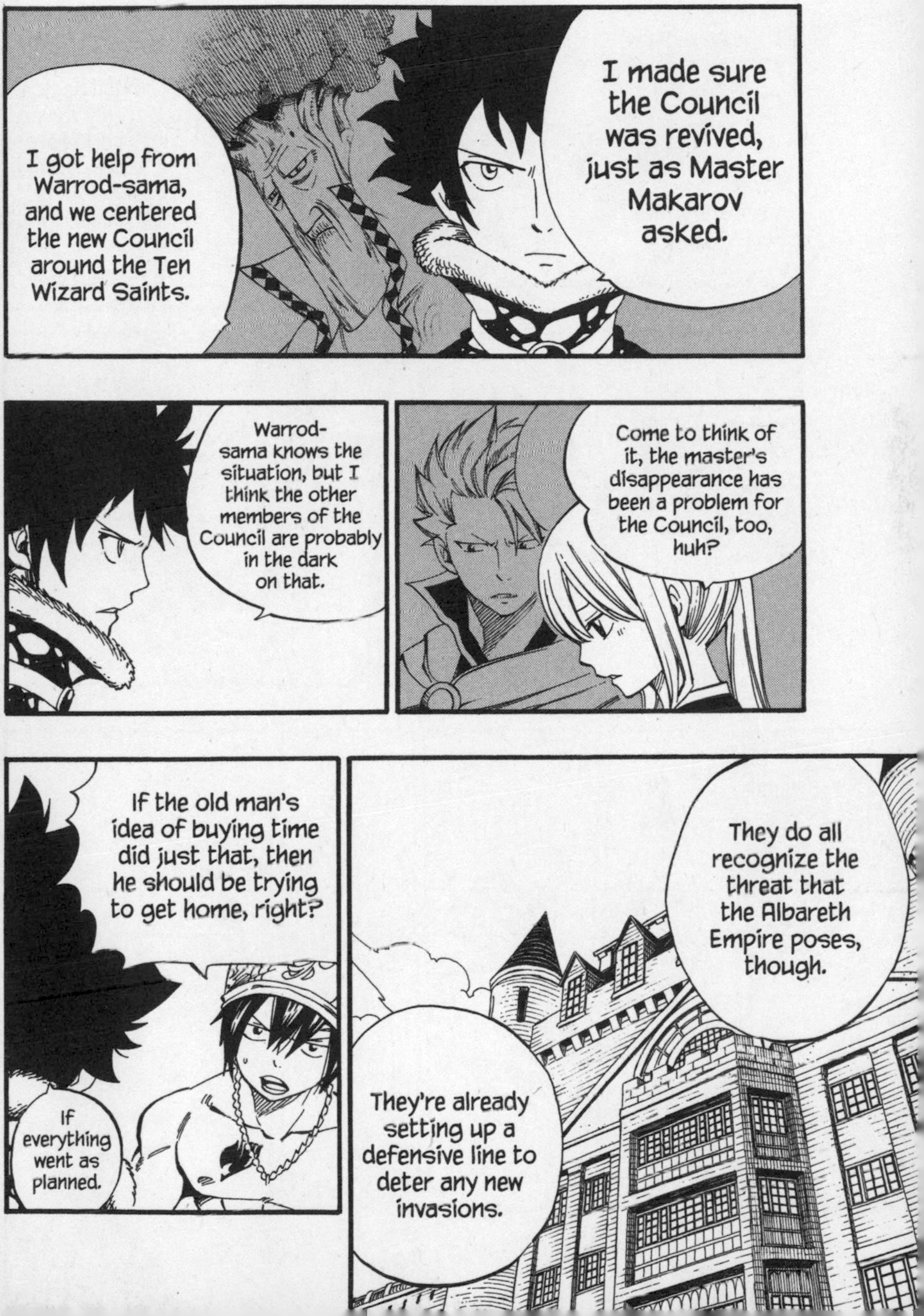
I made sure the Council was revived, just as Master Makarov asked.
I got help from Warrod-sama, and we centered the new Council around the Ten Wizard Saints.
Come to think of it, the master's disappearance has been a problem for the Council, too, huh?
Warrod-sama knows the situation, but I think the other members of the Council are probably in the dark on that.
They do all recognize the threat that the Albareth Empire poses, though.
They're already setting up a defensive line to deter any new invasions.
If the old man's idea of buying time did just that, then he should be trying to get home, right?
If everything went as planned.

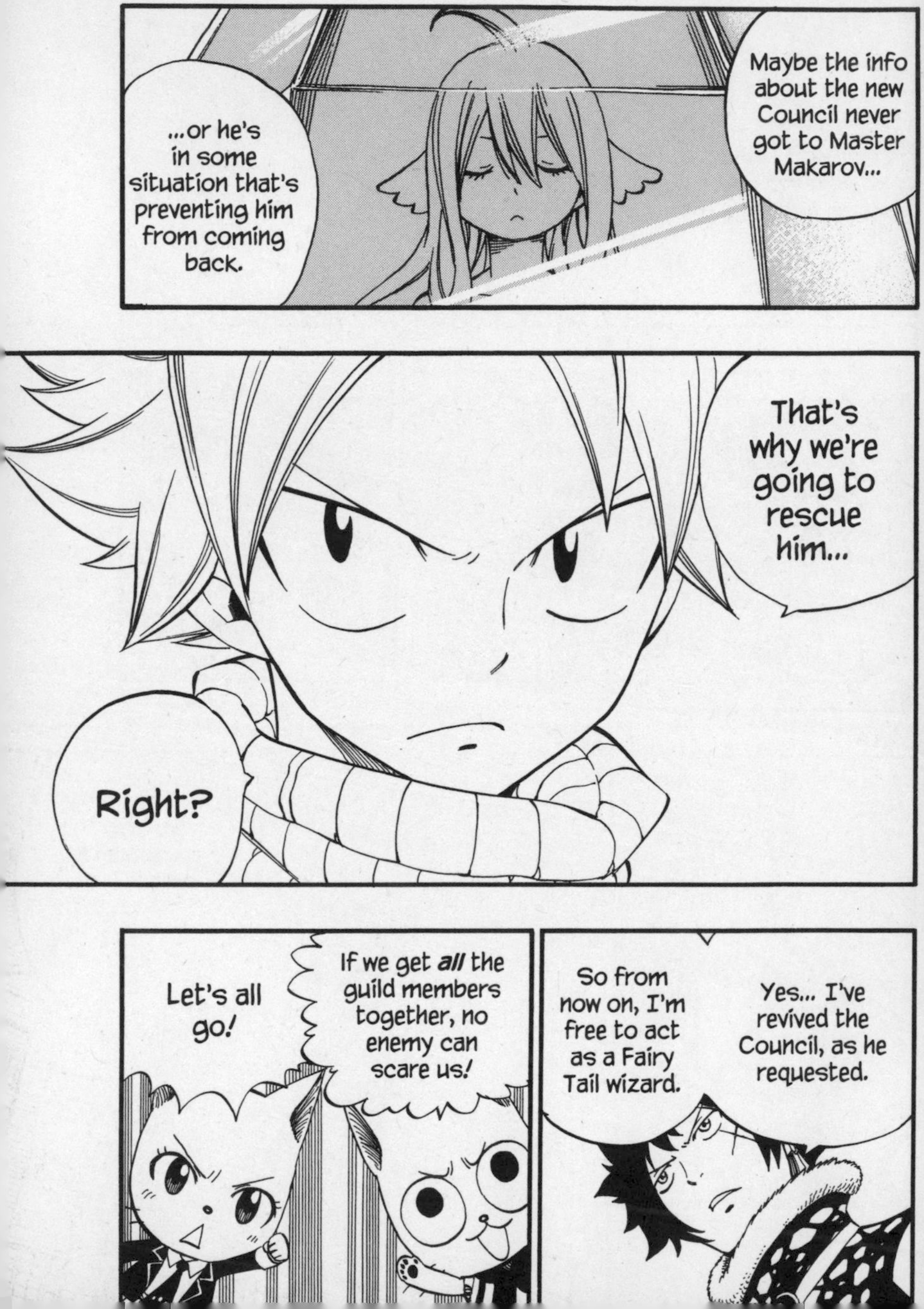
Maybe the info about the new Council never got to Master Makarov...
...or he's in some situation that's preventing him from coming back.
That's why we're going to rescue him...
Right?
Yes... I've revived the Council, as he requested.
So from now on, I'm free to act as a Fairy Tail wizard.
If we get *all* the guild members together, no enemy can scare us!
Let's all go!

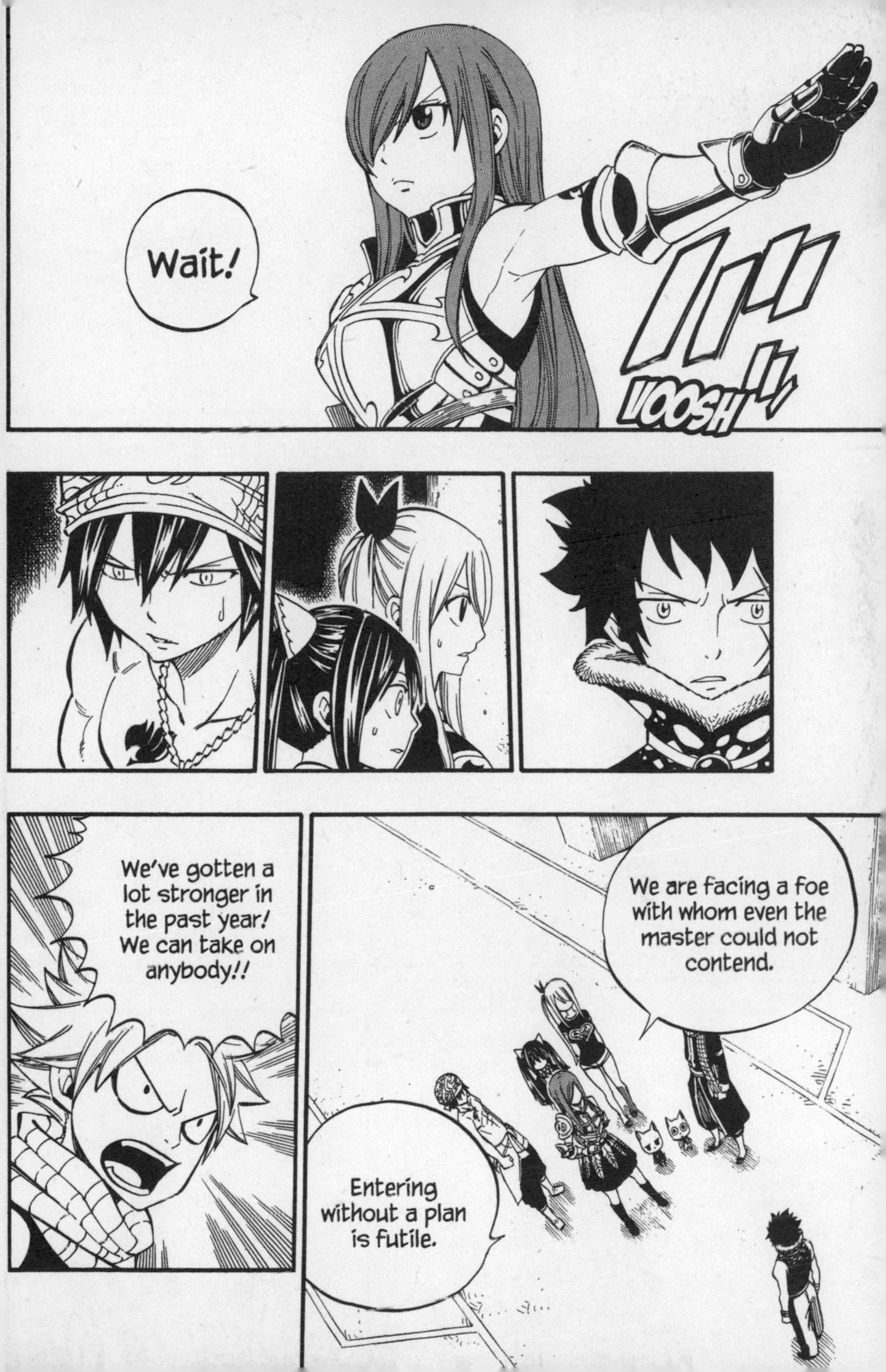
Wait!
VOOSH
We are facing a foe with whom even the master could not contend.
Entering without a plan is futile.
We've gotten a lot stronger in the past year! We can take on anybody!!

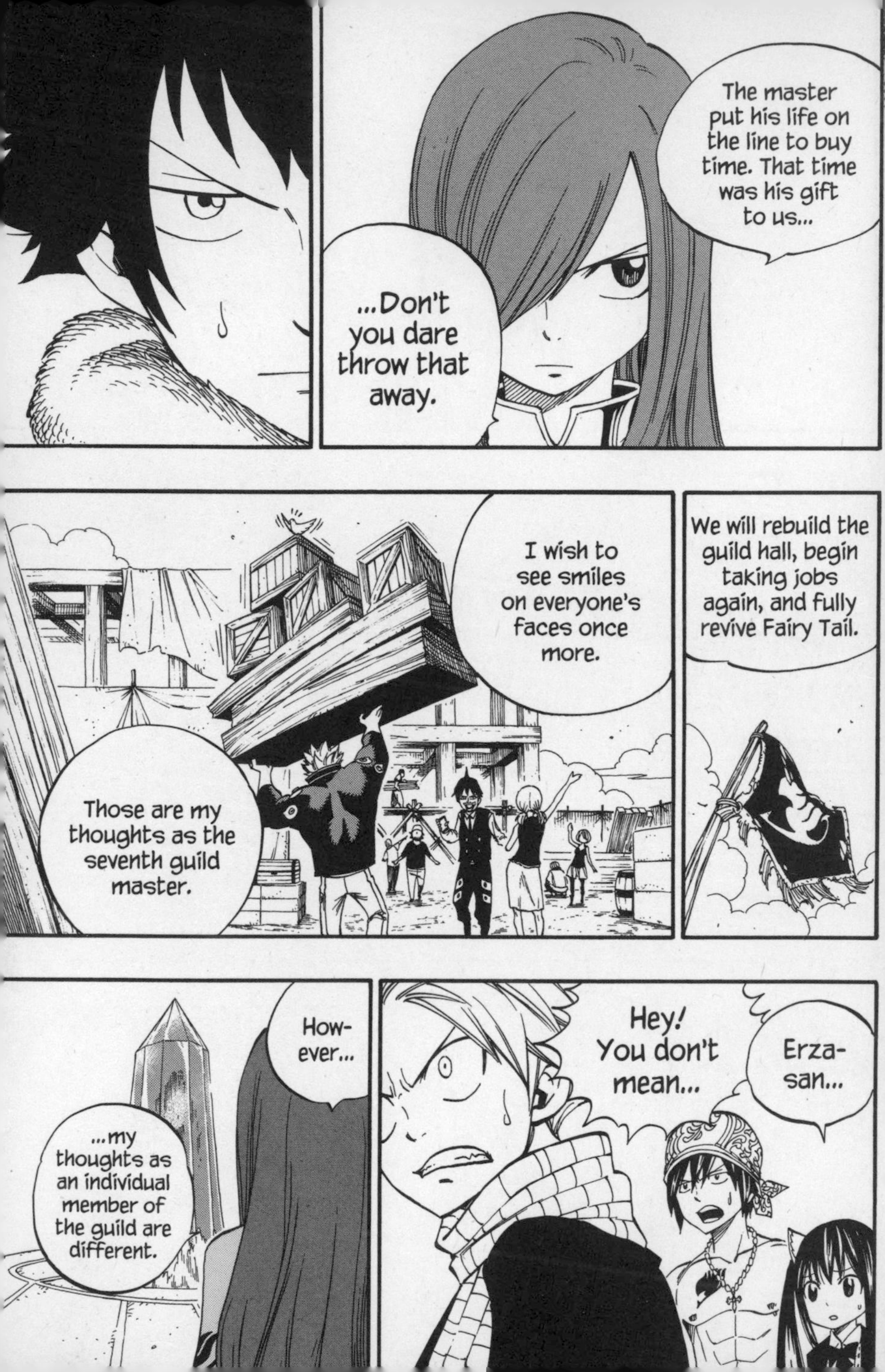
The master put his life on the line to buy time. That time was his gift to us...
...Don't you dare throw that away.
We will rebuild the guild hall, begin taking jobs again, and fully revive Fairy Tail.
I wish to see smiles on everyone's faces once more.
Those are my thoughts as the seventh guild master.
Erza-san...
Hey! You don't mean...
How-ever...
...my thoughts as an individual member of the guild are different.

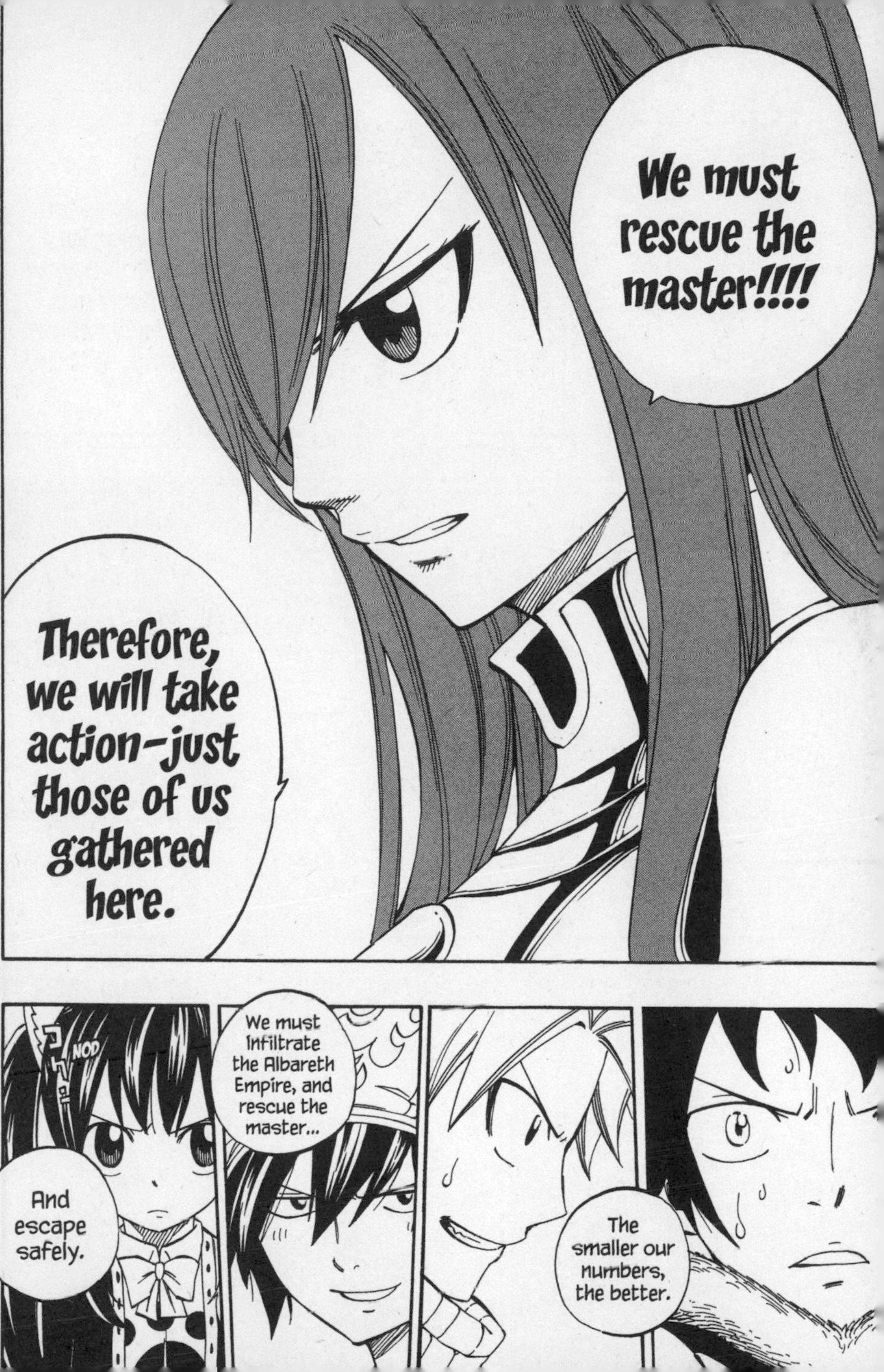
We must rescue the master!!!!
Therefore, we will take action–just those of us gathered here.
The smaller our numbers, the better.
We must infiltrate the Albareth Empire, and rescue the master...
NOD
And escape safely.

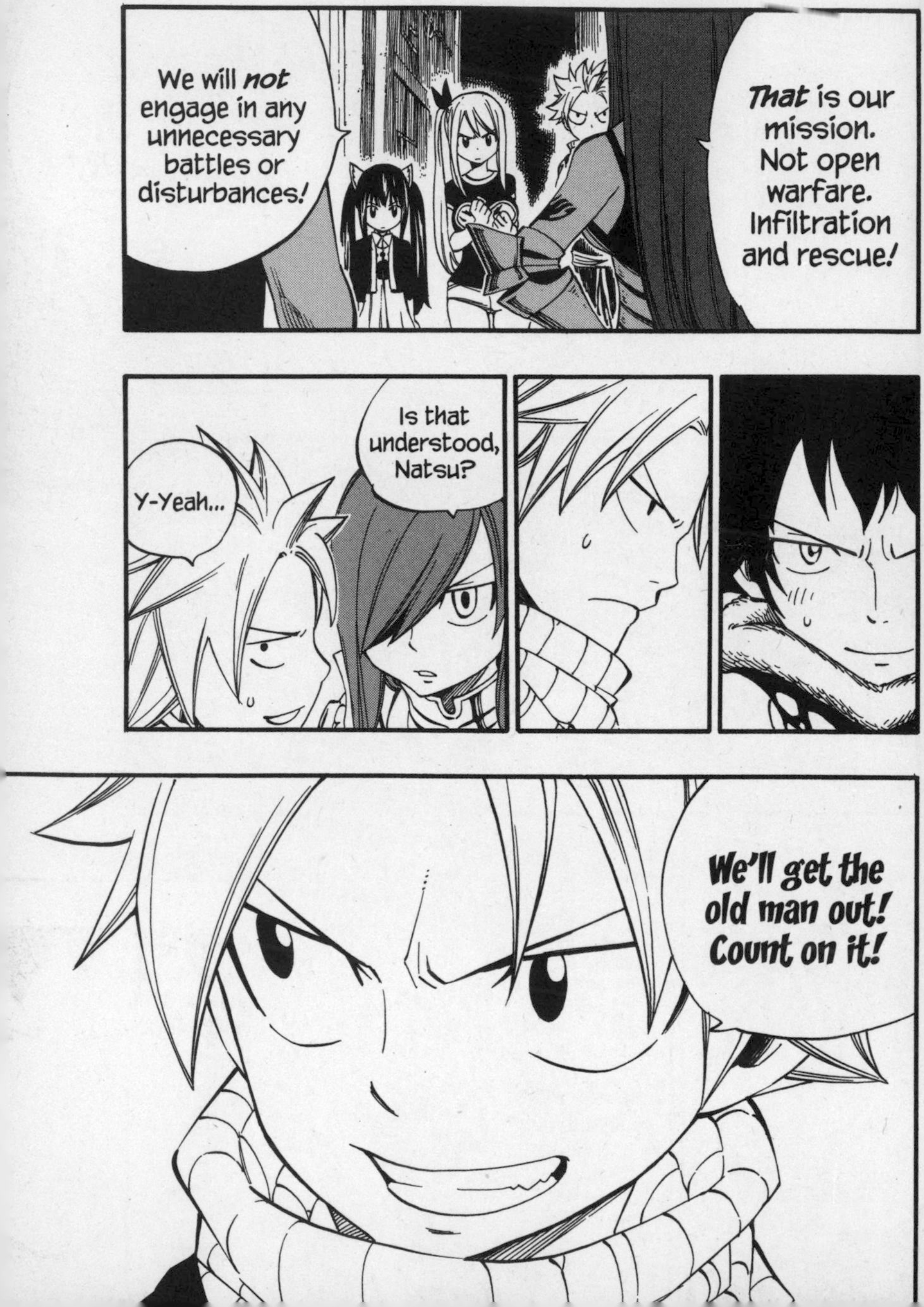

That is our mission. Not open warfare. Infiltration and rescue!
We will *not* engage in any unnecessary battles or disturbances!
Is that understood, Natsu?
Y-Yeah...
We'll get the old man out! Count on it!

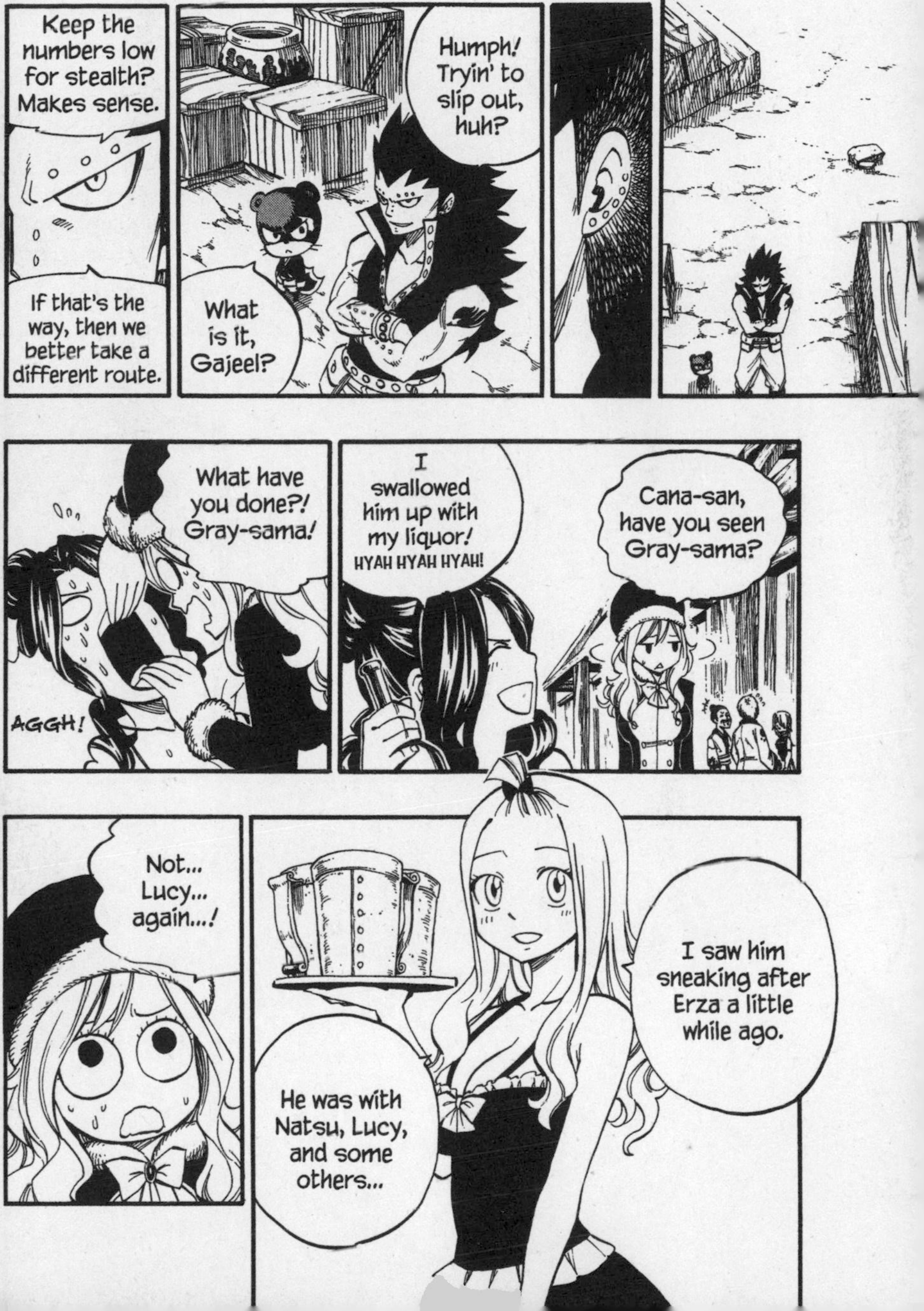
Humph! Tryin' to slip out, huh?
What is it, Gajeel?
Keep the numbers low for stealth? Makes sense.
If that's the way, then we better take a different route.
Cana-san, have you seen Gray-sama?
I swallowed him up with my liquor!
HYAH HYAH HYAH!
What have you done?! Gray-sama!
AGGH!
I saw him sneaking after Erza a little while ago.
He was with Natsu, Lucy, and some others...
Not... Lucy... again...!

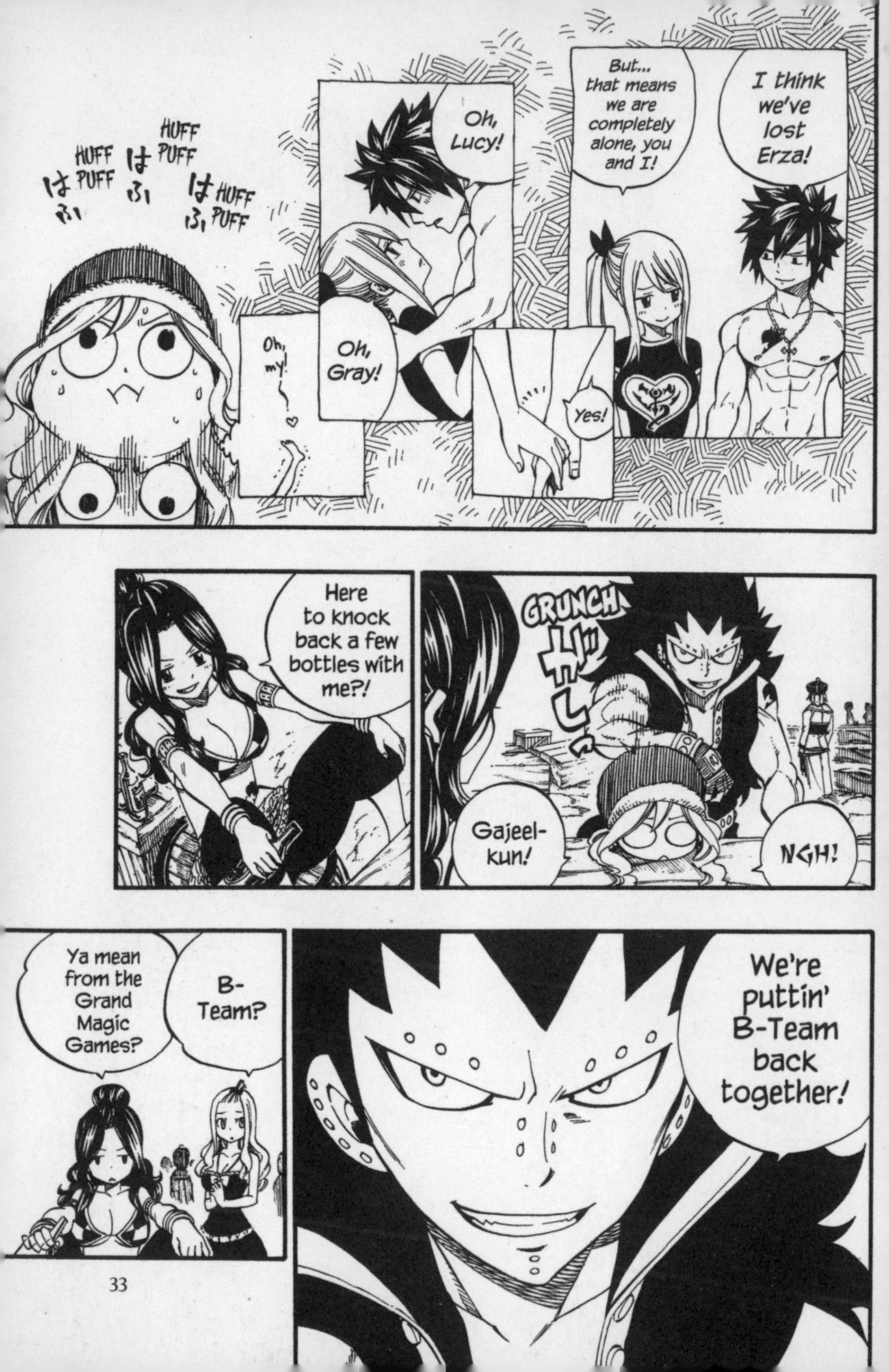
I think we've lost Erza!
But... that means we are completely alone, you and I!
Oh, Lucy!
Yes!
Oh, Gray!
Oh, my!
HUFF PUFF
はふ
HUFF PUFF
はふ
HUFF PUFF
はふ
GRUNCH
ガしっ
NGH!
Gajeel-kun!
Here to knock back a few bottles with me?!
We're puttin' B-Team back together!
B-Team?
Ya mean from the Grand Magic Games?

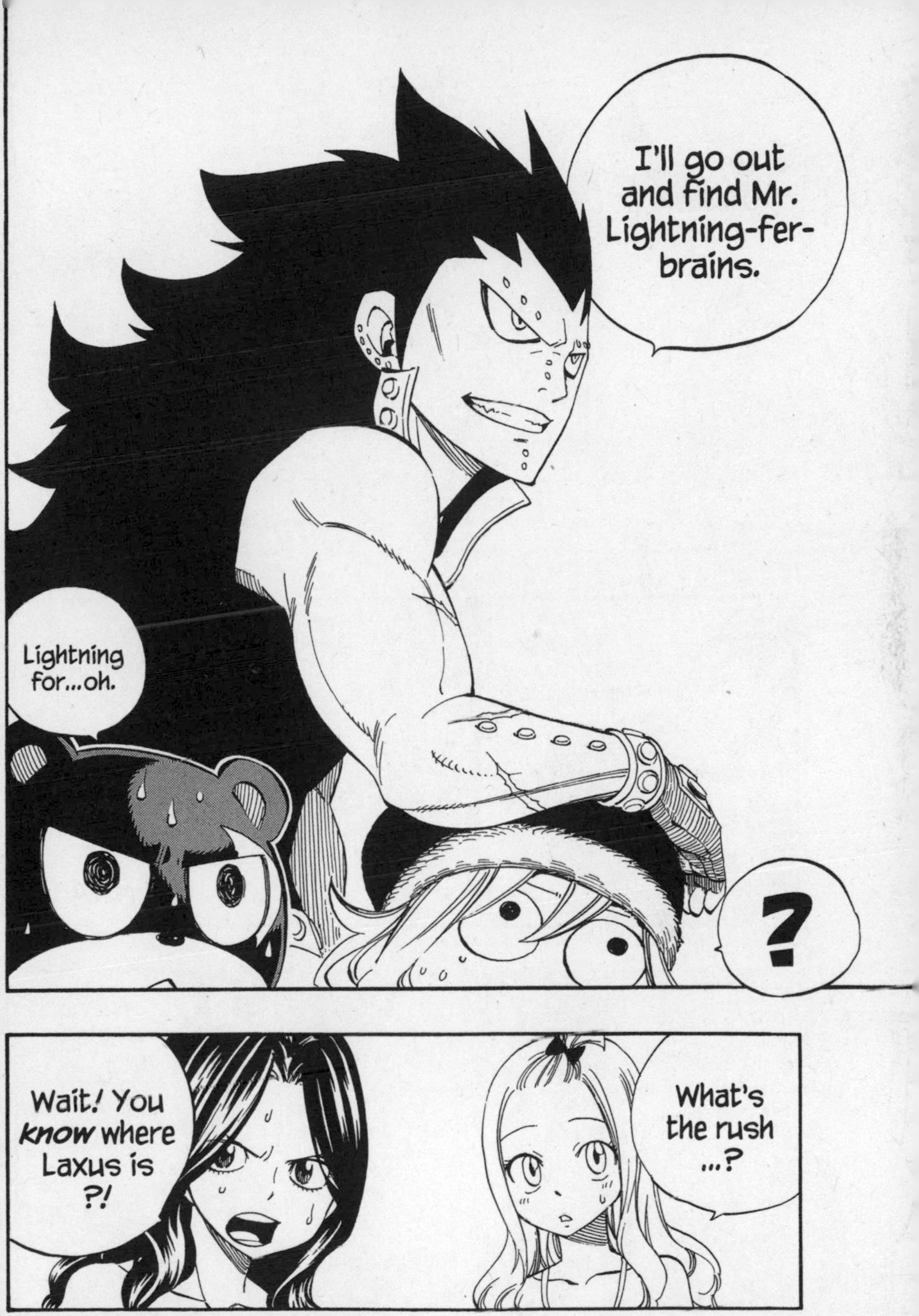
I'll go out and find Mr. Lightning-fer-brains.
Lightning for...oh.
?
What's the rush ...?
Wait! You *know* where Laxus is ?!

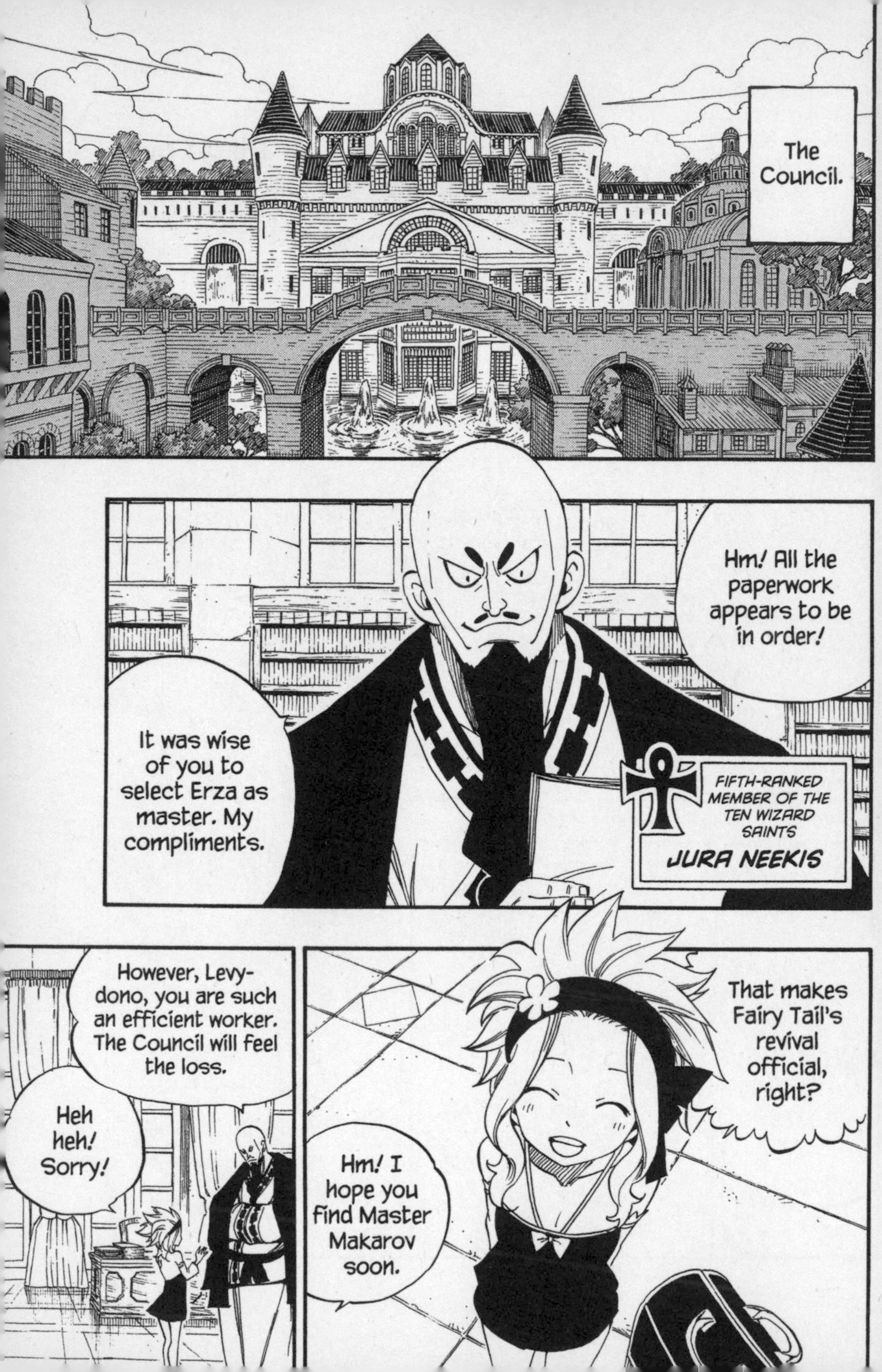
The Council.
Hm! All the paperwork appears to be in order!
It was wise of you to select Erza as master. My compliments.
FIFTH-RANKED MEMBER OF THE TEN WIZARD SAINTS
JURA NEEKIS
That makes Fairy Tail's revival official, right?
Hm! I hope you find Master Makarov soon.
However, Levy-dono, you are such an efficient worker. The Council will feel the loss.
Heh heh! Sorry!

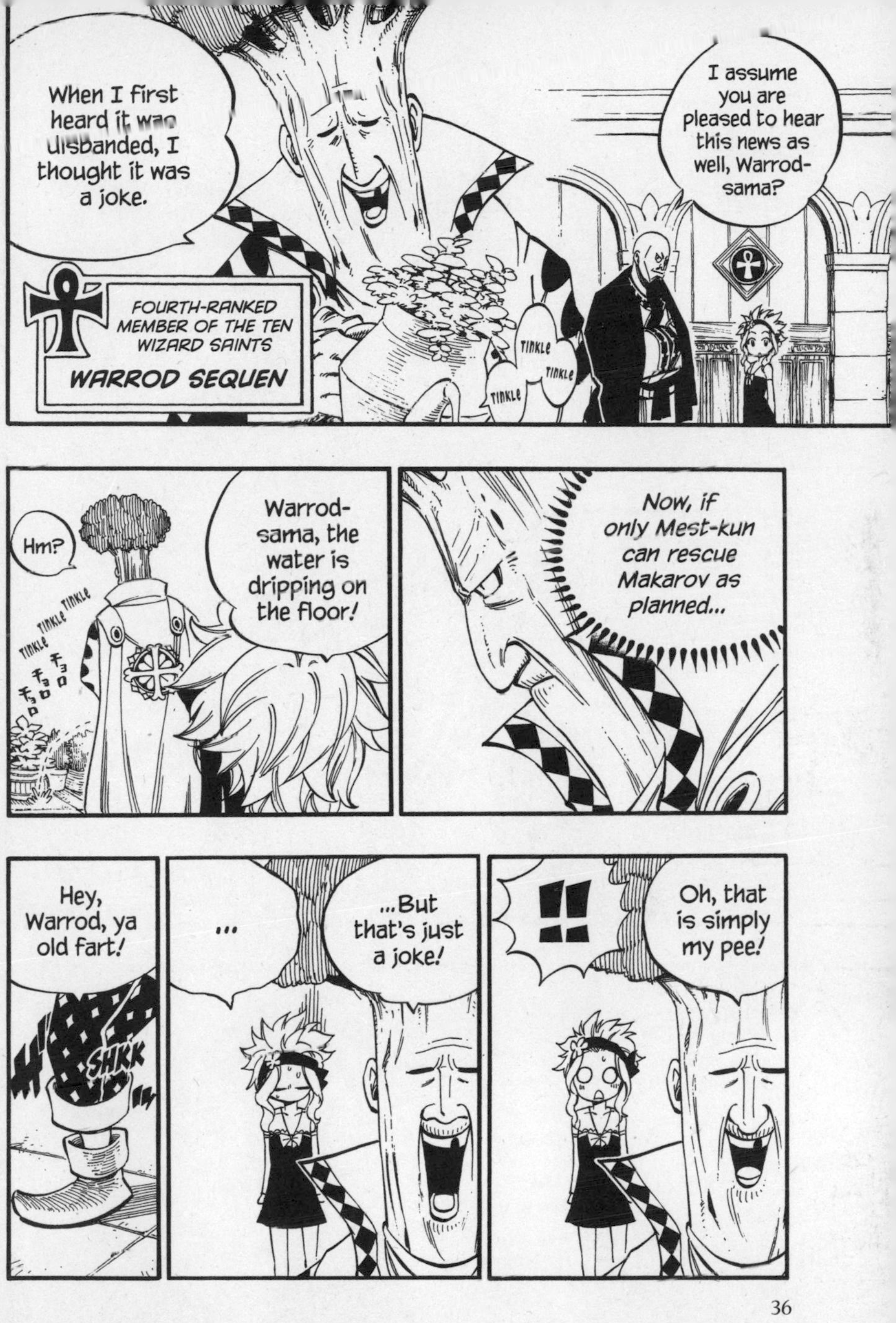
I assume you are pleased to hear this news as well, Warrod-sama?
When I first heard it was disbanded, I thought it was a joke.
FOURTH-RANKED MEMBER OF THE TEN WIZARD SAINTS
WARROD SEQUEN
TINKLE TINKLE TINKLE
Now, if only Mest-kun can rescue Makarov as planned...
Warrod-sama, the water is dripping on the floor!
Hm?
TINKLE TINKLE TINKLE
チョロ チョロ チョロ
!!
Oh, that is simply my pee!
...
...But that's just a joke!
Hey, Warrod, ya old fart!
SHKK

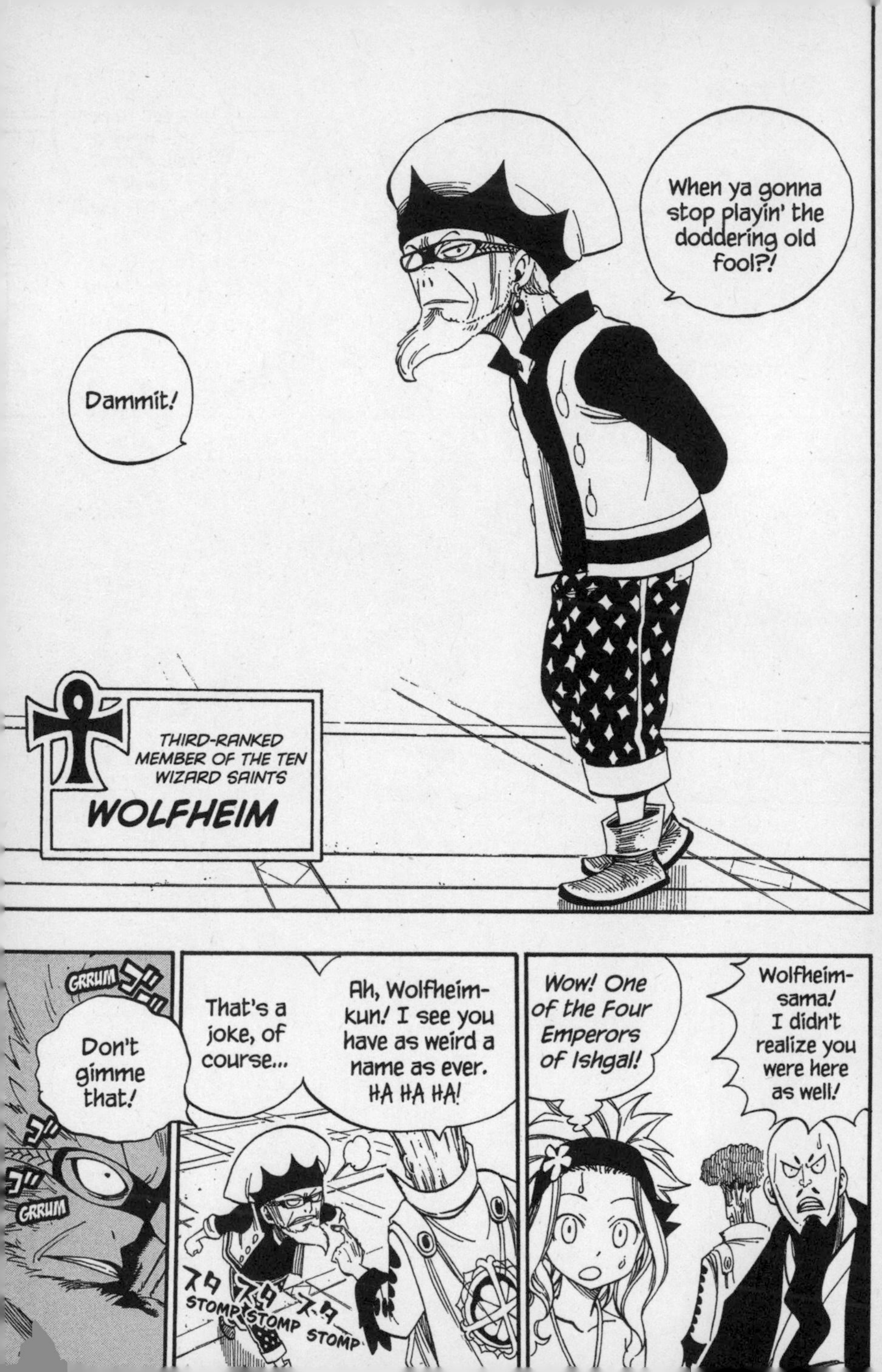
When ya gonna stop playin' the doddering old fool?!
Dammit!
THIRD-RANKED MEMBER OF THE TEN WIZARD SAINTS
WOLFHEIM
Wolfheim-sama! I didn't realize you were here as well!
Wow! One of the Four Emperors of Ishgal!
Ah, Wolfheim-kun! I see you have as weird a name as ever. HA HA HA!
That's a joke, of course...
STOMP STOMP STOMP
GRRUM
Don't gimme that!
GRRUM

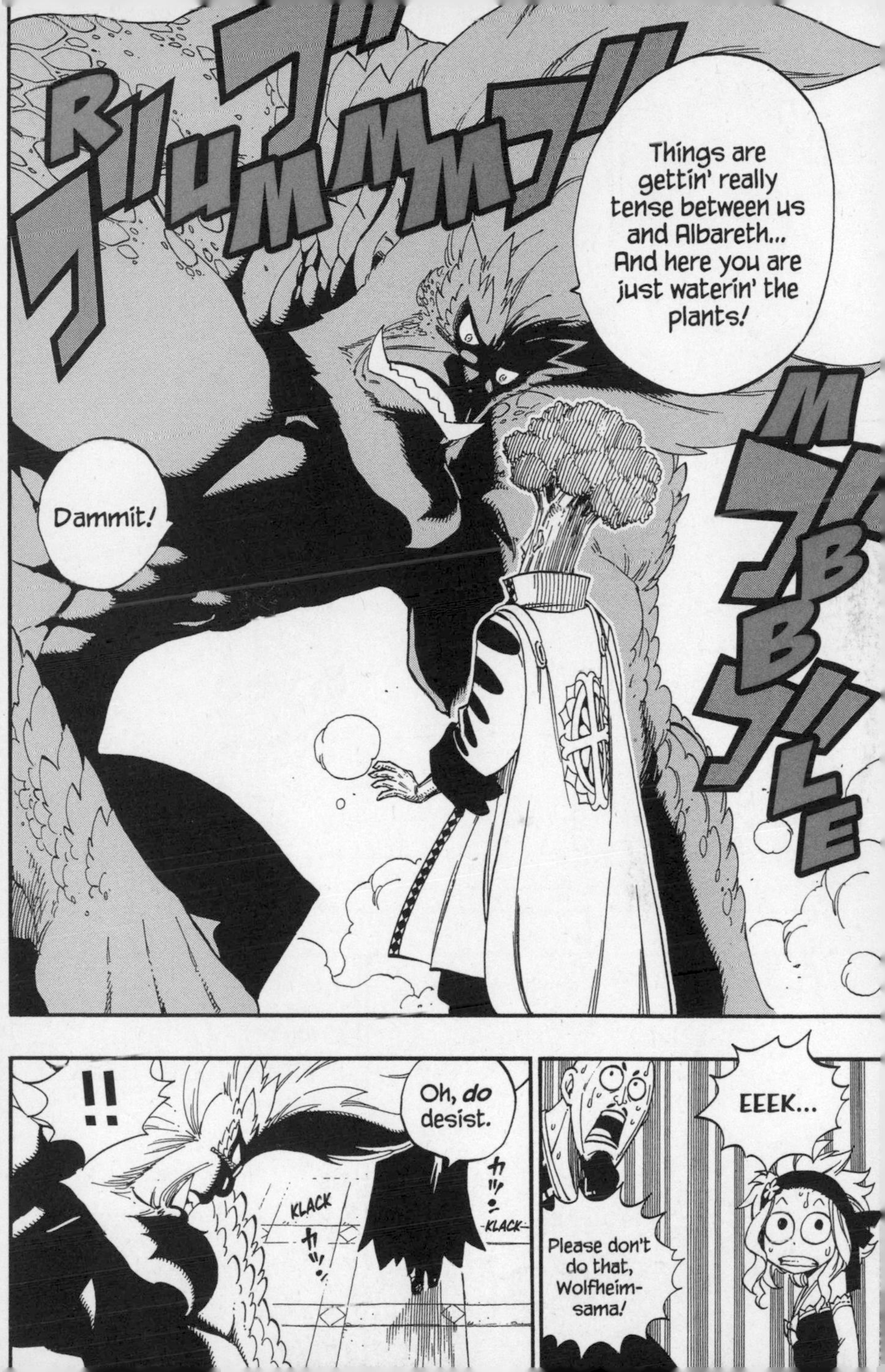
Things are gettin' really tense between us and Albareth... And here you are just waterin' the plants!
RUMMMM
MBBLE
Dammit!
EEEK...
Please don't do that, Wolfheim-sama!
!!
Oh, do desist.
KLACK
KLACK

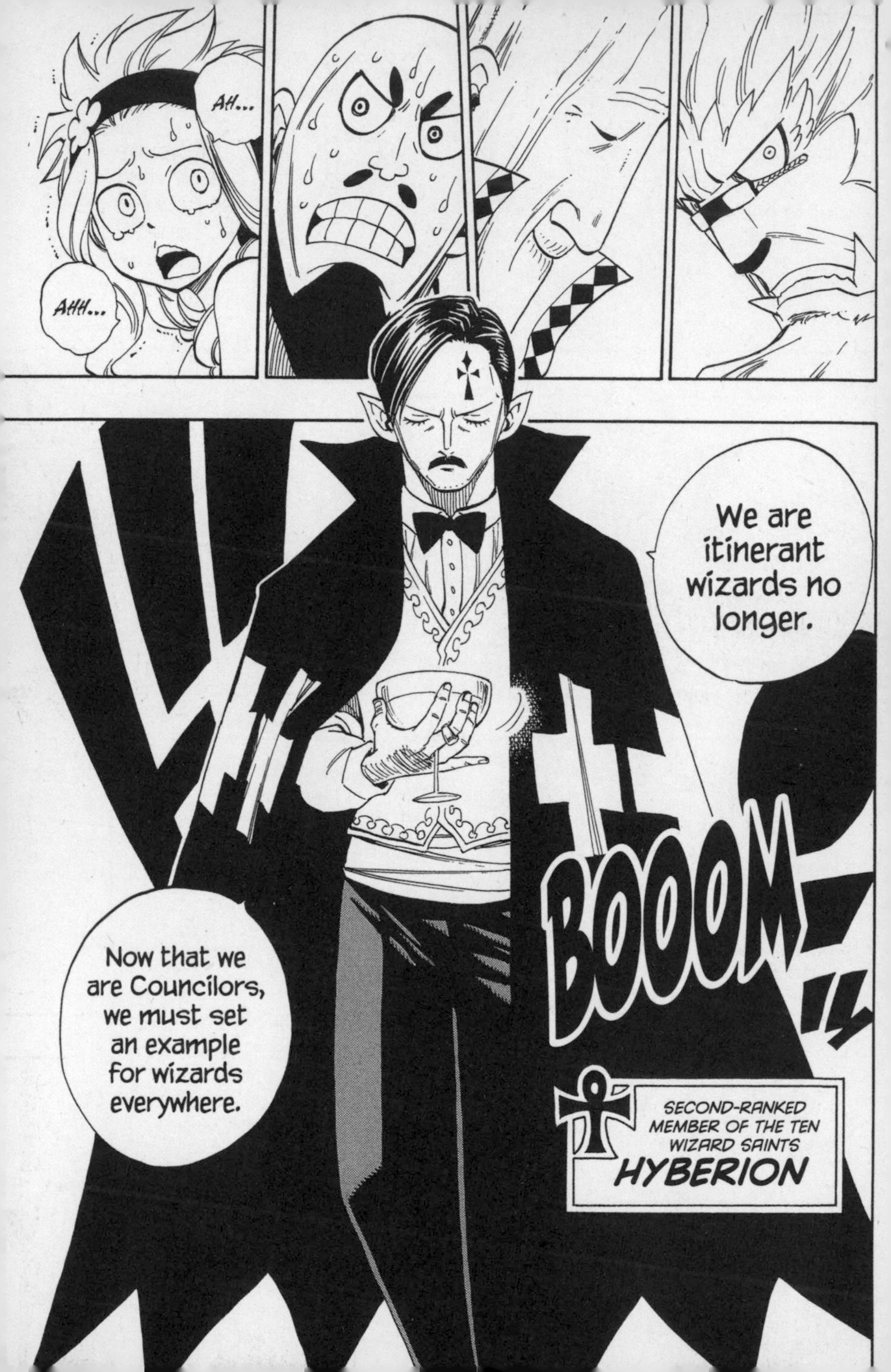

AH...
AHH...
We are itinerant wizards no longer.
BOOOM!!
Now that we are Councilors, we must set an example for wizards everywhere.
SECOND-RANKED MEMBER OF THE TEN WIZARD SAINTS
HYBERION

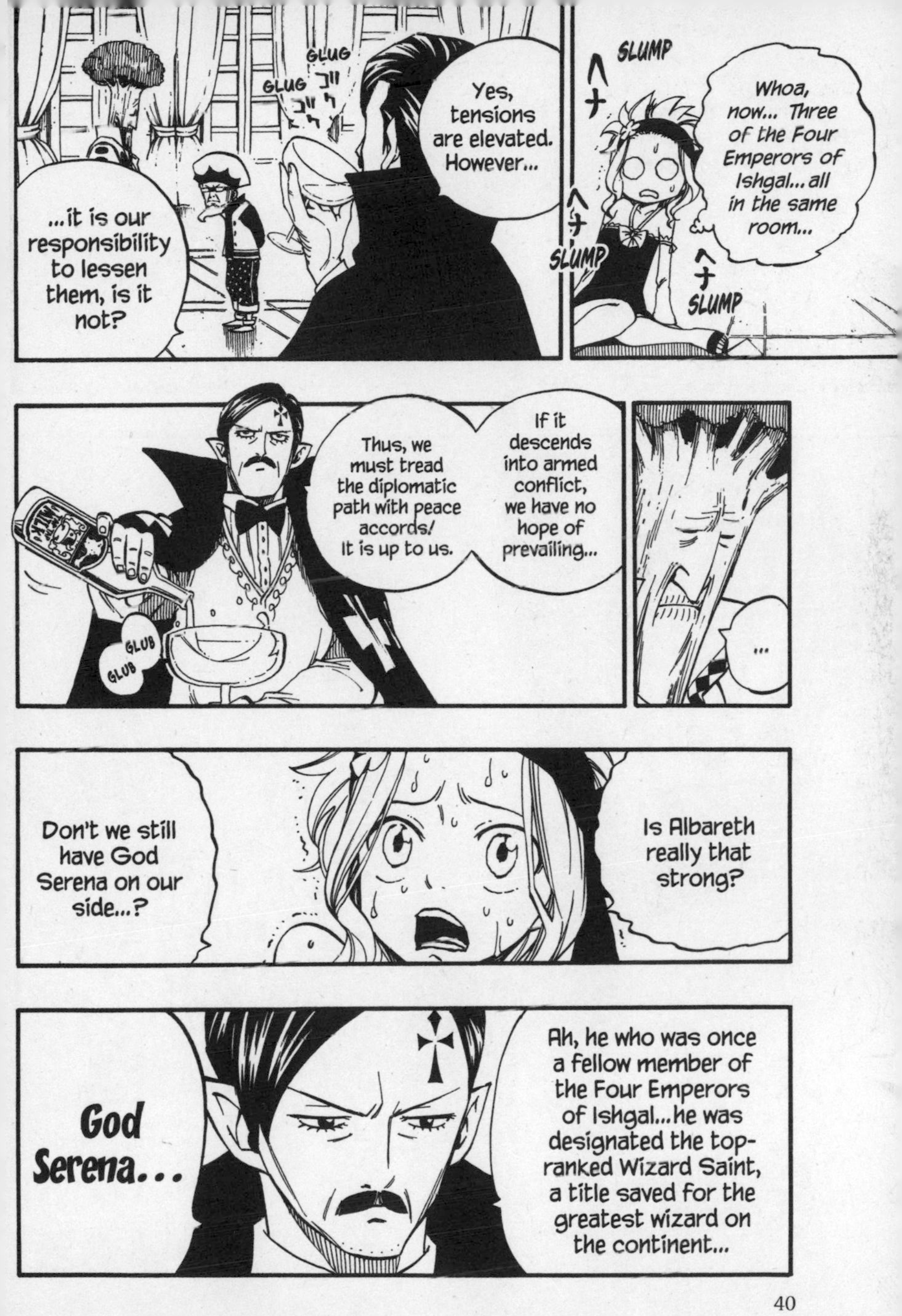
SLUMP
SLUMP
SLUMP
Whoa, now... Three of the Four Emperors of Ishgal... all in the same room...
Yes, tensions are elevated. However...
GLUG
GLUG
...it is our responsibility to lessen them, is it not?
...
If it descends into armed conflict, we have no hope of prevailing...
Thus, we must tread the diplomatic path with peace accords! It is up to us.
GLUB
GLUB
Is Albareth really that strong?
Don't we still have God Serena on our side...?
Ah, he who was once a fellow member of the Four Emperors of Ishgal... he was designated the top-ranked Wizard Saint, a title saved for the greatest wizard on the continent...
God Serena...

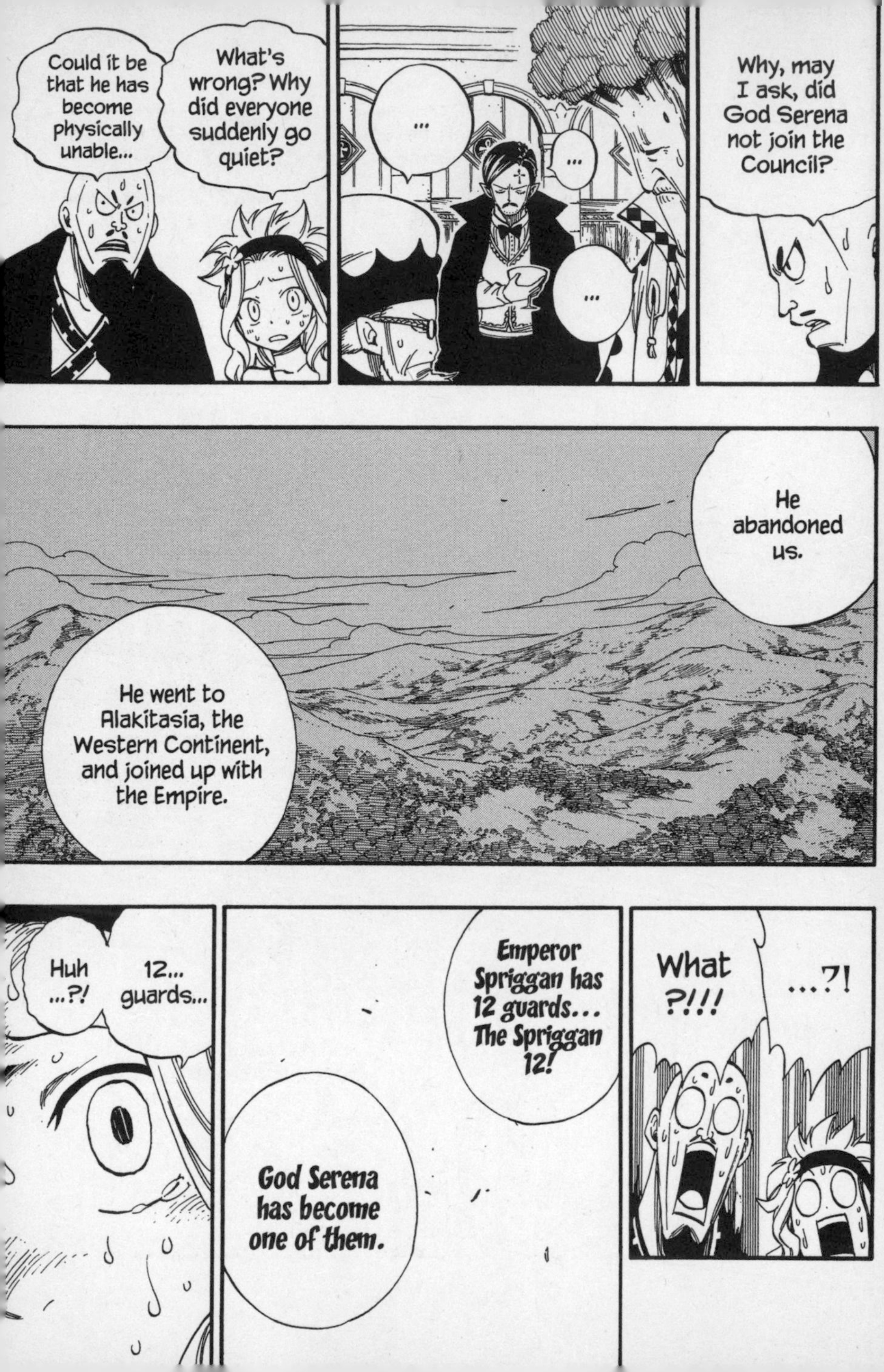
Why, may I ask, did God Serena not join the Council?
...
...
...
What's wrong? Why did everyone suddenly go quiet?
Could it be that he has become physically unable...
He abandoned us.
He went to Alakitasia, the Western Continent, and joined up with the Empire.
...?!
What ?!!!
Emperor Spriggan has 12 guards... The Spriggan 12!
God Serena has become one of them.
12... guards...
Huh ...?!

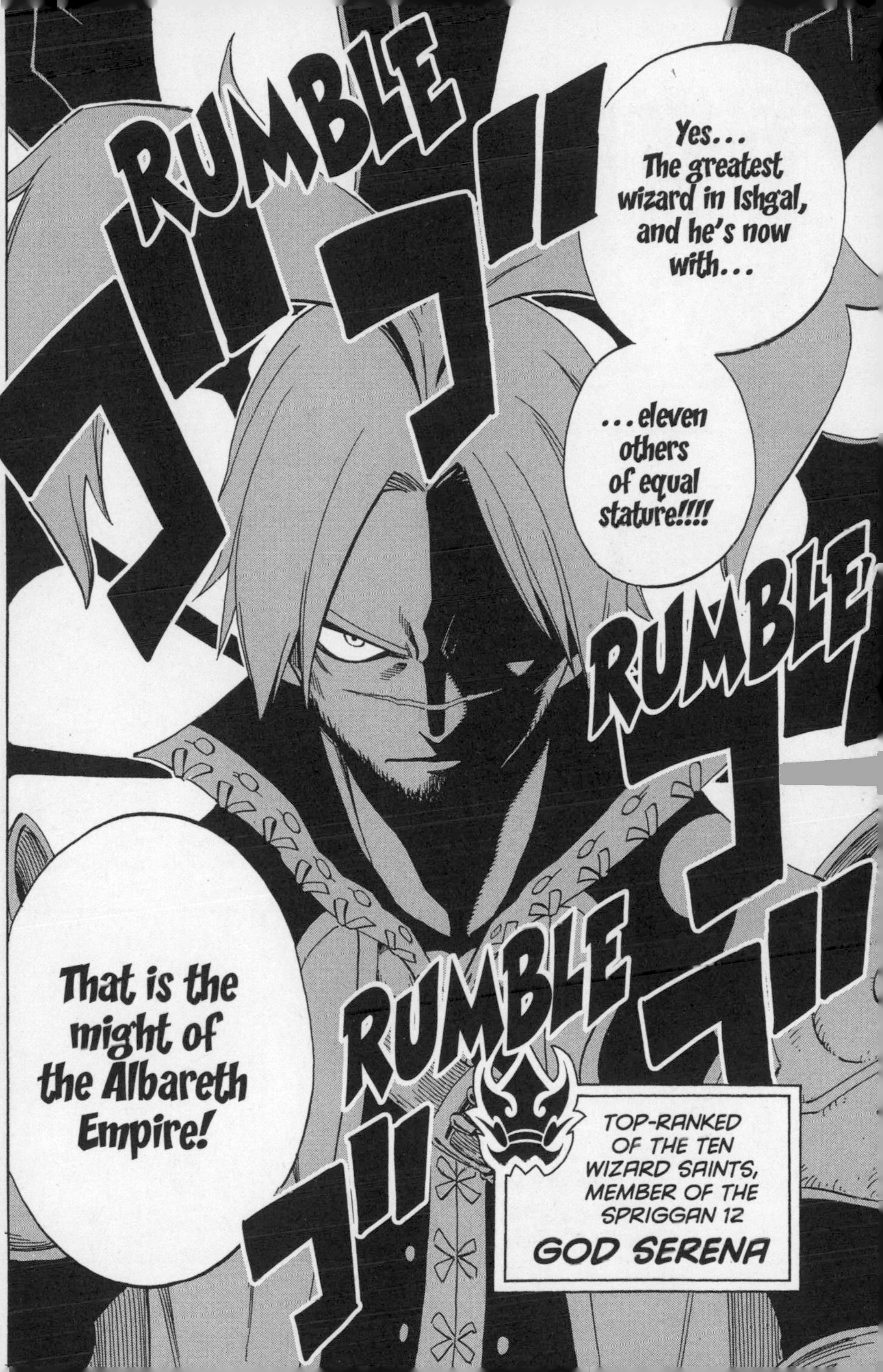
Yes... The greatest wizard in Ishgal, and he's now with...
RUMBLE
...eleven others of equal stature!!!!
RUMBLE
RUMBLE
That is the might of the Albareth Empire!
TOP-RANKED OF THE TEN WIZARD SAINTS, MEMBER OF THE SPRIGGAN 12
GOD SERENA

Chapter 441: Caracol Island

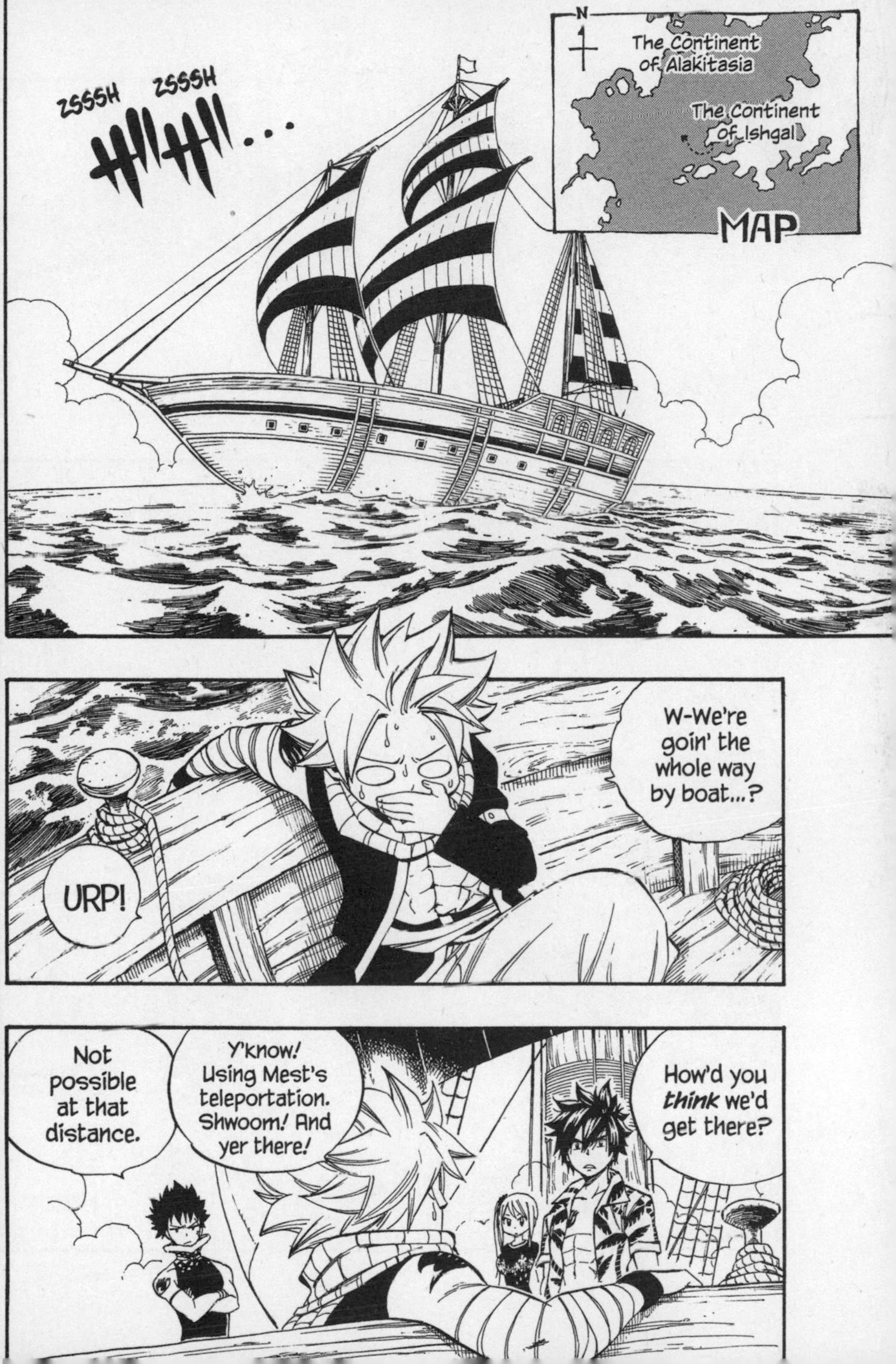
N
The Continent of Alakitasia
The Continent of Ishgal
MAP
ZSSSH ZSSSH
W-We're goin' the whole way by boat...?
URP!
How'd you *think* we'd get there?
Y'know! Using Mest's teleportation. Shwoom! And yer there!
Not possible at that distance.

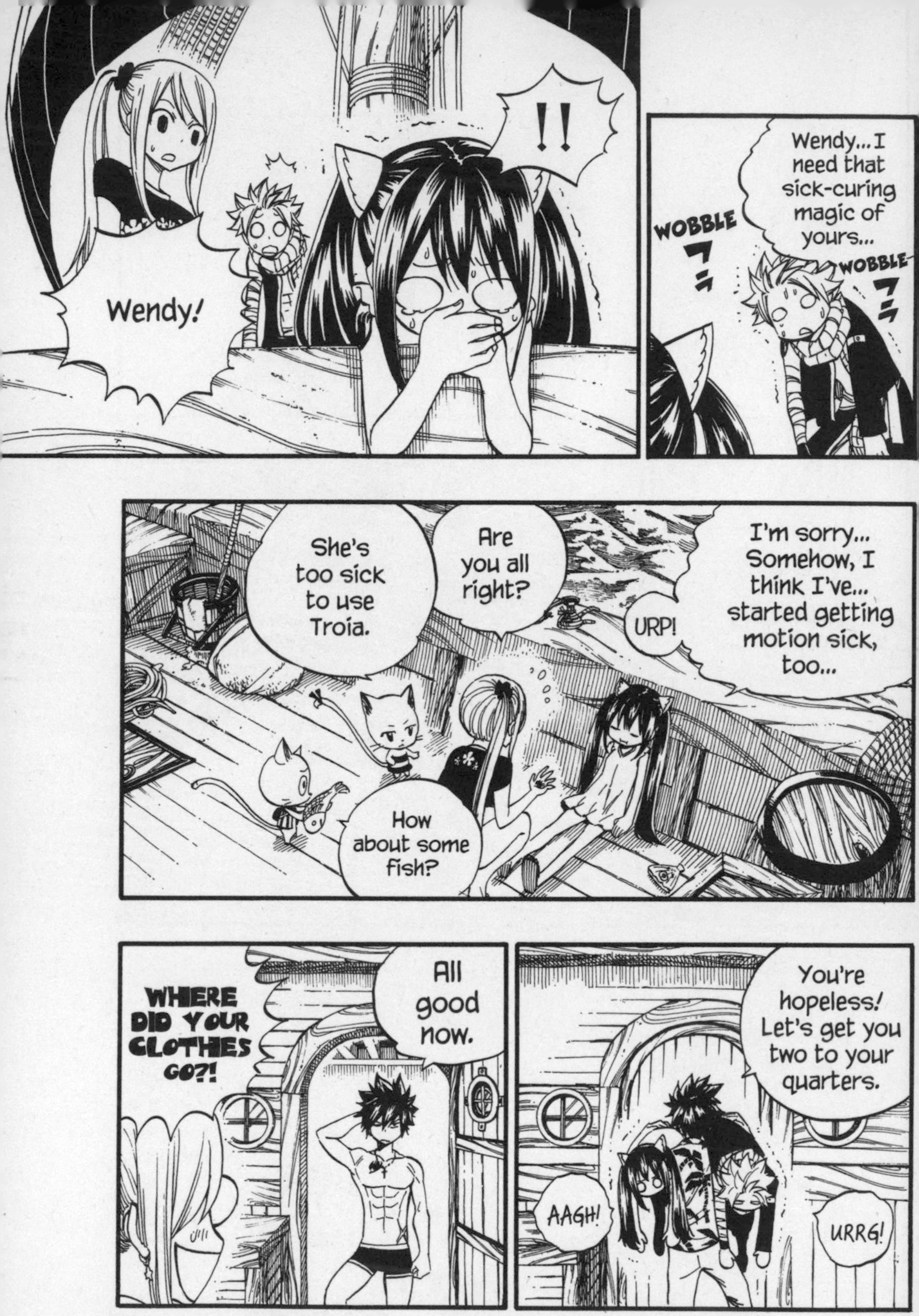

Wendy... I need that sick-curing magic of yours...
WOBBLE
WOBBLE
!!
Wendy!
I'm sorry... Somehow, I think I've... started getting motion sick, too...
URP!
Are you all right?
She's too sick to use Troia.
How about some fish?
You're hopeless! Let's get you two to your quarters.
URRG!
AAGH!
All good now.
WHERE DID YOUR CLOTHES GO?!

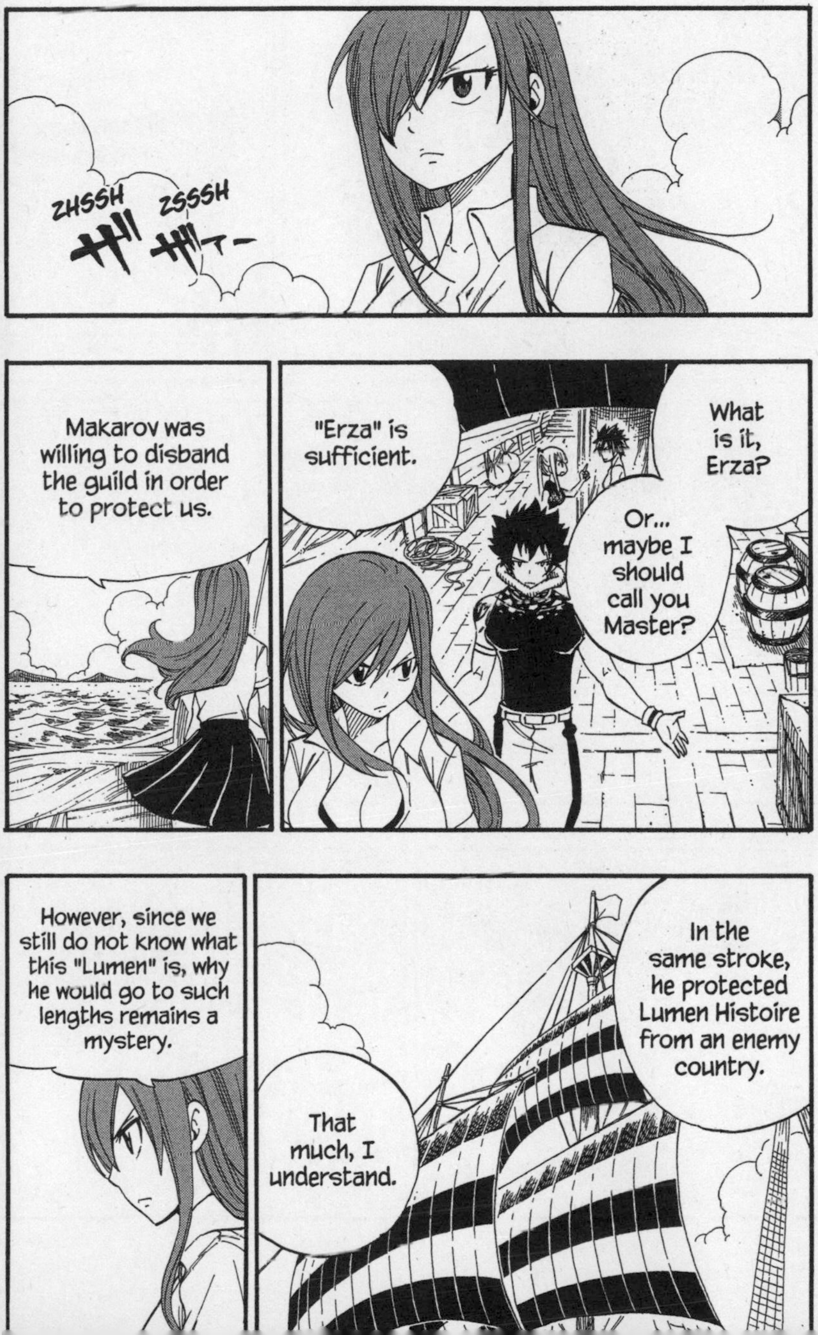
ZSSSH
ZHSSH
What is it, Erza?
Or... maybe I should call you Master?
"Erza" is sufficient.
Makarov was willing to disband the guild in order to protect us.
In the same stroke, he protected Lumen Histoire from an enemy country.
That much, I understand.
However, since we still do not know what this "Lumen" is, why he would go to such lengths remains a mystery.

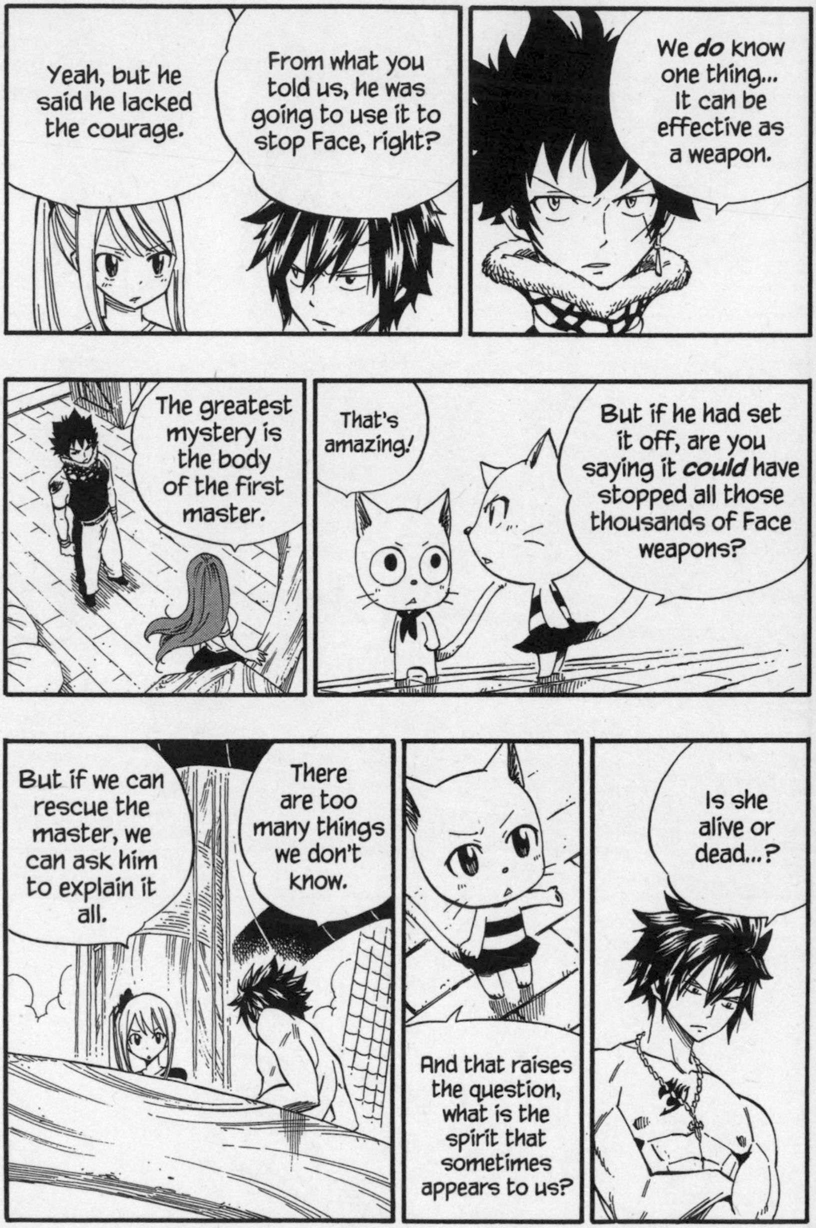
We do know one thing... It can be effective as a weapon.
From what you told us, he was going to use it to stop Face, right?
Yeah, but he said he lacked the courage.
But if he had set it off, are you saying it could have stopped all those thousands of Face weapons?
That's amazing!
The greatest mystery is the body of the first master.
Is she alive or dead...?
And that raises the question, what is the spirit that sometimes appears to us?
There are too many things we don't know.
But if we can rescue the master, we can ask him to explain it all.

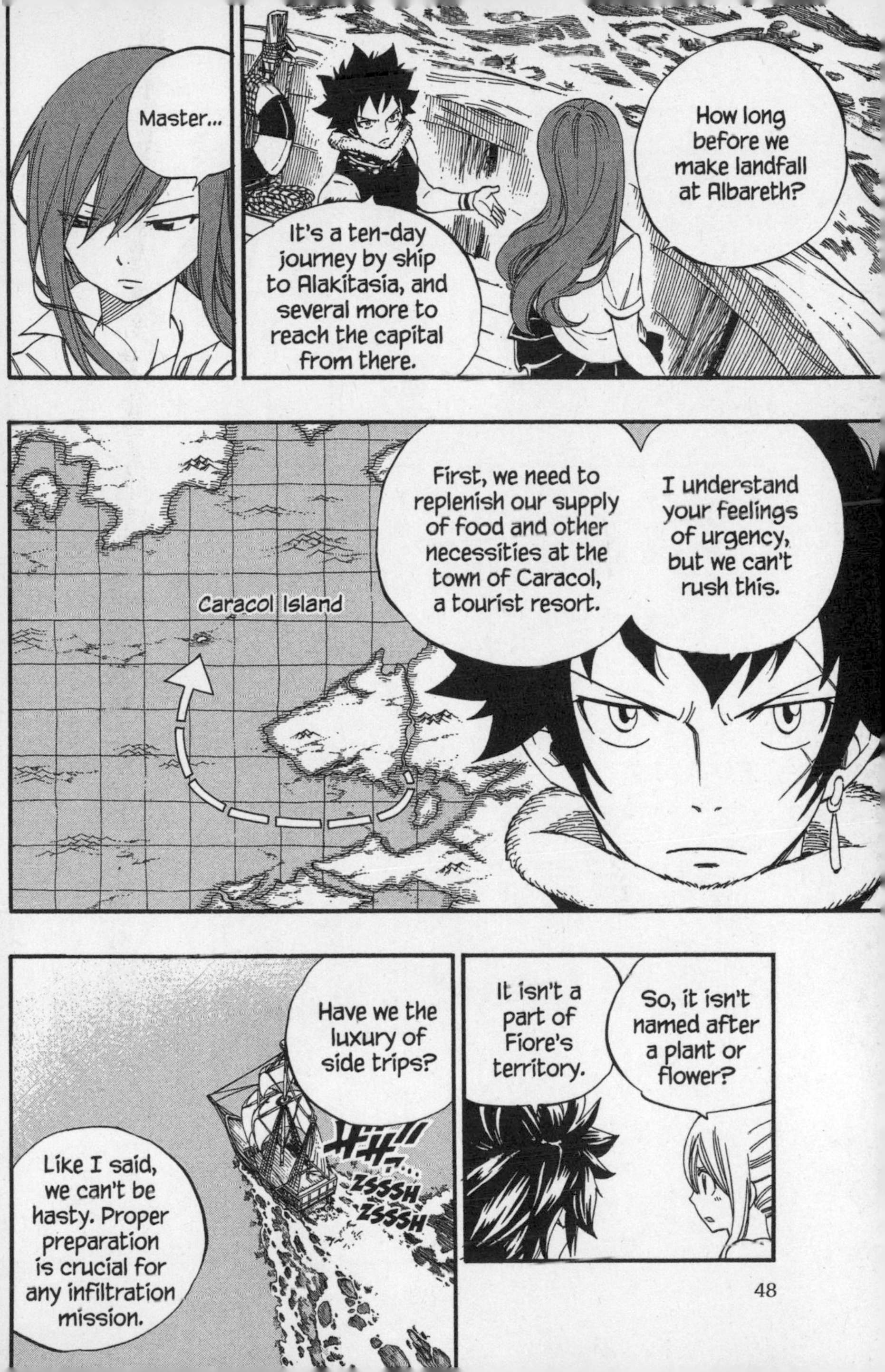
How long before we make landfall at Albareth?
It's a ten-day journey by ship to Alakitasia, and several more to reach the capital from there.
Master...
I understand your feelings of urgency, but we can't rush this.
First, we need to replenish our supply of food and other necessities at the town of Caracol, a tourist resort.
Caracol Island
So, it isn't named after a plant or flower?
It isn't a part of Fiore's territory.
Have we the luxury of side trips?
ZSSSH
ZSSSH
Like I said, we can't be hasty. Proper preparation is crucial for any infiltration mission.

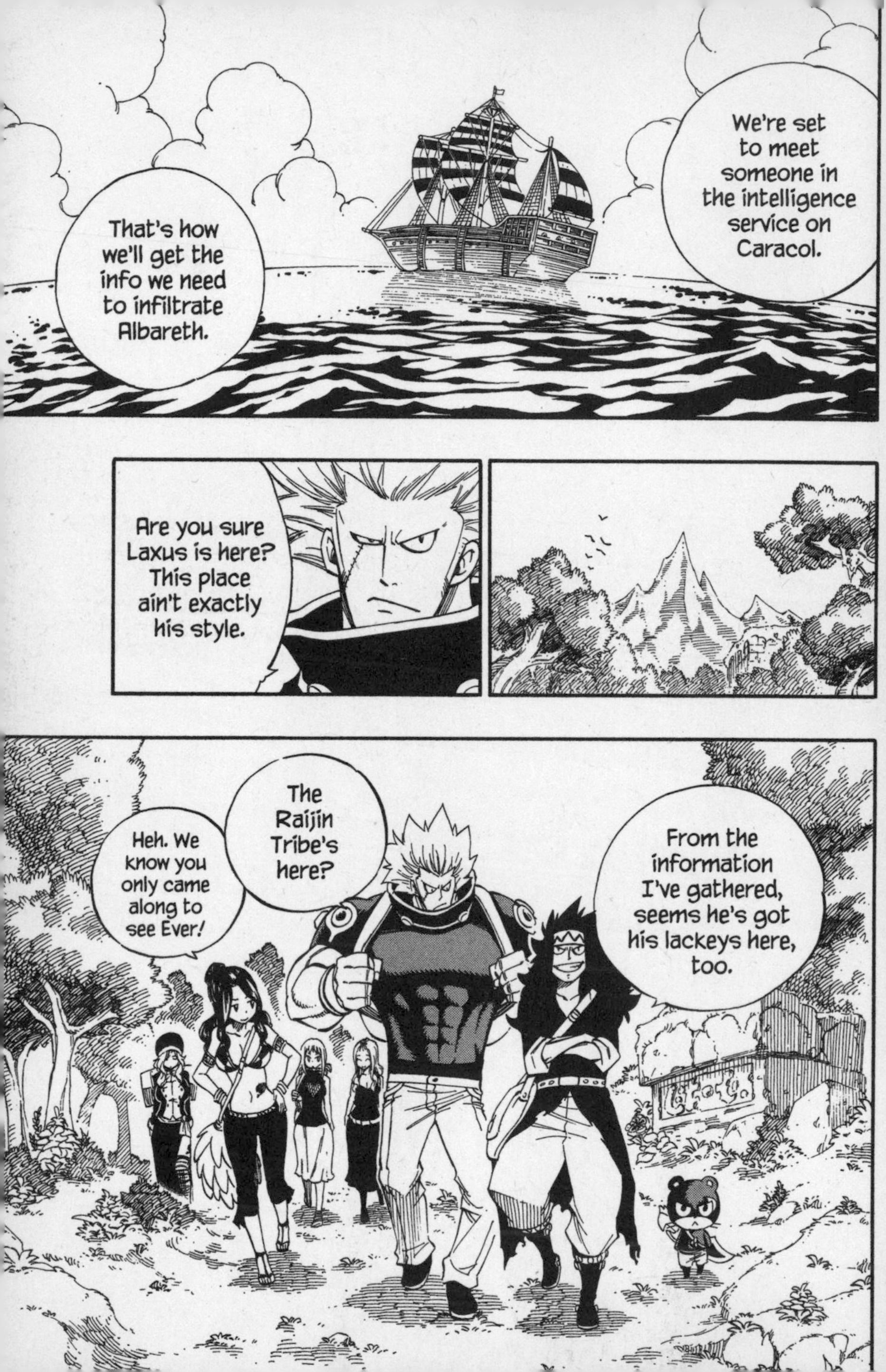
We're set to meet someone in the intelligence service on Caracol.
That's how we'll get the info we need to infiltrate Albareth.
Are you sure Laxus is here? This place ain't exactly his style.
From the information I've gathered, seems he's got his lackeys here, too.
The Raijin Tribe's here?
Heh. We know you only came along to see Ever!

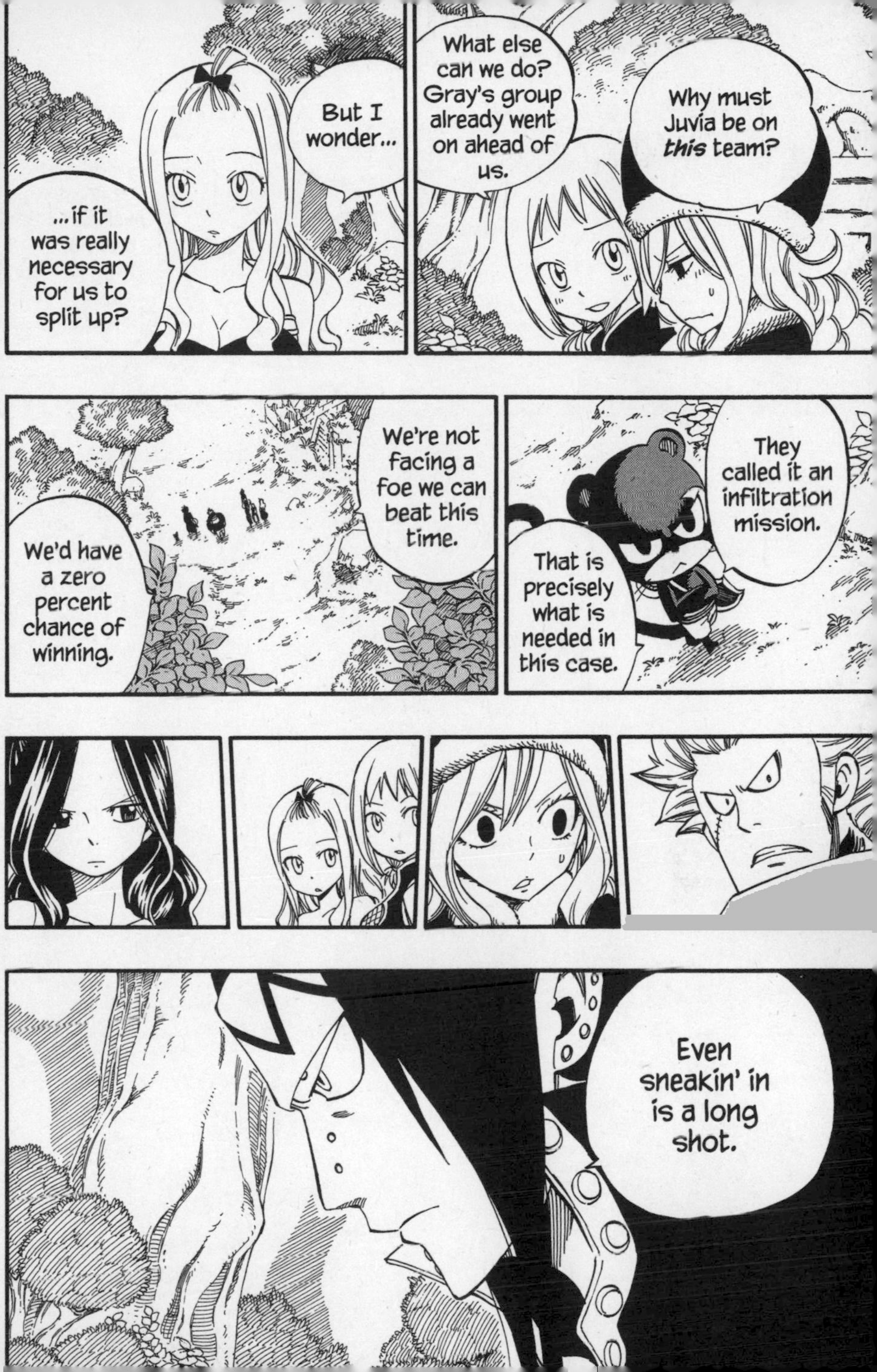
Why must Juvia be on *this* team?
What else can we do? Gray's group already went on ahead of us.
But I wonder...
...if it was really necessary for us to split up?
They called it an infiltration mission.
That is precisely what is needed in this case.
We're not facing a foe we can beat this time.
We'd have a zero percent chance of winning.
Even sneakin' in is a long shot.

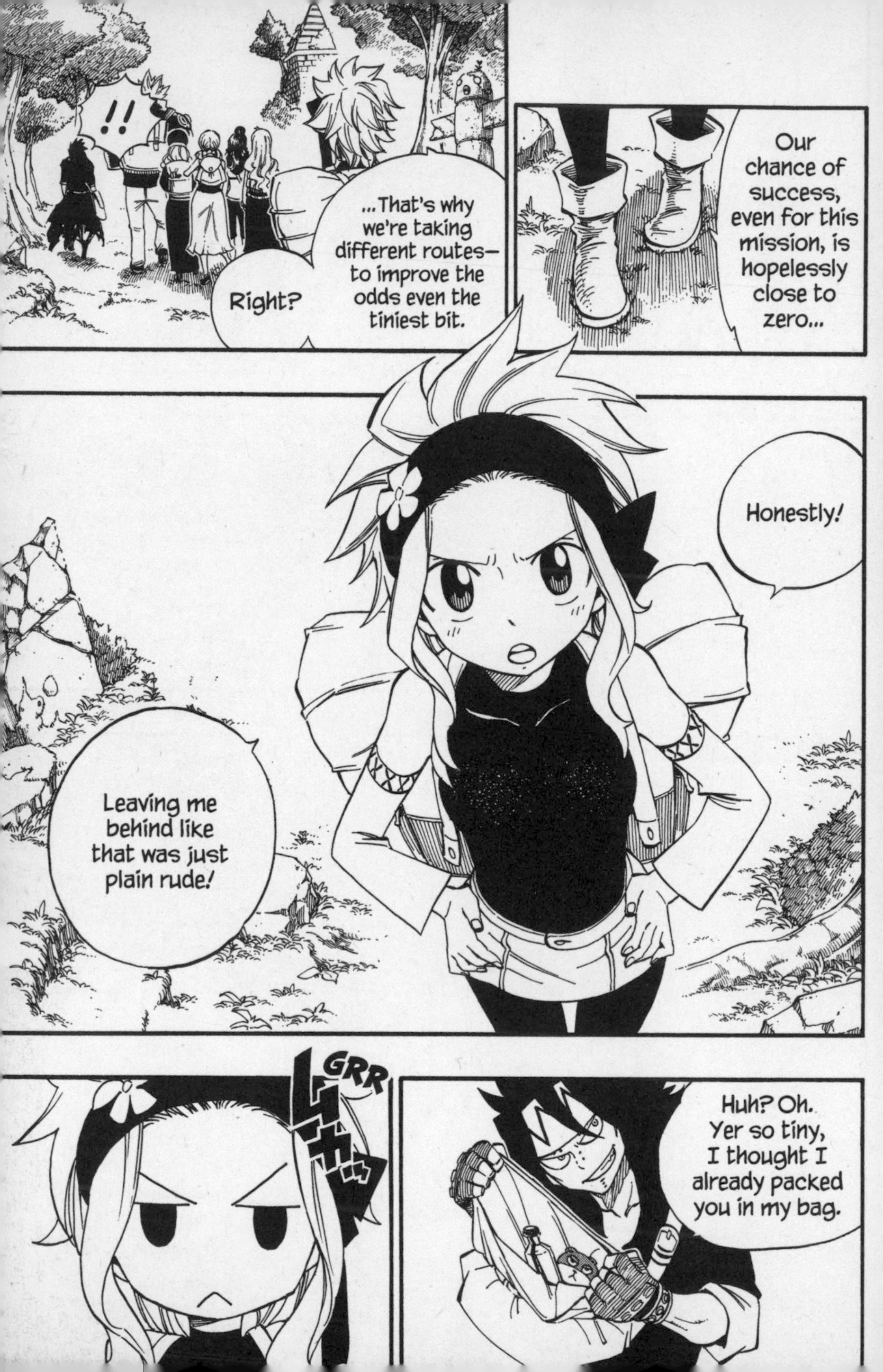
Our chance of success, even for this mission, is hopelessly close to zero...
...That's why we're taking different routes—to improve the odds even the tiniest bit.
Right?
!!
Honestly!
Leaving me behind like that was just plain rude!
Huh? Oh. Yer so tiny, I thought I already packed you in my bag.
GRR

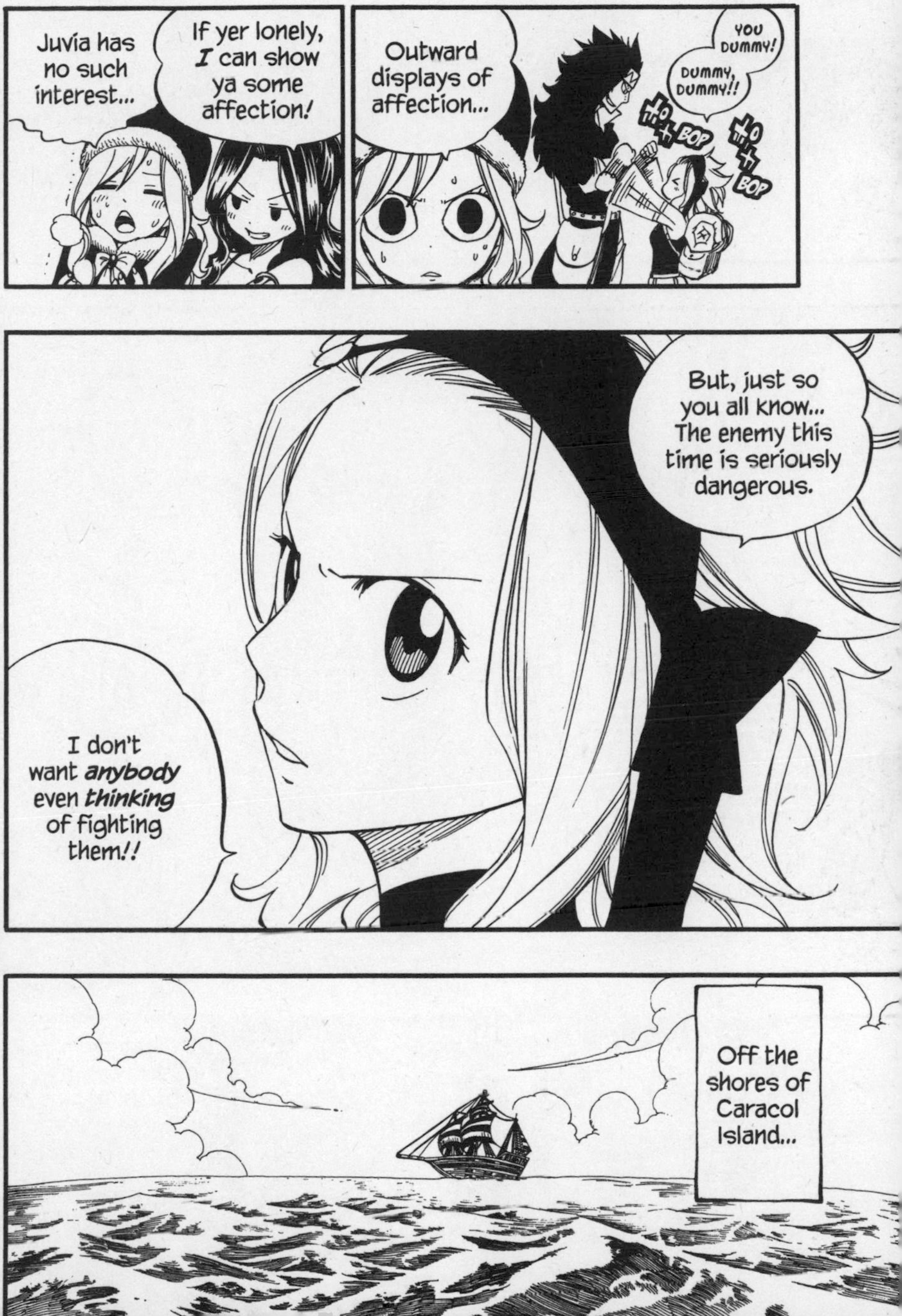
YOU DUMMY!
DUMMY, DUMMY!!
BOP
BOP
Outward displays of affection...
If yer lonely, *I* can show ya some affection!
Juvia has no such interest...
But, just so you all know... The enemy this time is seriously dangerous.
I don't want ***anybody*** even ***thinking*** of fighting them!!
Off the shores of Caracol Island...

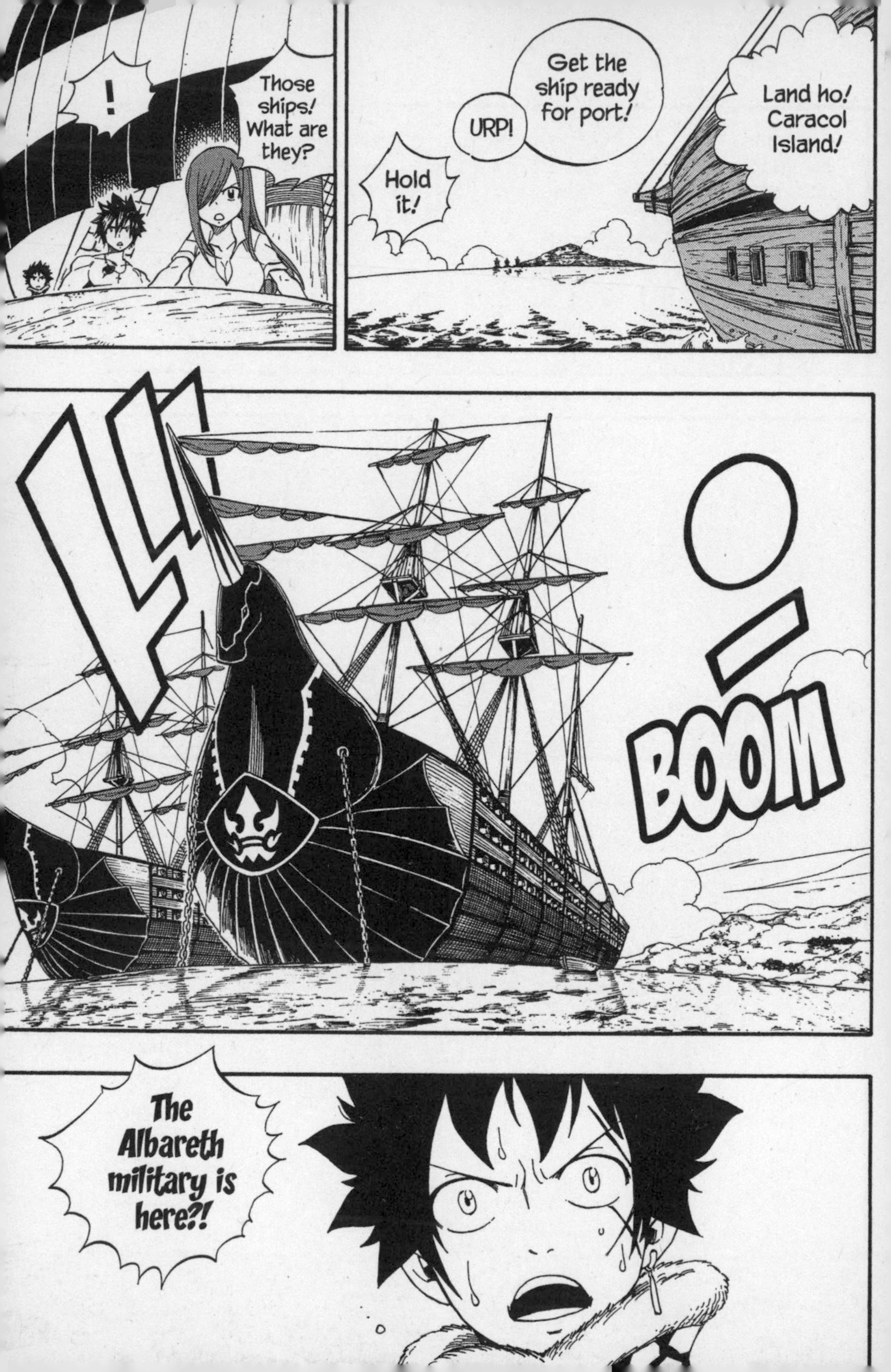
Land ho! Caracol Island!
Get the ship ready for port!
URP!
Hold it!
Those ships! What are they?
!
BOOM
!!
The Albareth military is here?!

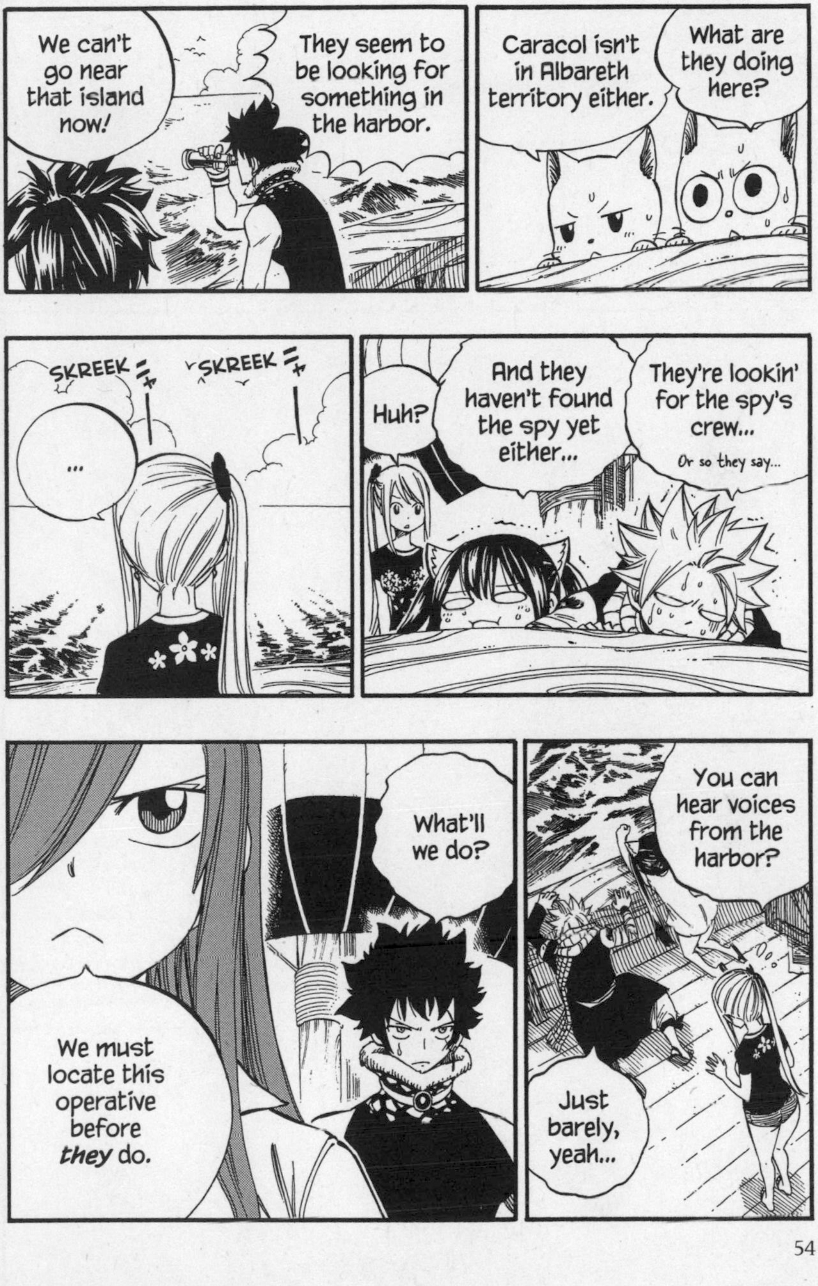
What are they doing here?
Caracol isn't in Albareth territory either.
They seem to be looking for something in the harbor.
We can't go near that island now!
They're lookin' for the spy's crew...
Or so they say...
And they haven't found the spy yet either...
Huh?
SKREEK
SKREEK
...
You can hear voices from the harbor?
Just barely, yeah...
What'll we do?
We must locate this operative before *they* do.

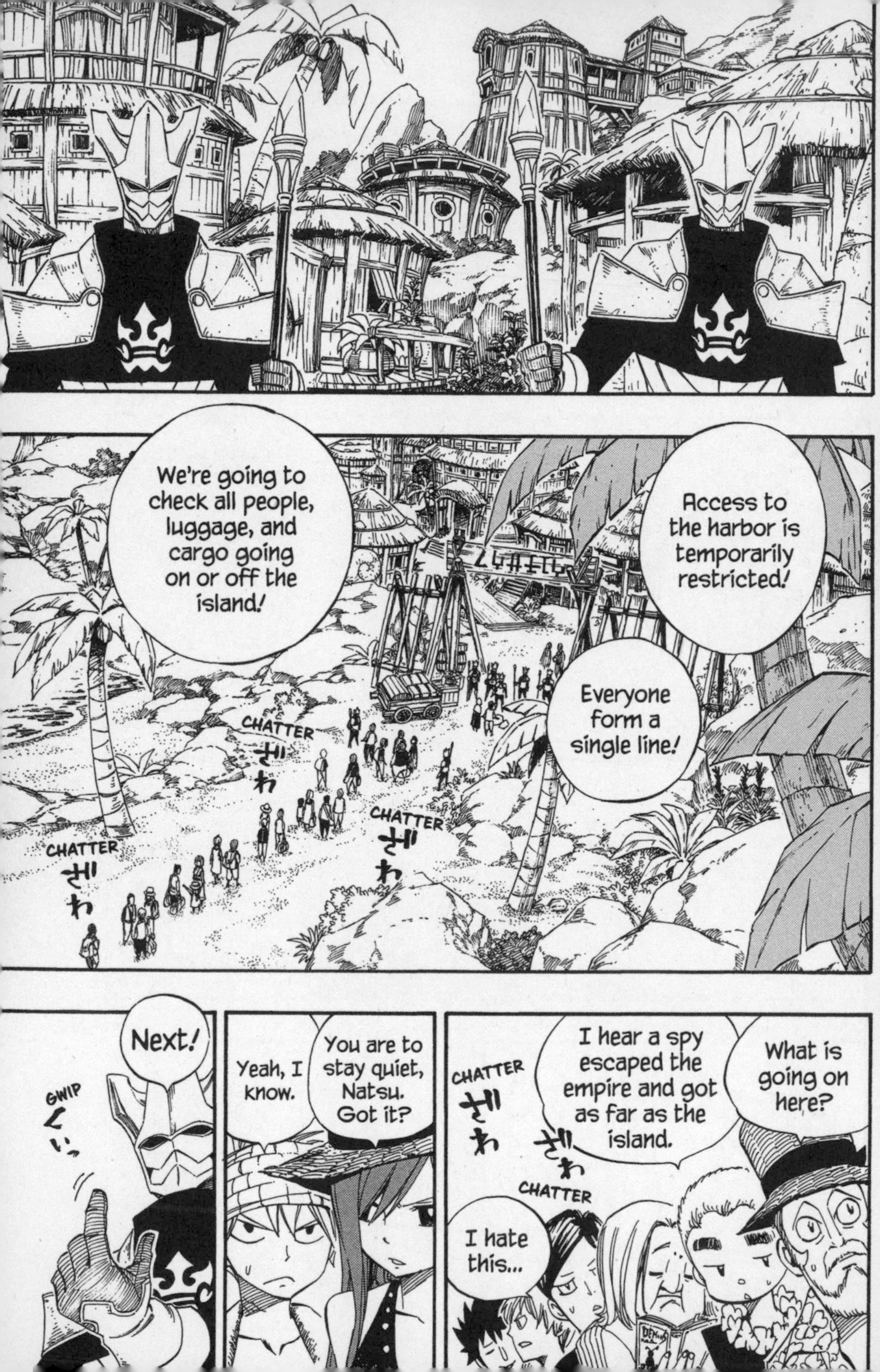
Access to the harbor is temporarily restricted!
Everyone form a single line!
We're going to check all people, luggage, and cargo going on or off the island!
CHATTER
ざわ
CHATTER
ざわ
CHATTER
ざわ
What is going on here?
I hear a spy escaped the empire and got as far as the island.
CHATTER
ざわ
ざわ
CHATTER
I hate this...
You are to stay quiet, Natsu. Got it?
Yeah, I know.
Next!
GWIP
くいっ

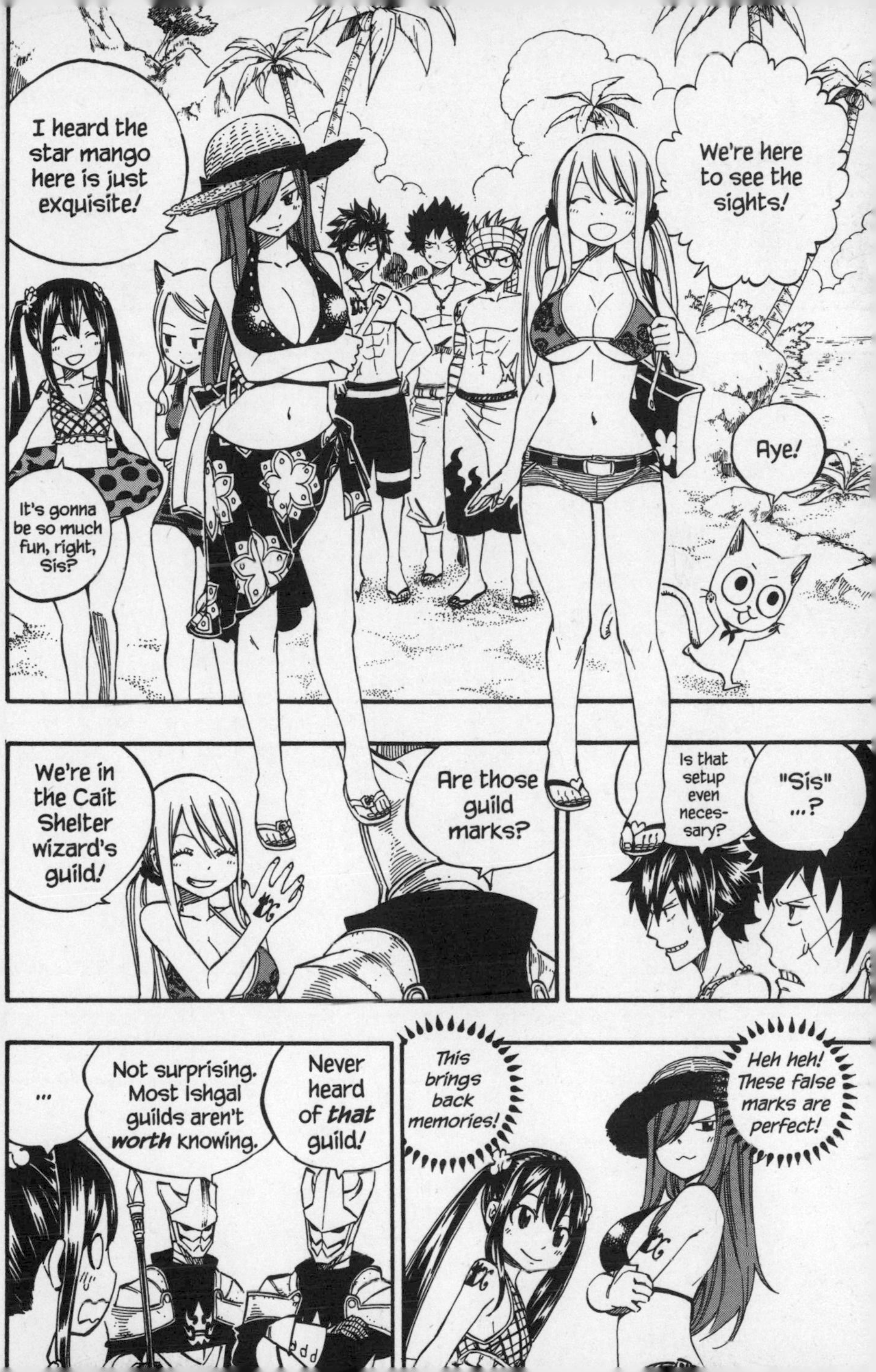
We're here to see the sights!
Aye!
I heard the star mango here is just exquisite!
It's gonna be so much fun, right, Sis?
"Sis" ...?
Is that setup even neces-sary?
Are those guild marks?
We're in the Cait Shelter wizard's guild!
Heh heh! These false marks are perfect!
This brings back memories!
Never heard of *that* guild!
Not surprising. Most Ishgal guilds aren't *worth* knowing.
...

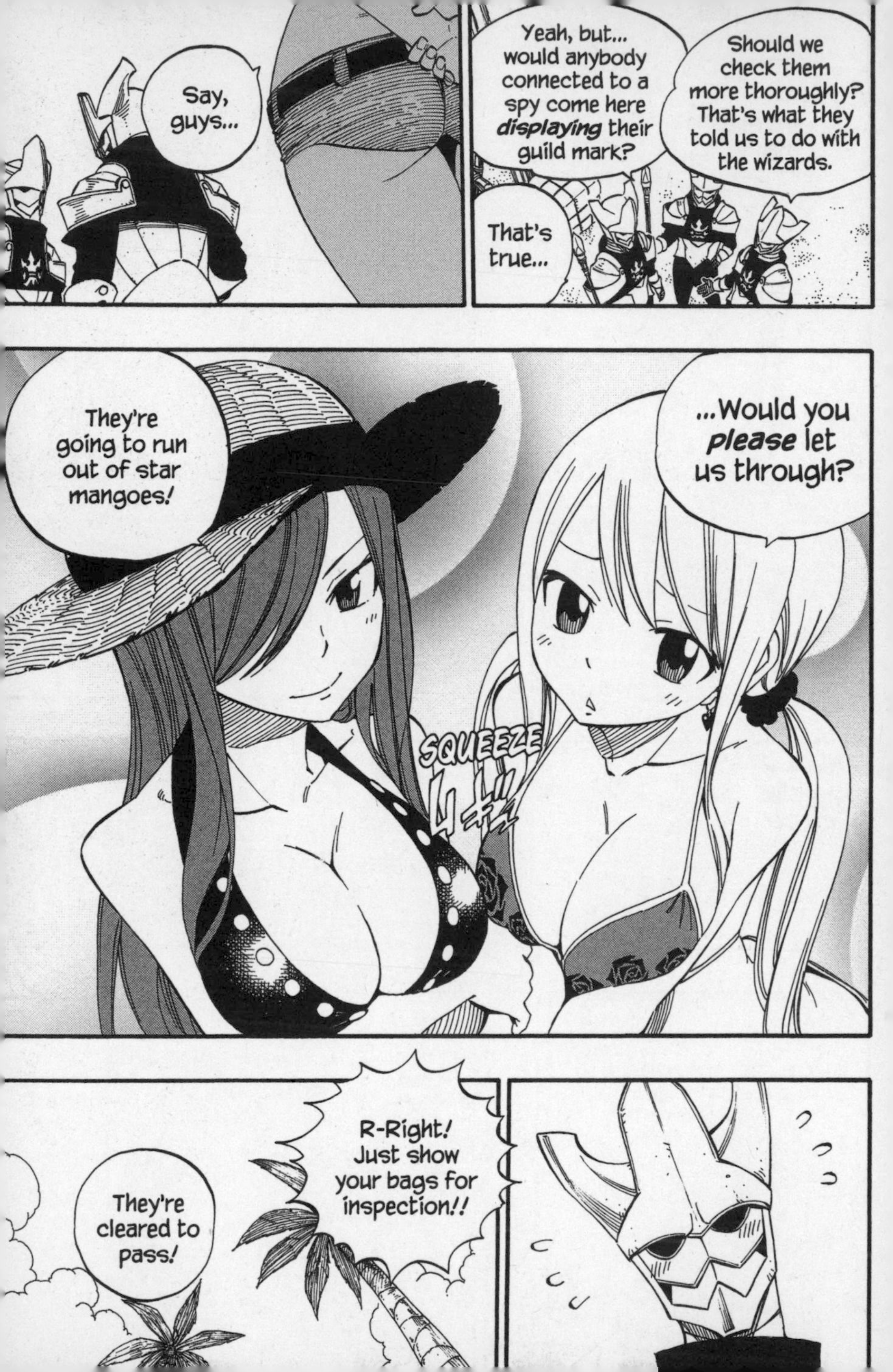
Should we check them more thoroughly? That's what they told us to do with the wizards.
Yeah, but... would anybody connected to a spy come here *displaying* their guild mark?
That's true...
Say, guys...
...Would you *please* let us through?
They're going to run out of star mangoes!
SQUEEZE
R-Right! Just show your bags for inspection!!
They're cleared to pass!

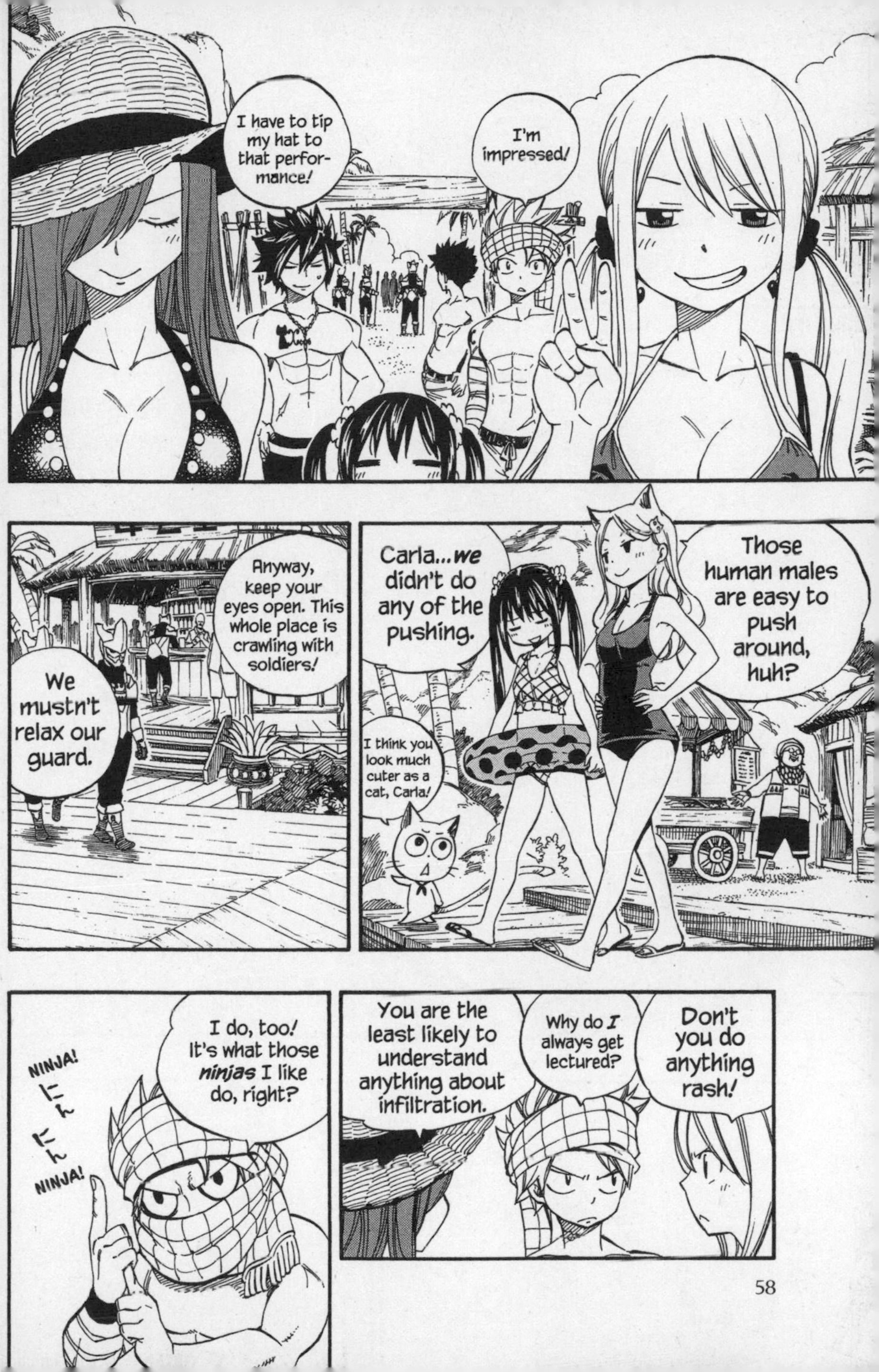
I'm impressed!
I have to tip my hat to that performance!
Those human males are easy to push around, huh?
Carla...*we* didn't do any of the pushing.
I think you look much cuter as a cat, Carla!
Anyway, keep your eyes open. This whole place is crawling with soldiers!
We mustn't relax our guard.
Don't you do anything rash!
Why do *I* always get lectured?
You are the least likely to understand anything about infiltration.
I do, too! It's what those *ninjas* I like do, right?
NINJA!
にん
にん
NINJA!

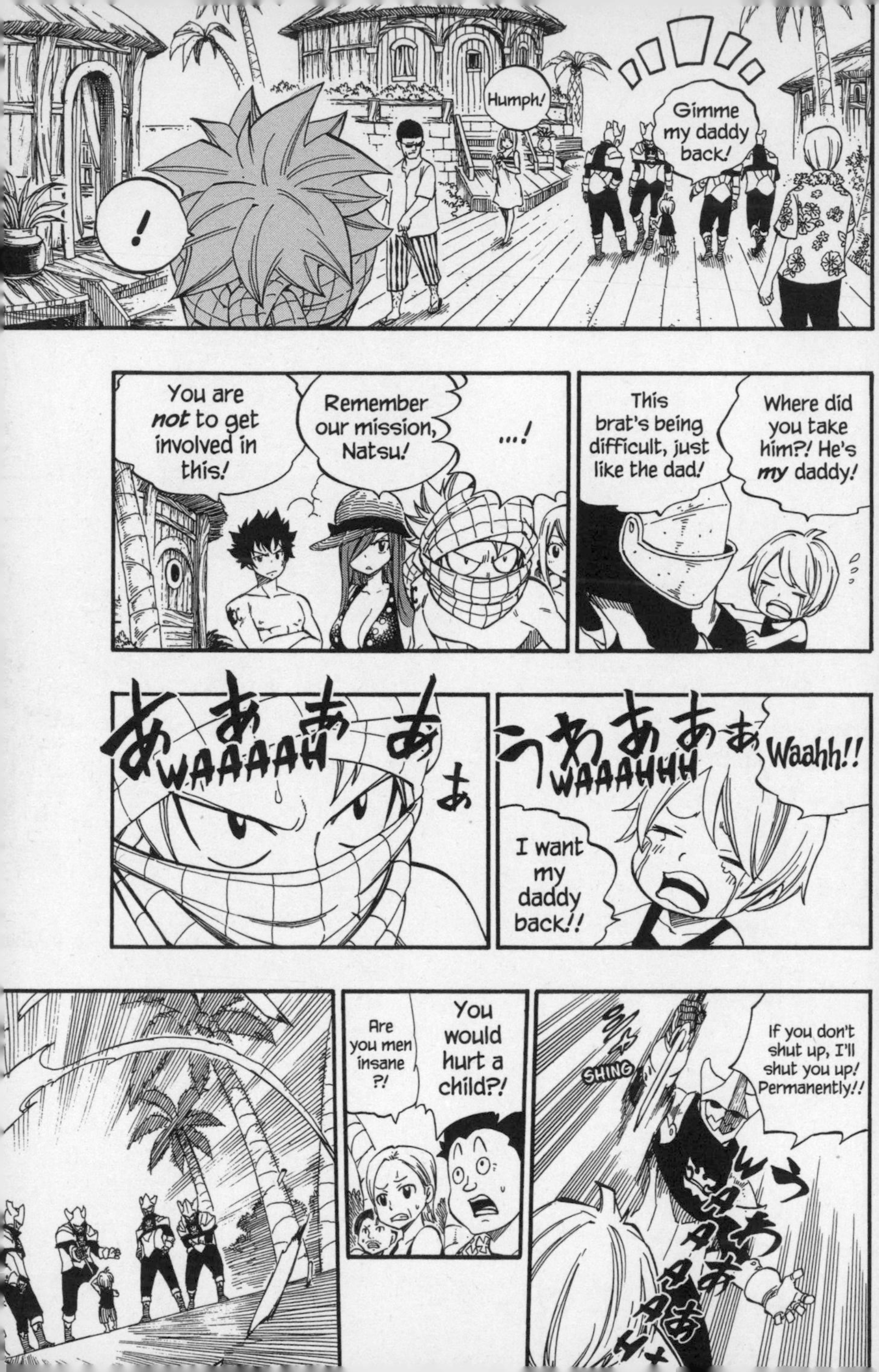
Gimme my daddy back!
Humph!
!
Where did you take him?! He's my daddy!
This brat's being difficult, just like the dad!
...!
Remember our mission, Natsu!
You are not to get involved in this!
Waahh!!
うわあああ
WAAAHHH
I want my daddy back!!
あああ
WAAAAH
あ あ
If you don't shut up, I'll shut you up! Permanently!!
SHING
You would hurt a child?!
Are you men insane?!

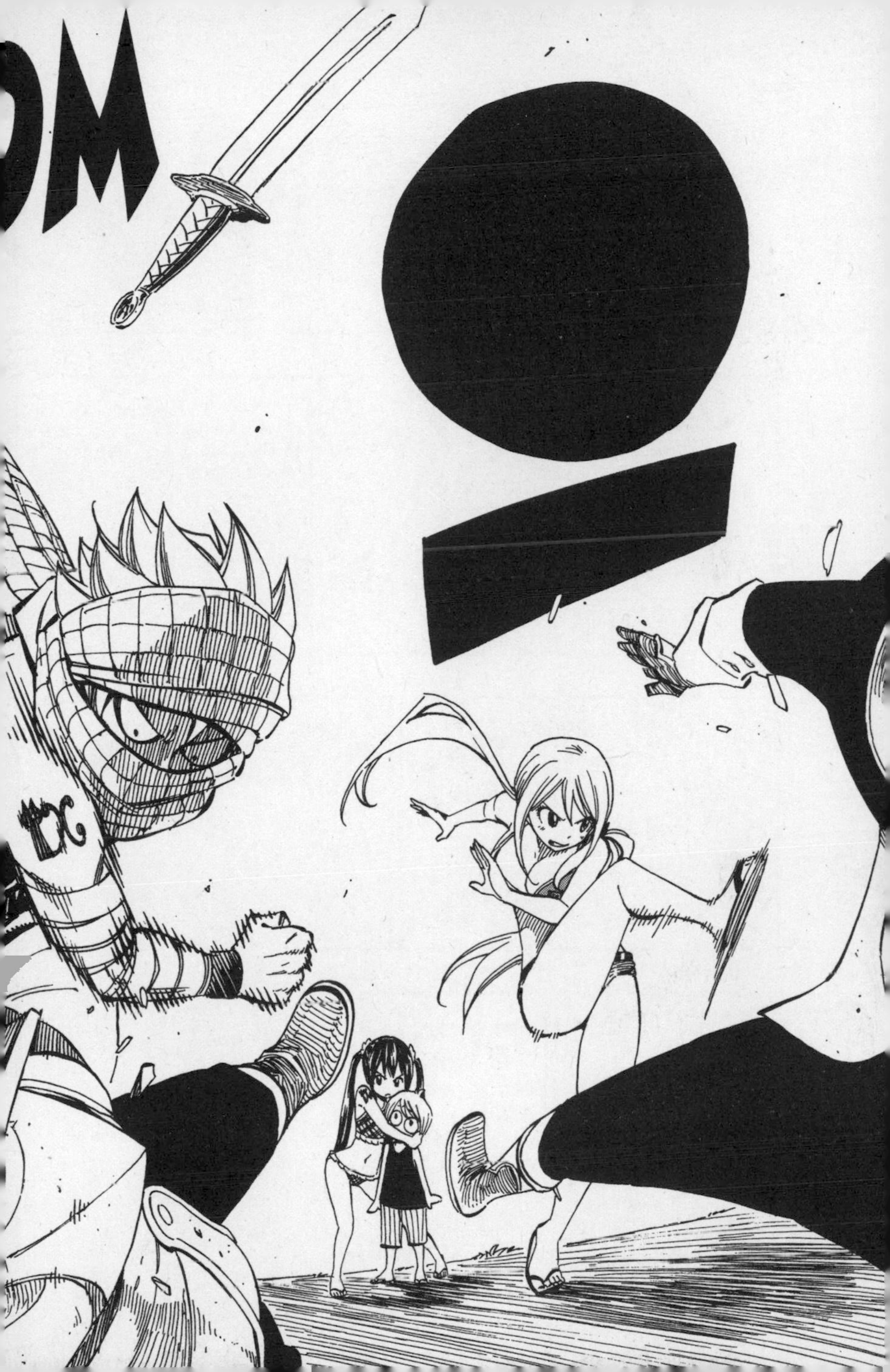
OM

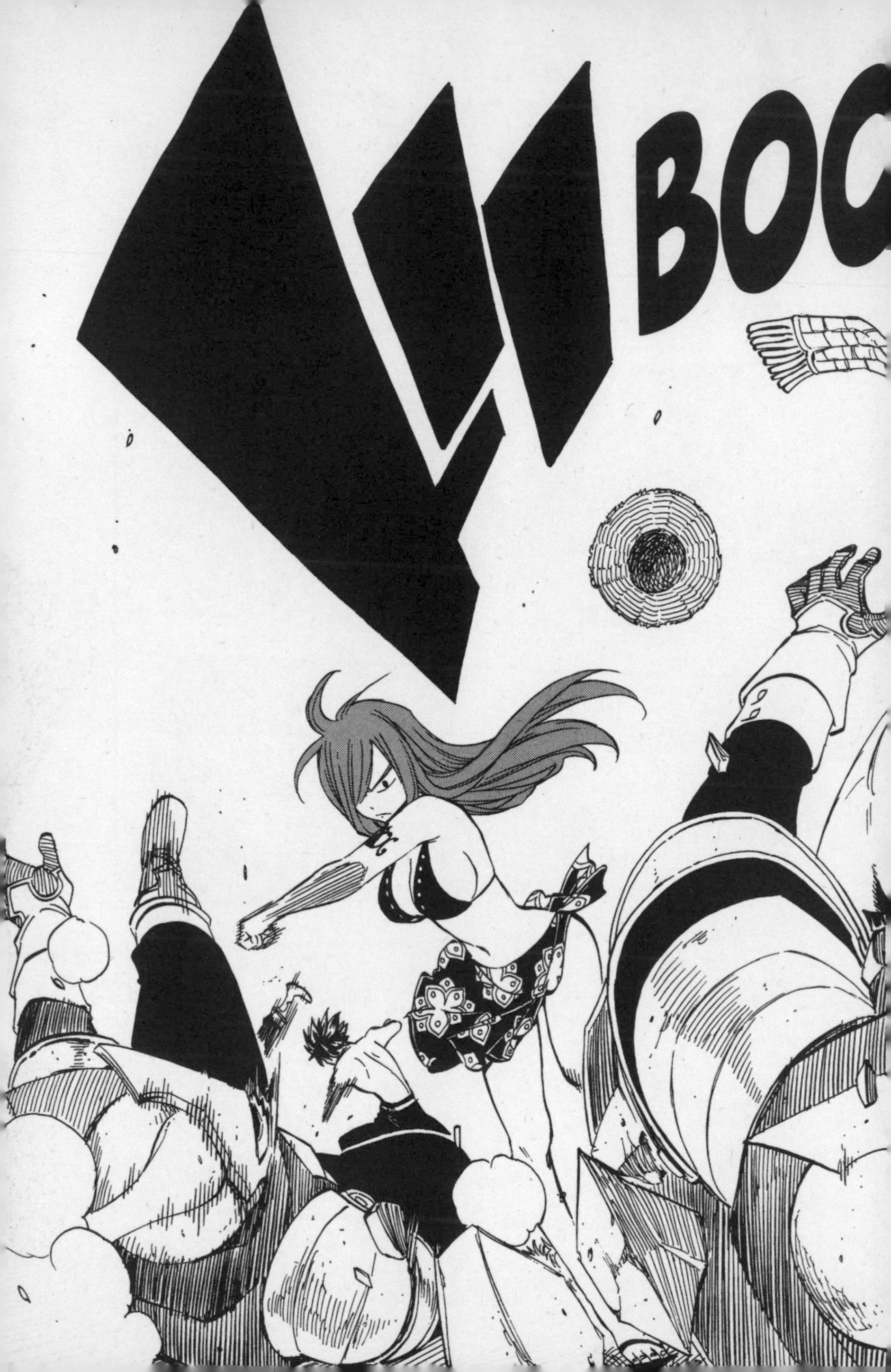
BOC

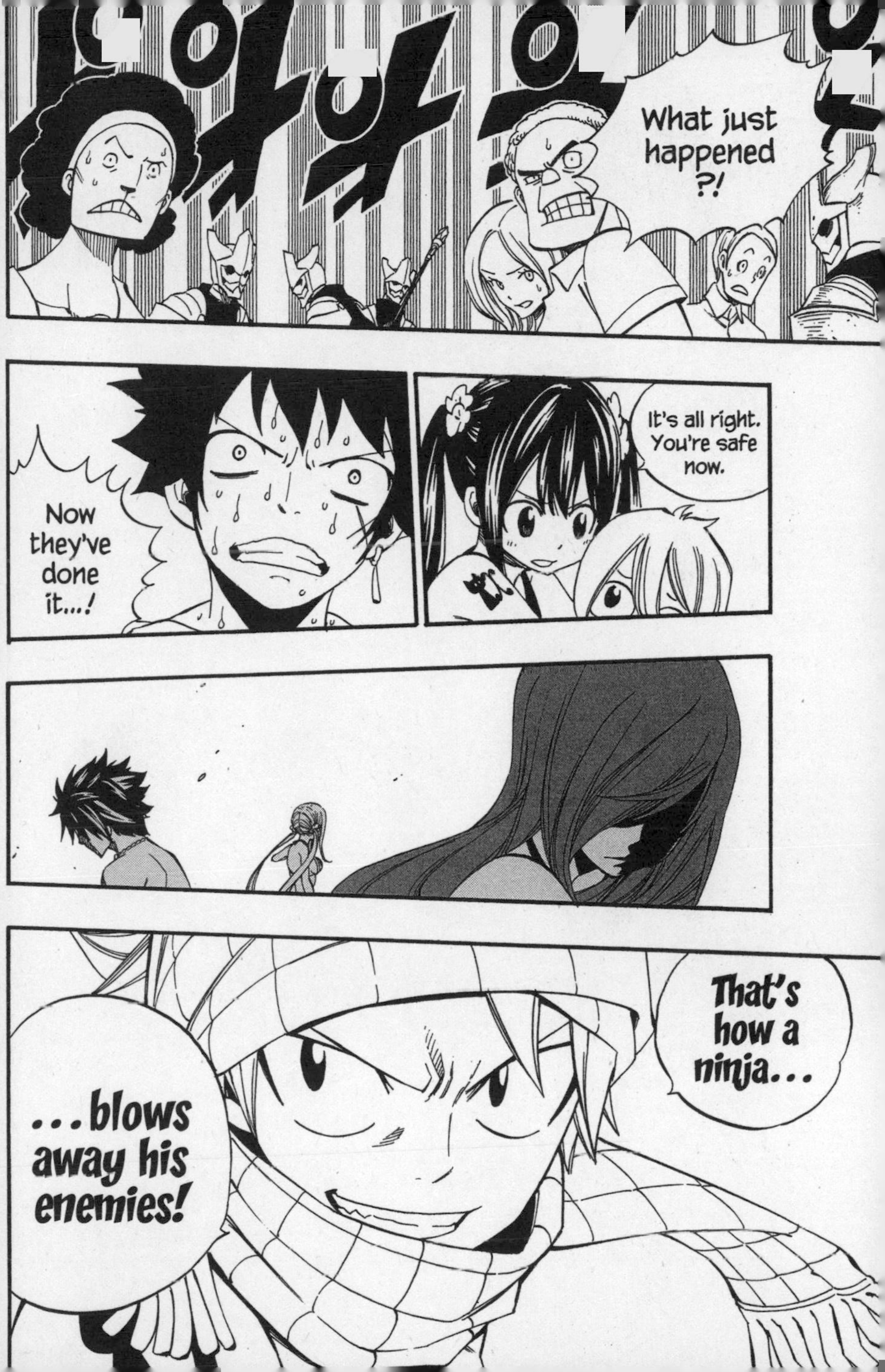
What just happened ?!
It's all right. You're safe now.
Now they've done it...!
That's how a ninja...
...blows away his enemies!

FAIRY TAIL
フェアリーテイル

Chapter 442: Rules of the Area

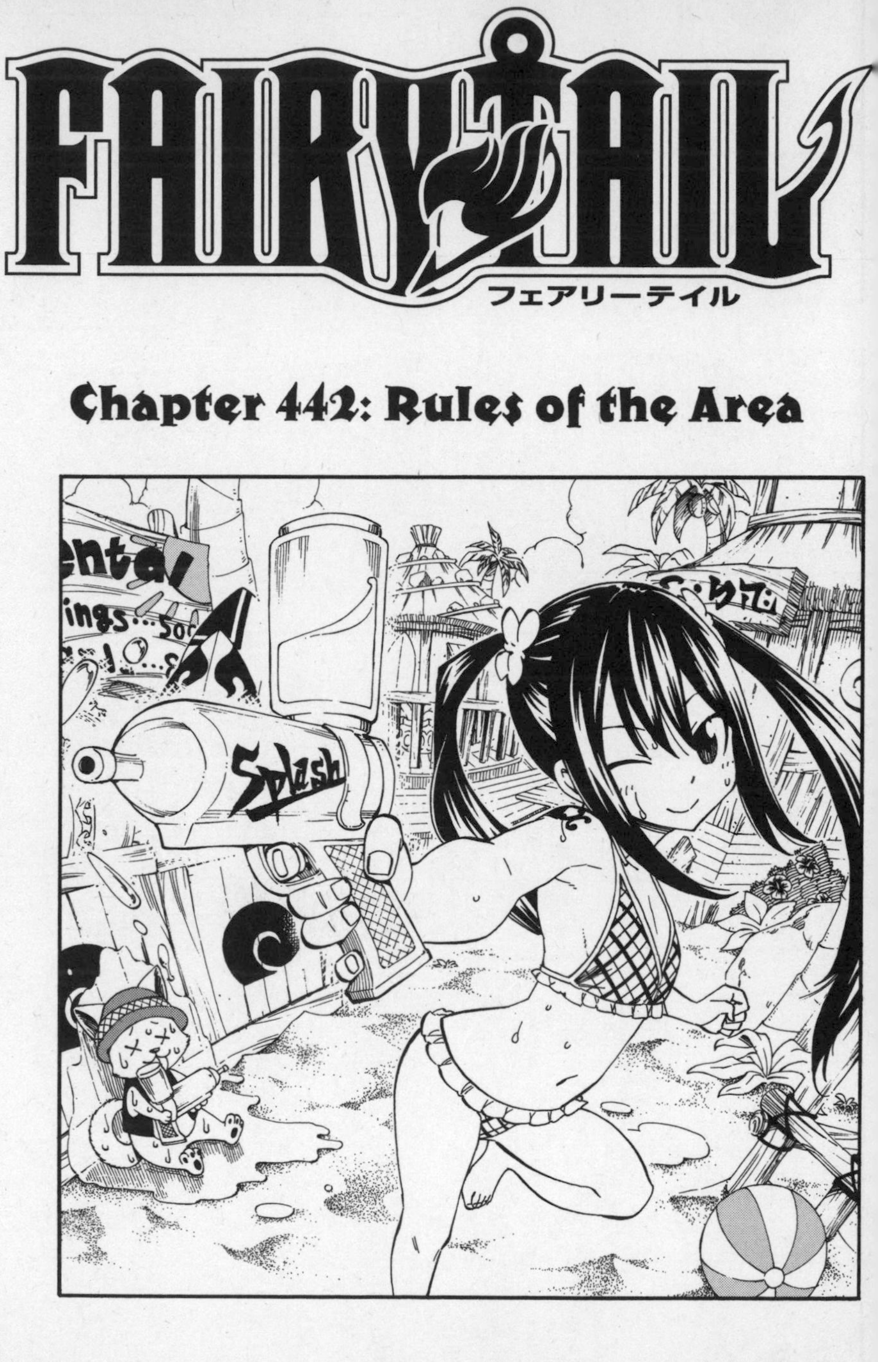
Splash

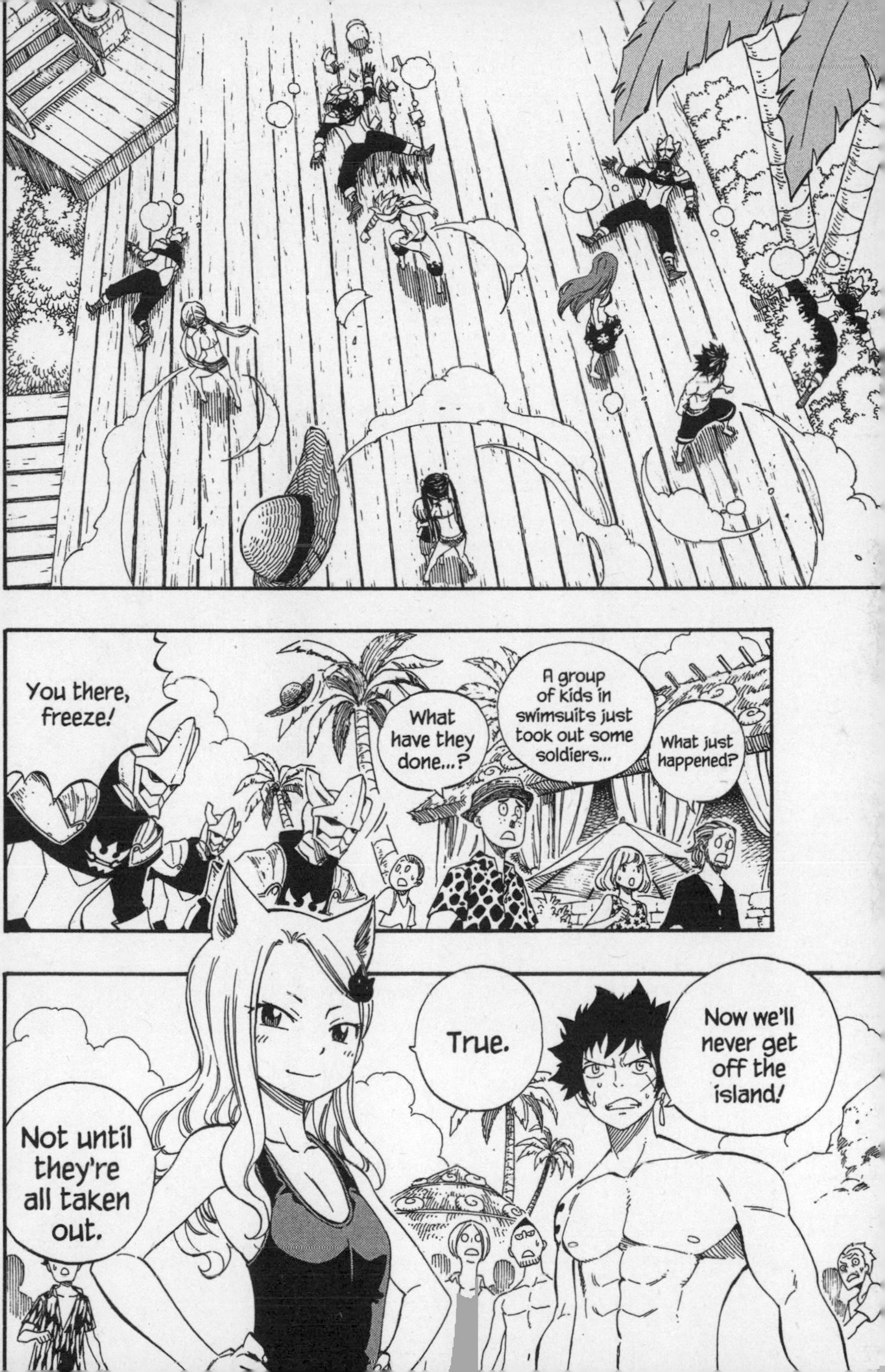

What just happened?
A group of kids in swimsuits just took out some soldiers...
What have they done...?
You there, freeze!
Now we'll never get off the island!
True.
Not until they're all taken out.

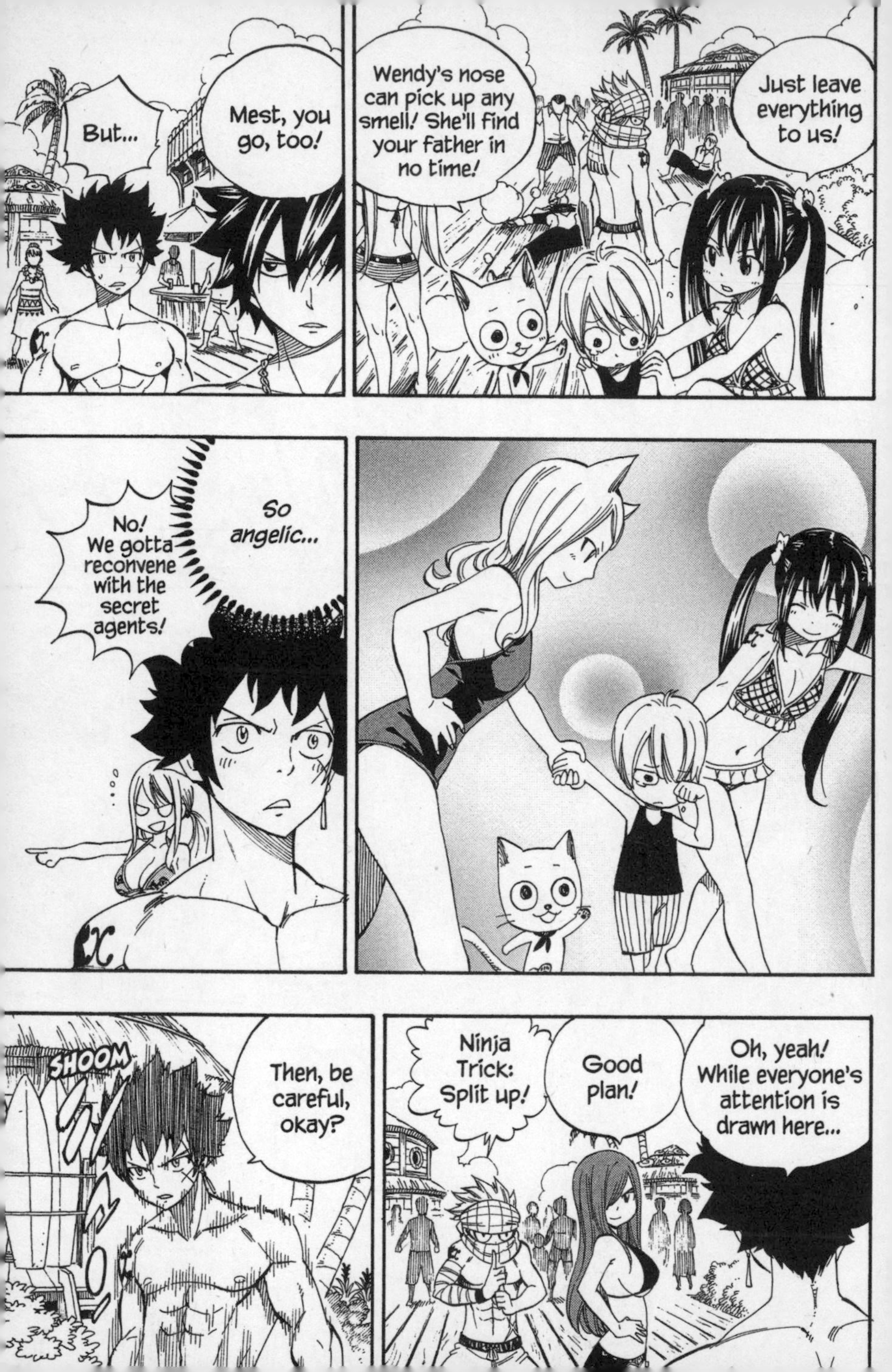
Just leave everything to us!
Wendy's nose can pick up any smell! She'll find your father in no time!
Mest, you go, too!
But...
So angelic...
No! We gotta reconvene with the secret agents!
Oh, yeah! While everyone's attention is drawn here...
Good plan!
Ninja Trick: Split up!
Then, be careful, okay?
SHOOM

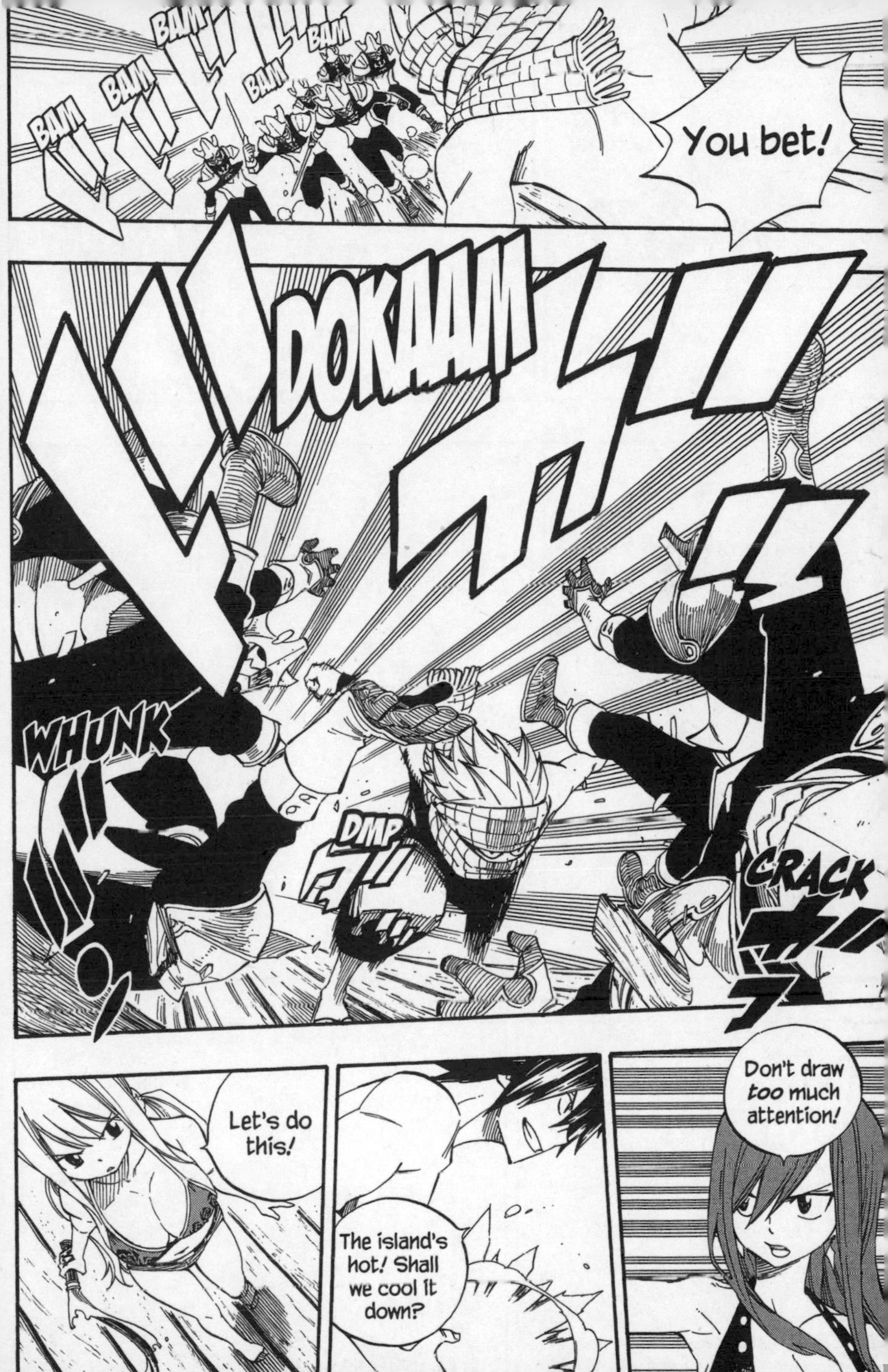
You bet!
BAM
BAM
BAM
BAM
BAM
DOKAAM
CRACK
DMP
WHUNK
Don't draw *too* much attention!
The island's hot! Shall we cool it down?
Let's do this!

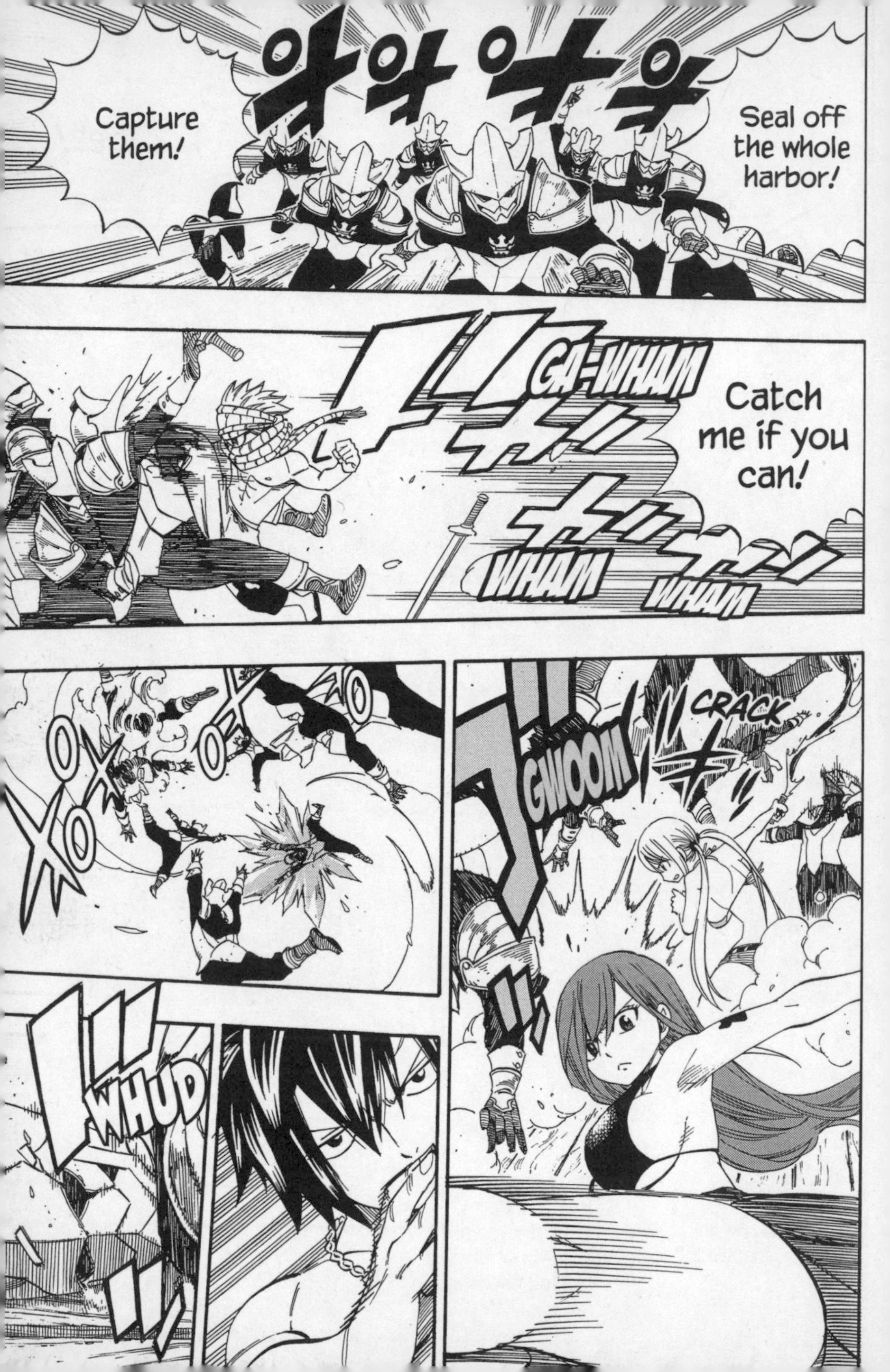
Seal off the whole harbor!
Capture them!
Catch me if you can!
GA-WHAM
WHAM
WHAM
CRACK
GWOOM
WHUD

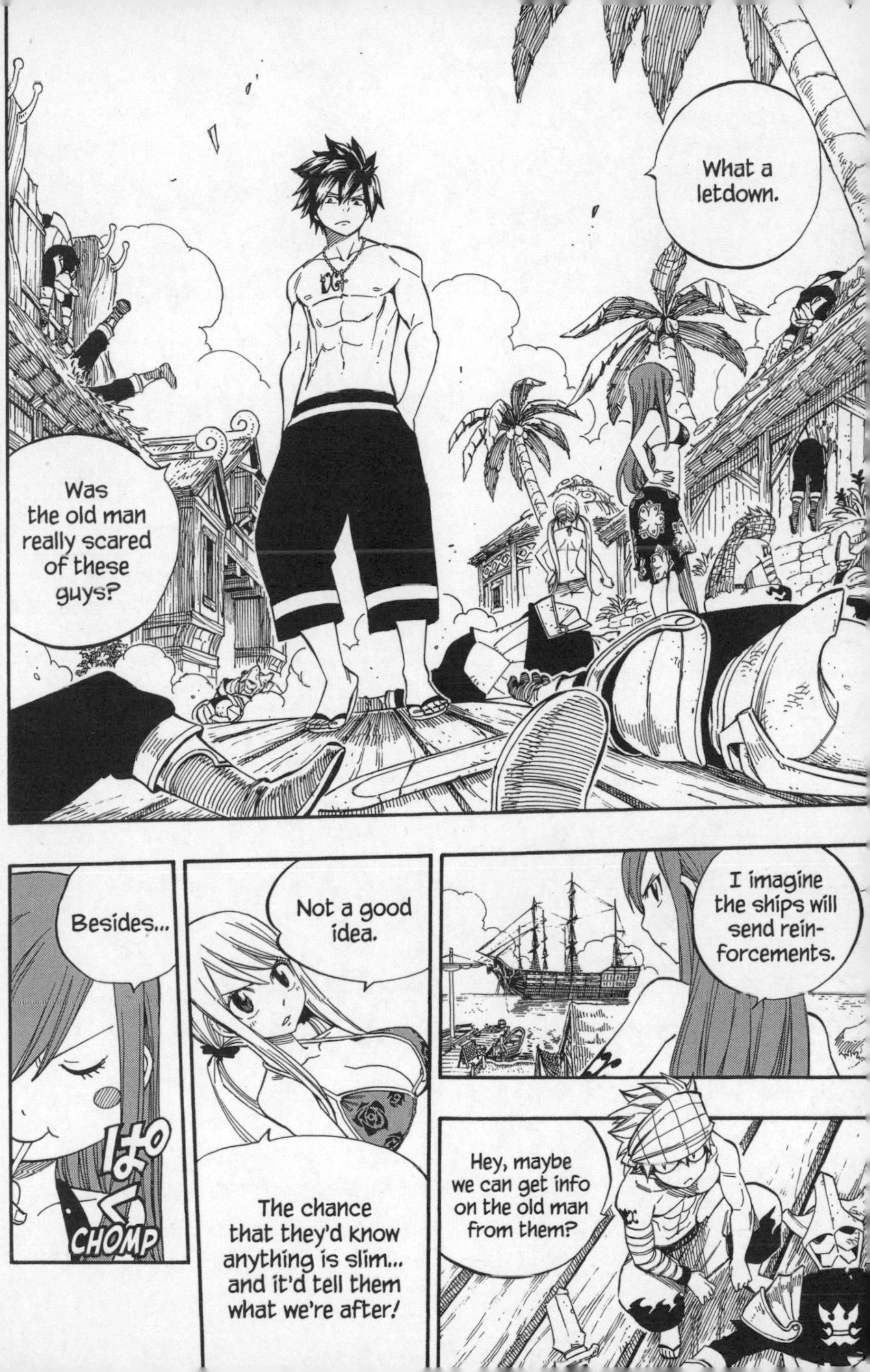
What a letdown.
Was the old man really scared of these guys?
I imagine the ships will send reinforcements.
Hey, maybe we can get info on the old man from them?
Not a good idea.
The chance that they'd know anything is slim... and it'd tell them what we're after!
Besides...
ぱく
CHOMP

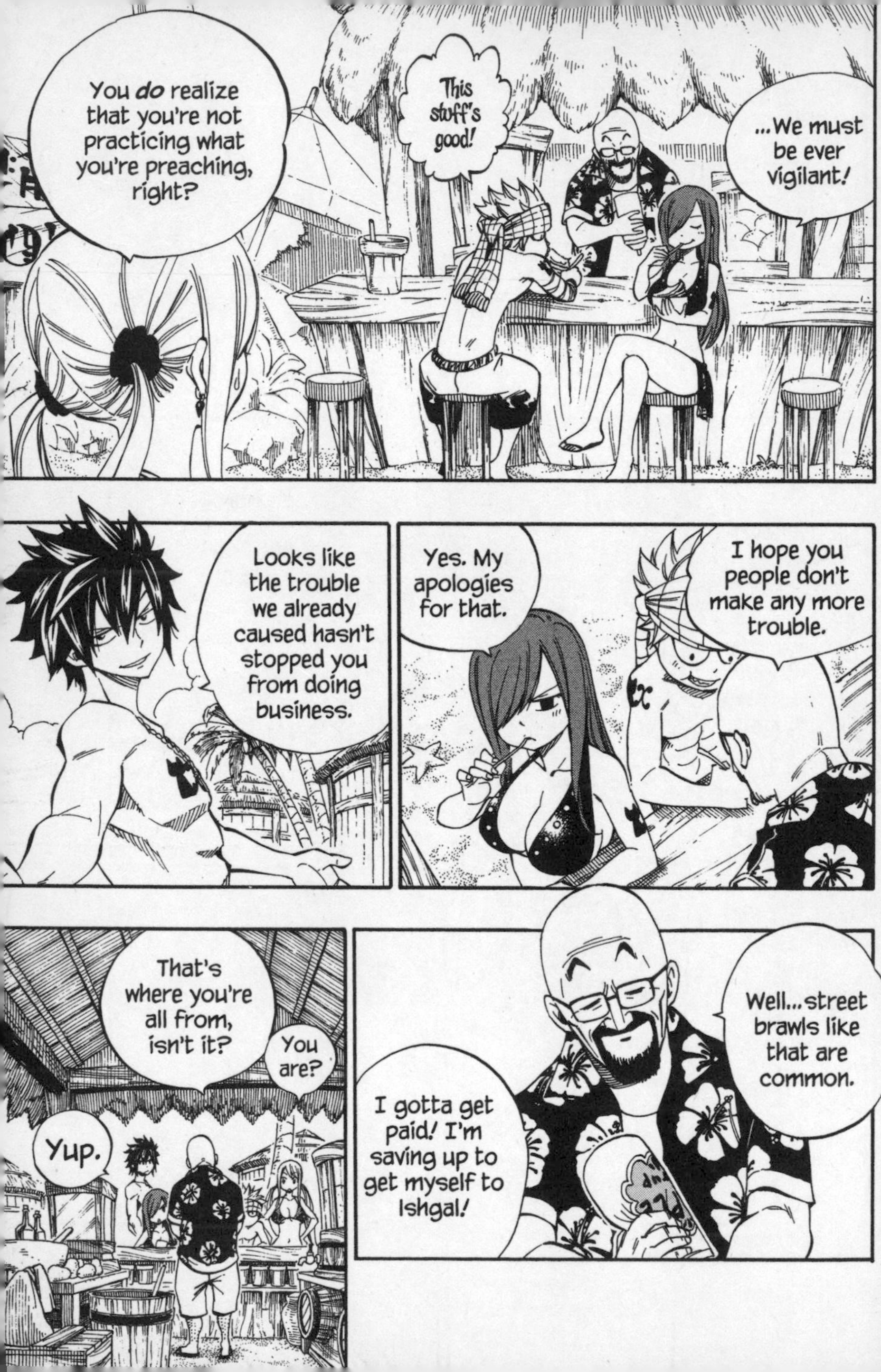
...We must be ever vigilant!
This stuff's good!
You *do* realize that you're not practicing what you're preaching, right?
I hope you people don't make any more trouble.
Yes. My apologies for that.
Looks like the trouble we already caused hasn't stopped you from doing business.
Well...street brawls like that are common.
I gotta get paid! I'm saving up to get myself to Ishgal!
That's where you're all from, isn't it?
You are?
Yup.

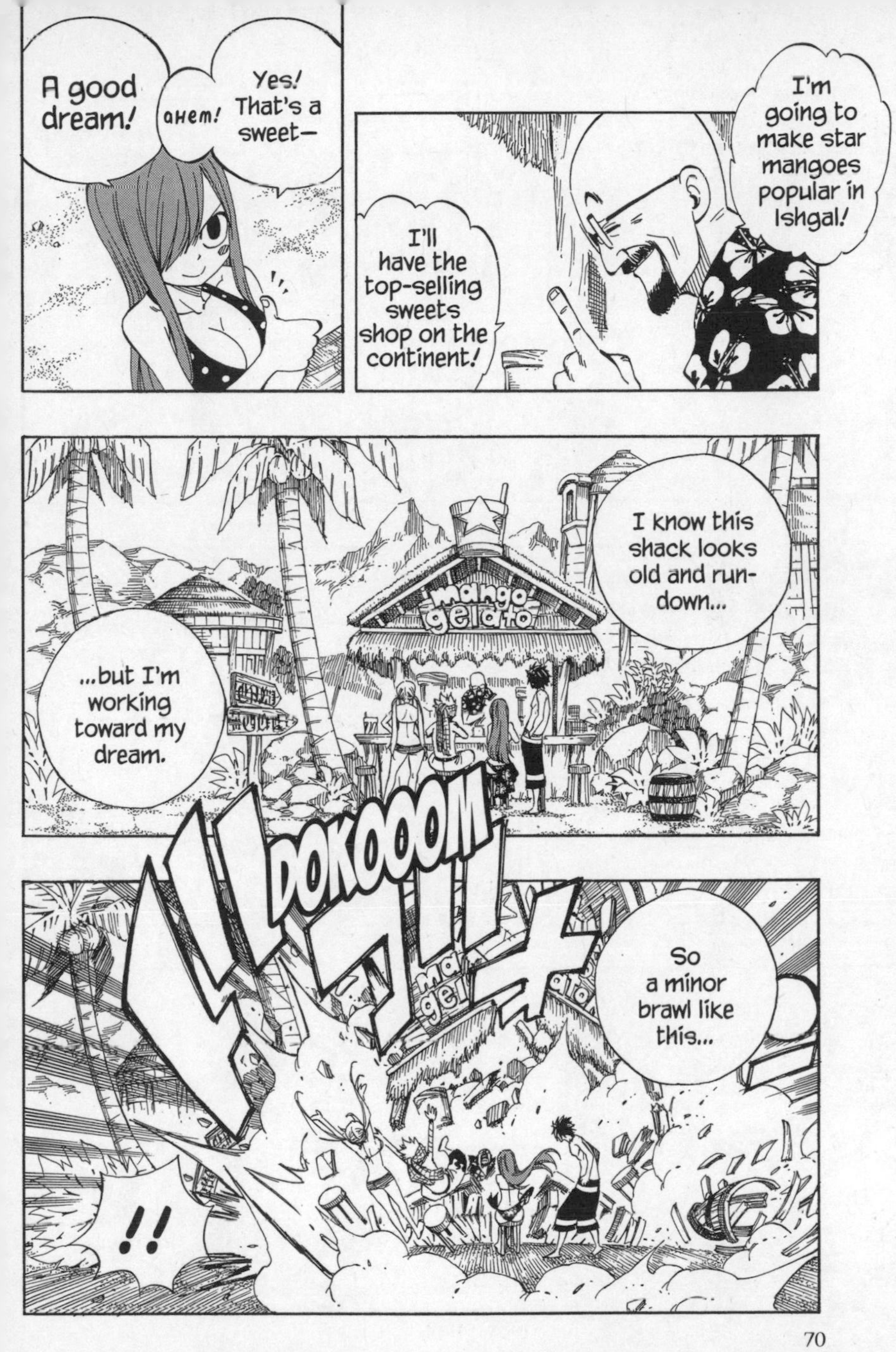
I'm going to make star mangoes popular in Ishgal!
I'll have the top-selling sweets shop on the continent!
Yes! That's a sweet—
AHEM!
A good dream!
I know this shack looks old and run-down...
mango gelato
...but I'm working toward my dream.
DOKOOOM
So a minor brawl like this...
!!

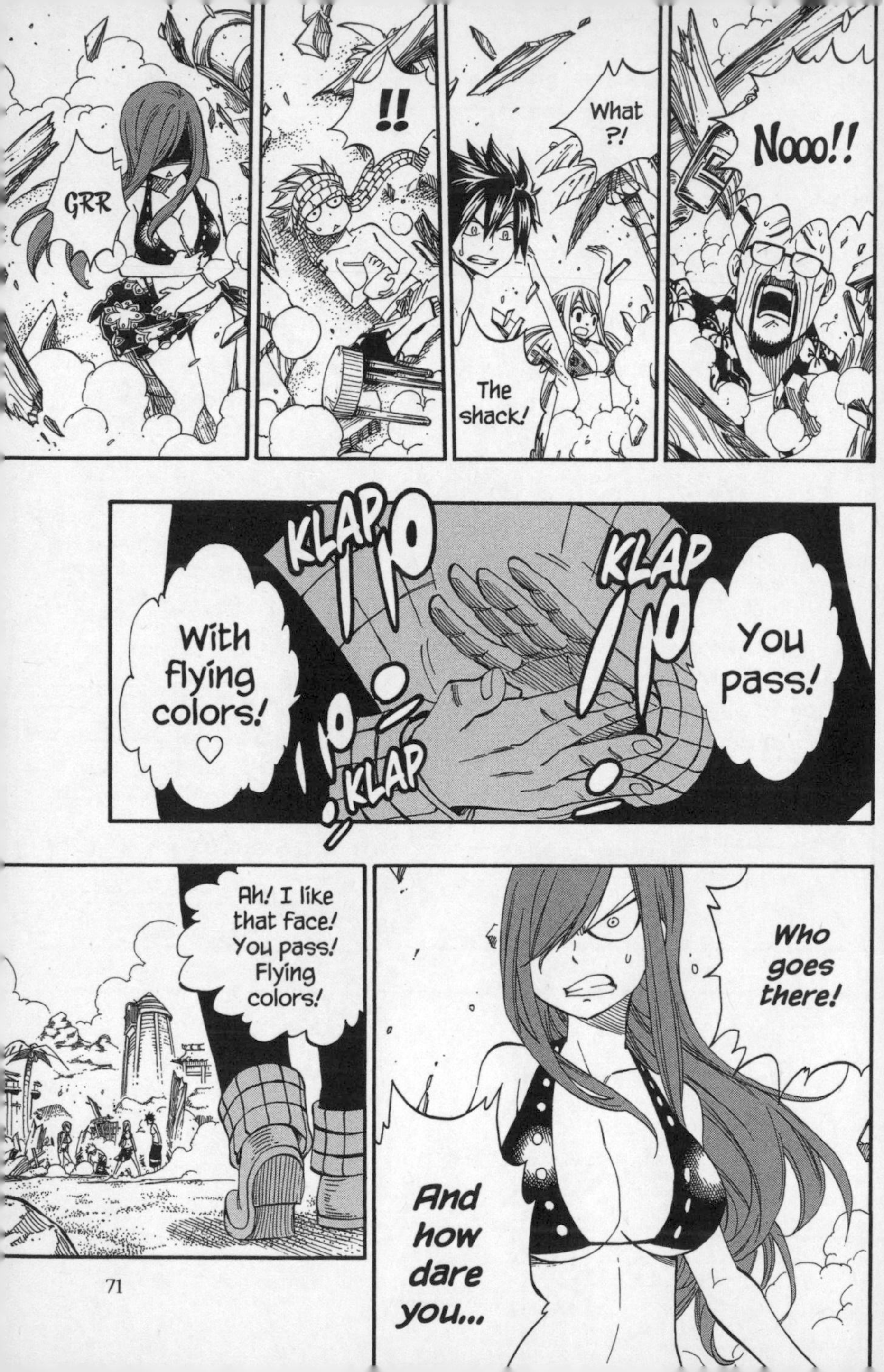
Nooo!!
What ?!
The shack!
!!
GRR
KLAP
You pass!
KLAP
With flying colors! ♡
KLAP
Who goes there!
And how dare you...
Ah! I like that face! You pass! Flying colors!

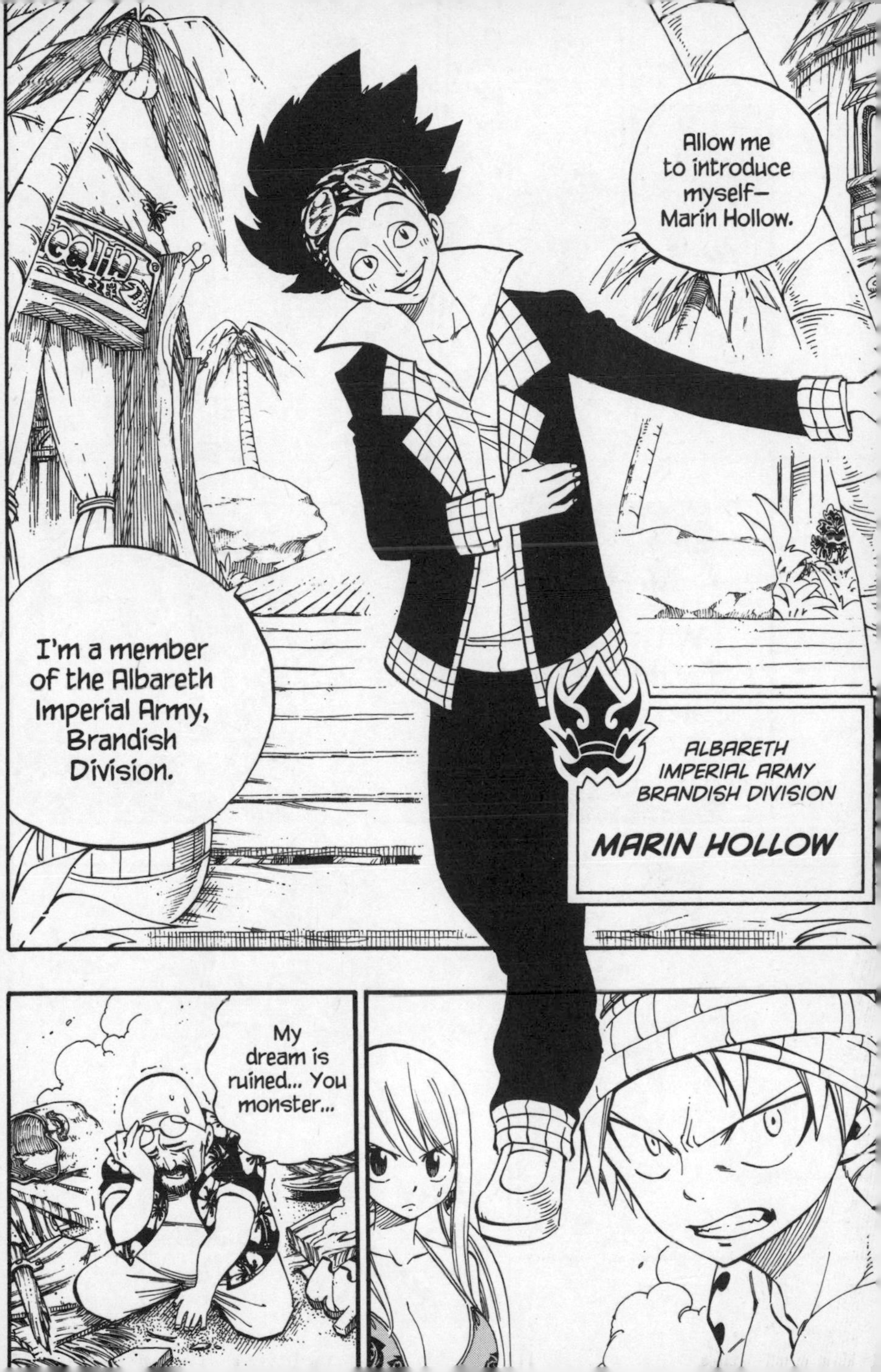
Allow me to introduce myself—Marin Hollow.
I'm a member of the Albareth Imperial Army, Brandish Division.
ALBARETH IMPERIAL ARMY BRANDISH DIVISION
MARIN HOLLOW
My dream is ruined... You monster...

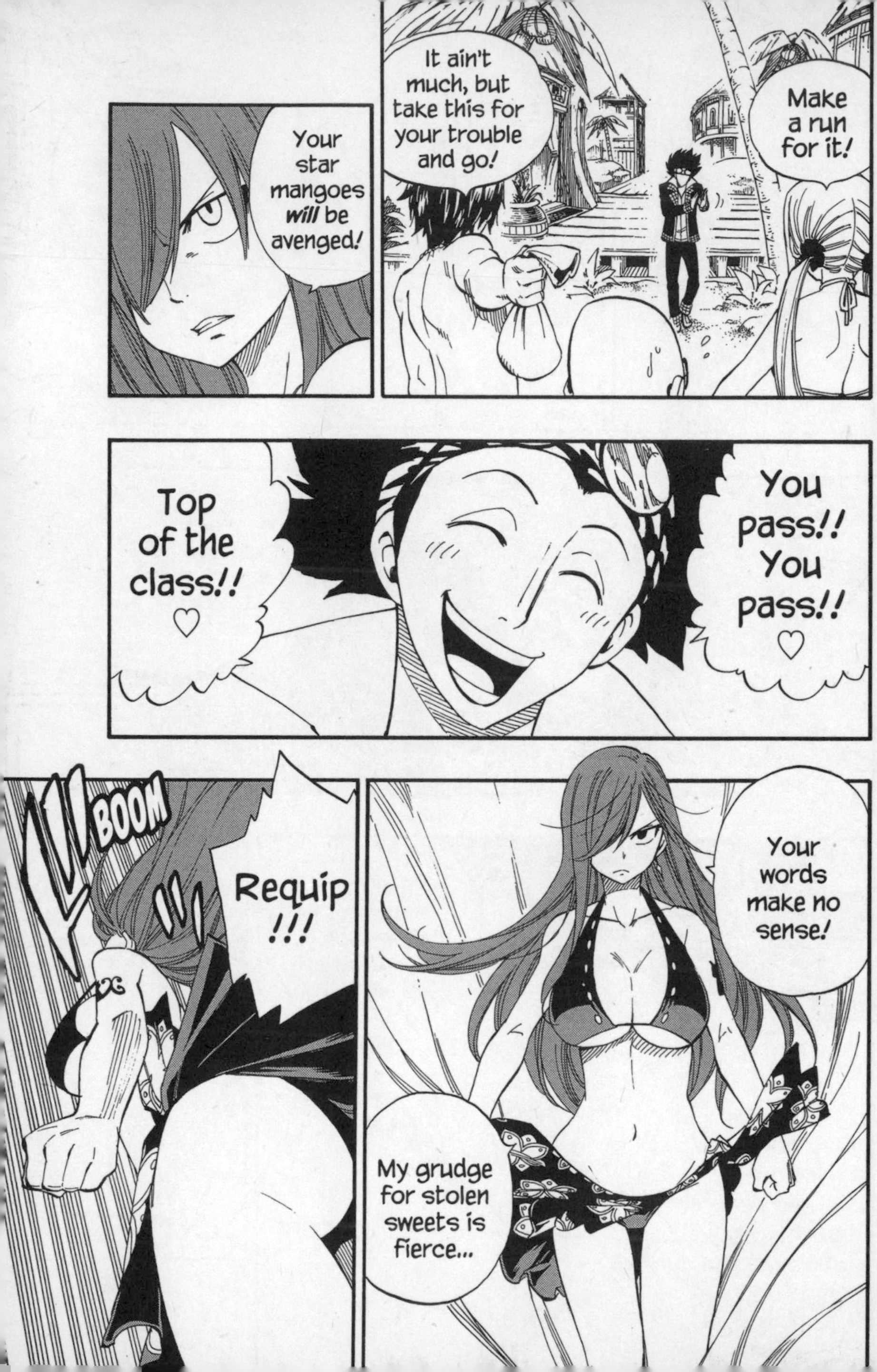
Make a run for it!
It ain't much, but take this for your trouble and go!
Your star mangoes *will* be avenged!
You pass!! You pass!! ♡
Top of the class!! ♡
Your words make no sense!
My grudge for stolen sweets is fierce...
BOOM
Requip!!!

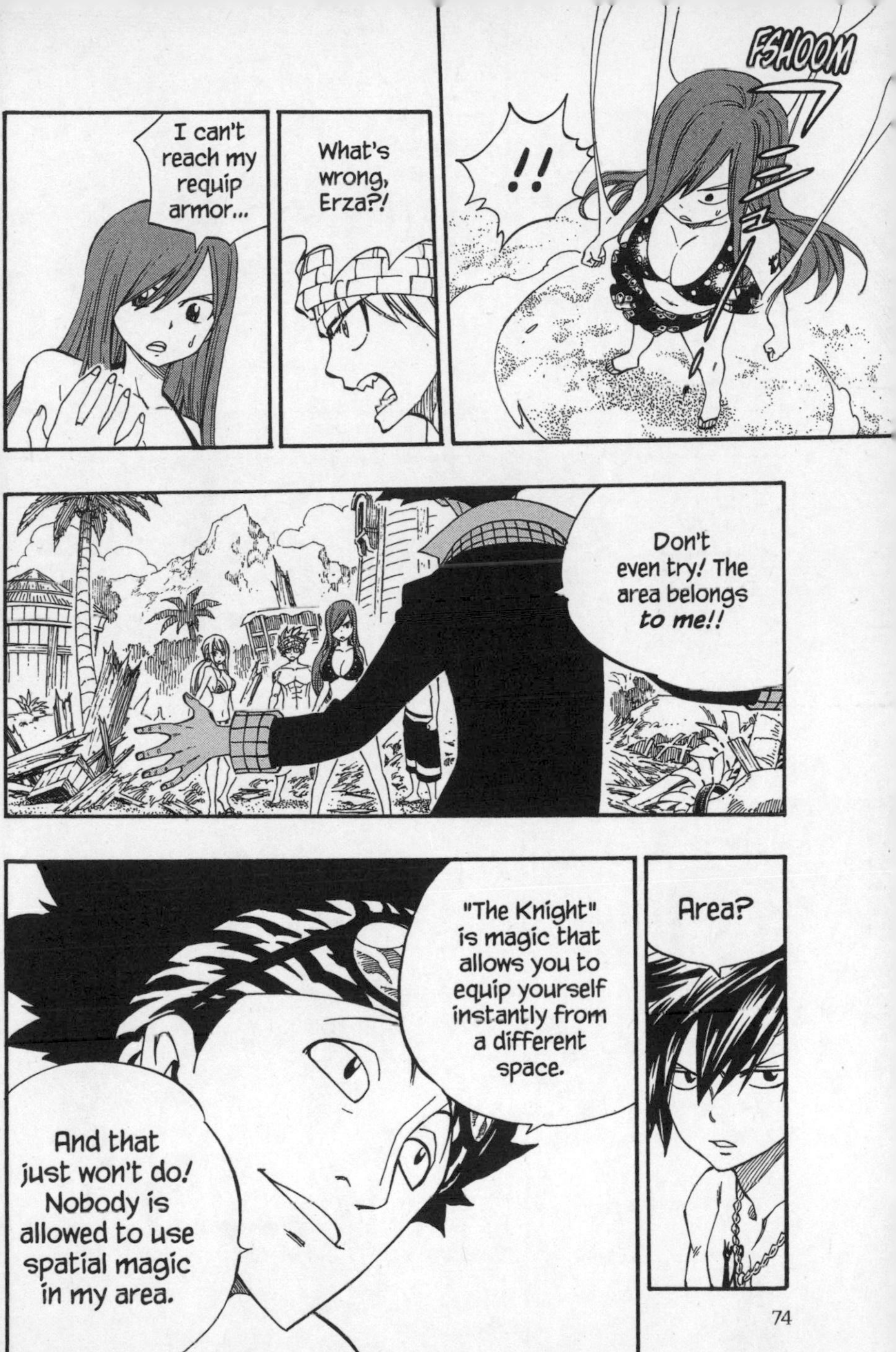
FSHOOM
!!
What's wrong, Erza?!
I can't reach my requip armor...
Don't even try! The area belongs to me!!
Area?
"The Knight" is magic that allows you to equip yourself instantly from a different space.
And that just won't do! Nobody is allowed to use spatial magic in my area.

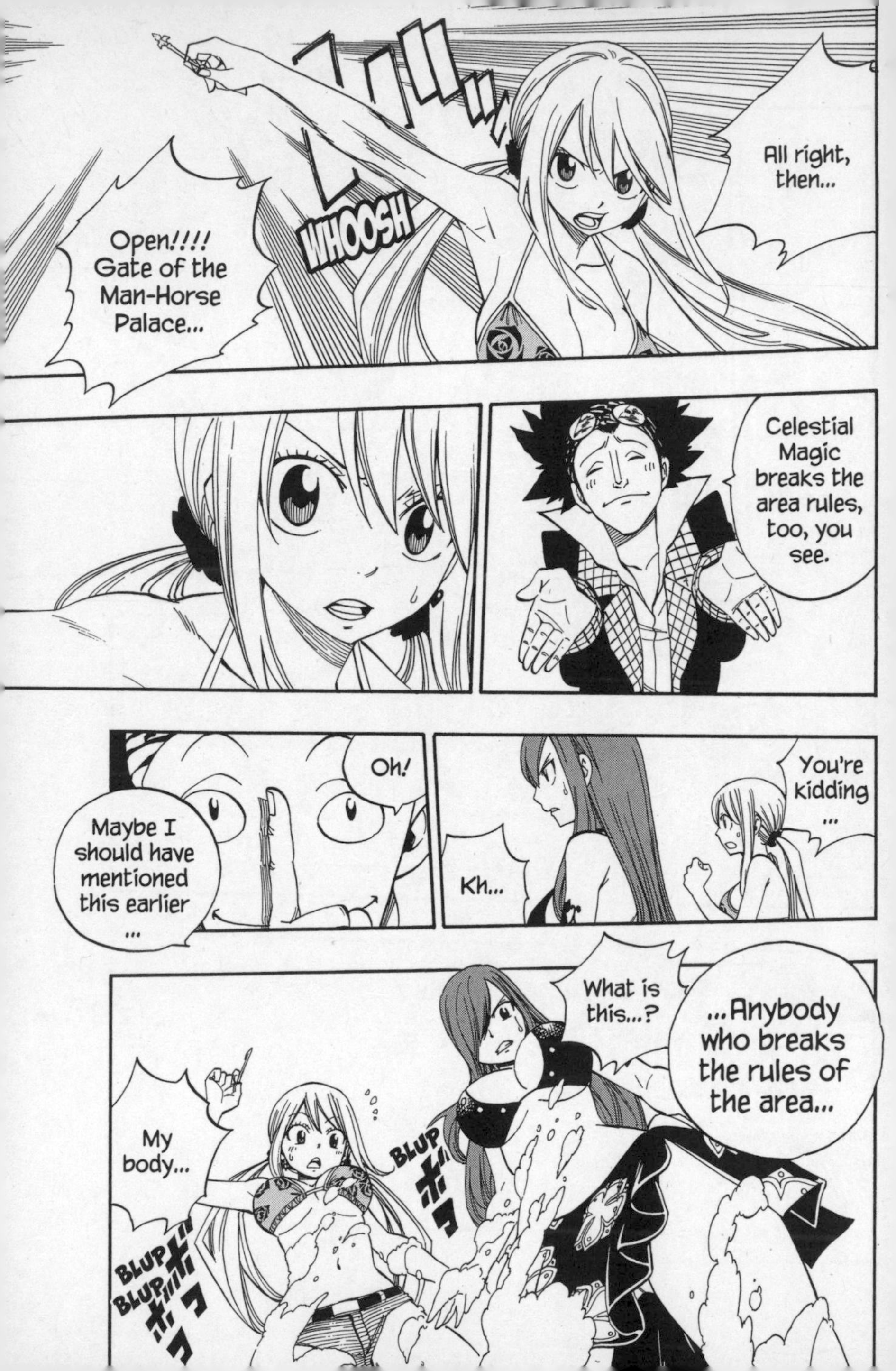
All right, then...
WHOOSH
Open!!!! Gate of the Man-Horse Palace...
Celestial Magic breaks the area rules, too, you see.
You're kidding ...
Kh...
Oh!
Maybe I should have mentioned this earlier ...
...Anybody who breaks the rules of the area...
What is this...?
BLUP
My body...
BLUP BLUP

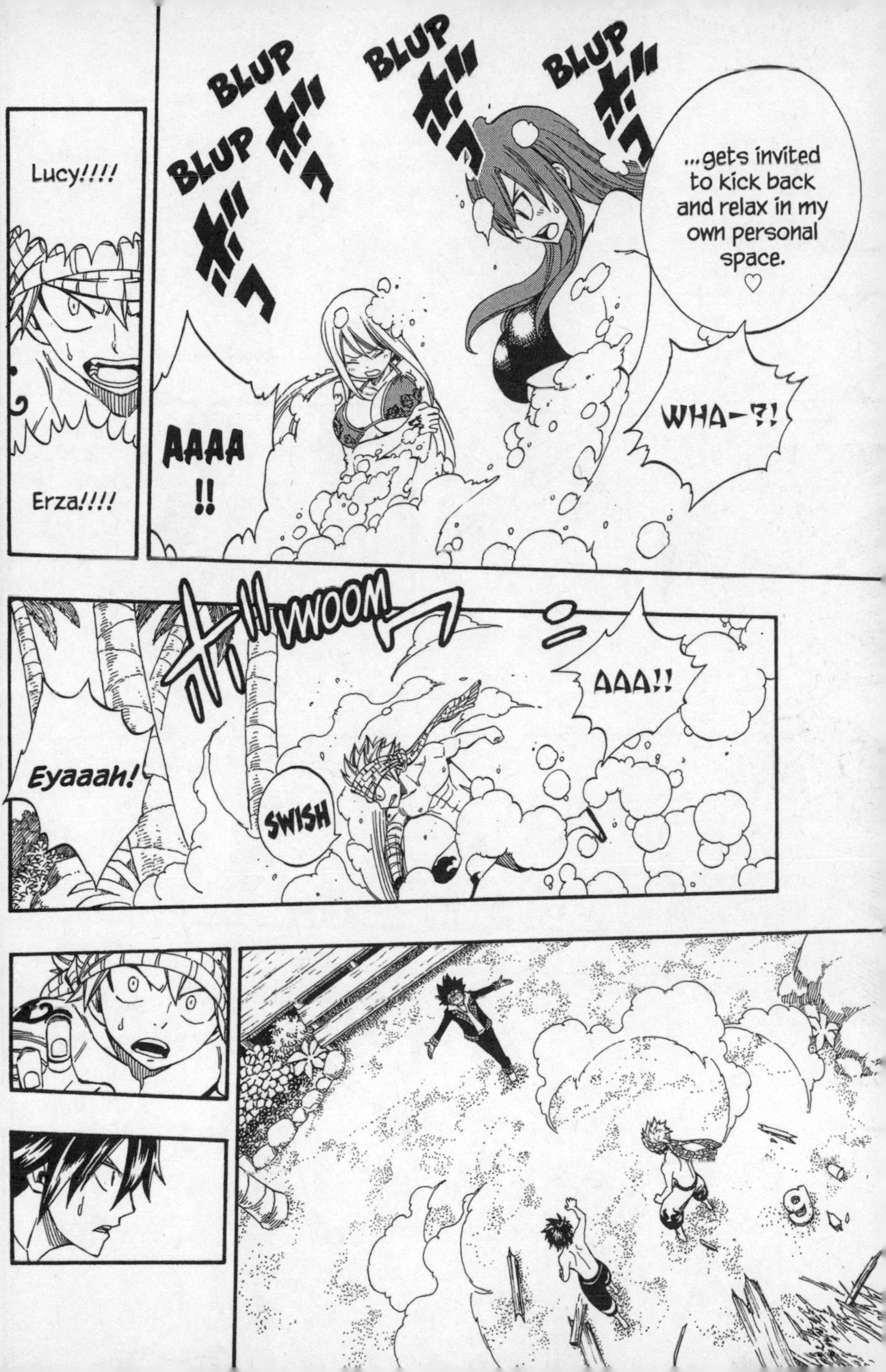
BLUP
BLUP
BLUP
BLUP
...gets invited to kick back and relax in my own personal space. ♡
WHA-?!
AAAA !!
Lucy!!!!
Erza!!!!
VVOOM
AAA!!
SWISH
Eyaaah!

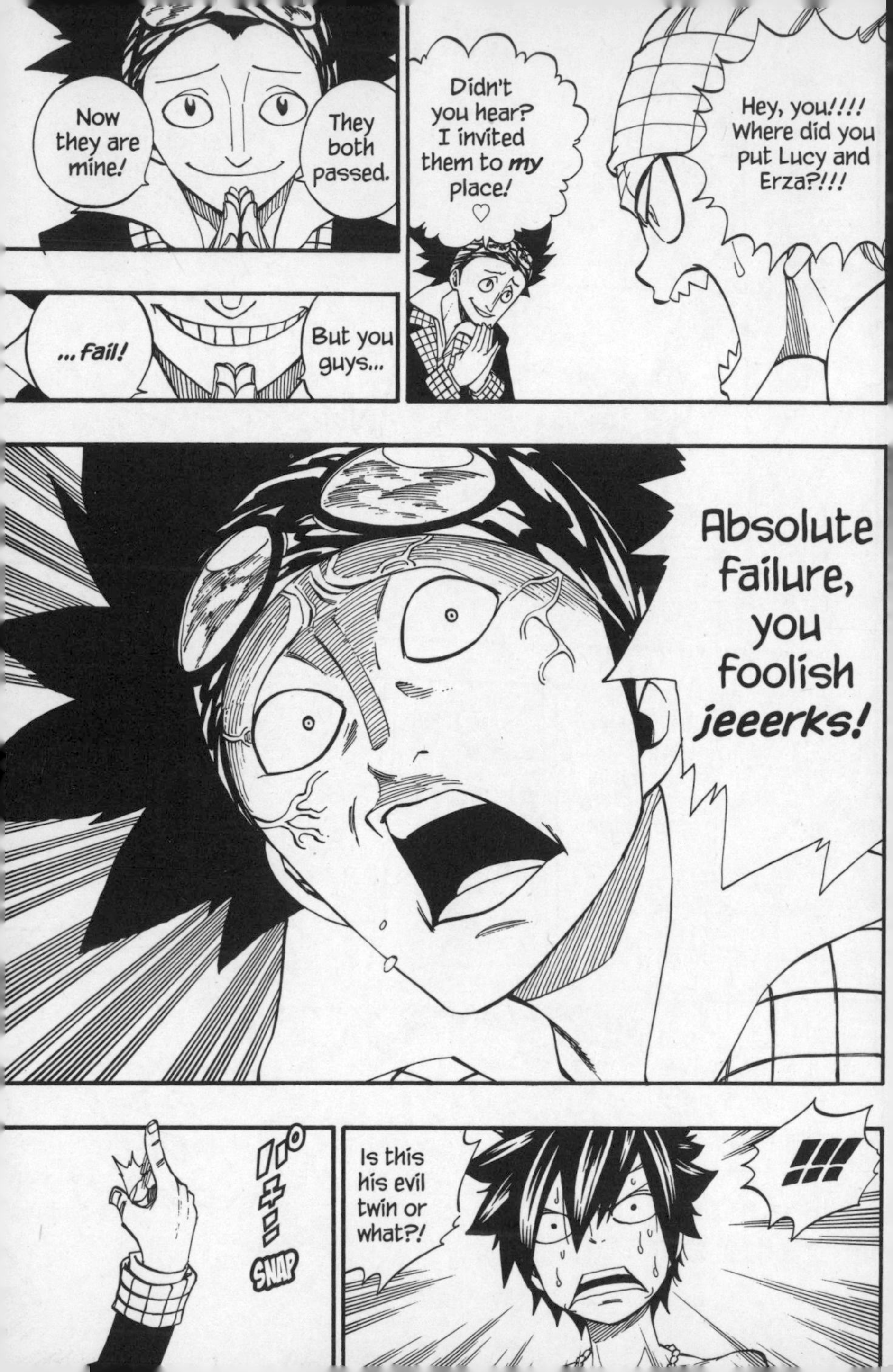
Hey, you!!!! Where did you put Lucy and Erza?!!!
Didn't you hear? I invited them to *my* place! ♡
They both passed.
Now they are mine!
But you guys...
...fail!
Absolute failure, you foolish *jeeerks!*
!!!
Is this his evil twin or what?!
SNAP

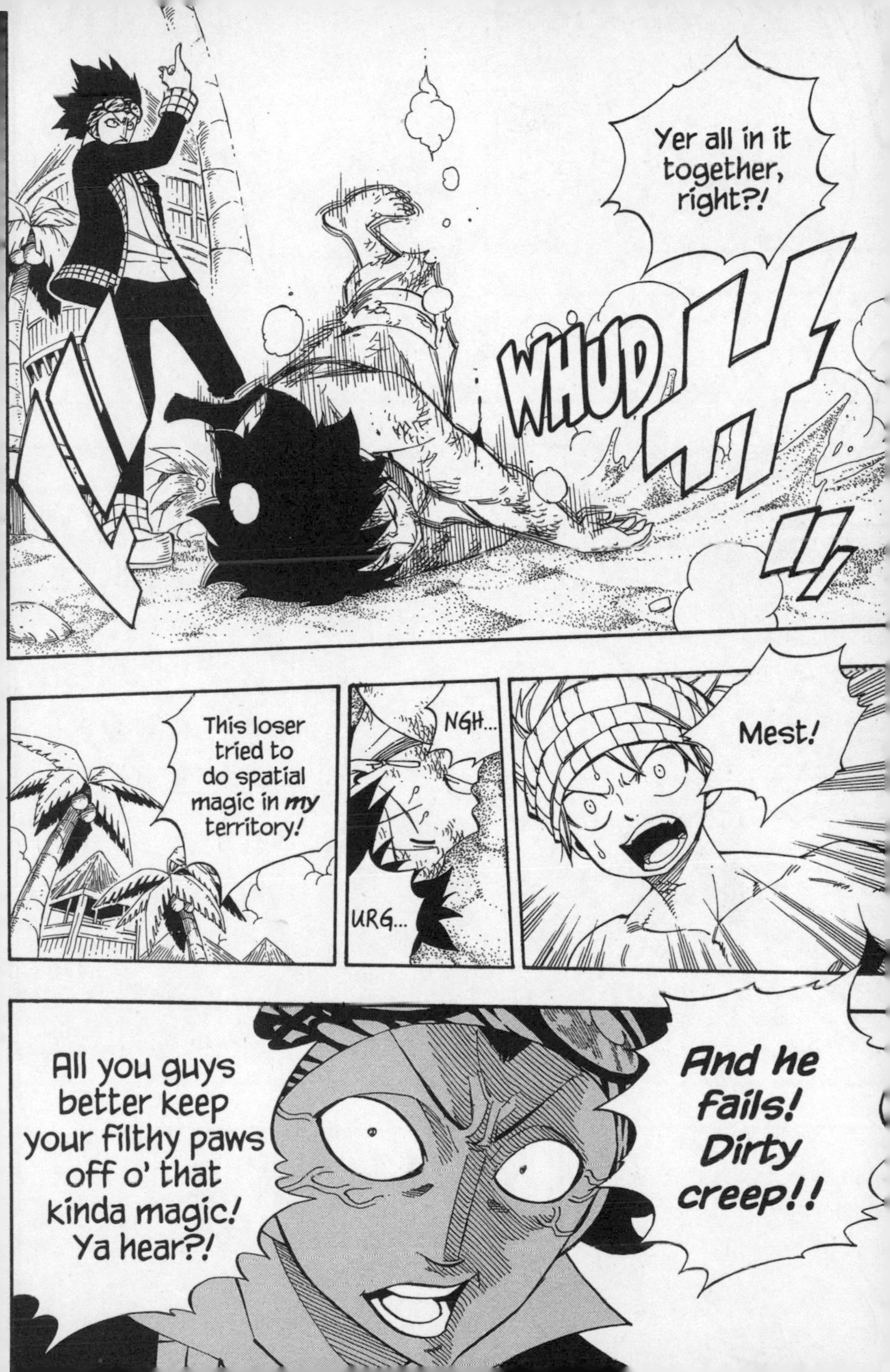
Yer all in it together, right?!
WHUDH
Mest!
NGH...
URG...
This loser tried to do spatial magic in *my* territory!
And he fails! Dirty creep!!
All you guys better keep your filthy paws off o' that kinda magic! Ya hear?!

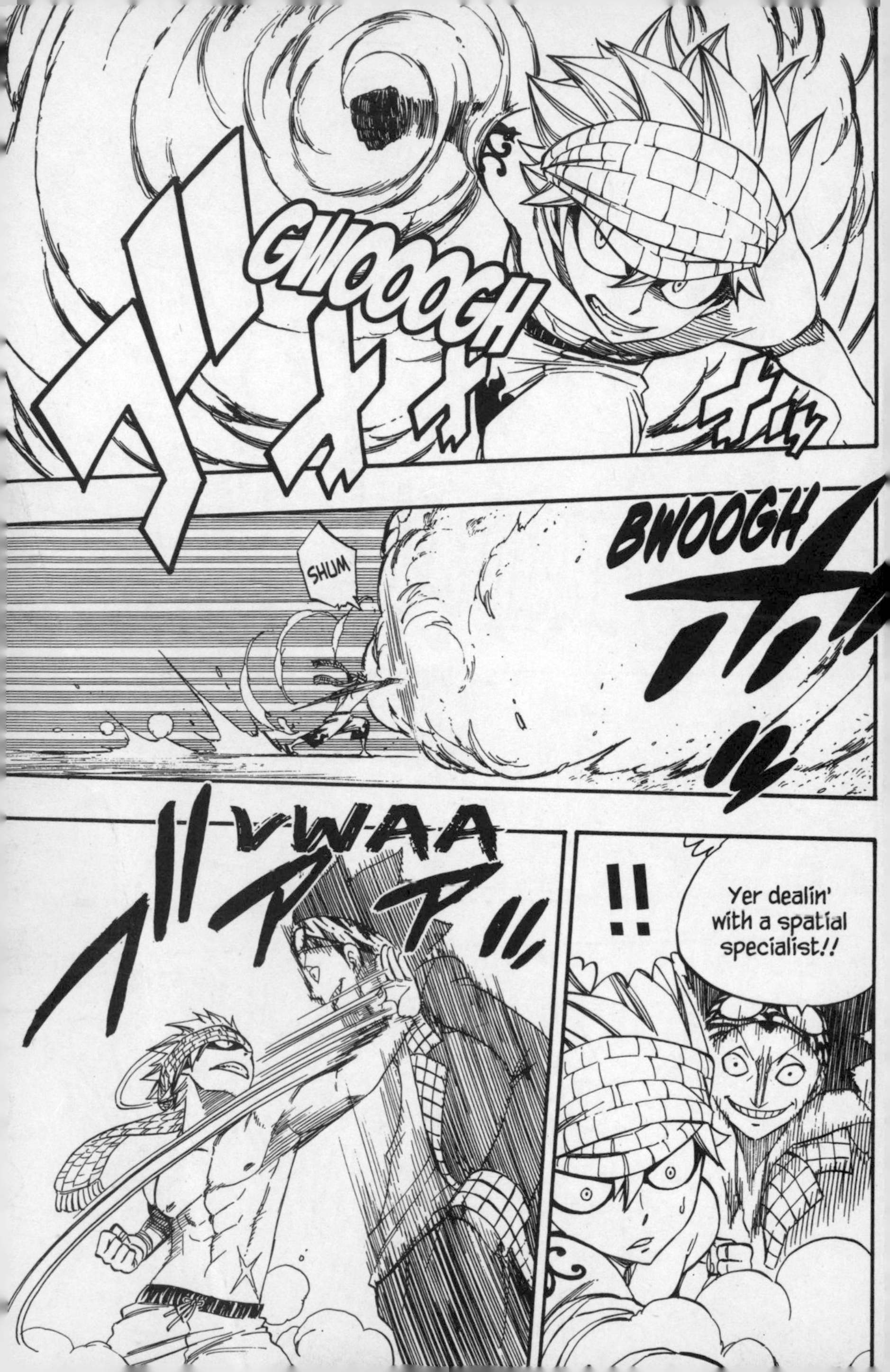
GWOOOGH
BWOOGH
SHUM
!!
Yer dealin' with a spatial specialist!!
VWAA

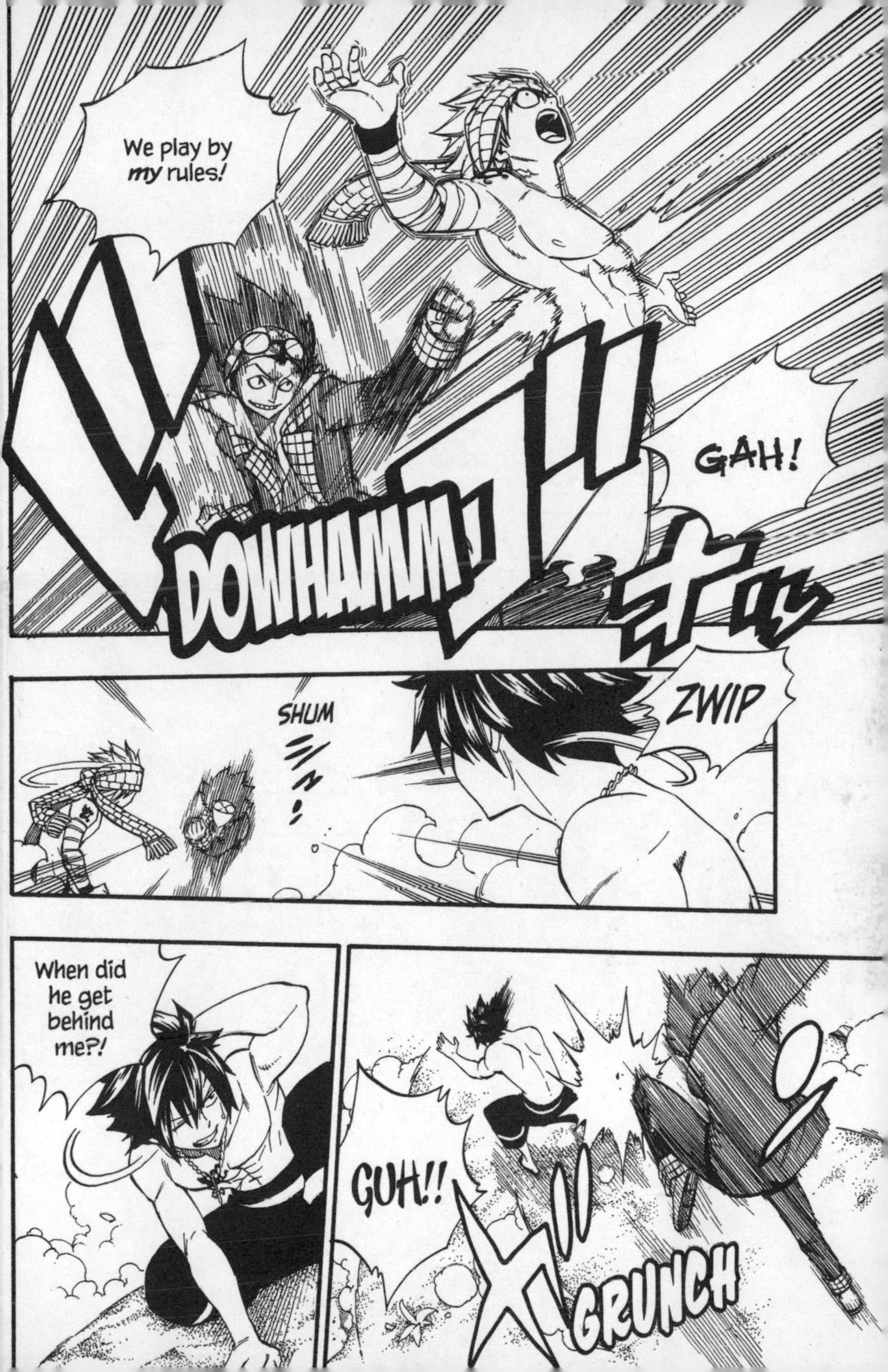
We play by *my* rules!
GAH!
DOWHAMM
ZWIP
SHUM
GUH!!
GRUNCH
When did he get behind me?!

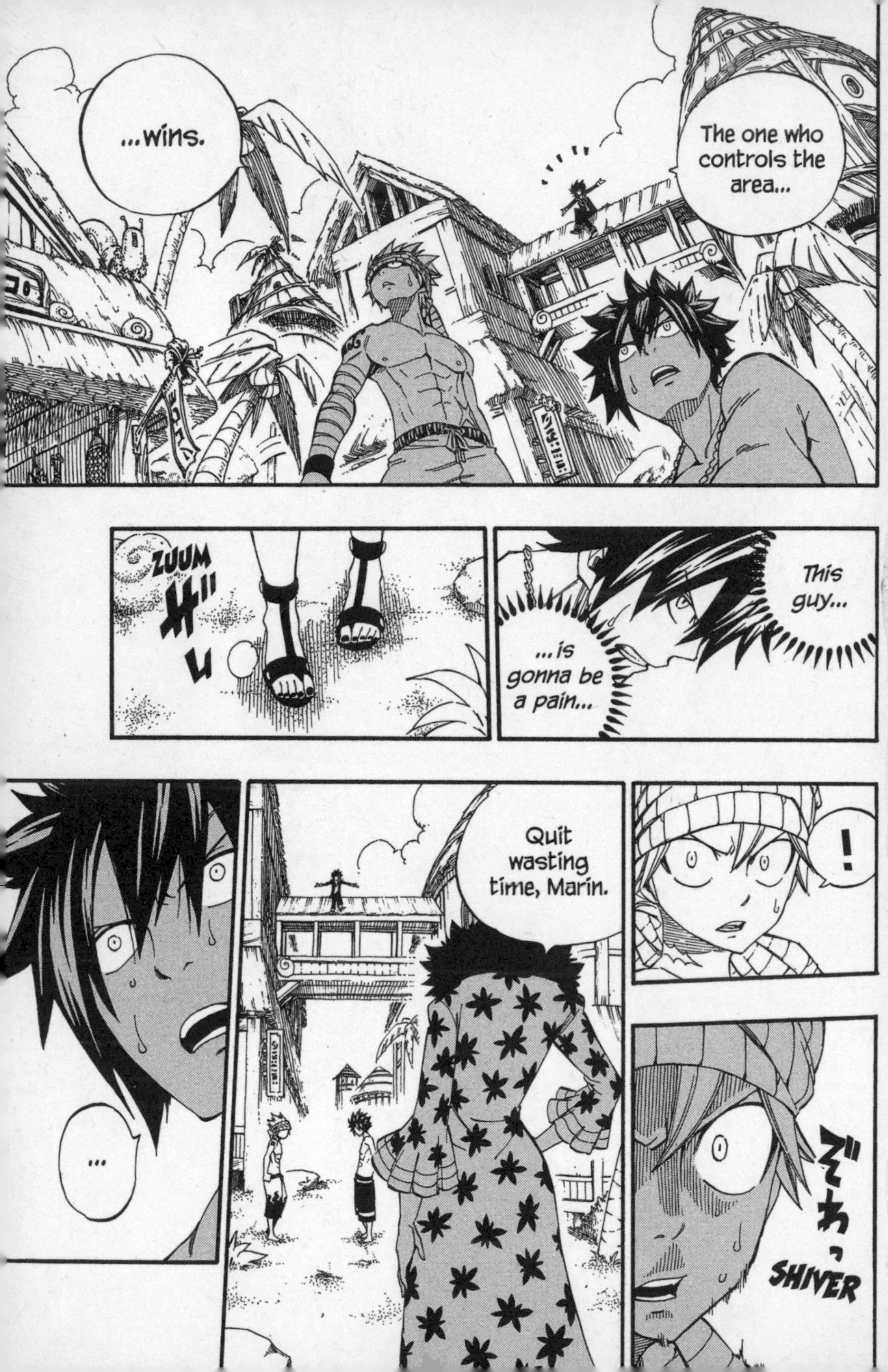

The one who controls the area...
...wins.
This guy...
...is gonna be a pain...
ZUUM
!
SHIVER
Quit wasting time, Marin.
...

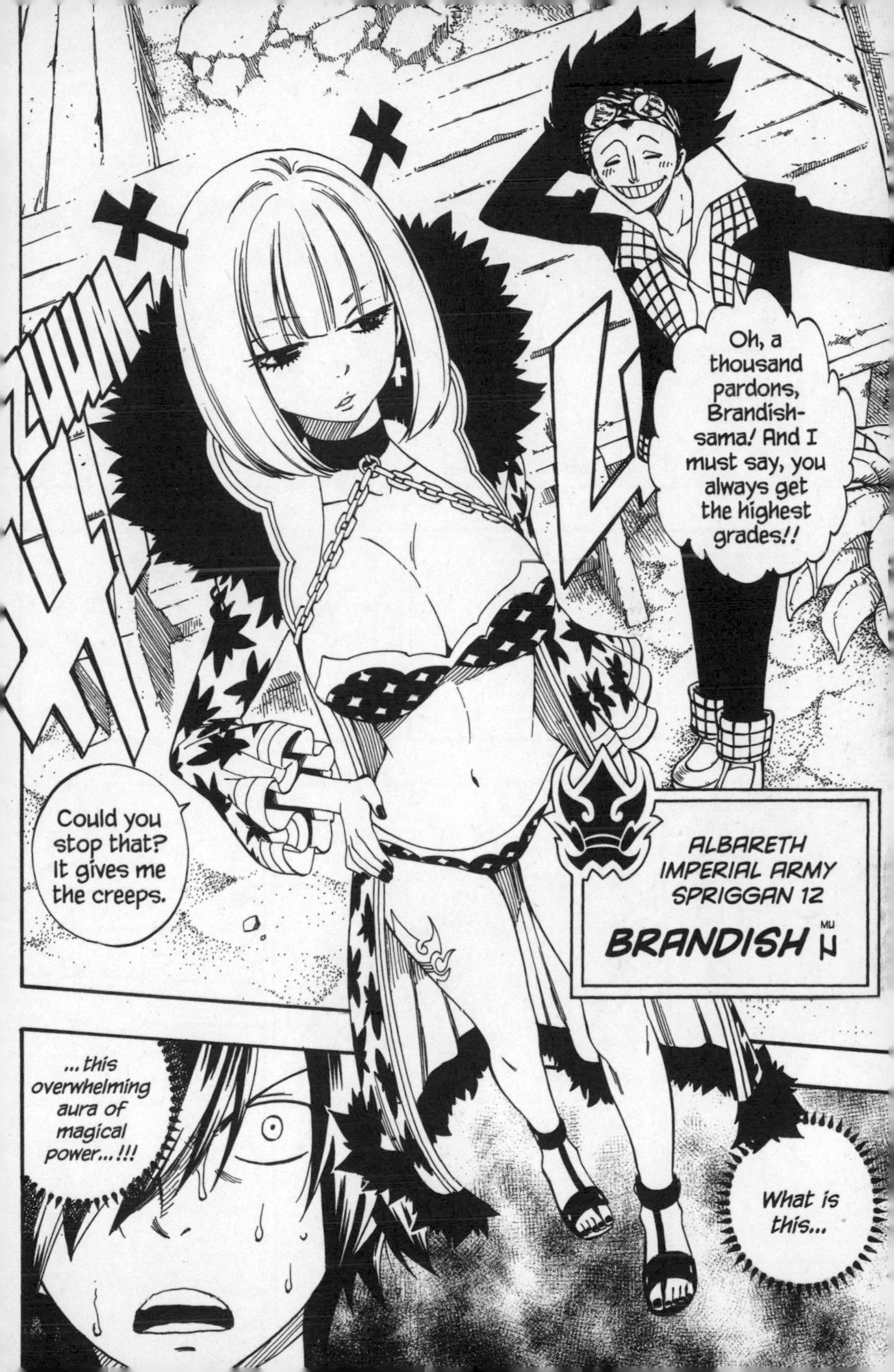
Oh, a thousand pardons, Brandish-sama! And I must say, you always get the highest grades!!
ALBARETH IMPERIAL ARMY SPRIGGAN 12
BRANDISH μ (MU)
Could you stop that? It gives me the creeps.
What is this...
...this overwhelming aura of magical power...!!!

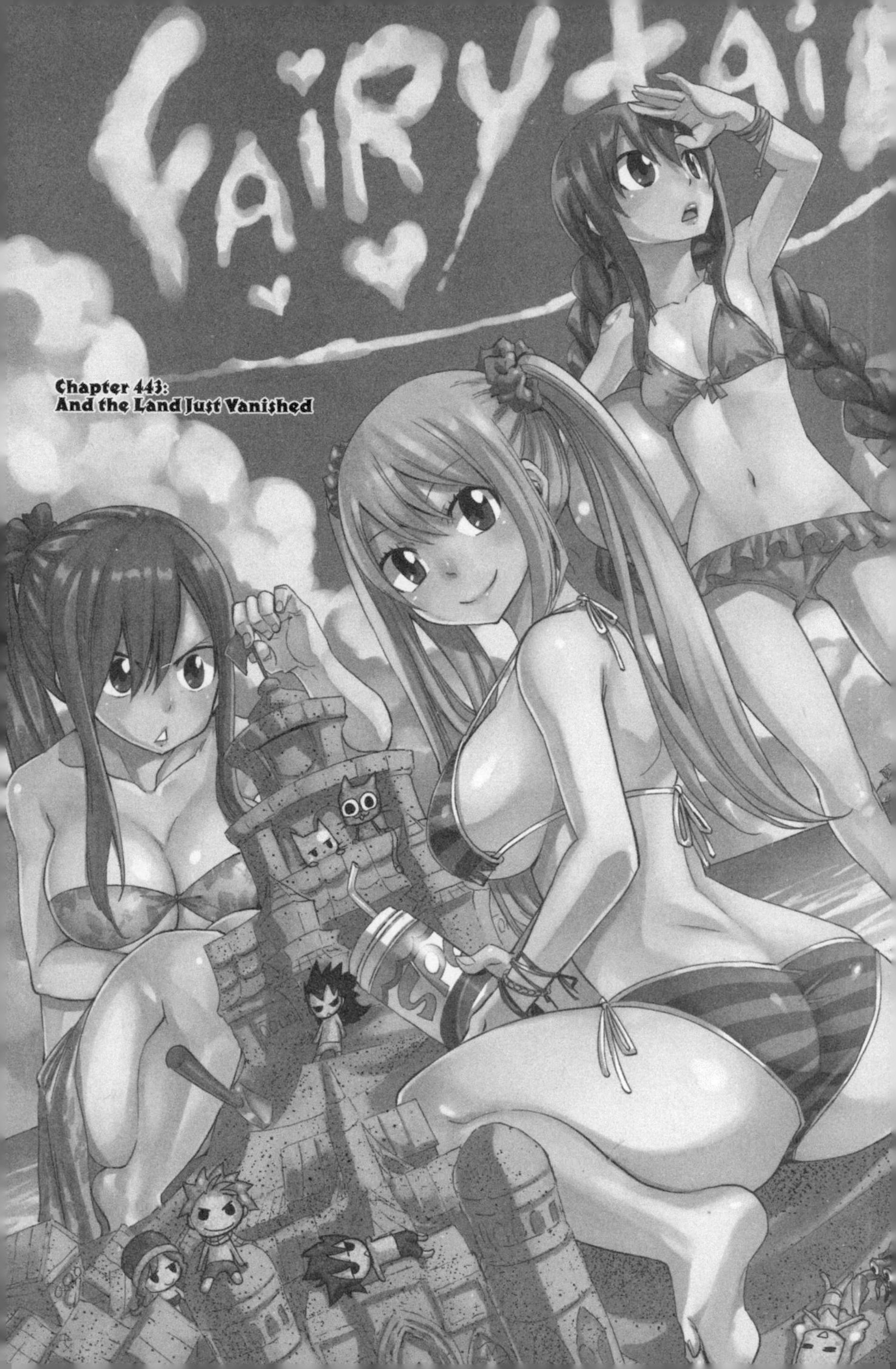
Chapter 443:
And the Land Just Vanished

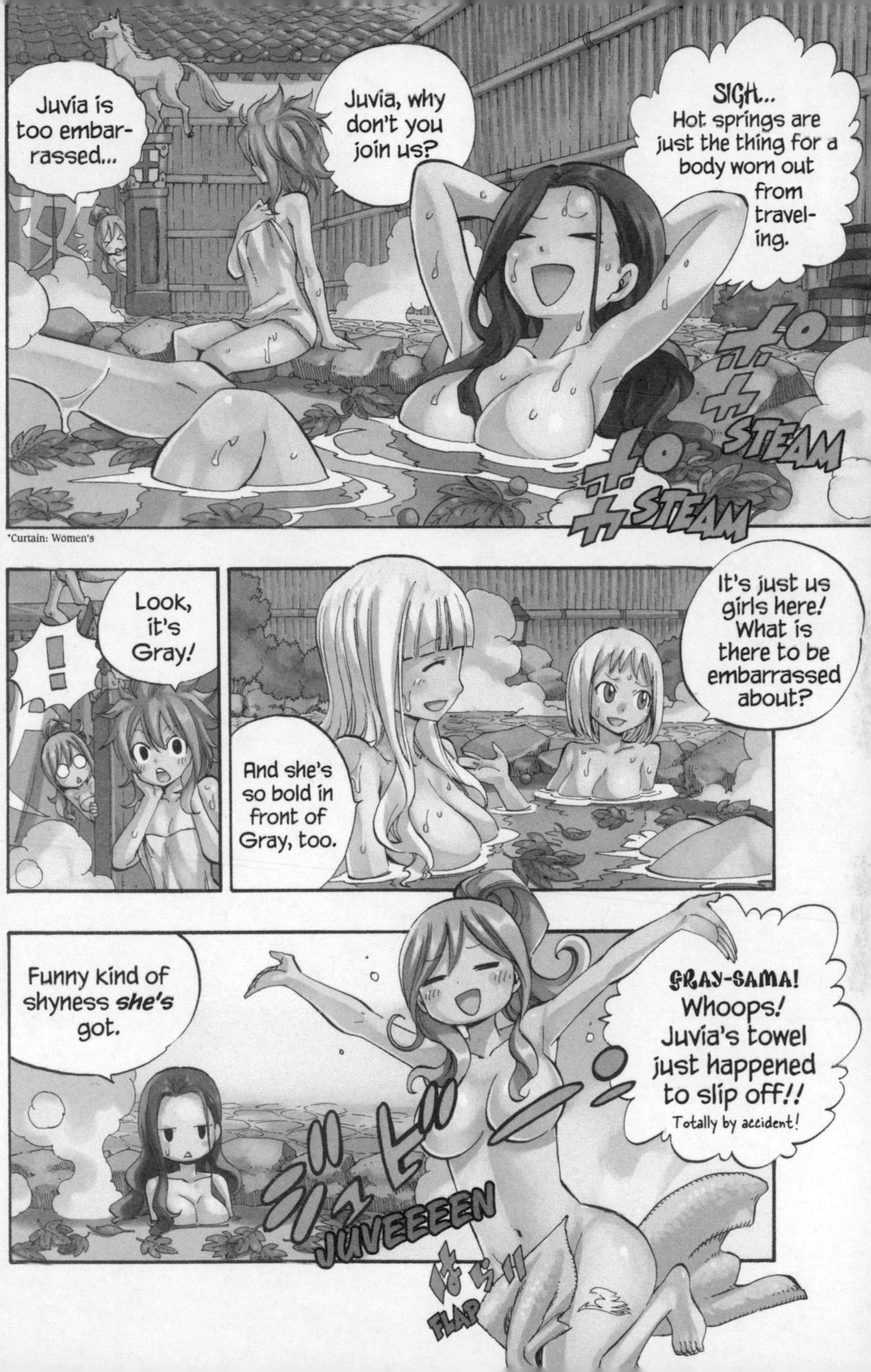
SIGH... Hot springs are just the thing for a body worn out from traveling.
Juvia, why don't you join us?
Juvia is too embarrassed...
STEAM
STEAM
It's just us girls here! What is there to be embarrassed about?
And she's so bold in front of Gray, too.
Look, it's Gray!
GRAY-SAMA! Whoops! Juvia's towel just happened to slip off!! Totally by accident!
JUVEEEEN
FLAP
Funny kind of shyness *she's* got.

*Curtain: Women's

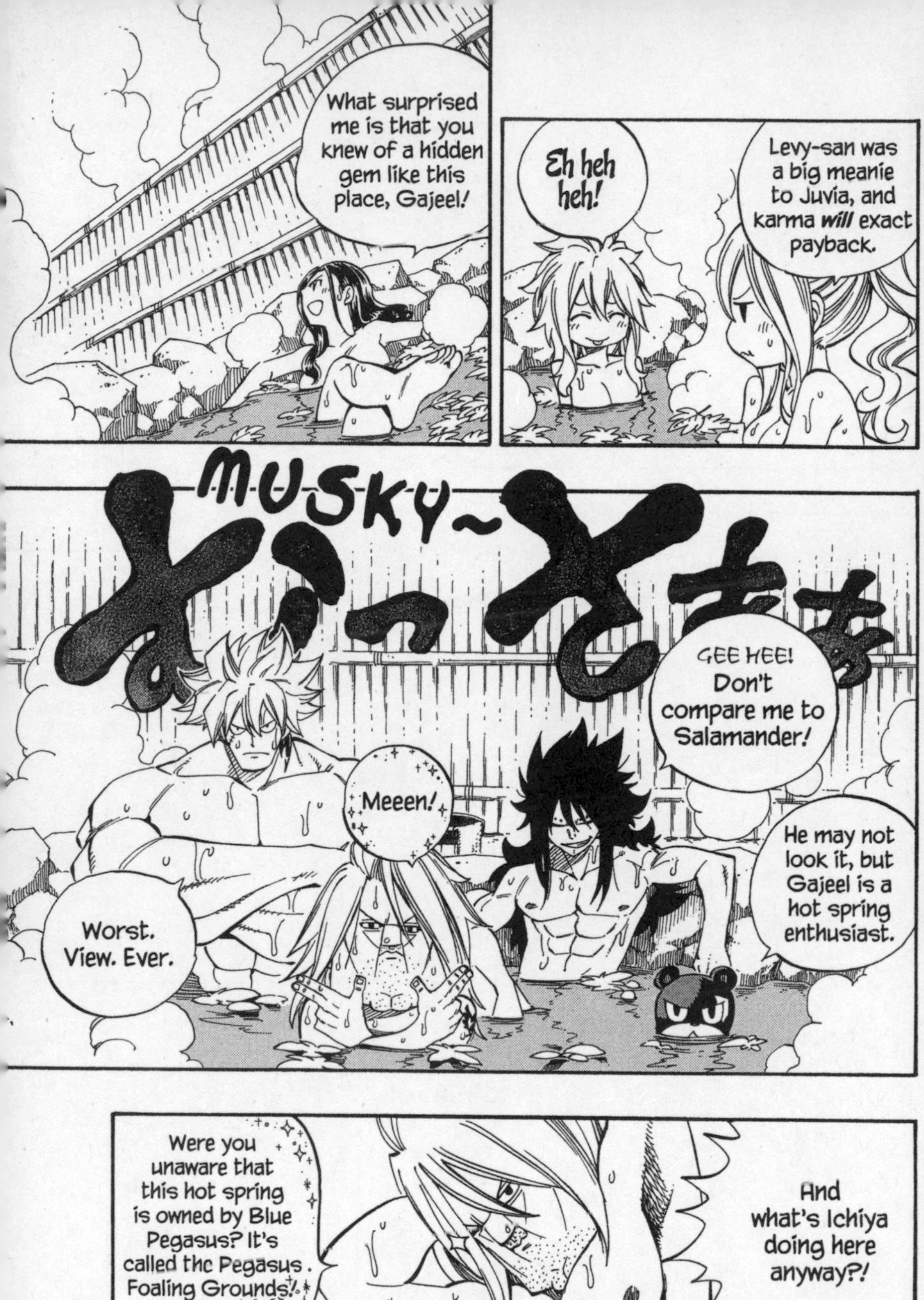

Levy-san was a big meanie to Juvia, and karma *will* exact payback.
Eh heh heh!
What surprised me is that you knew of a hidden gem like this place, Gajeel!
MUSKY~
GEE HEE! Don't compare me to Salamander!
He may not look it, but Gajeel is a hot spring enthusiast.
Meeen!
Worst. View. Ever.
And what's Ichiya doing here anyway?!
Were you unaware that this hot spring is owned by Blue Pegasus? It's called the Pegasus Foaling Grounds!

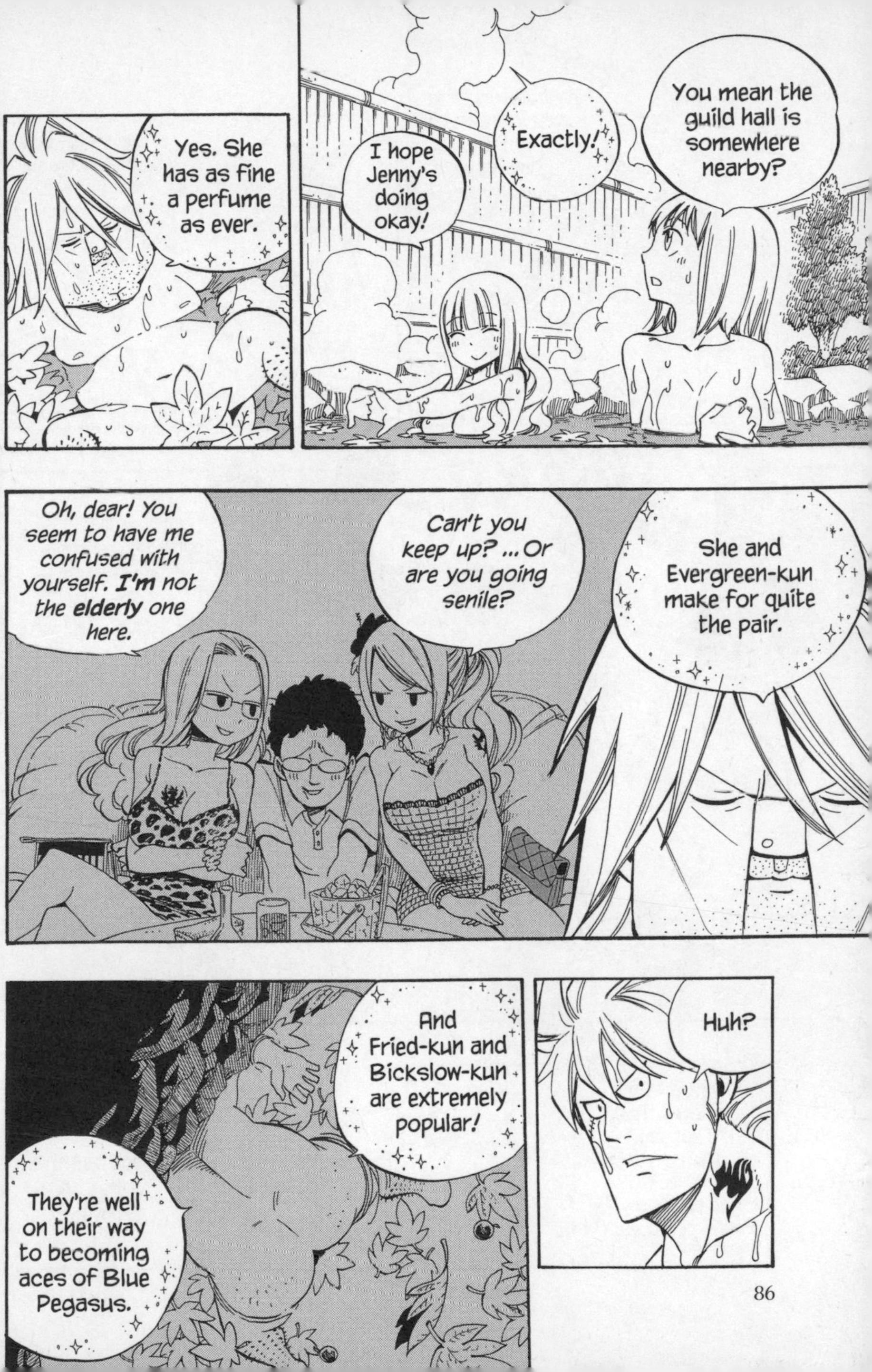
You mean the guild hall is somewhere nearby?
Exactly!
I hope Jenny's doing okay!
Yes. She has as fine a perfume as ever.
She and Evergreen-kun make for quite the pair.
Can't you keep up? ...Or are you going senile?
Oh, dear! You seem to have me confused with yourself. **I'm** not the **elderly** one here.
Huh?
And Fried-kun and Bickslow-kun are extremely popular!
They're well on their way to becoming aces of Blue Pegasus.

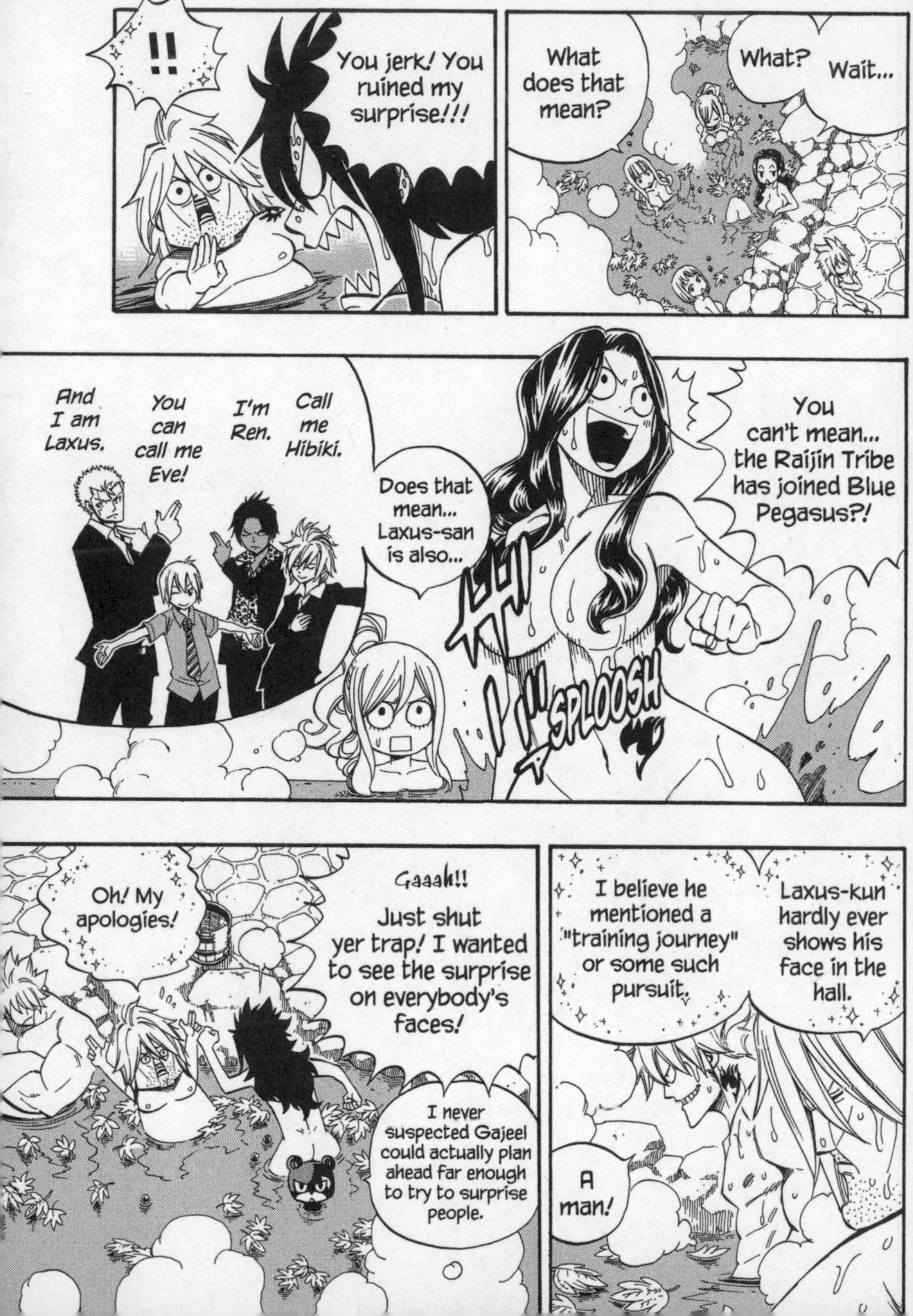
Wait...
What?
What does that mean?
!!
You jerk! You ruined my surprise!!!
You can't mean... the Raijin Tribe has joined Blue Pegasus?!
SPLOOSH
Does that mean... Laxus-san is also...
Call me Hibiki.
I'm Ren.
You can call me Eve!
And I am Laxus.
Laxus-kun hardly ever shows his face in the hall.
I believe he mentioned a "training journey" or some such pursuit.
A man!
Gaaah!!
Just shut yer trap! I wanted to see the surprise on everybody's faces!
Oh! My apologies!
I never suspected Gajeel could actually plan ahead far enough to try to surprise people.

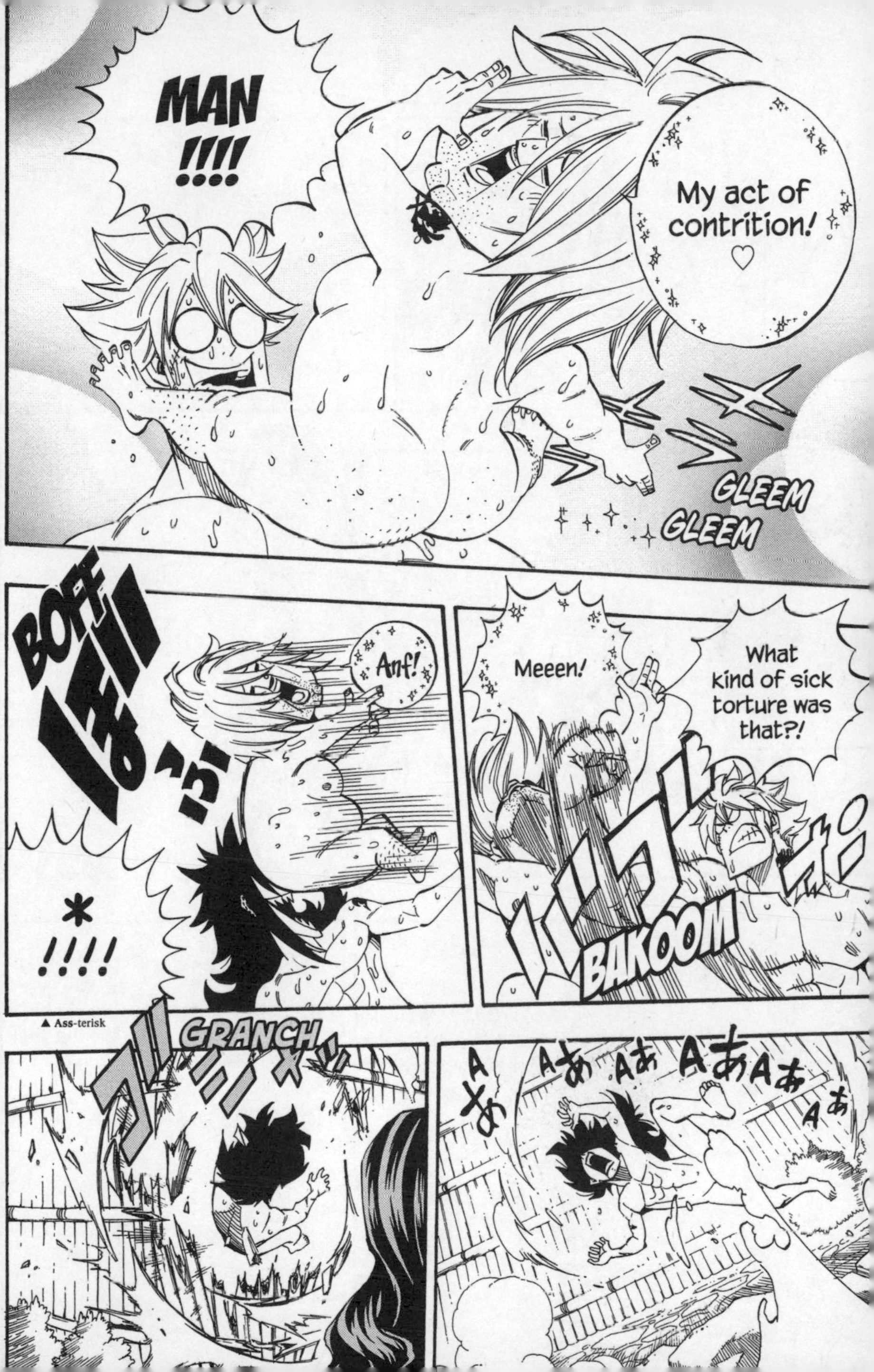
My act of contrition! ♡
MAN !!!!
GLEEM GLEEM
What kind of sick torture was that?!
Meeen!
BAKOOM
Anf!
BOFF
* !!!!
▲ Ass-terisk
Aあ Aあ Aあ Aあ Aあ Aあ Aあ
GRANCH

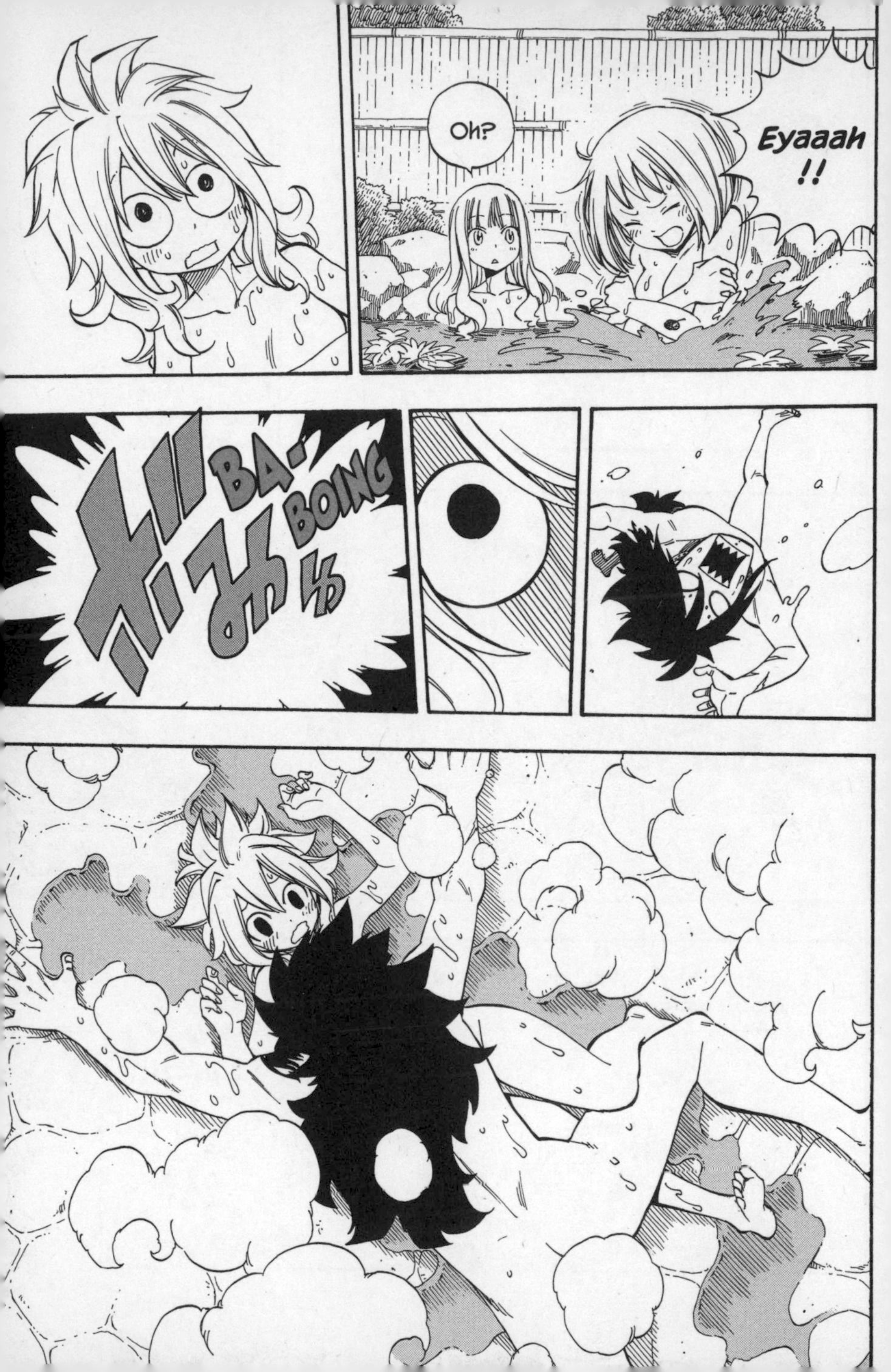
Eyaaah !!
Oh?
BA-BOING

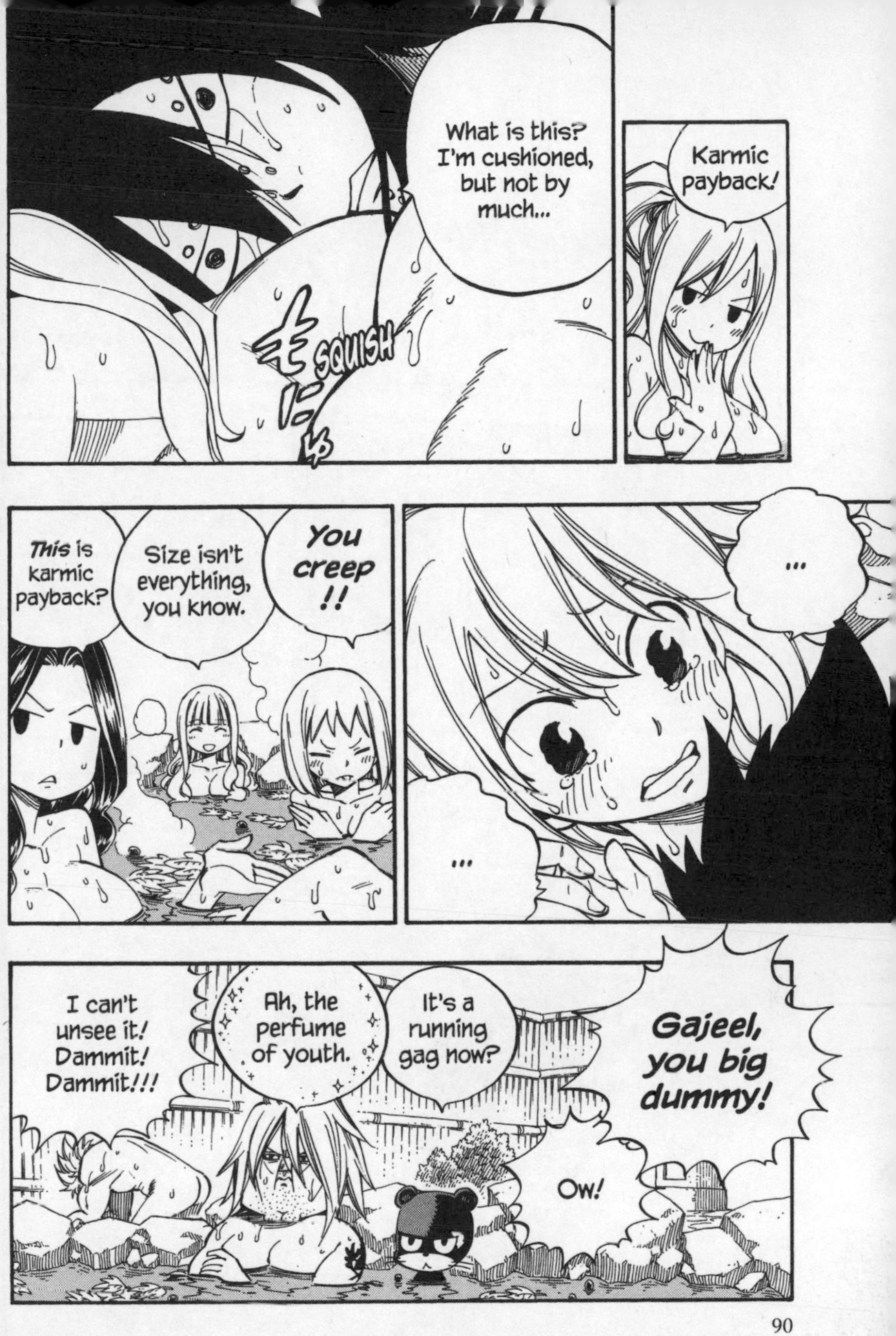
Karmic payback!
What is this? I'm cushioned, but not by much...
SQUISH
...
...
You creep!!
Size isn't everything, you know.
This is karmic payback?
Gajeel, you big dummy!
Ow!
It's a running gag now?
Ah, the perfume of youth.
I can't unsee it! Dammit! Dammit!!!

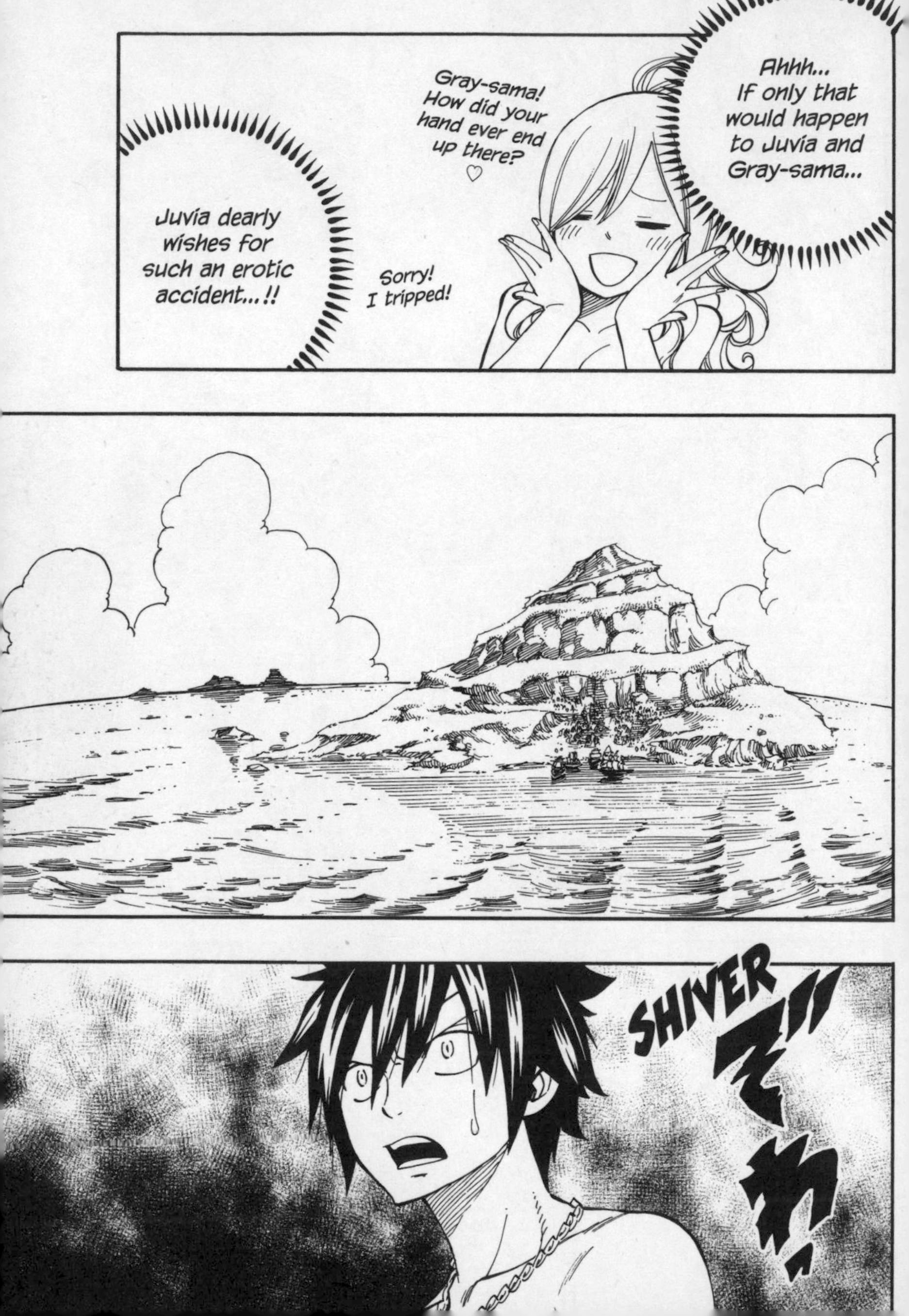
Ahhh... If only that would happen to Juvia and Gray-sama...
Gray-sama! How did your hand ever end up there? ♡
Sorry! I tripped!
Juvia dearly wishes for such an erotic accident...!!
SHIVER

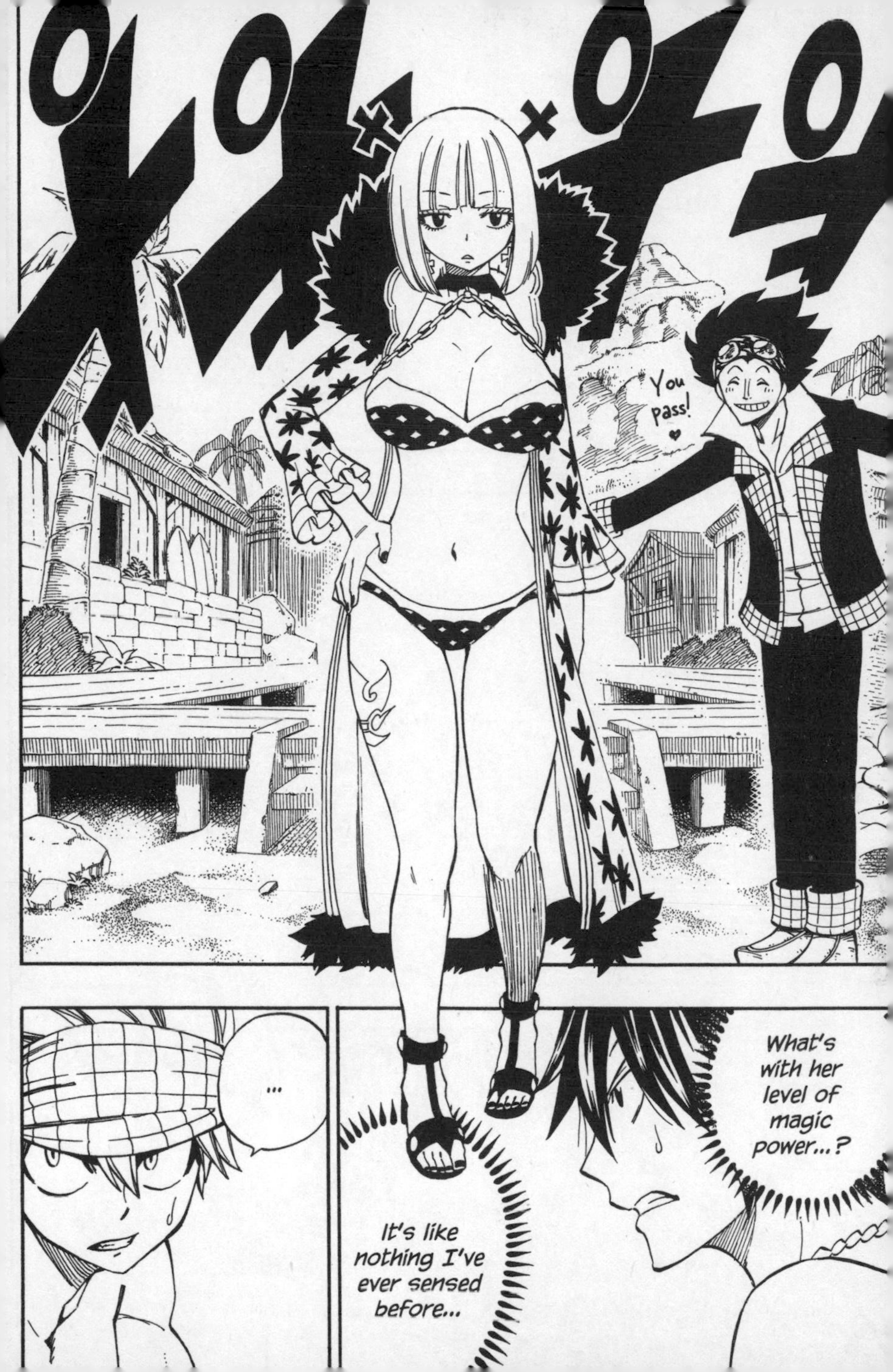
You pass! ♥
What's with her level of magic power...?
It's like nothing I've ever sensed before...
...

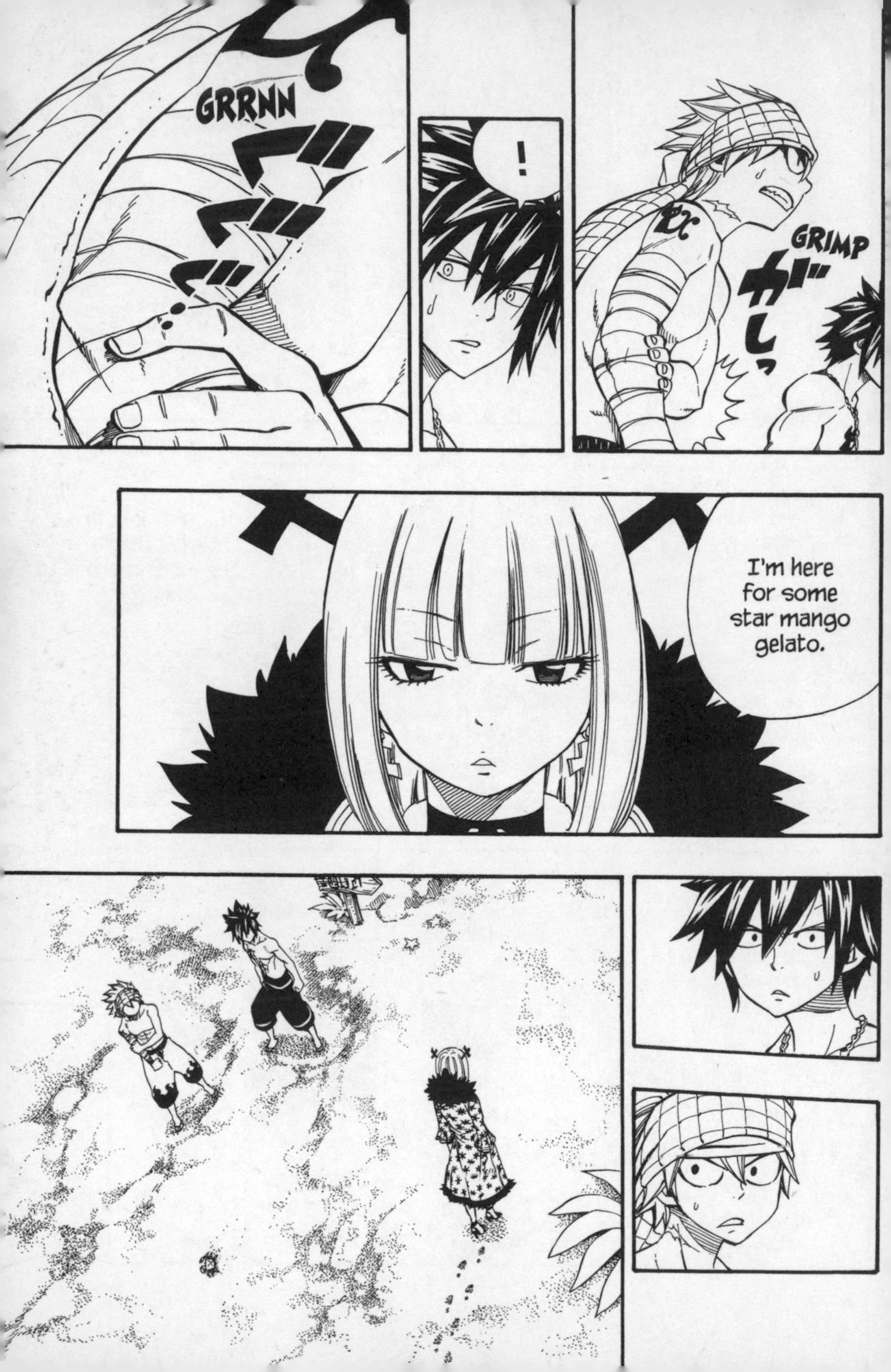
GRIMP
がしっ
!
GRRNN
ゴゴゴ
I'm here for some star mango gelato.

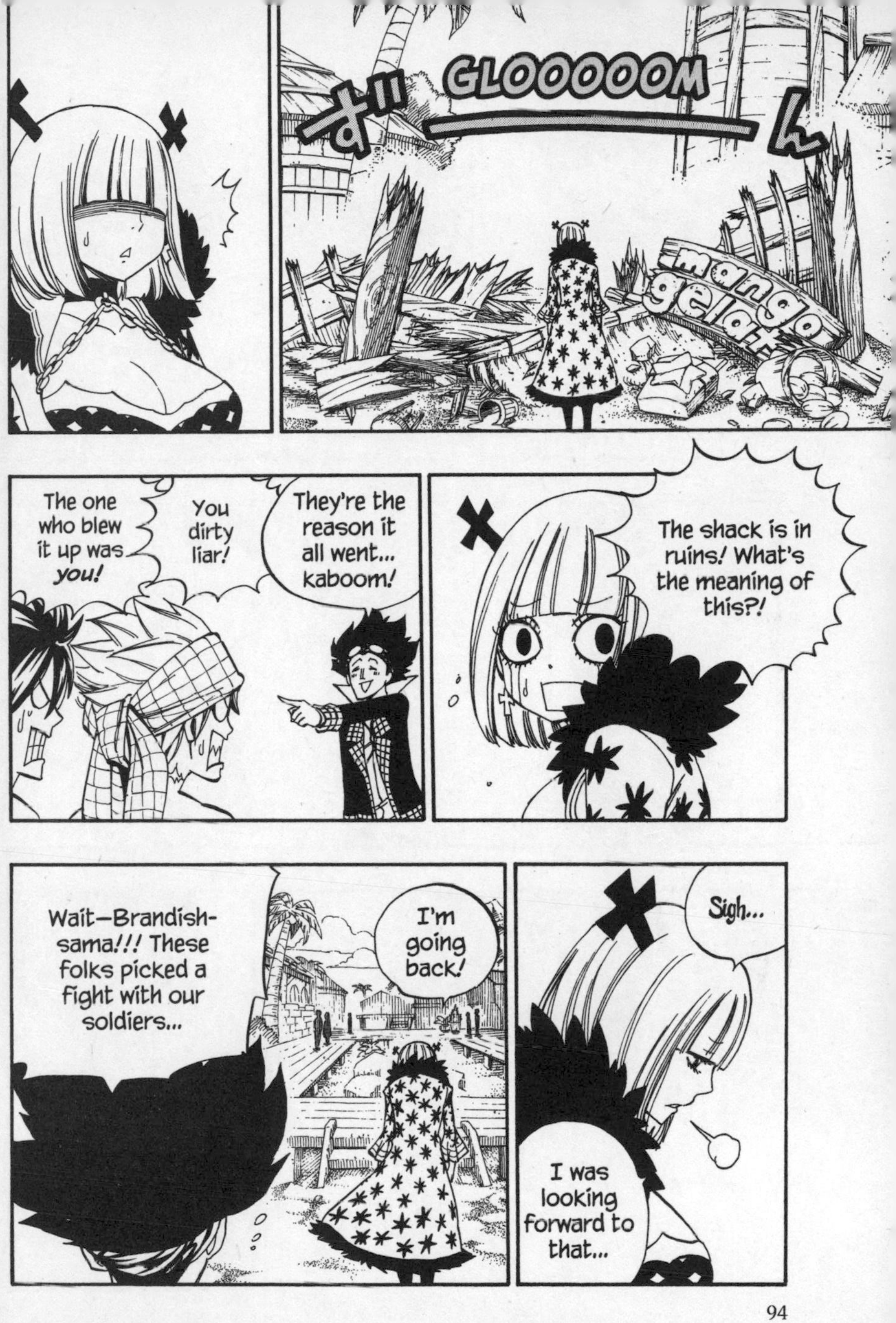

GLOOOOOM
mango gelato
The shack is in ruins! What's the meaning of this?!
They're the reason it all went... kaboom!
You dirty liar!
The one who blew it up was *you!*
Sigh...
I was looking forward to that...
I'm going back!
Wait—Brandish-sama!!! These folks picked a fight with our soldiers...

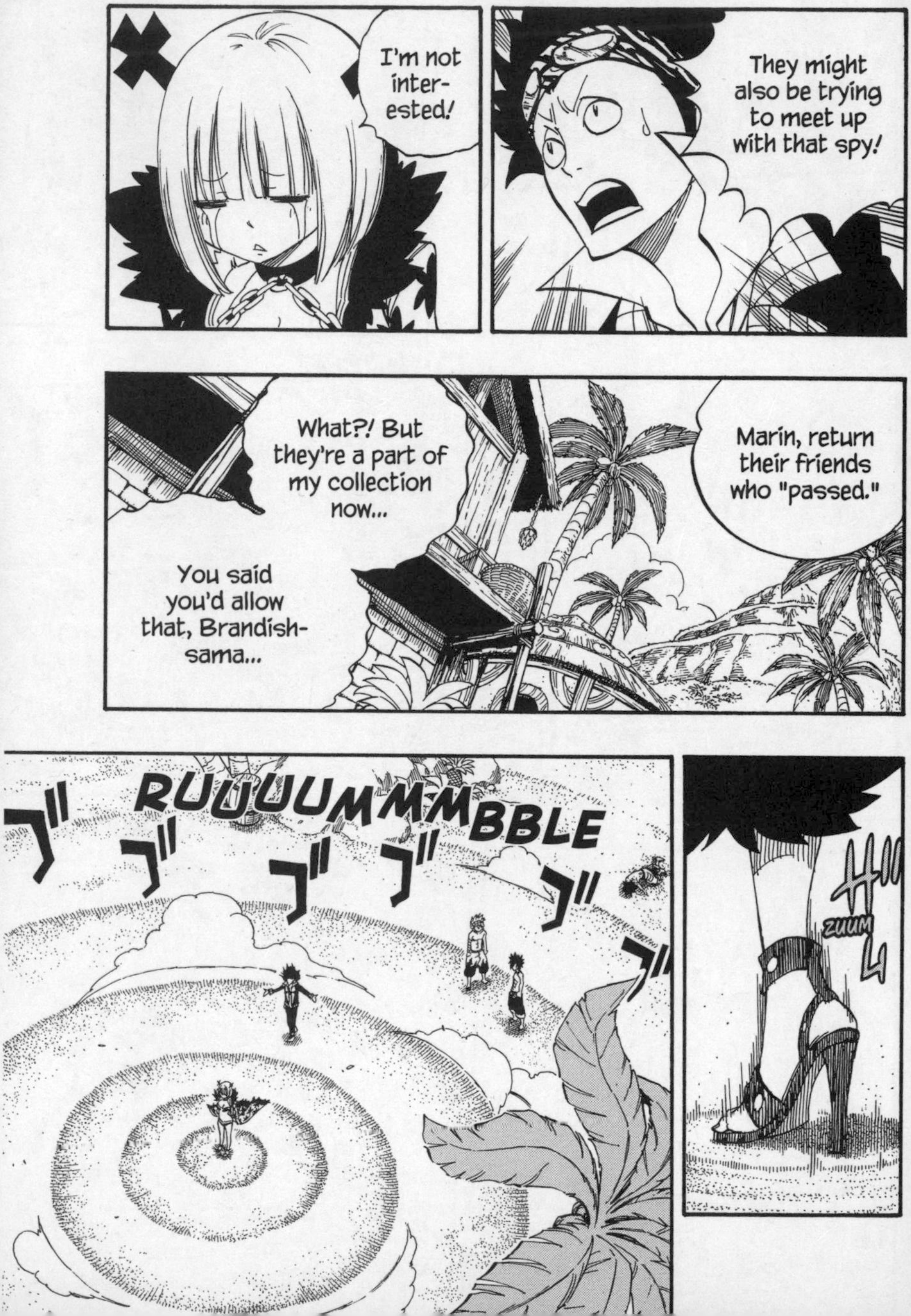
They might also be trying to meet up with that spy!
I'm not interested!
Marin, return their friends who "passed."
What?! But they're a part of my collection now...
You said you'd allow that, Brandish-sama...
ZUUM
RUUUUMMMBBLE

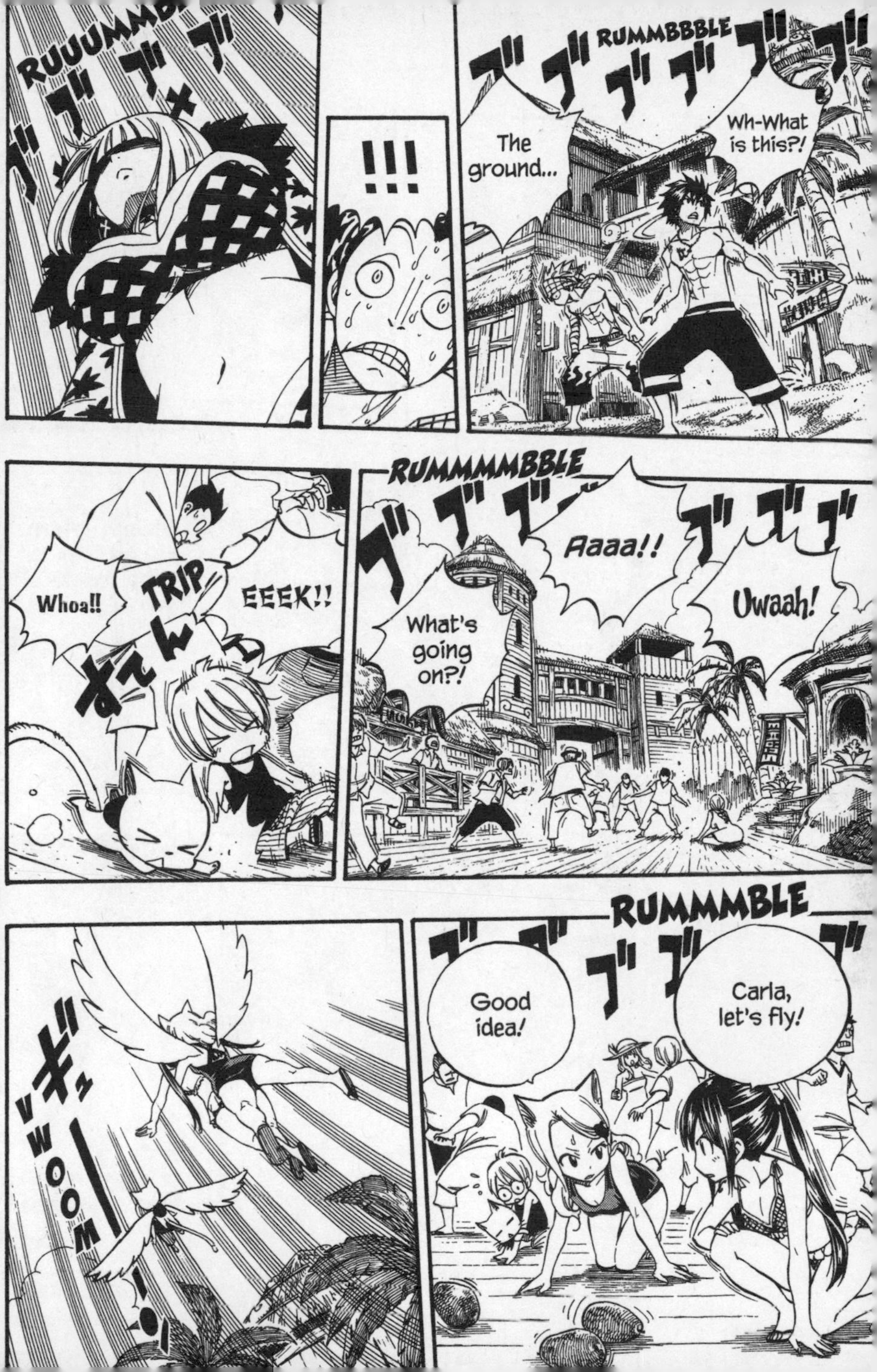
RUMMBBBLE
Wh-What is this?!
The ground...
!!!
RUUUMMBL
RUMMMMBBLE
Uwaah!
Aaaa!!
What's going on?!
EEEK!!
TRIP
Whoa!!
RUMMMBLE
Carla, let's fly!
Good idea!
VWOOM

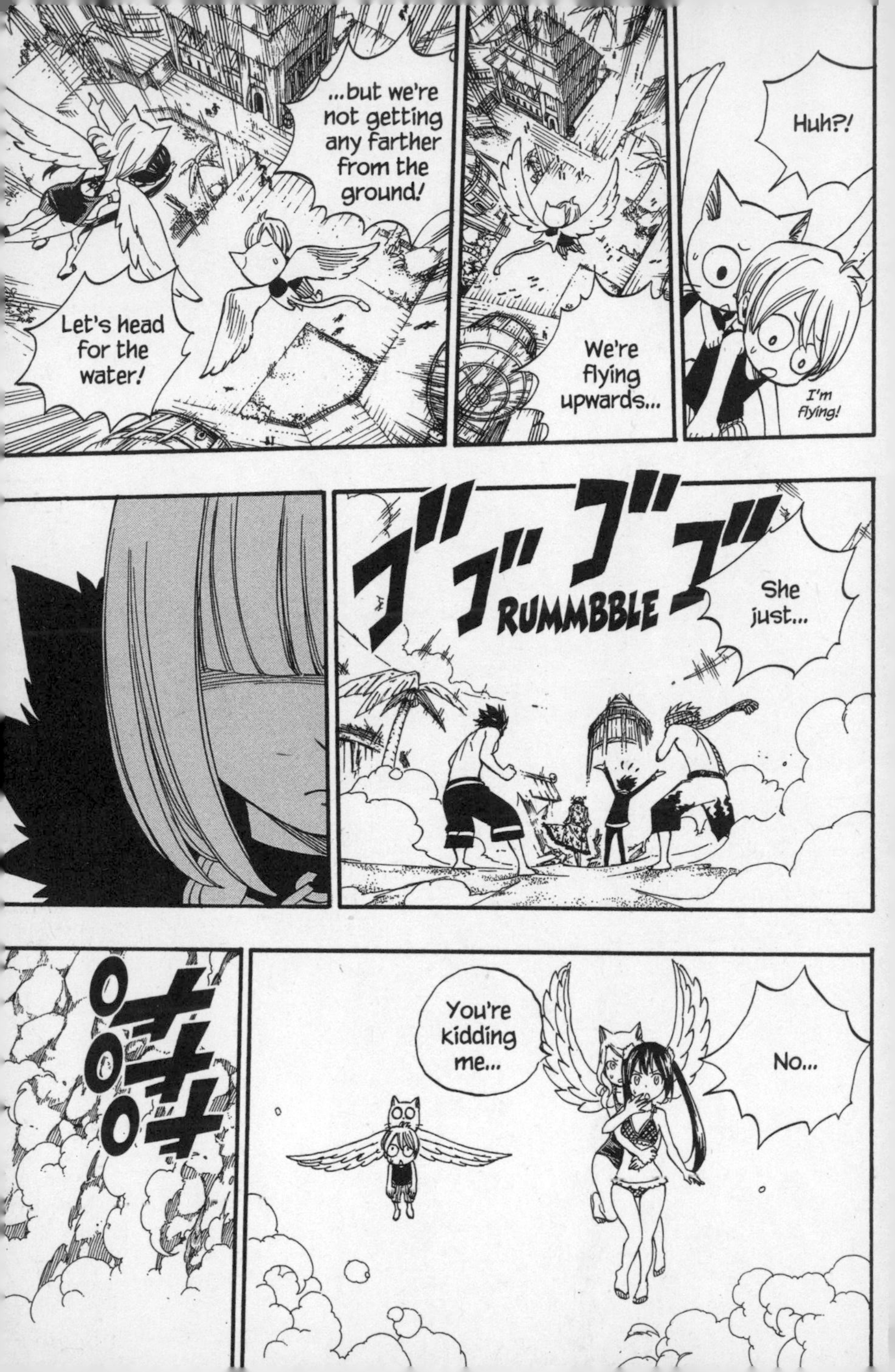
Huh?!
I'm flying!
We're flying upwards...
...but we're not getting any farther from the ground!
Let's head for the water!
ゴゴゴゴ
RUMMBBLE
She just...
No...
You're kidding me...

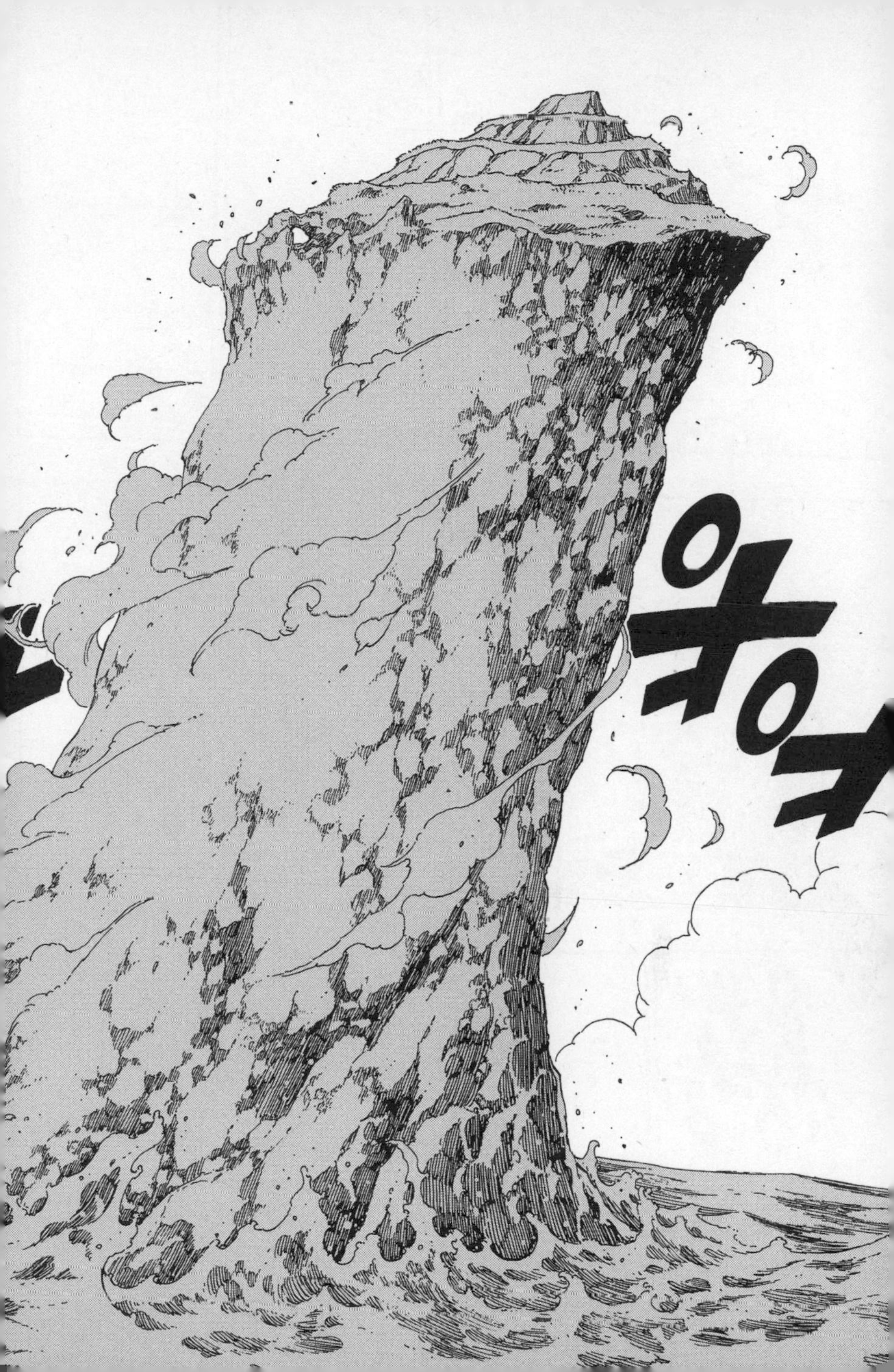
워어

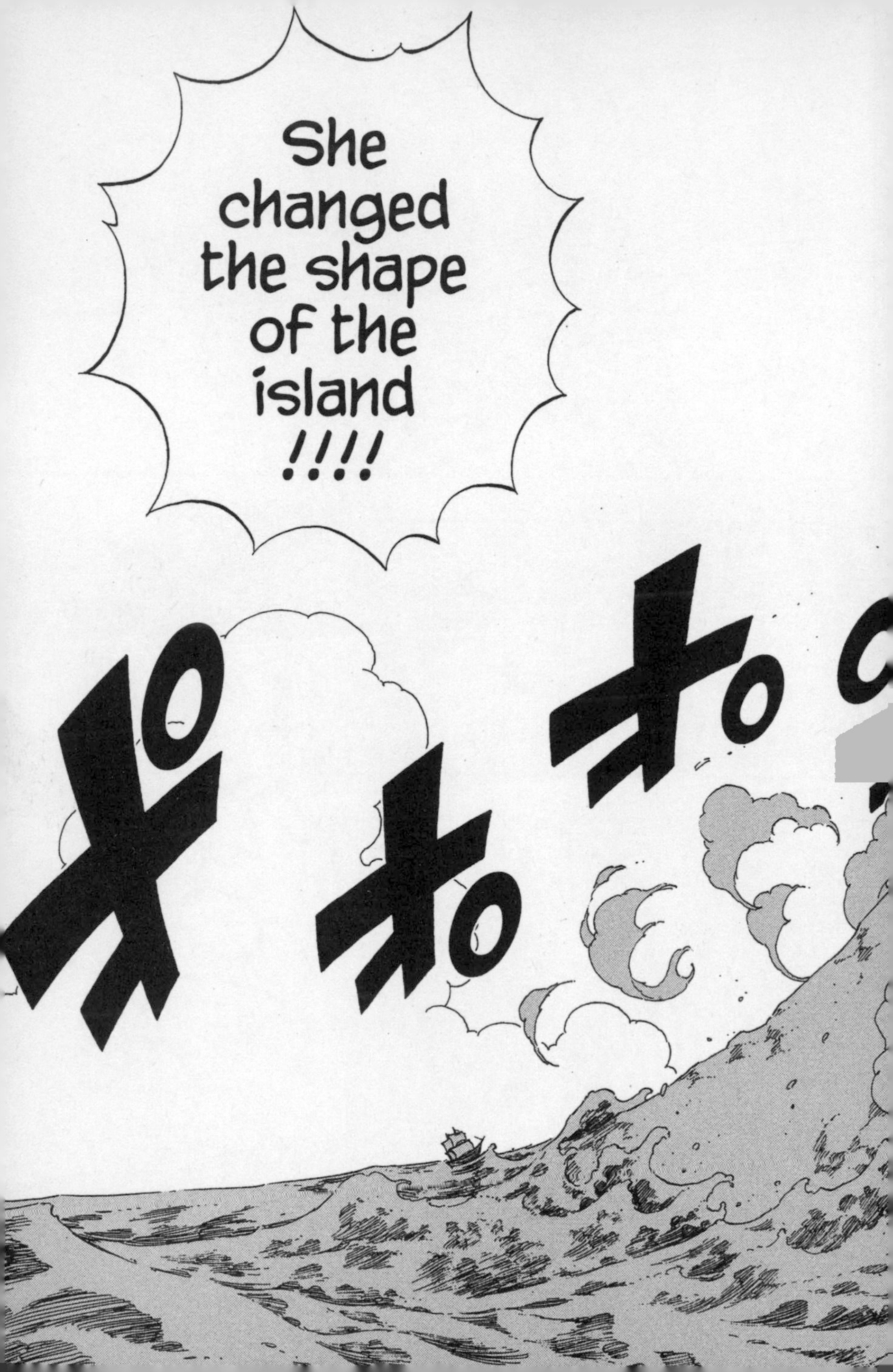
She changed the shape of the island !!!!

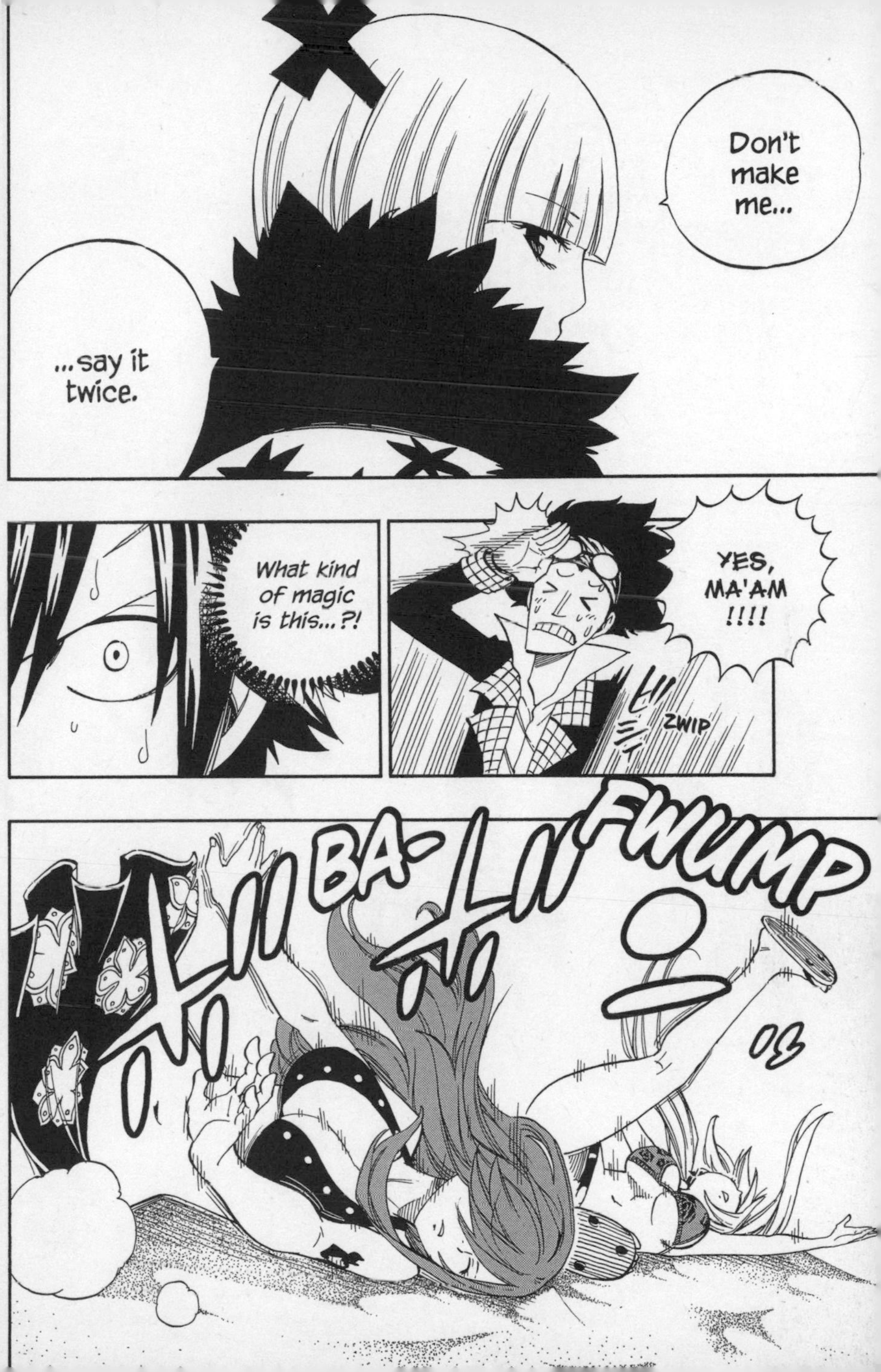
Don't make me...
...say it twice.
YES, MA'AM !!!!
ZWIP
What kind of magic is this...?!
BA-FWUMP

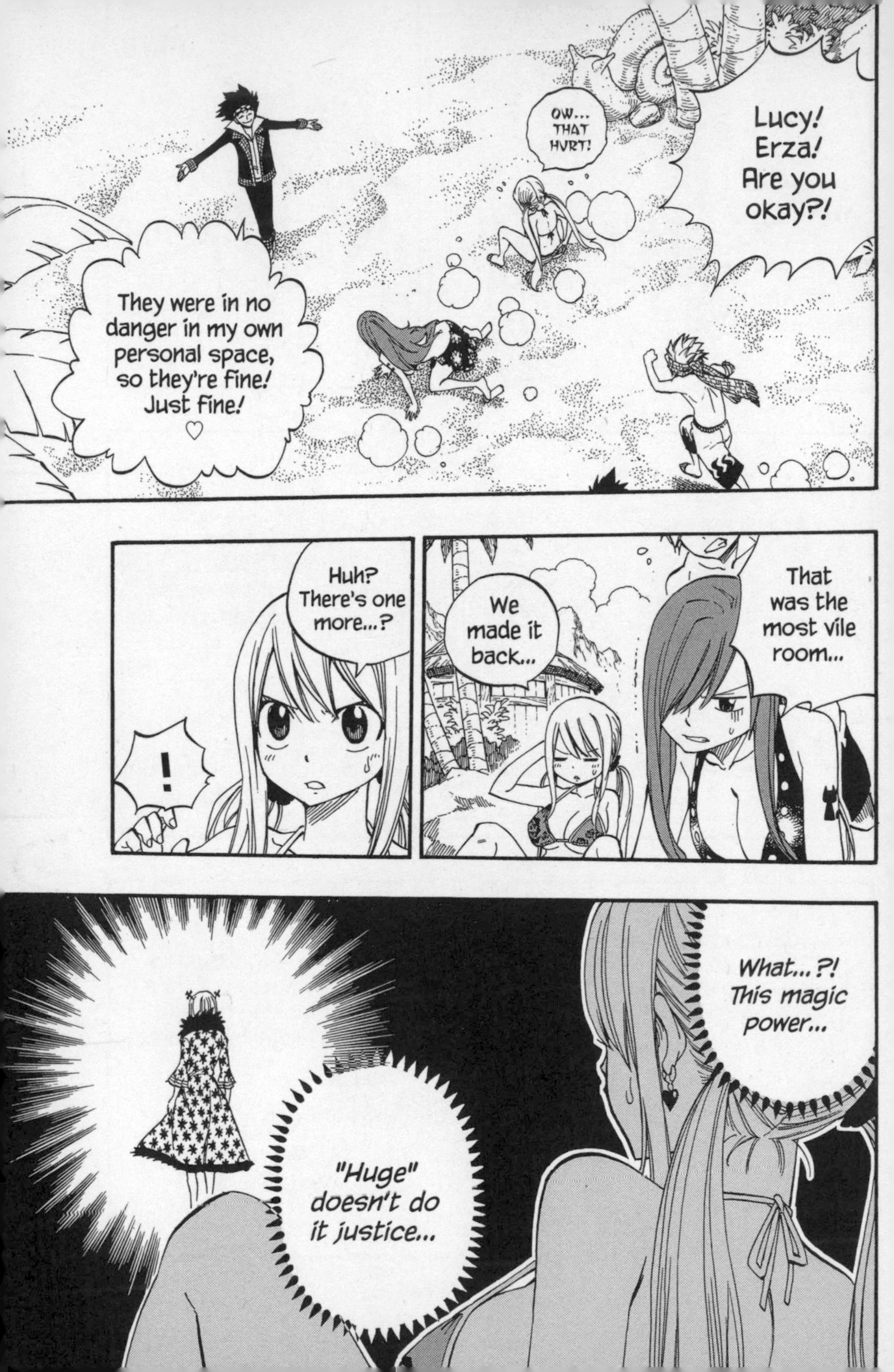
Lucy! Erza! Are you okay?!
OW... THAT HURT!
They were in no danger in my own personal space, so they're fine! Just fine! ♡
That was the most vile room...
We made it back...
Huh? There's one more...?
!
What...?! This magic power...
"Huge" doesn't do it justice...

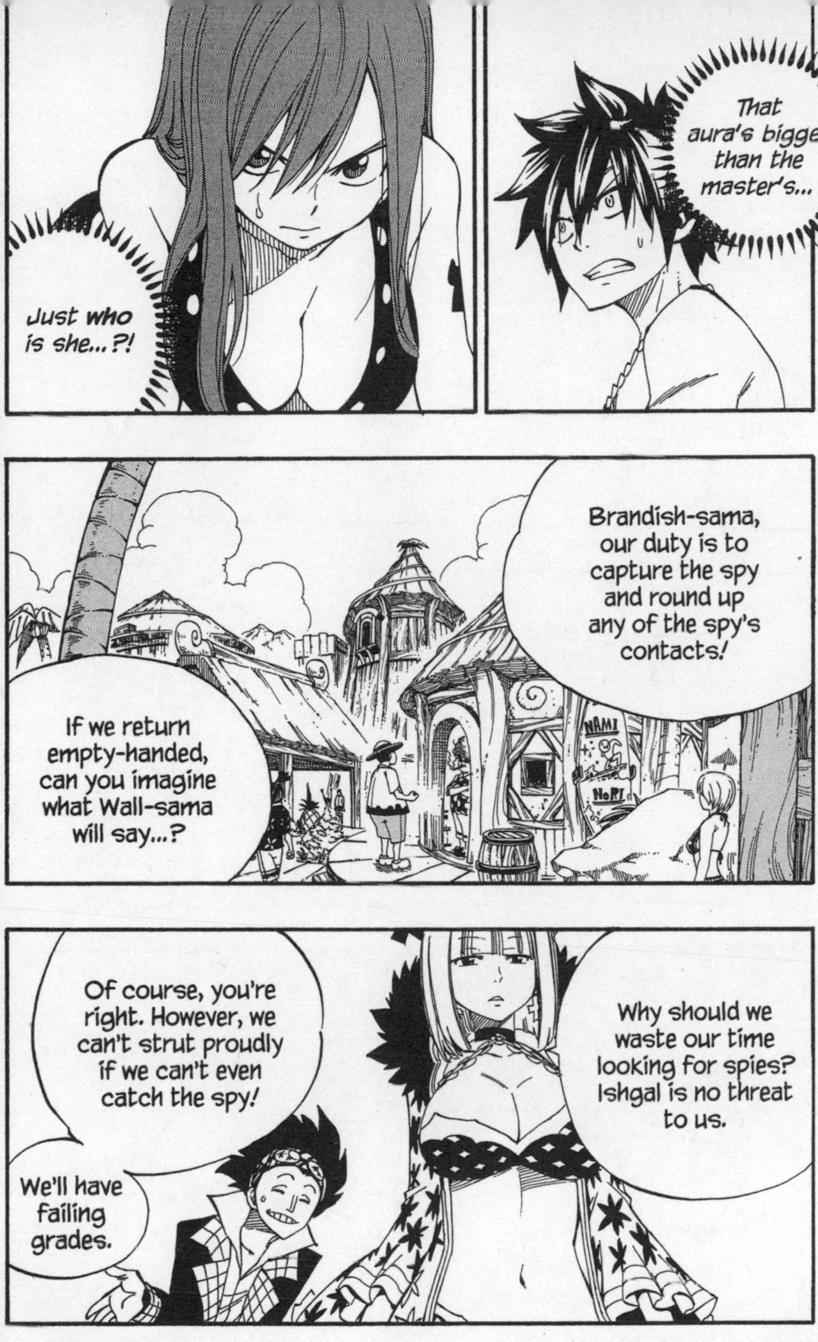
That aura's bigger than the master's...
Just who is she...?!
Brandish-sama, our duty is to capture the spy and round up any of the spy's contacts!
If we return empty-handed, can you imagine what Wall-sama will say...?
NAMI
NORI
Why should we waste our time looking for spies? Ishgal is no threat to us.
Of course, you're right. However, we can't strut proudly if we can't even catch the spy!
We'll have failing grades.

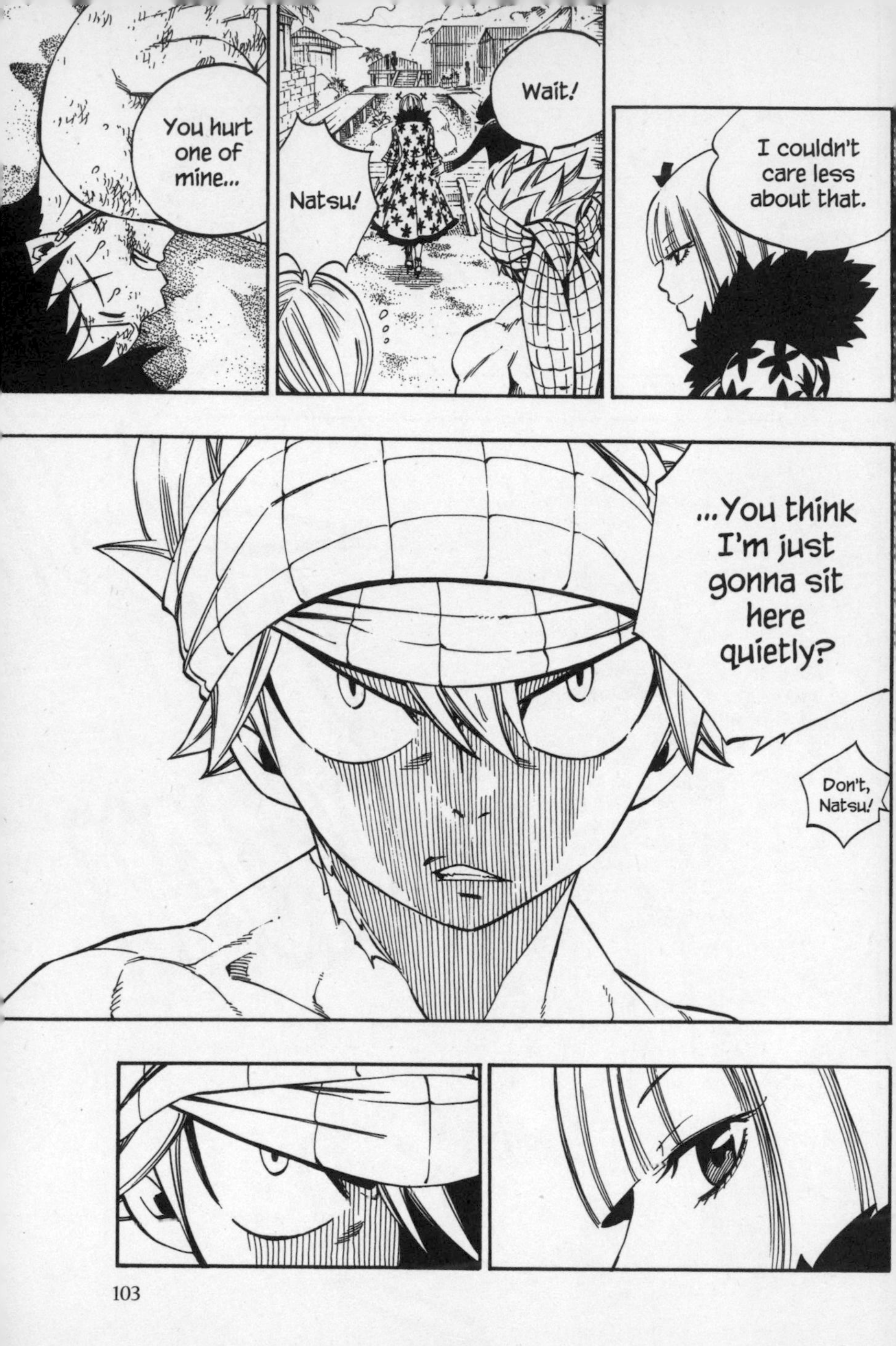
I couldn't care less about that.
Wait!
Natsu!
You hurt one of mine...
...You think I'm just gonna sit here quietly?
Don't, Natsu!

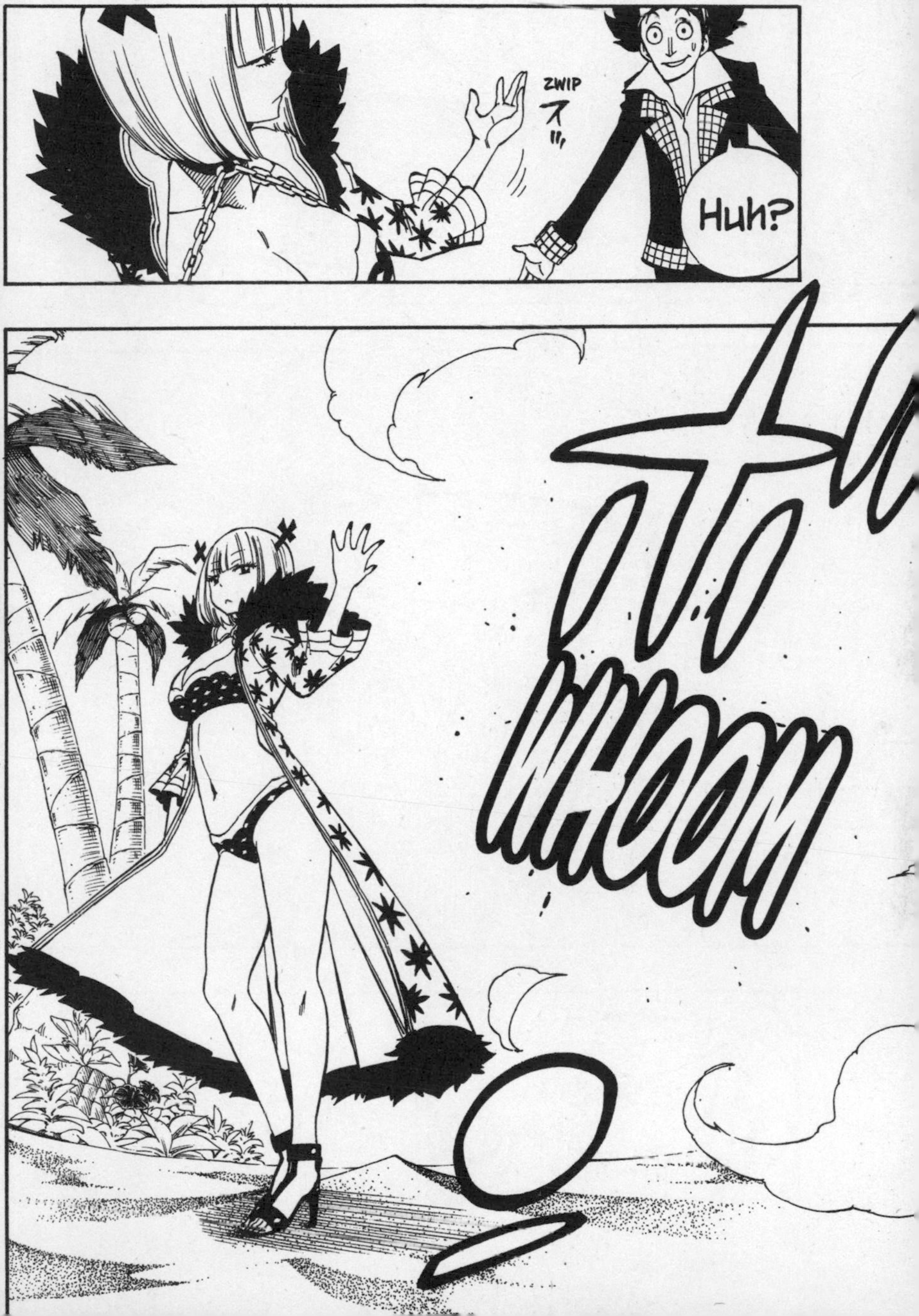
ZWIP
Huh?

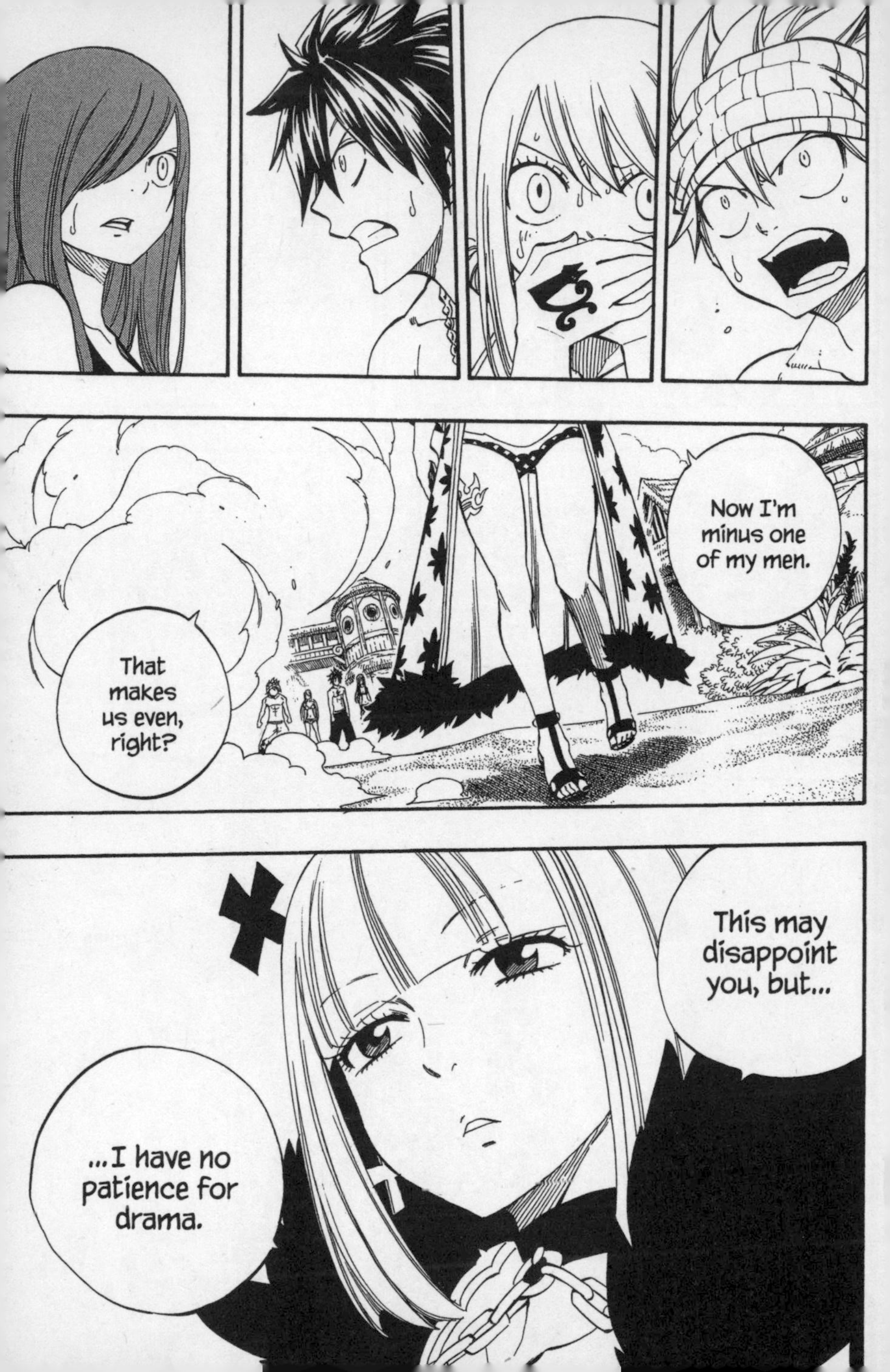
Now I'm minus one of my men.
That makes us even, right?
This may disappoint you, but...
...I have no patience for drama.

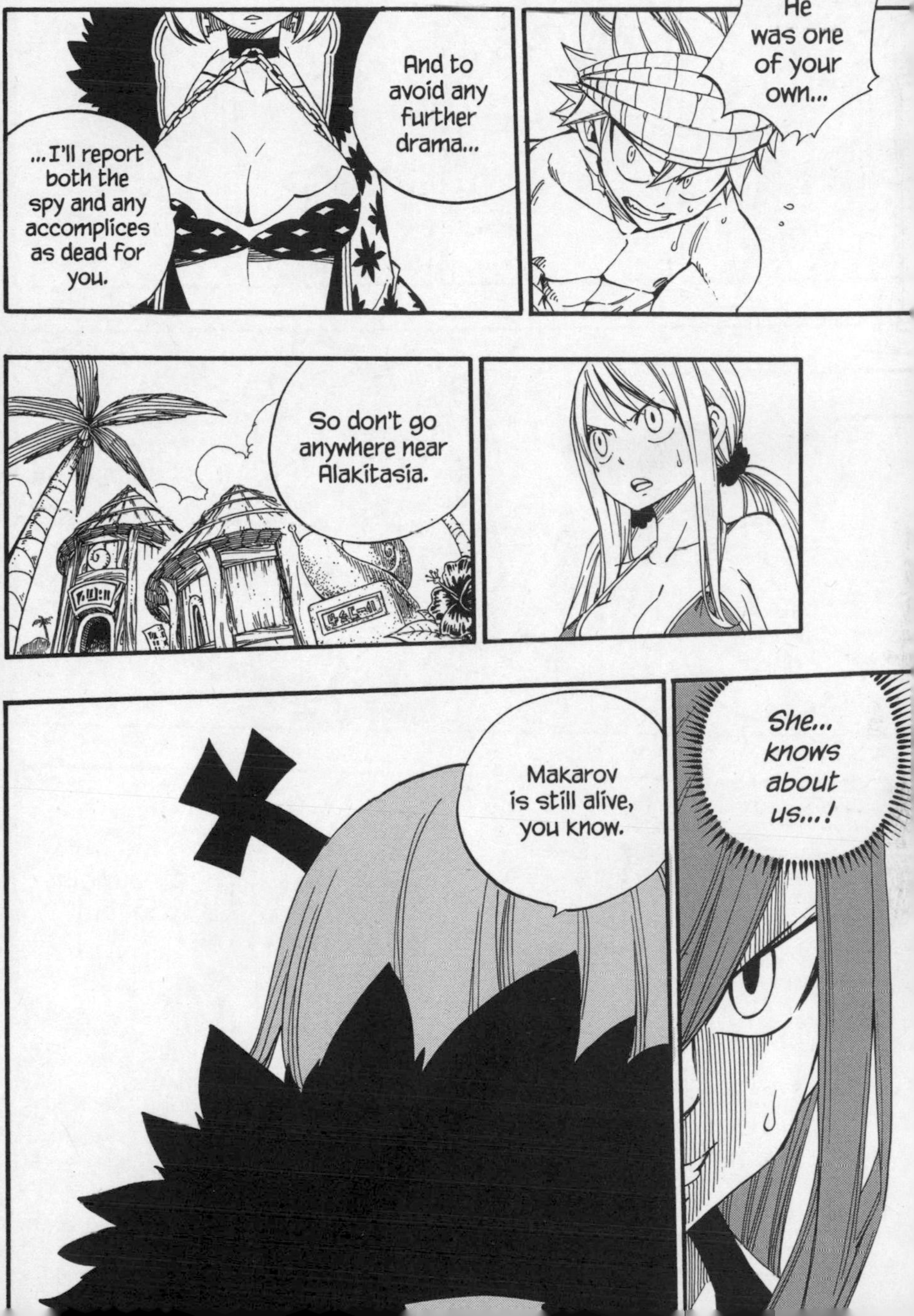
He was one of your own...
And to avoid any further drama...
...I'll report both the spy and any accomplices as dead for you.
So don't go anywhere near Alakitasia.
She... knows about us...!
Makarov is still alive, you know.

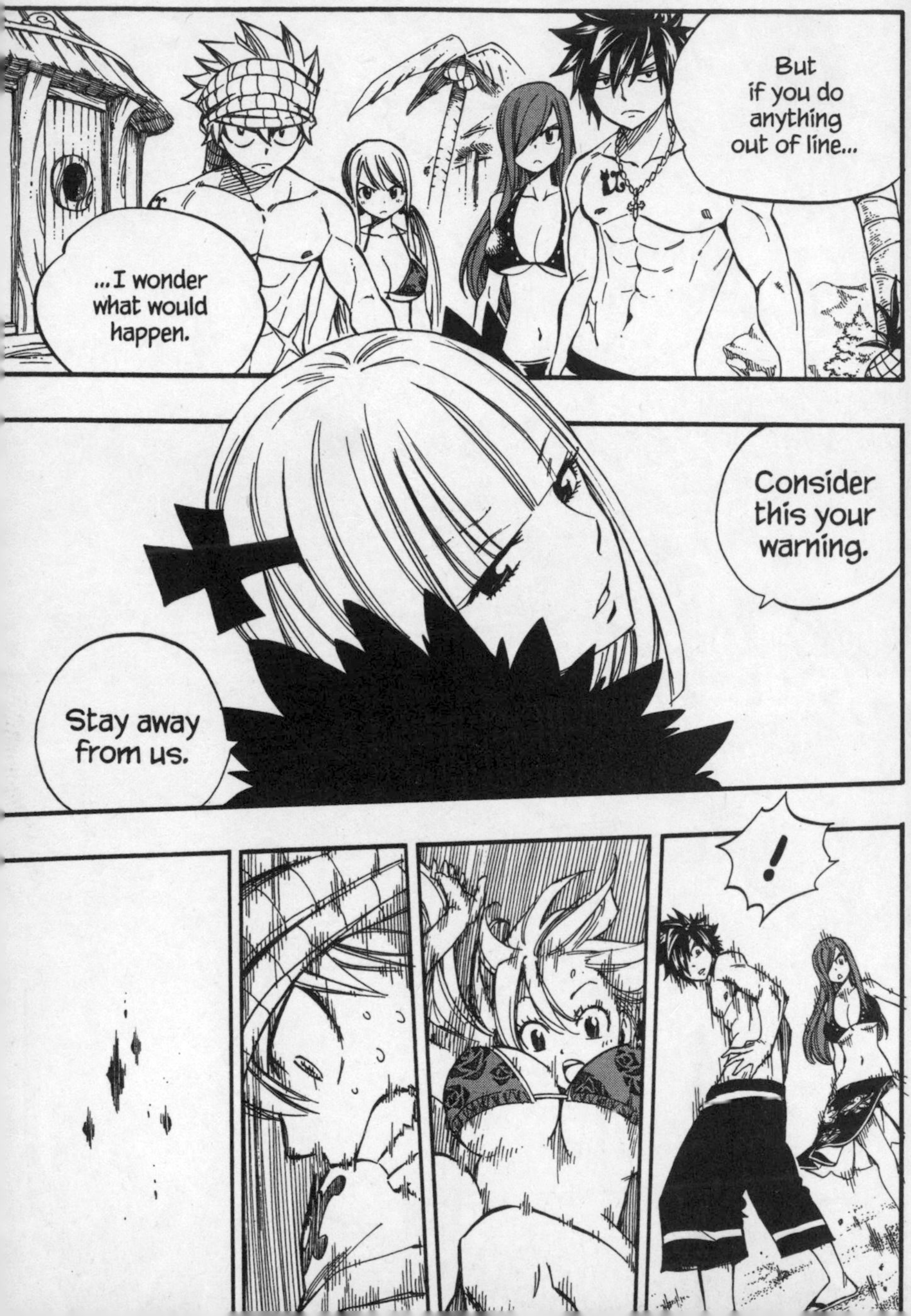
But if you do anything out of line...
...I wonder what would happen.
Consider this your warning.
Stay away from us.
!

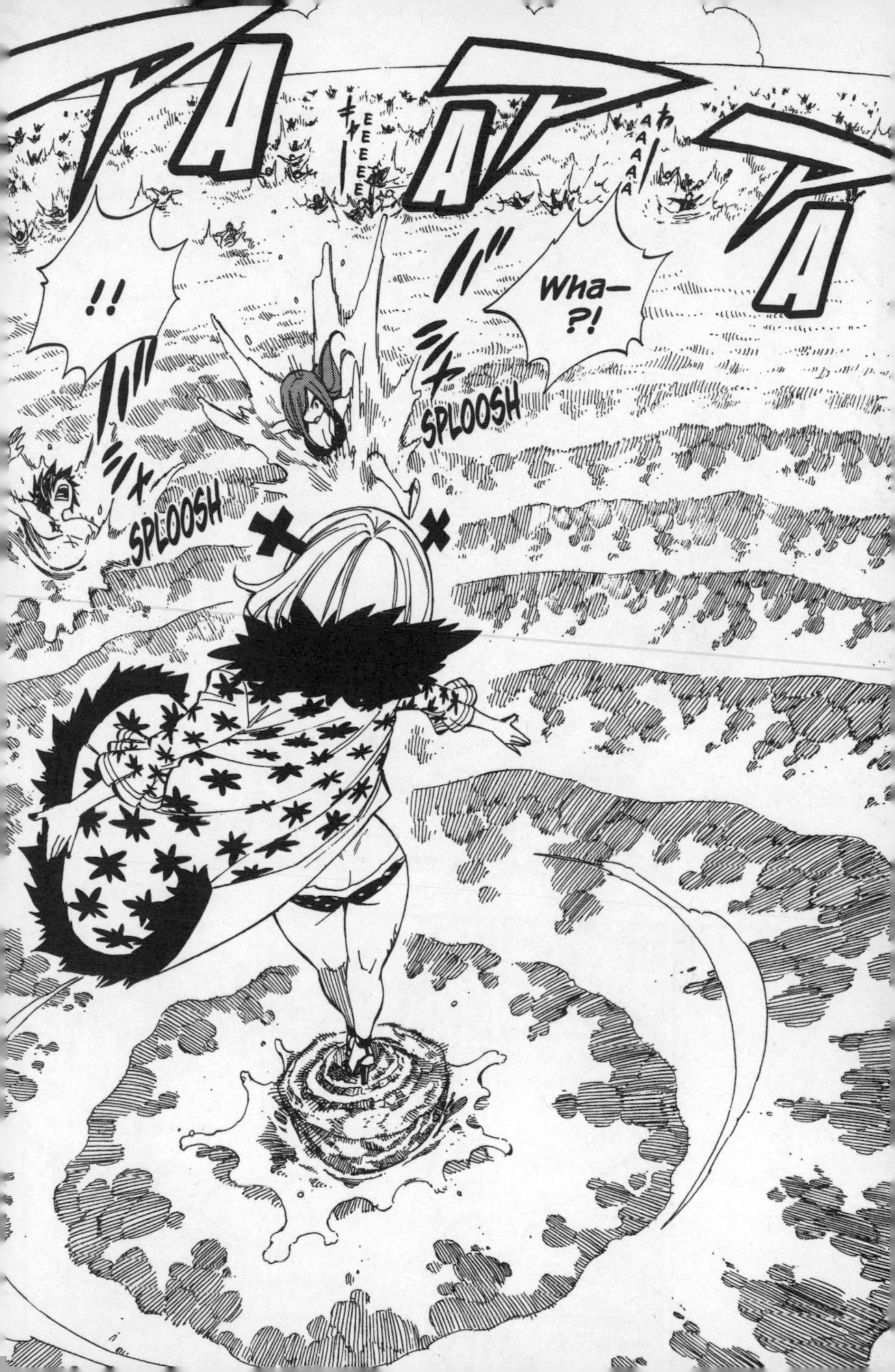
YAAAA
AAAAAA
EEEEEE
Wha—?!
SPLOOSH
!!
SPLOOSH

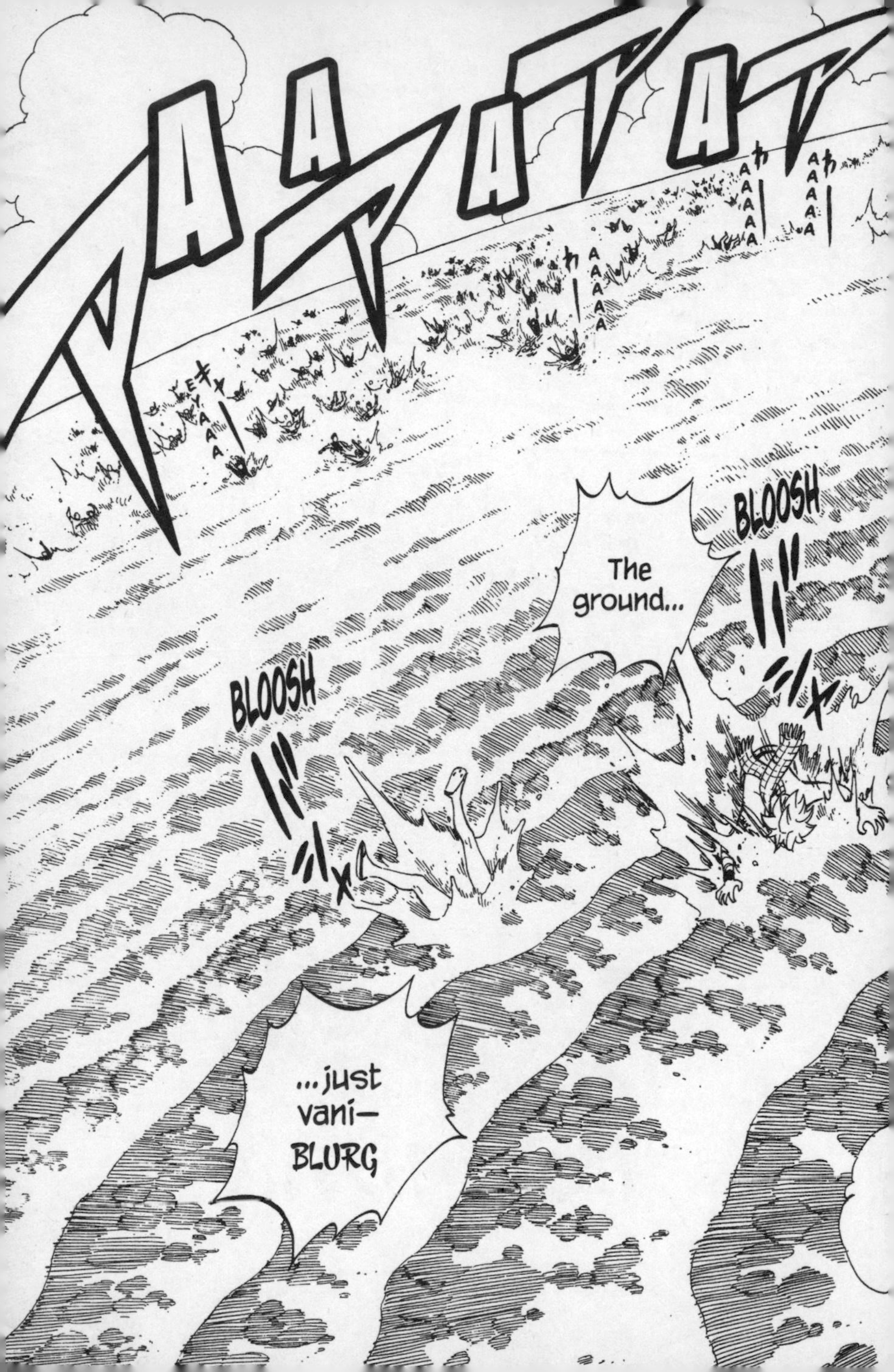

AAAAA
AAAAA
AAAAA
BLOOSH
The ground...
BLOOSH
...just vani— BLURG

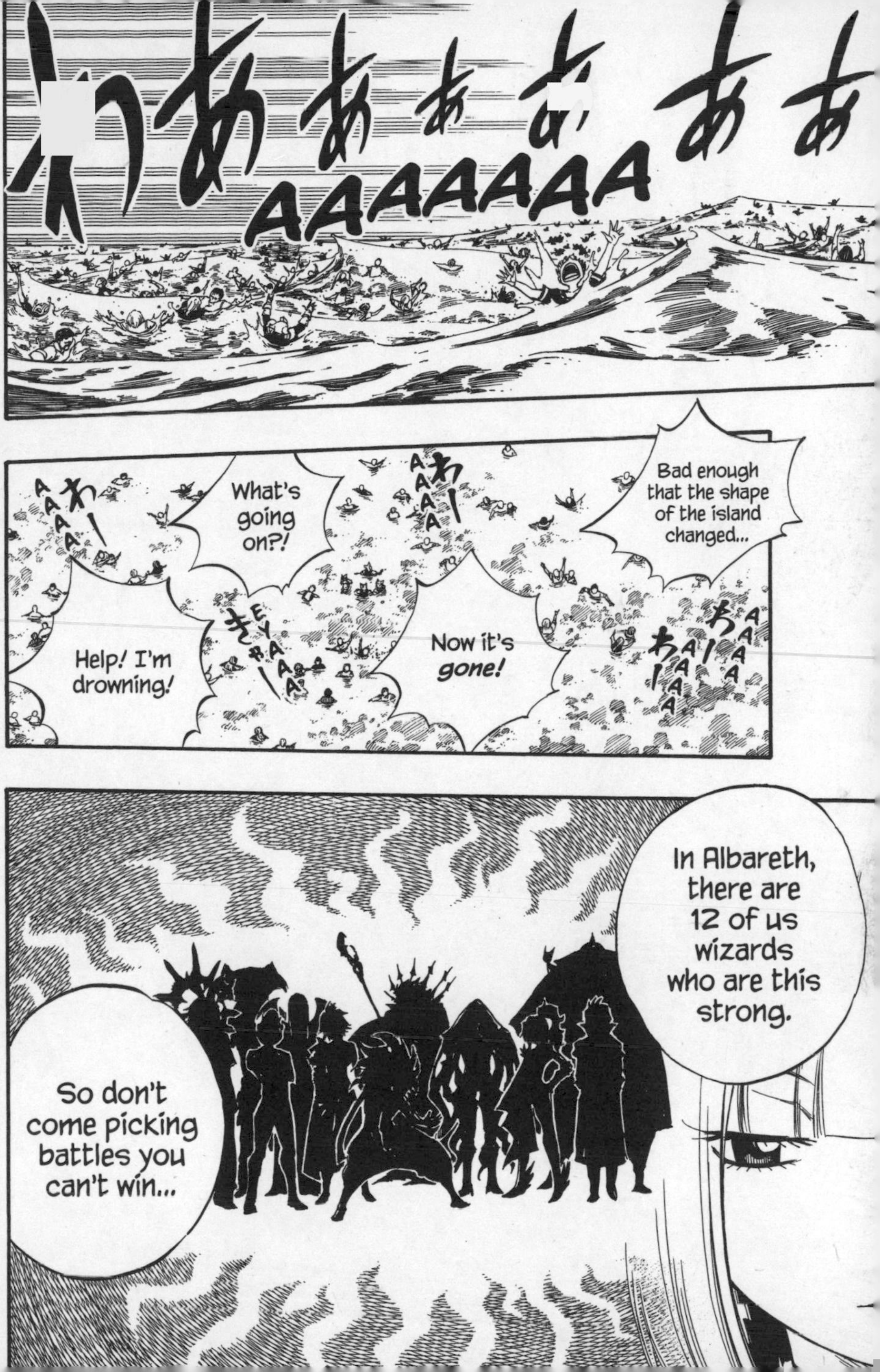
AAAAAAA
Bad enough that the shape of the island changed...
Now it's *gone!*
What's going on?!
Help! I'm drowning!
EYAAAA
In Albareth, there are 12 of us wizards who are this strong.
So don't come picking battles you can't win...

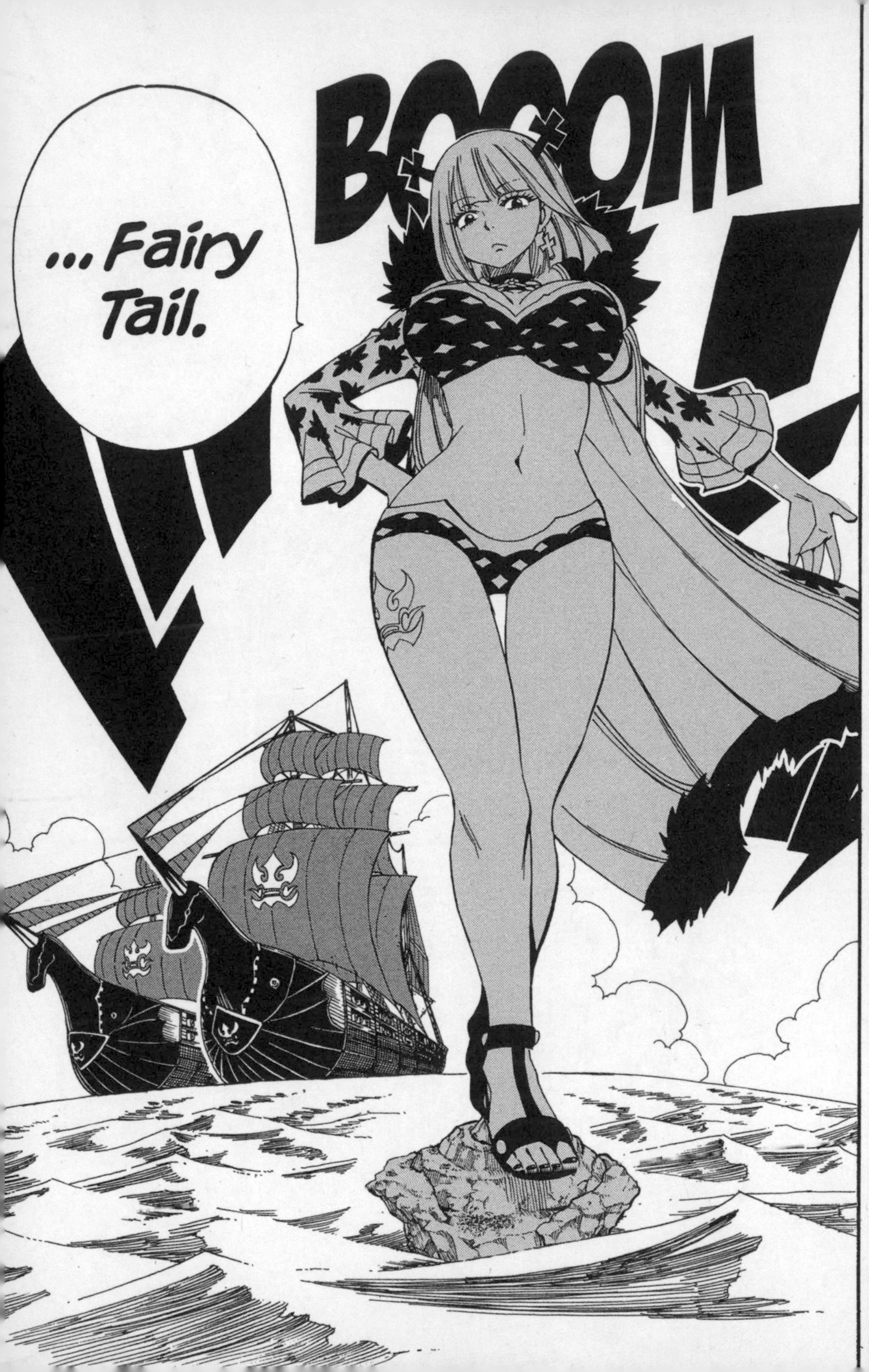

BOOOM
...Fairy Tail.

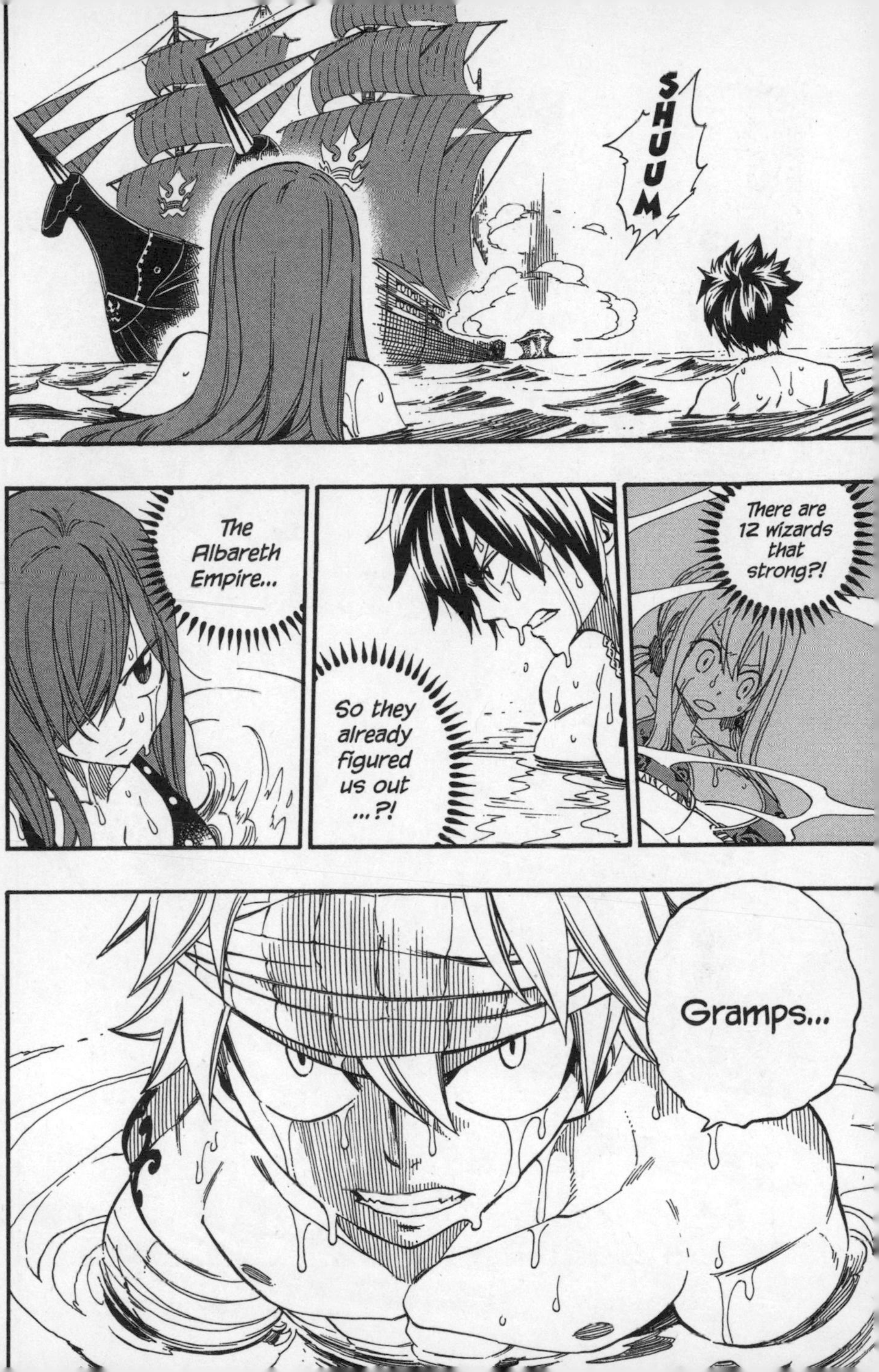
SHUUM
There are 12 wizards that strong?!
So they already figured us out ...?!
The Albareth Empire...
Gramps...

FAIRY TAIL

フェアリーテイル

Chapter 444: Emperor Spriggan

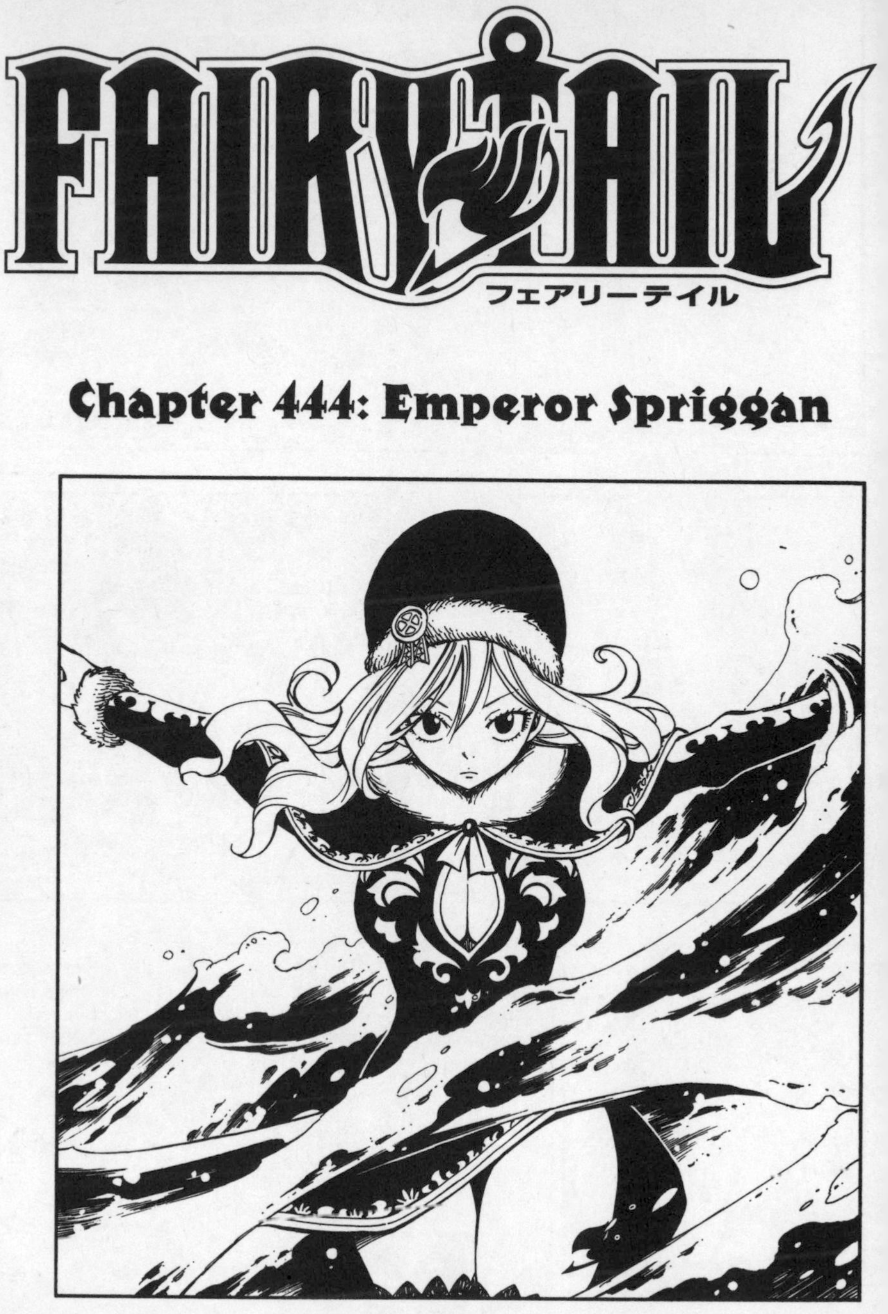

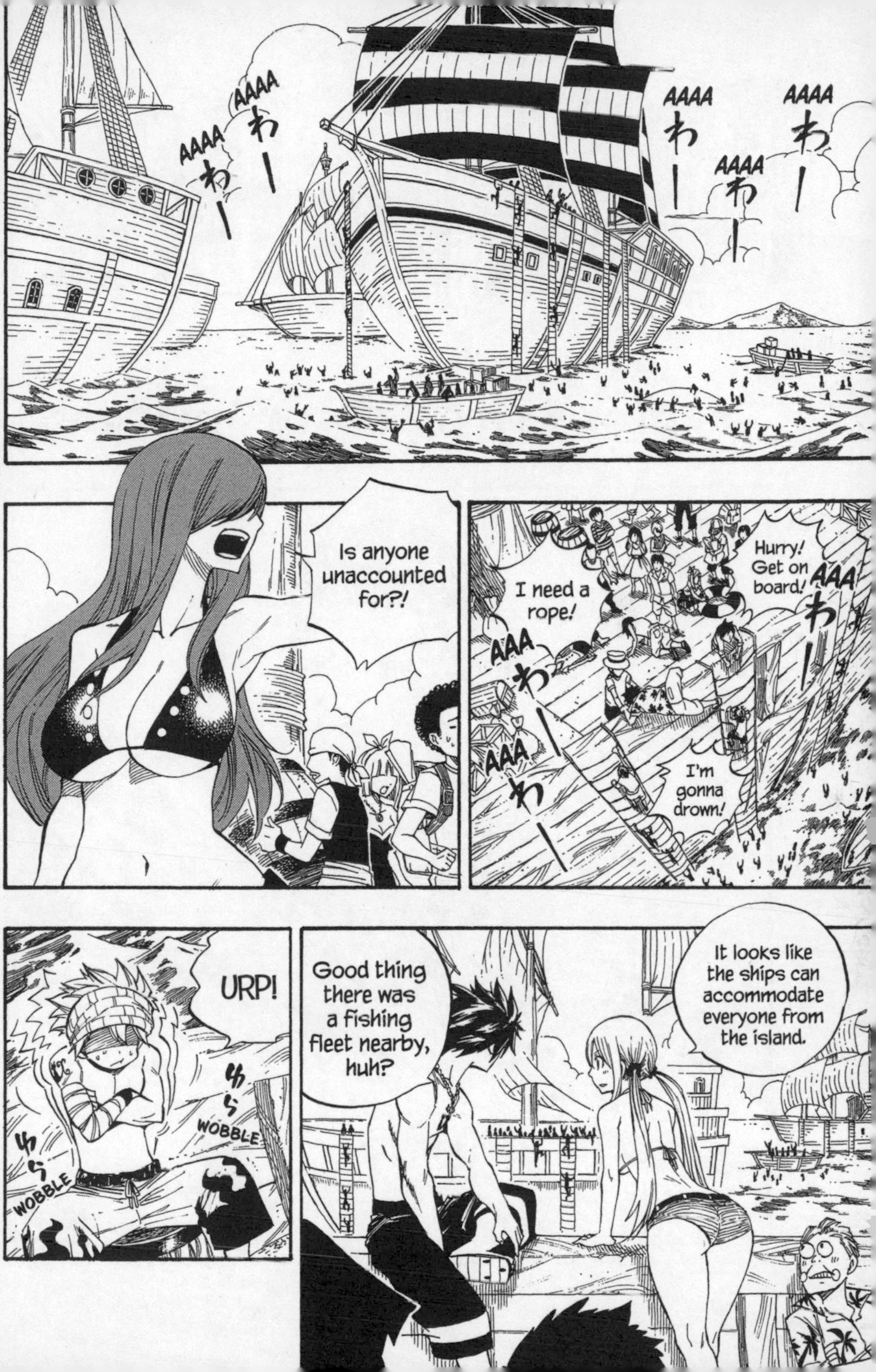
AAAA
わー
AAAA
わー
AAAA
わー
AAAA
わー
AAAA
わー
Hurry! Get on board!
AAA
わー
I need a rope!
AAA
わー
AAA
わー
I'm gonna drown!
Is anyone unaccounted for?!
It looks like the ships can accommodate everyone from the island.
Good thing there was a fishing fleet nearby, huh?
URP!
ゆら
WOBBLE
ゆら
WOBBLE

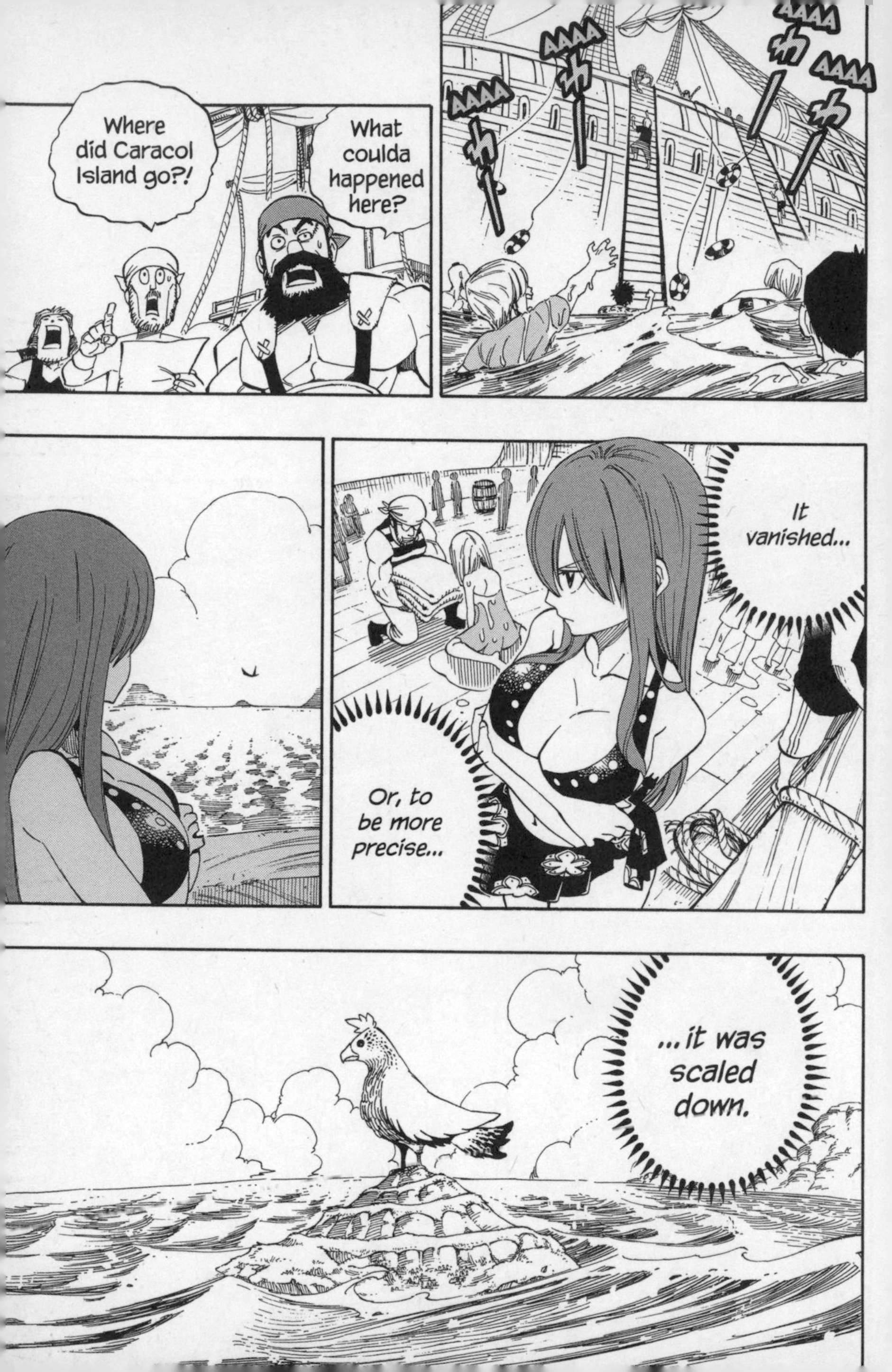
AAAA
AAAA
AAAA
AAAA
What coulda happened here?
Where did Caracol Island go?!
It vanished...
Or, to be more precise...
...it was scaled down.

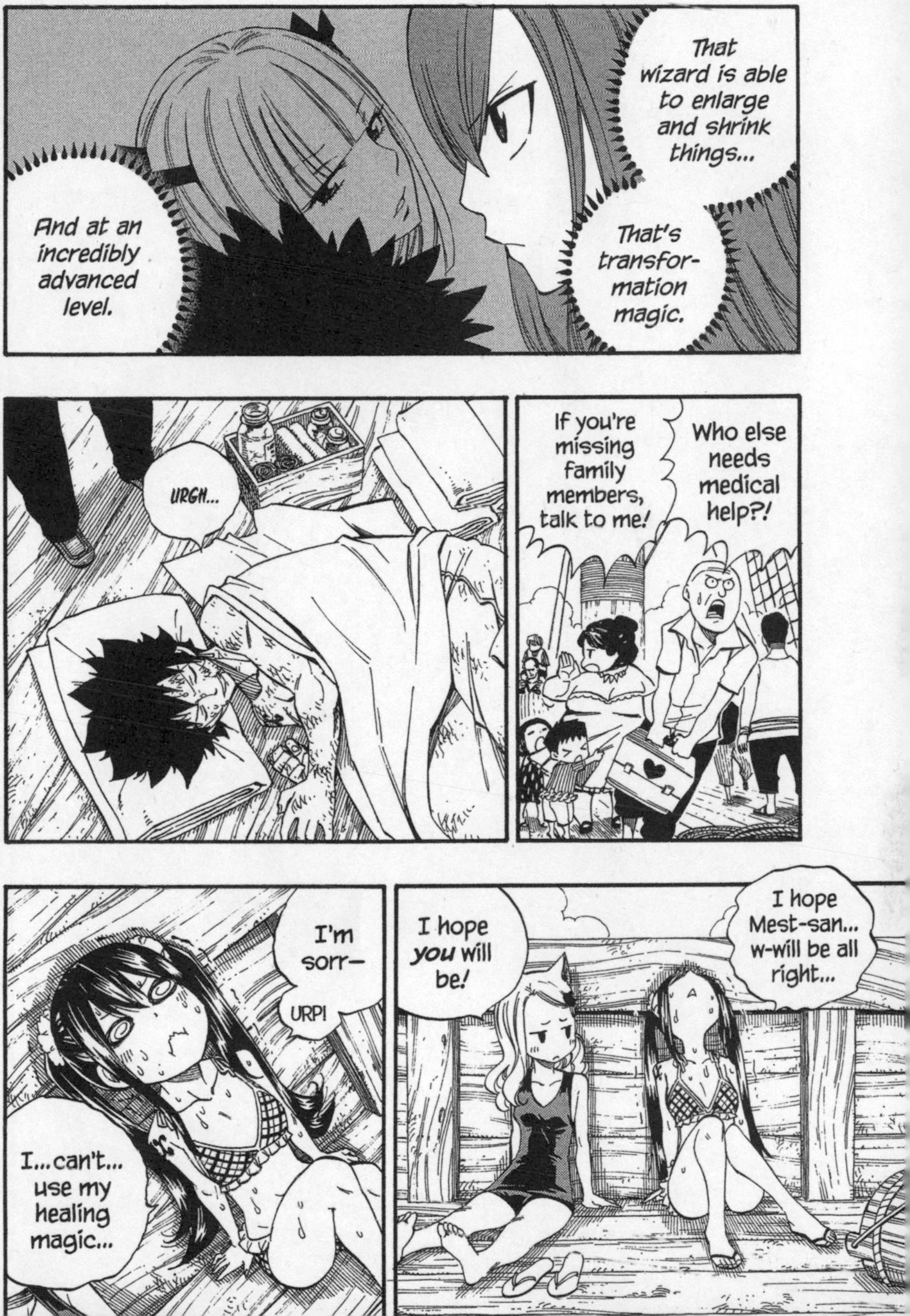
That wizard is able to enlarge and shrink things...
That's transformation magic.
And at an incredibly advanced level.
Who else needs medical help?!
If you're missing family members, talk to me!
URGH...
I hope Mest-san... w-will be all right...
I hope *you* will be!
I'm sorr—
URP!
I...can't... use my healing magic...

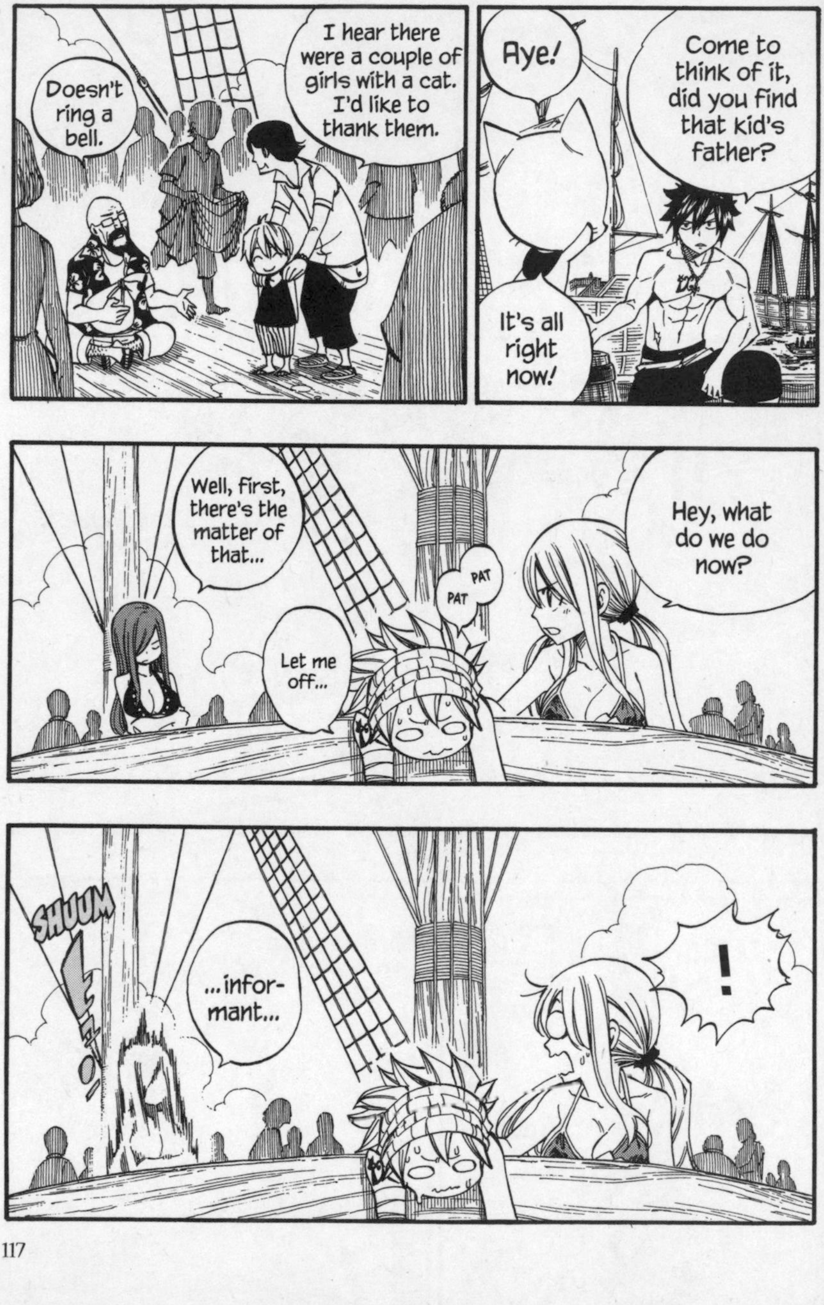
Come to think of it, did you find that kid's father?
Aye!
It's all right now!
I hear there were a couple of girls with a cat. I'd like to thank them.
Doesn't ring a bell.
Hey, what do we do now?
PAT PAT
Well, first, there's the matter of that...
Let me off...
!
...infor-mant...
SHUUM

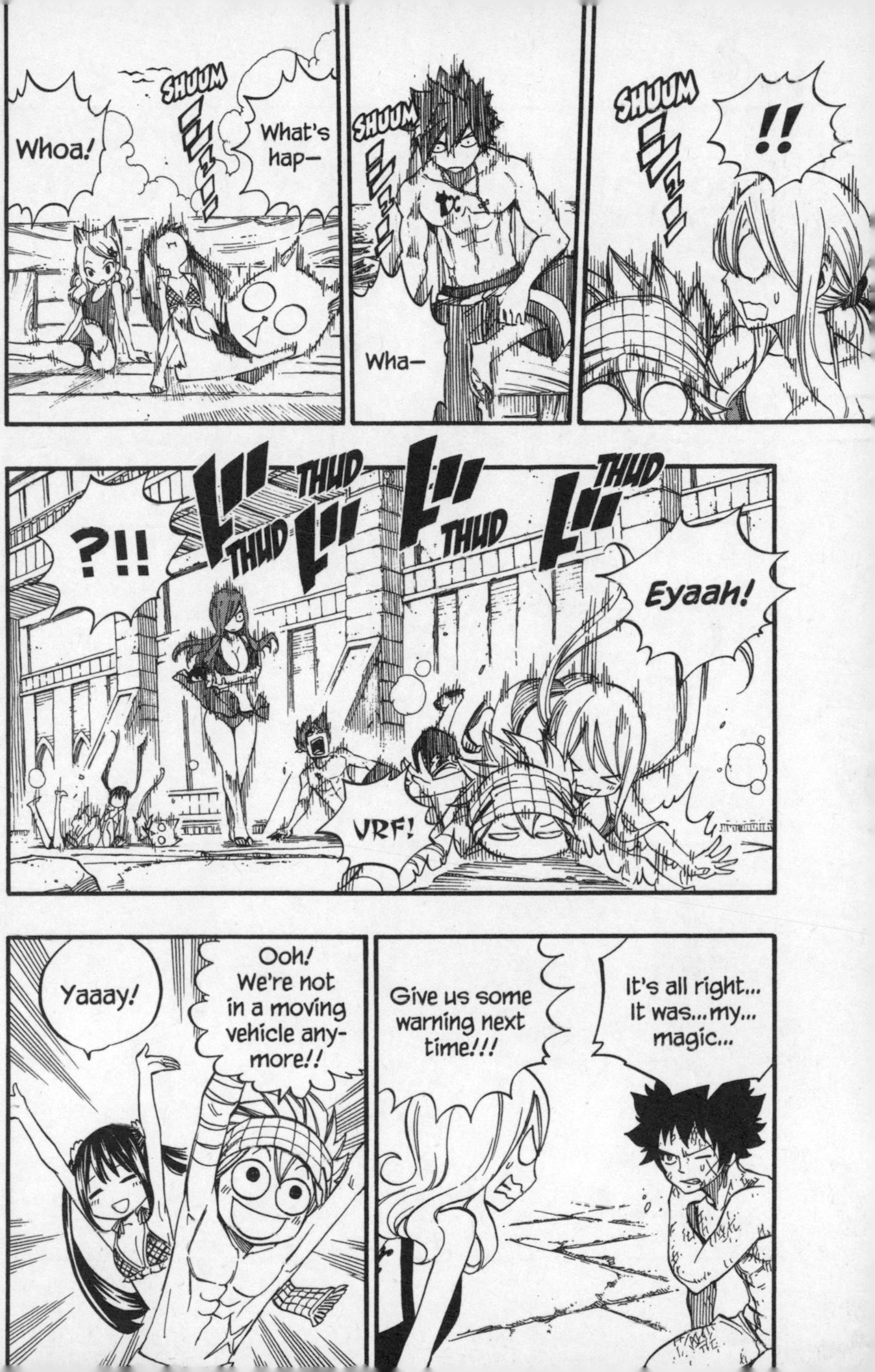
SHUUM
!!
SHUUM
Wha–
SHUUM
What's hap–
Whoa!
THUD
Eyaah!
THUD
THUD
THUD
?!!
VRF!
It's all right... It was...my... magic...
Give us some warning next time!!!
Ooh! We're not in a moving vehicle any-more!!
Yaaay!

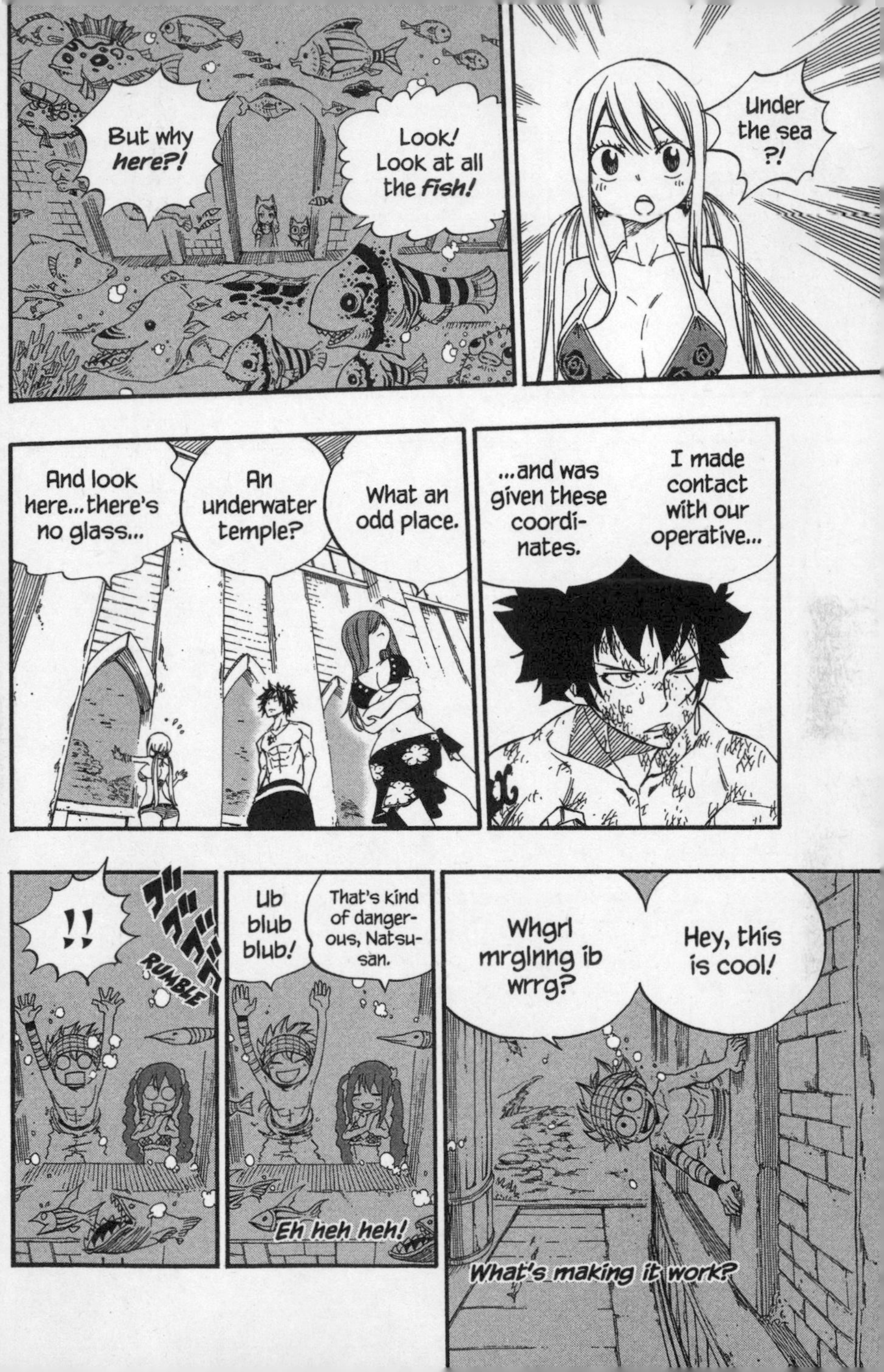
Under the sea ?!
Look! Look at all the fish!
But why here?!
I made contact with our operative...
...and was given these coordinates.
What an odd place.
An underwater temple?
And look here...there's no glass...
Hey, this is cool!
Whgrl mrglnng ib wrrg?
What's making it work?
That's kind of dangerous, Natsu-san.
Ub blub blub!
Eh heh heh!
!!
RUMBLE

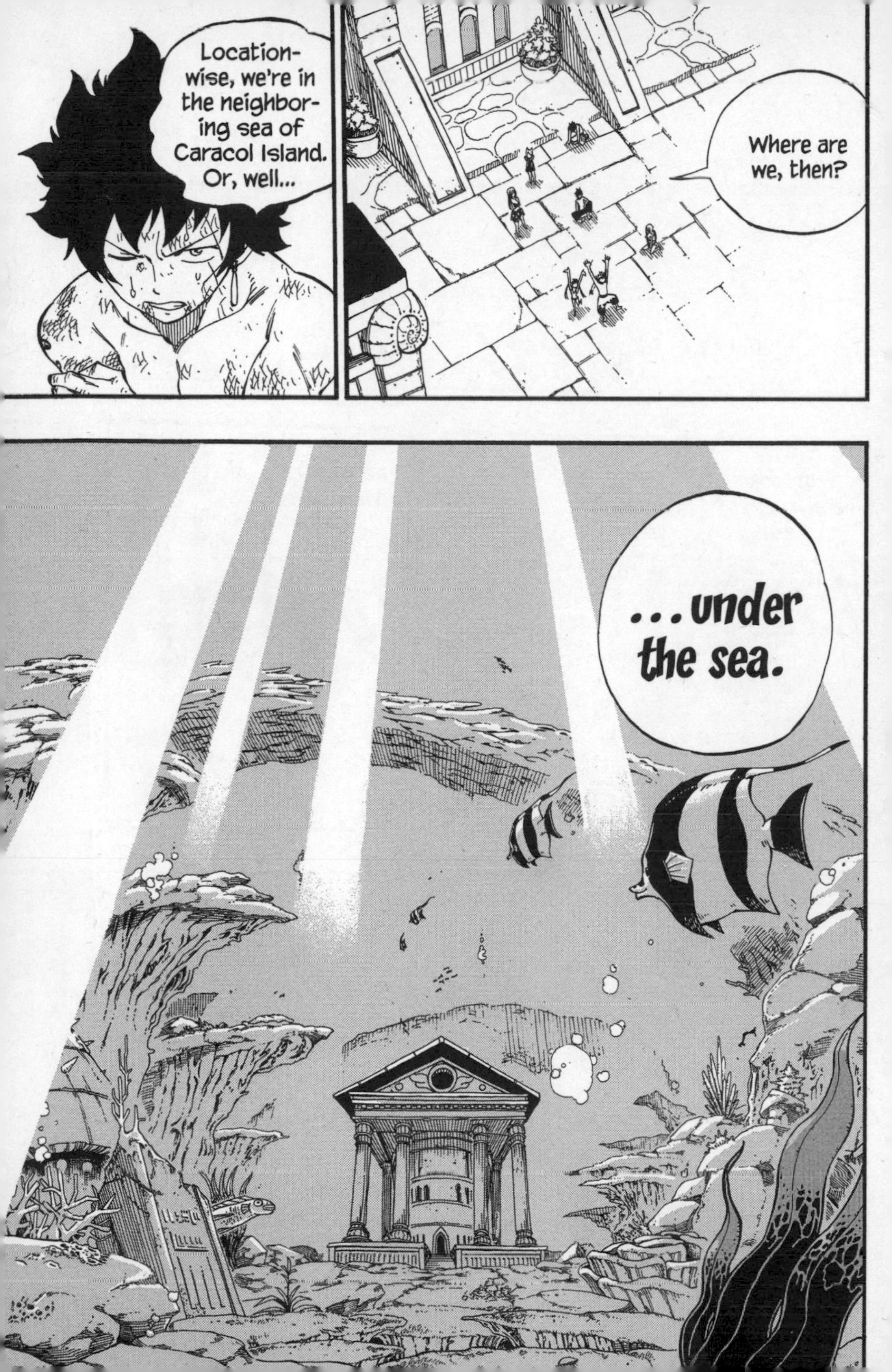
Where are we, then?
Location-wise, we're in the neighbor-ing sea of Caracol Island. Or, well...
...under the sea.

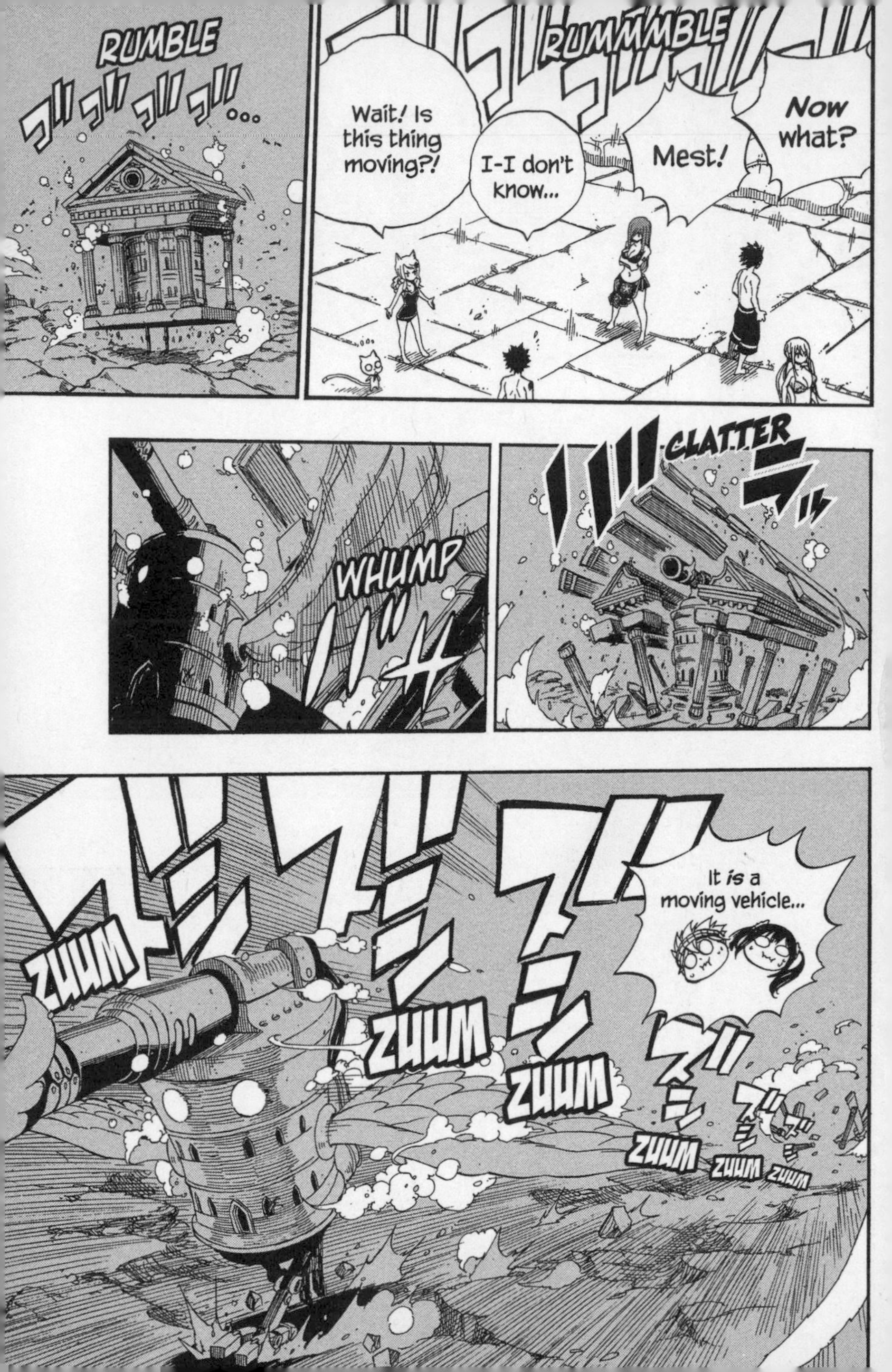

RUMMMBLE
Now what?
Mest!
I-I don't know...
Wait! Is this thing moving?!
RUMBLE
CLATTER
WHUMP
It *is* a moving vehicle...
ZUUM
ZUUM
ZUUM
ZUUM
ZUUM
ZUUM

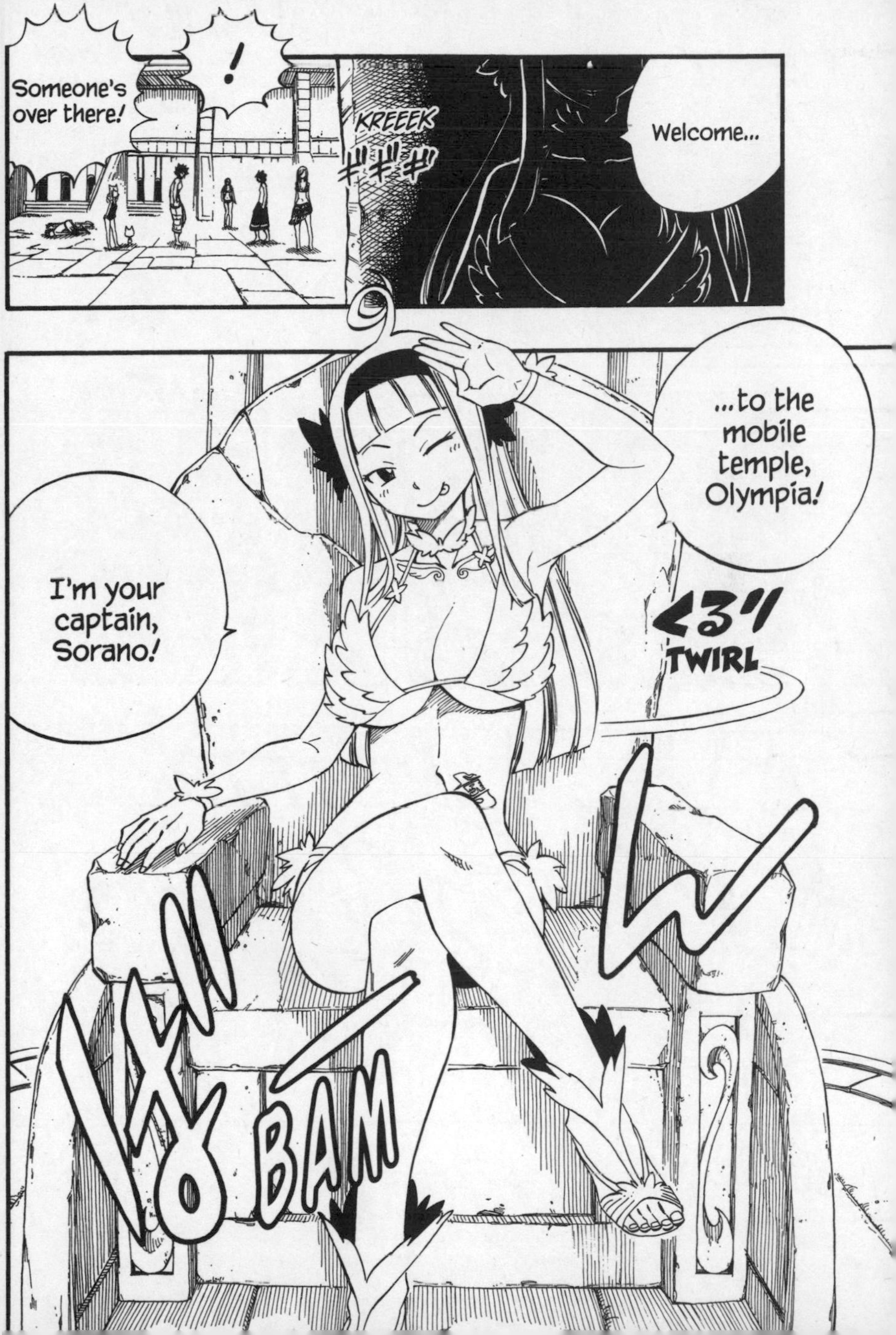
KREEEK
Welcome...
!
Someone's over there!
...to the mobile temple, Olympia!
I'm your captain, Sorano!
くるッ
TWIRL
BAM

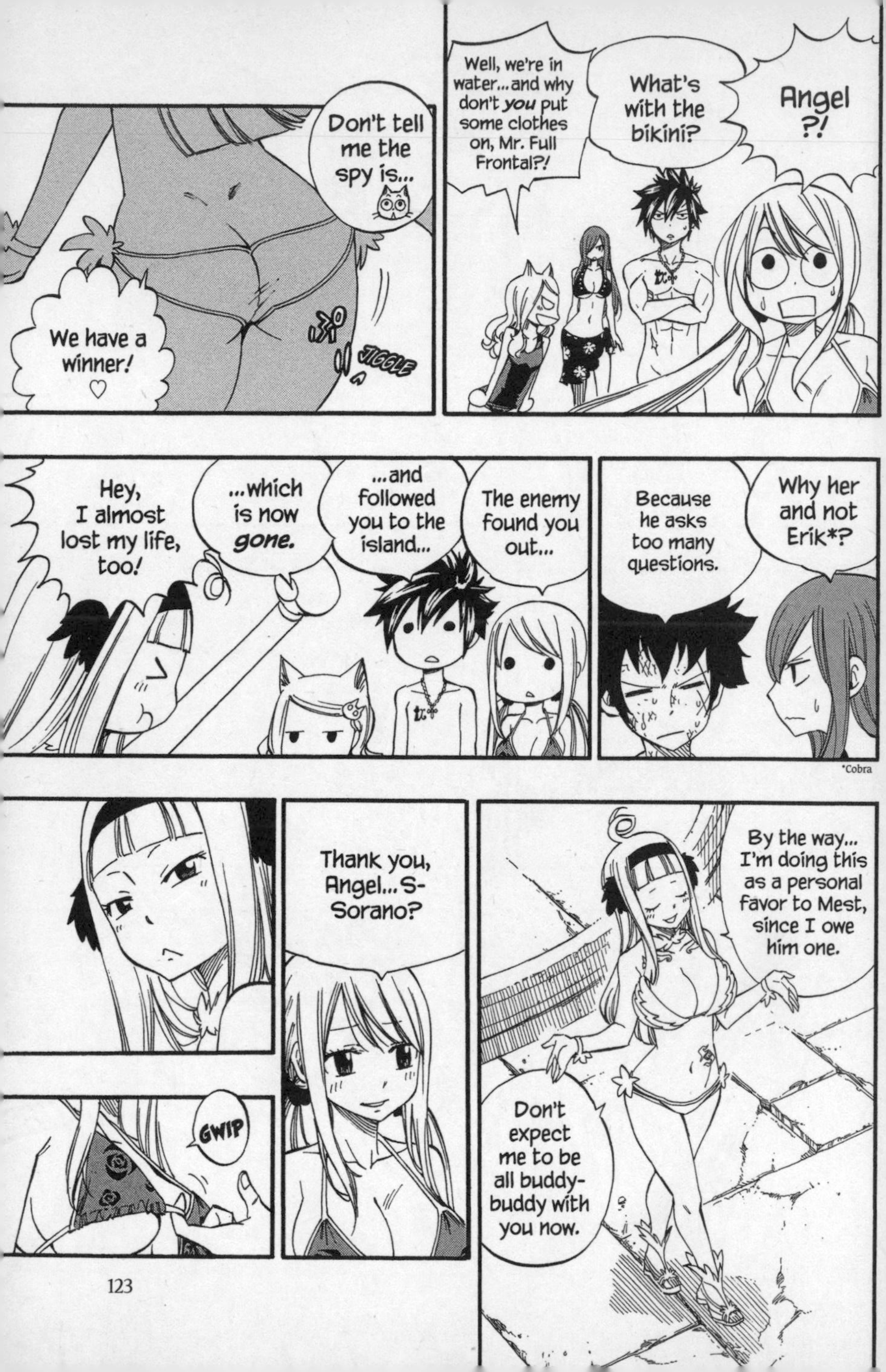
Angel ?!
What's with the bikini?
Well, we're in water...and why don't *you* put some clothes on, Mr. Full Frontal?!
Don't tell me the spy is...
JIGGLE
We have a winner! ♡
Why her and not Erik*?
Because he asks too many questions.
The enemy found you out...
...and followed you to the island...
...which is now *gone.*
Hey, I almost lost my life, too!
By the way... I'm doing this as a personal favor to Mest, since I owe him one.
Don't expect me to be all buddy-buddy with you now.
Thank you, Angel... S-Sorano?
GWIP

*Cobra

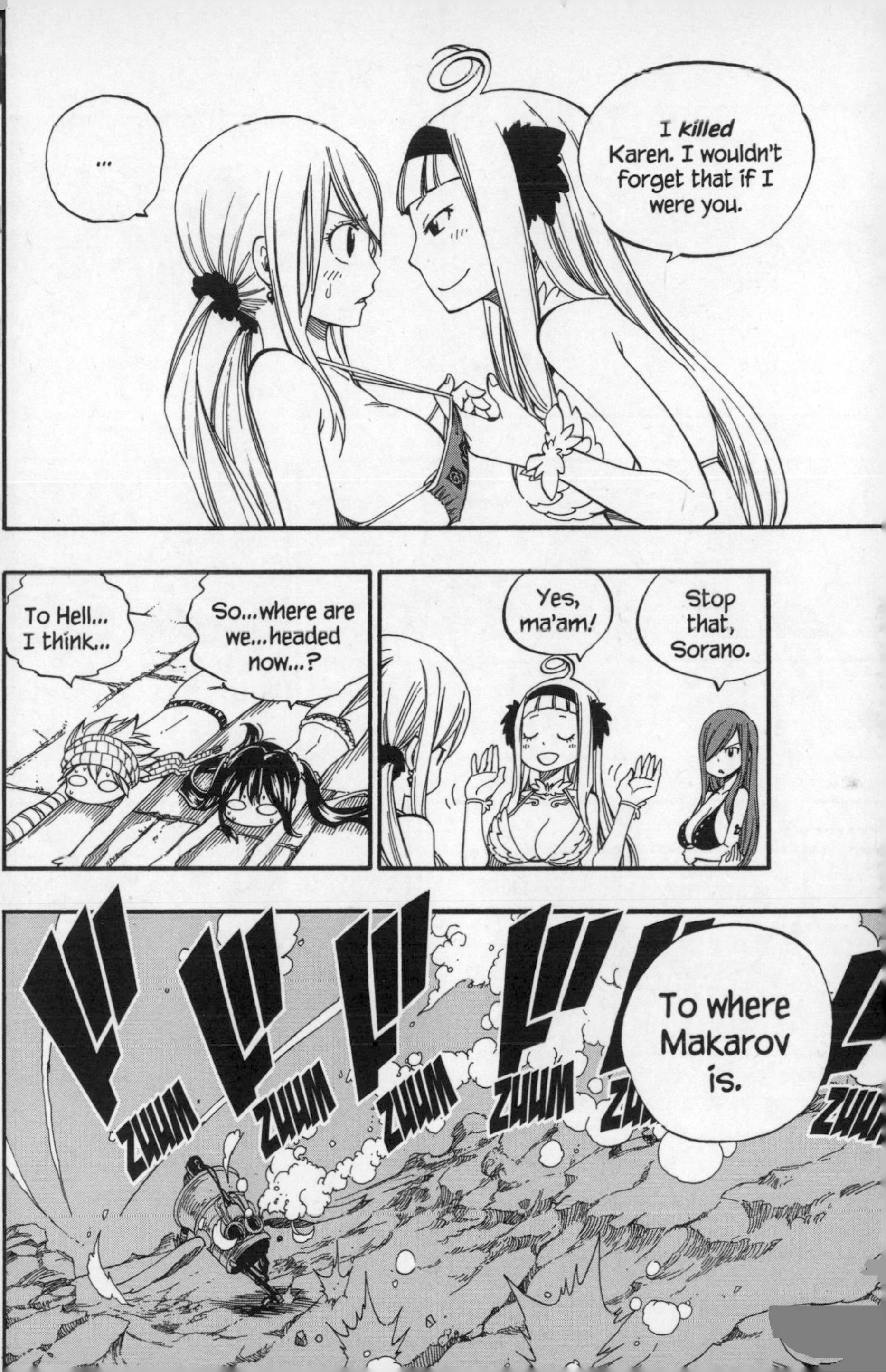
I *killed* Karen. I wouldn't forget that if I were you.
...
Stop that, Sorano.
Yes, ma'am!
So...where are we...headed now...?
To Hell... I think...
To where Makarov is.
ZUUM
ZUUM
ZUUM
ZUUM

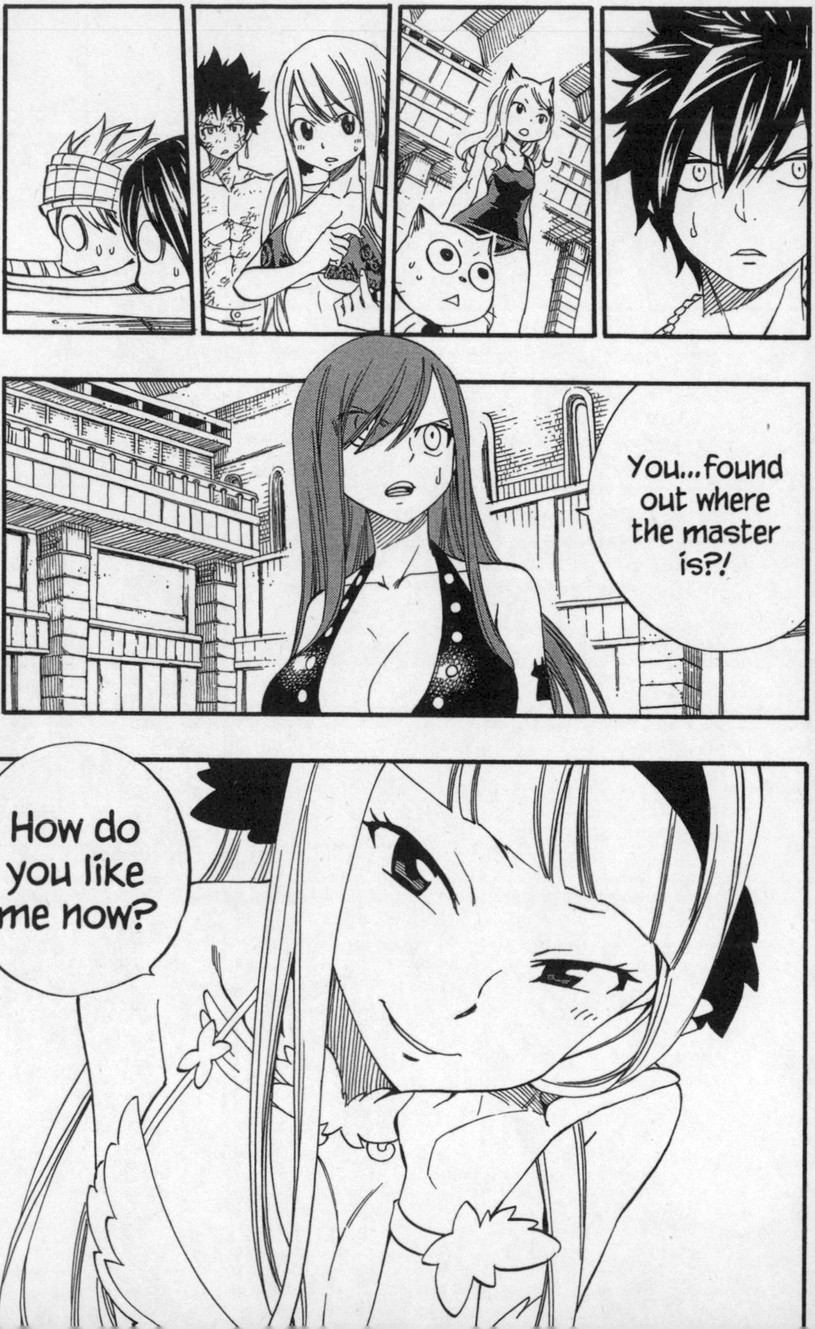
You...found out where the master is?!
How do you like me now?

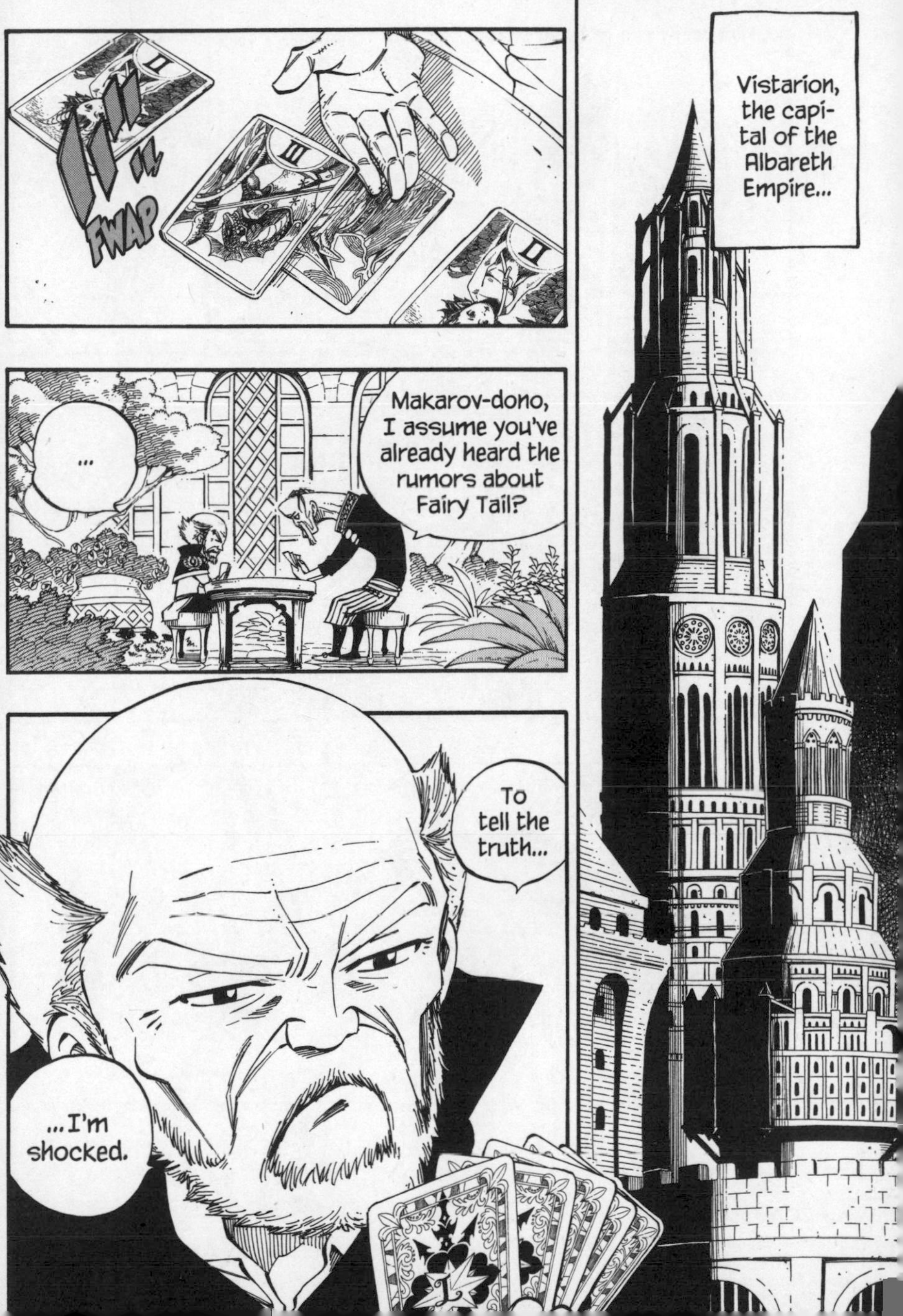

Vistarion, the capital of the Albareth Empire...
FWAP
Makarov-dono, I assume you've already heard the rumors about Fairy Tail?
...
To tell the truth...
...I'm shocked.

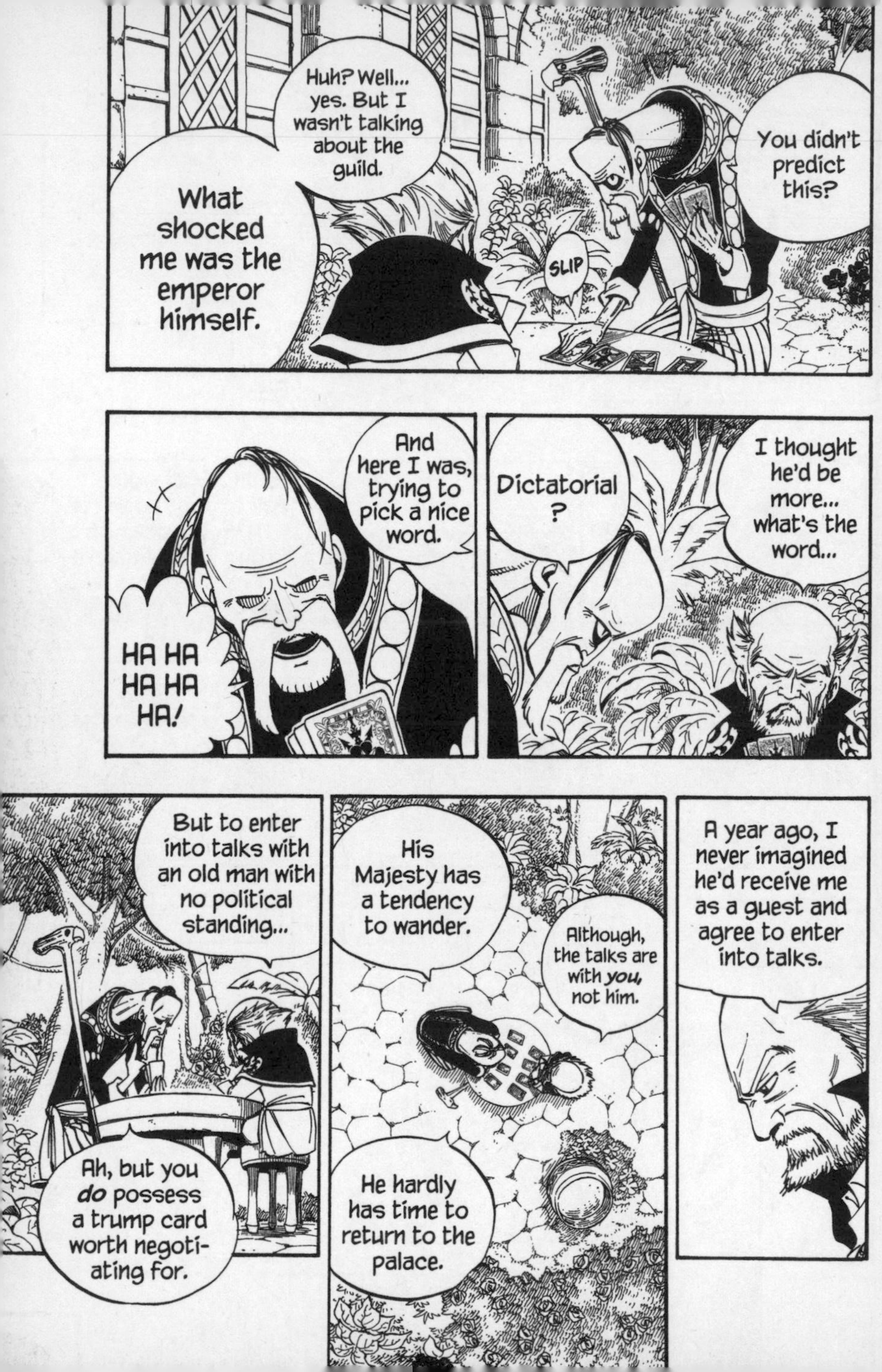

You didn't predict this?
Huh? Well... yes. But I wasn't talking about the guild.
What shocked me was the emperor himself.
SLIP
I thought he'd be more... what's the word...
Dictatorial?
And here I was, trying to pick a nice word.
HA HA HA HA HA!
A year ago, I never imagined he'd receive me as a guest and agree to enter into talks.
His Majesty has a tendency to wander.
Although, the talks are with *you*, not him.
He hardly has time to return to the palace.
But to enter into talks with an old man with no political standing...
Ah, but you *do* possess a trump card worth negoti-ating for.

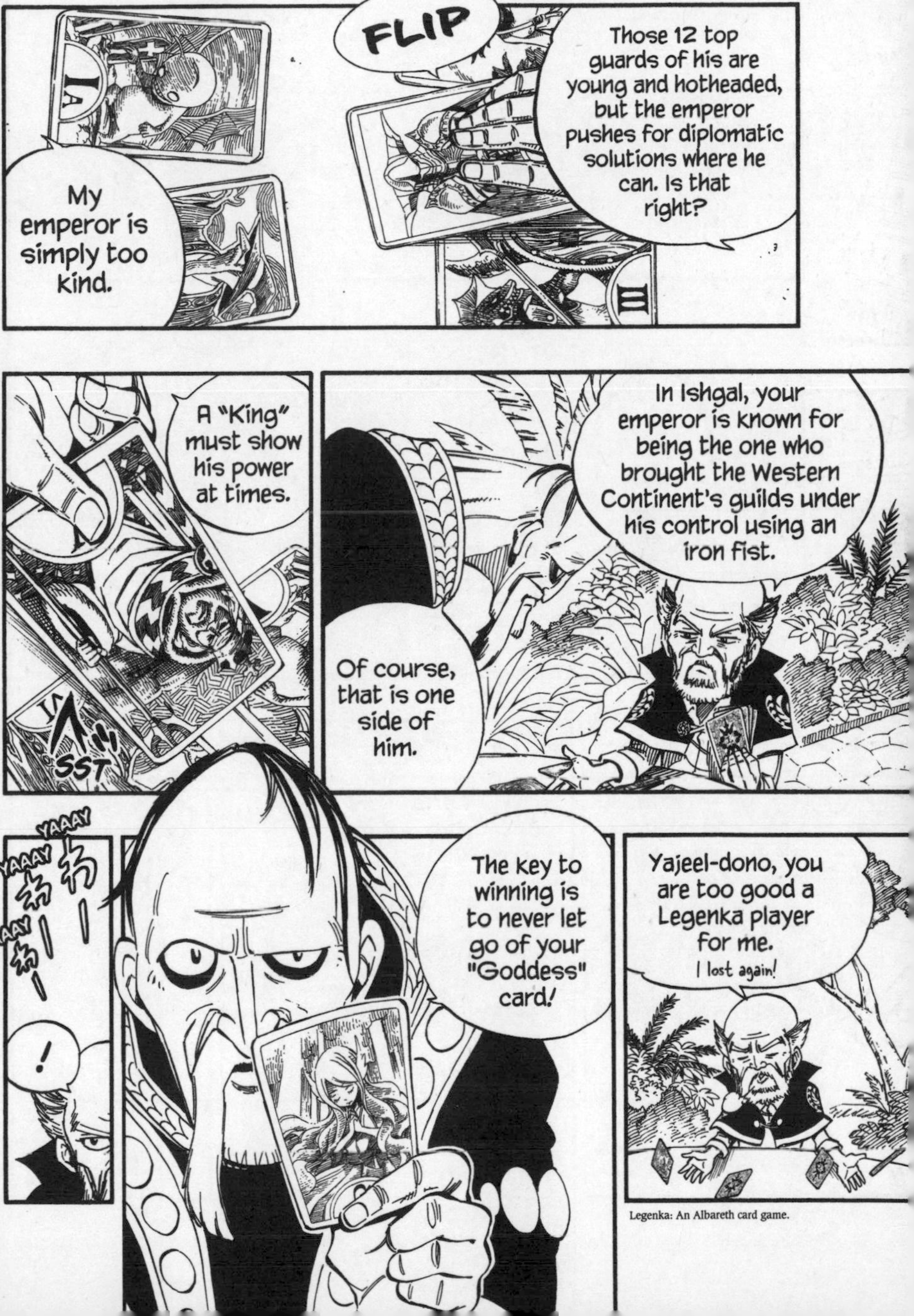

FLIP
Those 12 top guards of his are young and hotheaded, but the emperor pushes for diplomatic solutions where he can. Is that right?
My emperor is simply too kind.
In Ishgal, your emperor is known for being the one who brought the Western Continent's guilds under his control using an iron fist.
Of course, that is one side of him.
A "King" must show his power at times.
SST
Yajeel-dono, you are too good a Legenka player for me.
I lost again!
The key to winning is to never let go of your "Goddess" card!
YAAAY
YAAAY
AAAY
!

Legenka: An Albareth card game.

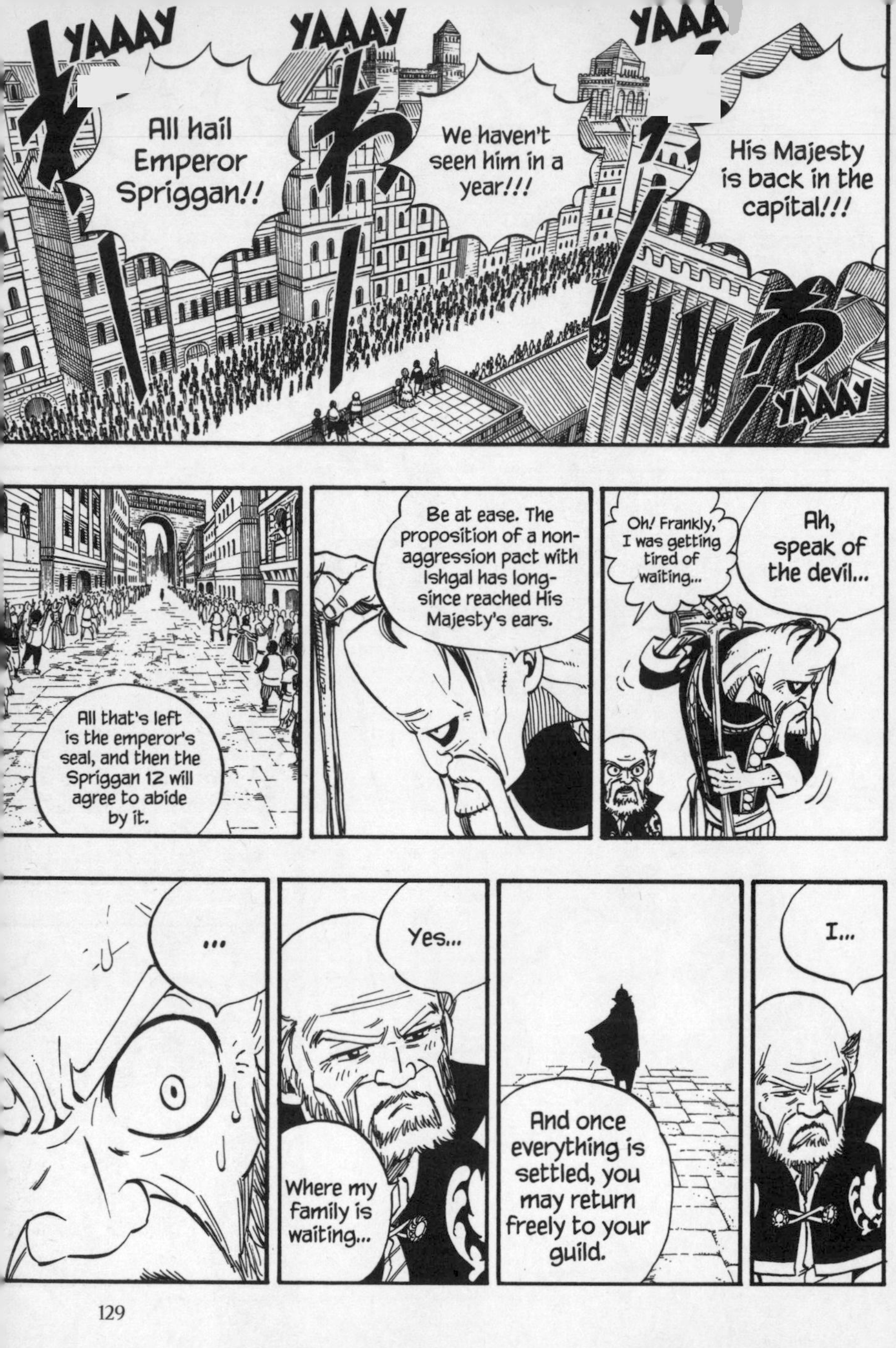
YAAA
His Majesty is back in the capital!!!
YAAAY
We haven't seen him in a year!!!
YAAAY
All hail Emperor Spriggan!!
YAAAY
Ah, speak of the devil...
Oh! Frankly, I was getting tired of waiting...
Be at ease. The proposition of a non-aggression pact with Ishgal has long-since reached His Majesty's ears.
All that's left is the emperor's seal, and then the Spriggan 12 will agree to abide by it.
I...
And once everything is settled, you may return freely to your guild.
Yes...
Where my family is waiting...
...

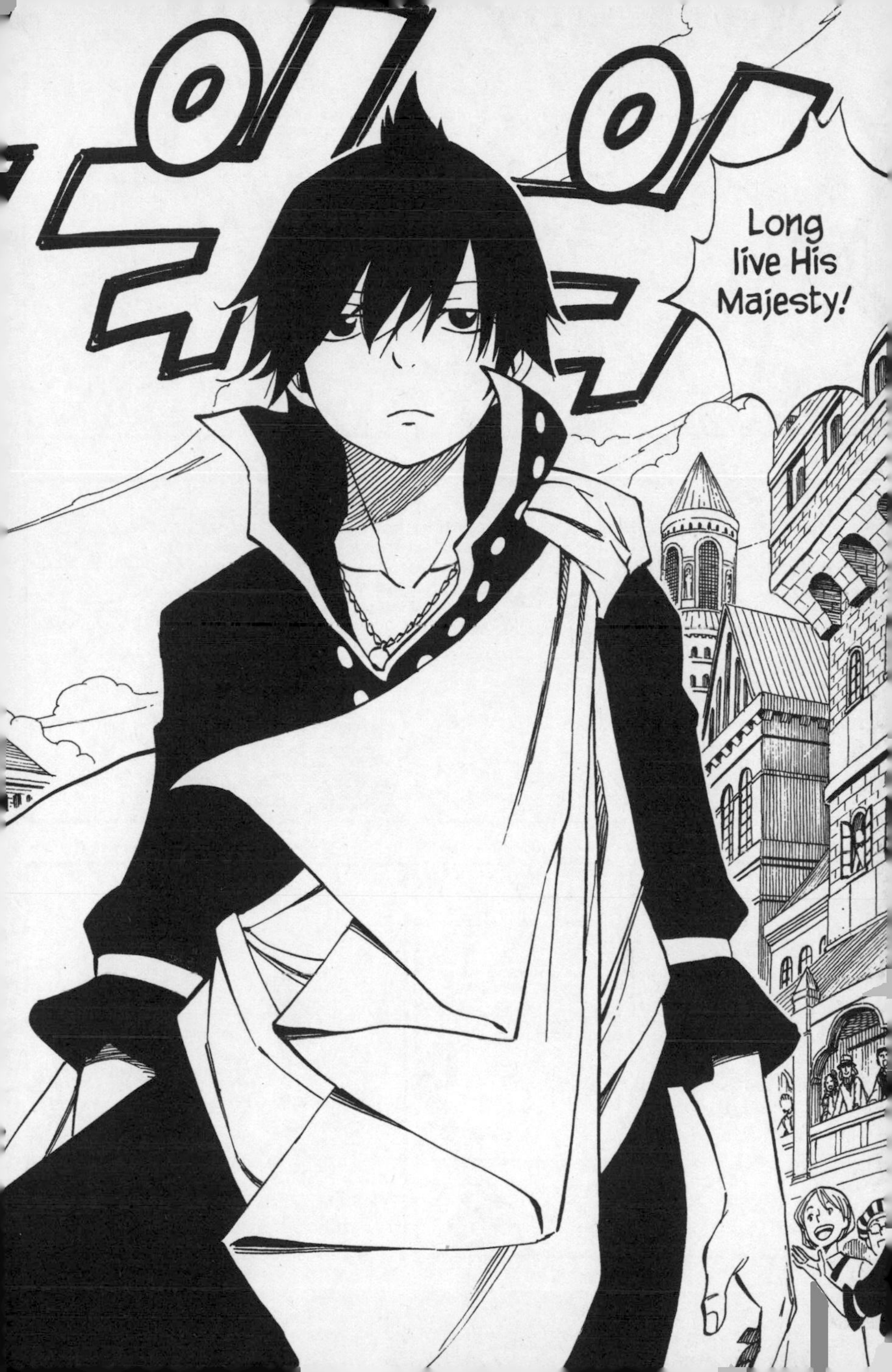
Long live His Majesty!

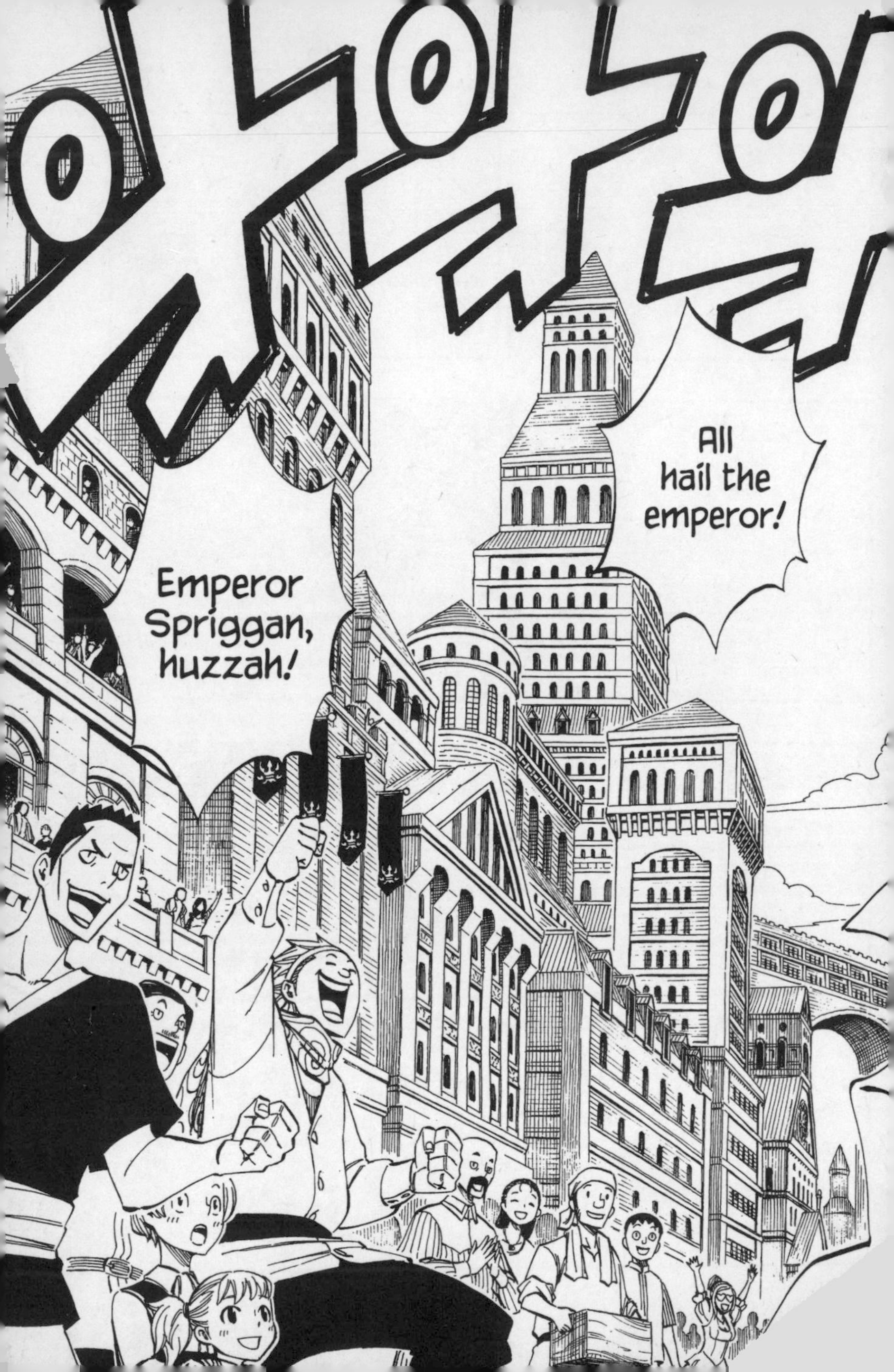
All hail the emperor!
Emperor Spriggan, huzzah!

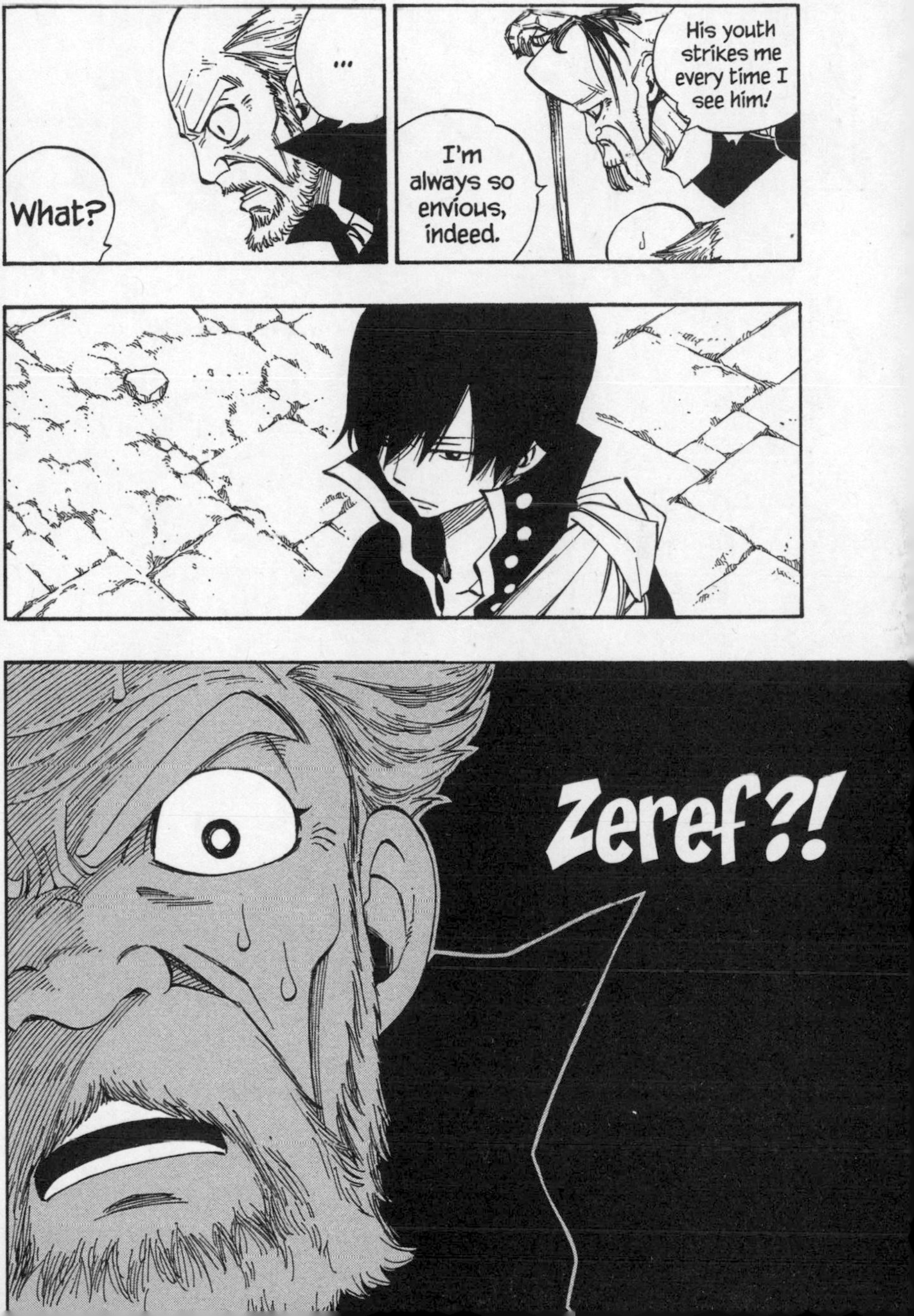
His youth strikes me every time I see him!
I'm always so envious, indeed.
...
What?
Zeref?!

Chapter 445: The Grotesque Fairy

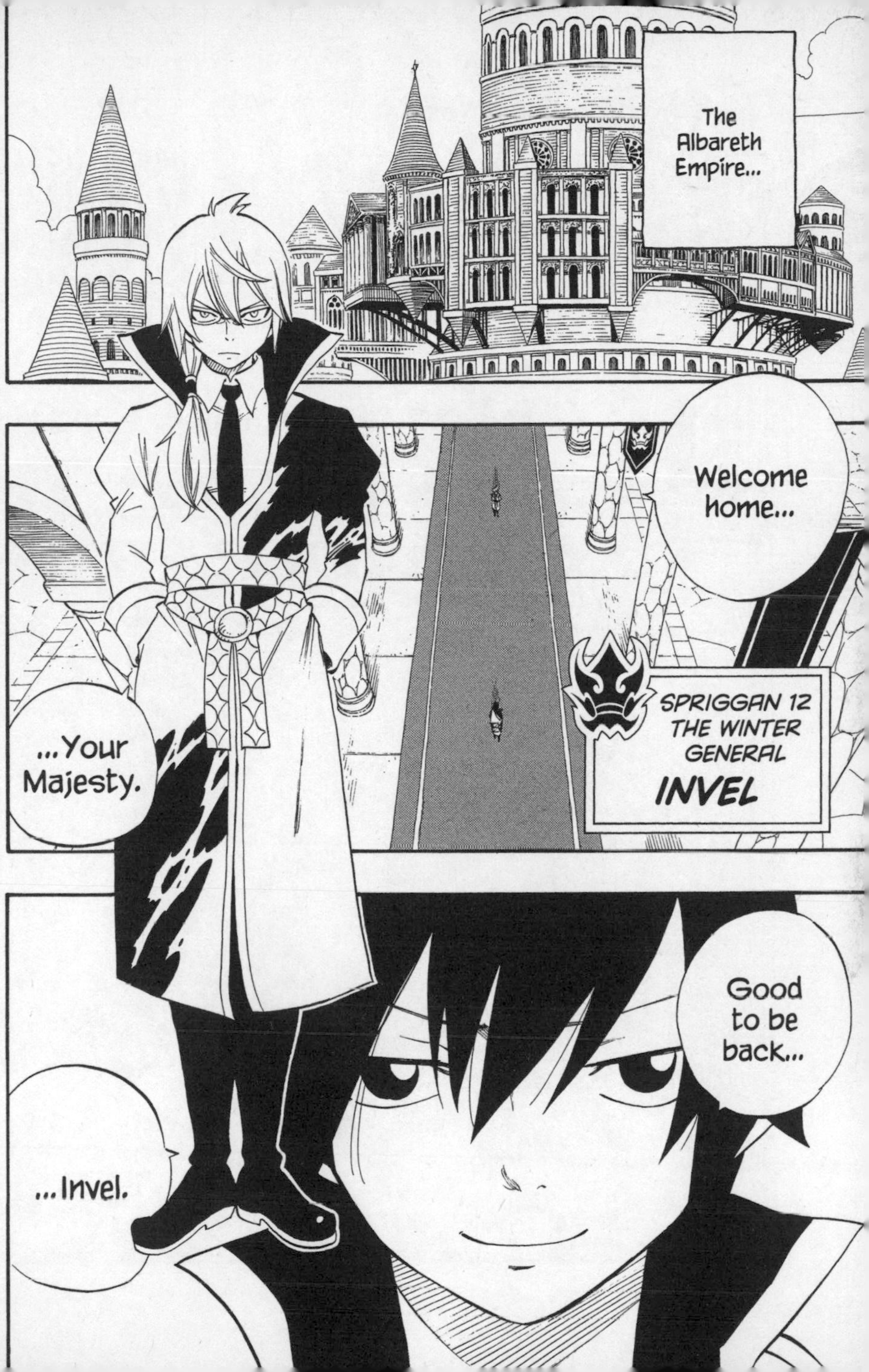
The Albareth Empire...
Welcome home...
SPRIGGAN 12 THE WINTER GENERAL
INVEL
...Your Majesty.
Good to be back...
...Invel.

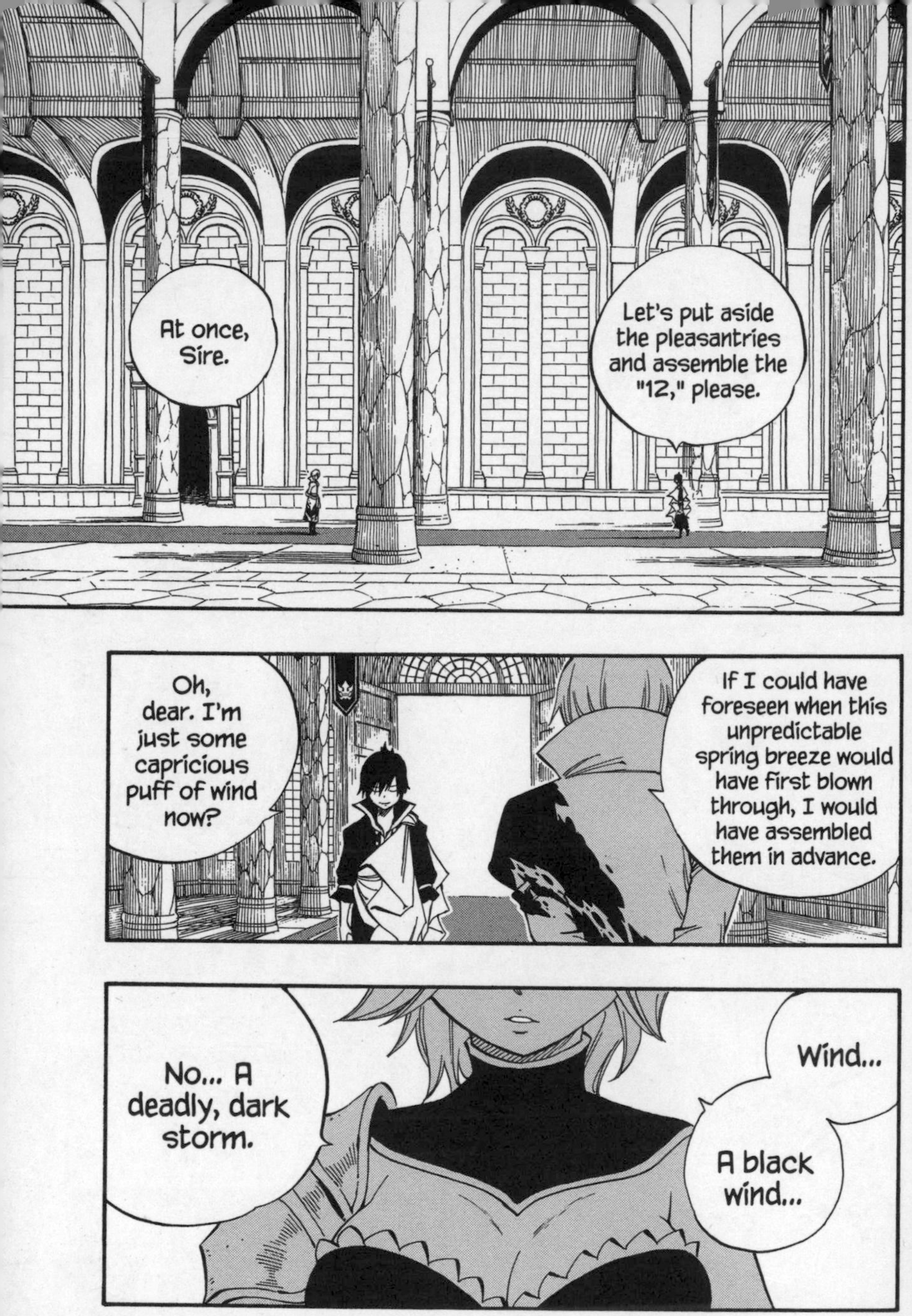
Let's put aside the pleasantries and assemble the "12," please.
At once, Sire.
If I could have foreseen when this unpredictable spring breeze would have first blown through, I would have assembled them in advance.
Oh, dear. I'm just some capricious puff of wind now?
Wind...
A black wind...
No... A deadly, dark storm.

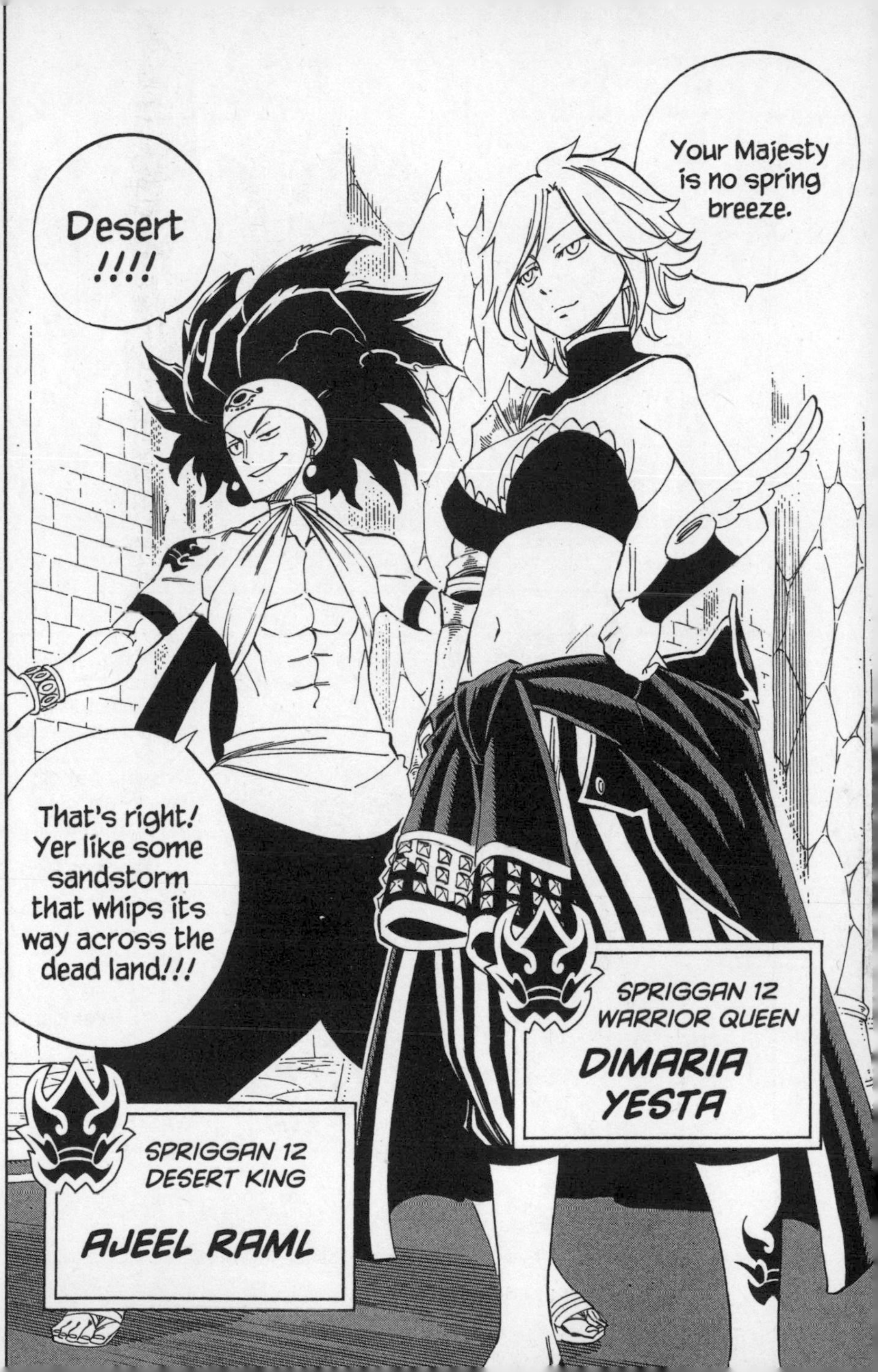
Your Majesty is no spring breeze.
Desert !!!!
That's right! Yer like some sandstorm that whips its way across the dead land!!!
SPRIGGAN 12 WARRIOR QUEEN
DIMARIA YESTA
SPRIGGAN 12 DESERT KING
AJEEL RAML

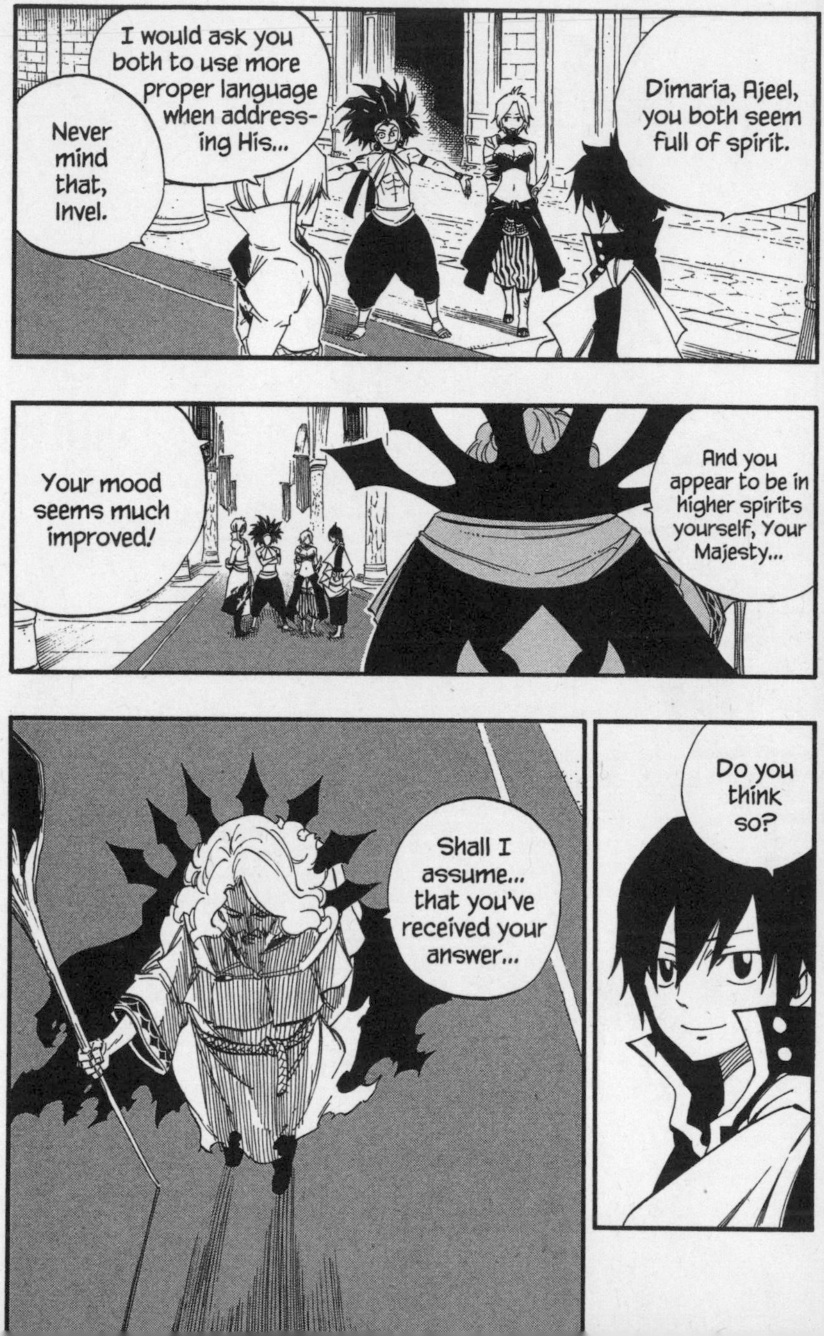
Dimaria, Ajeel, you both seem full of spirit.
I would ask you both to use more proper language when address-ing His...
Never mind that, Invel.
And you appear to be in higher spirits yourself, Your Majesty...
Your mood seems much improved!
Do you think so?
Shall I assume... that you've received your answer...

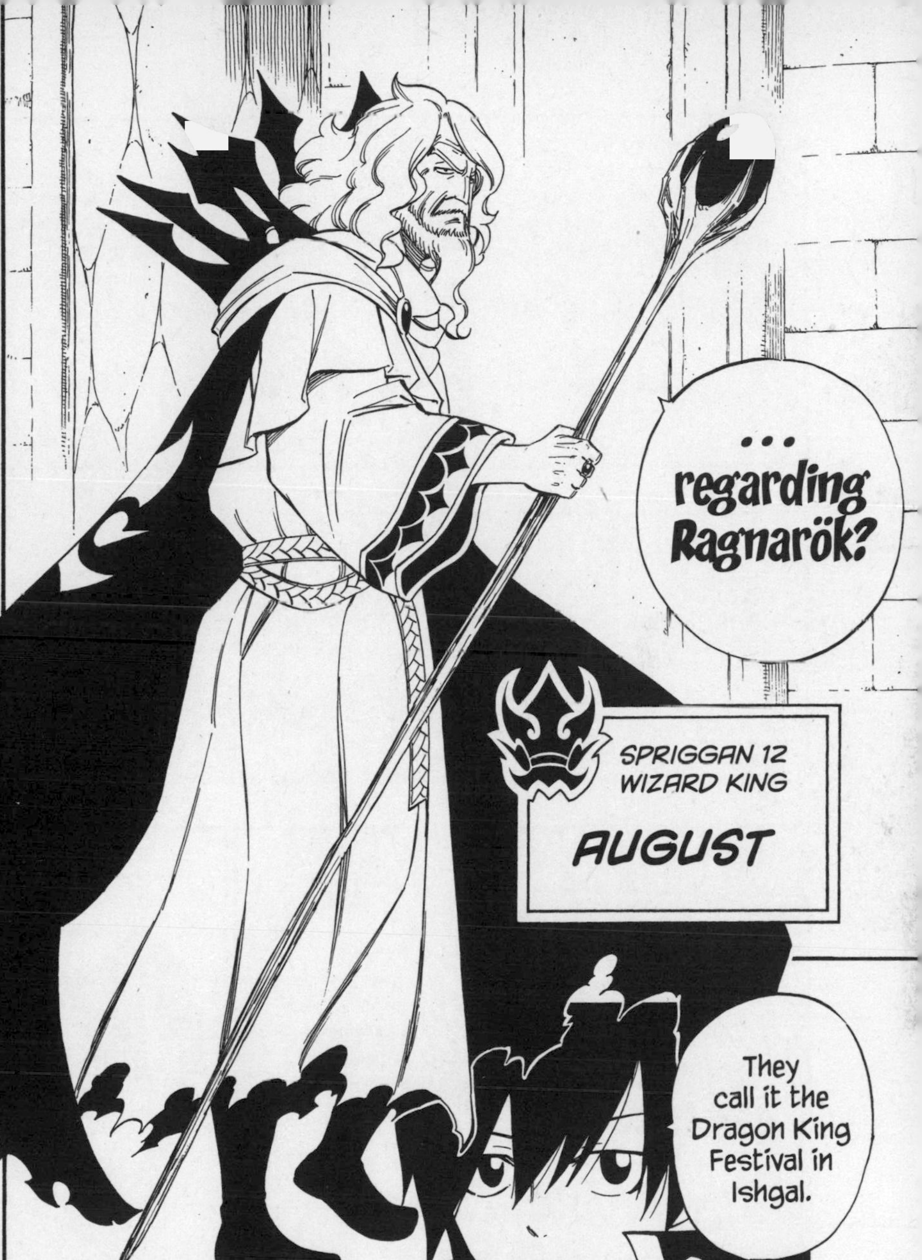
...regarding Ragnarök?
SPRIGGAN 12 WIZARD KING
AUGUST
They call it the Dragon King Festival in Ishgal.

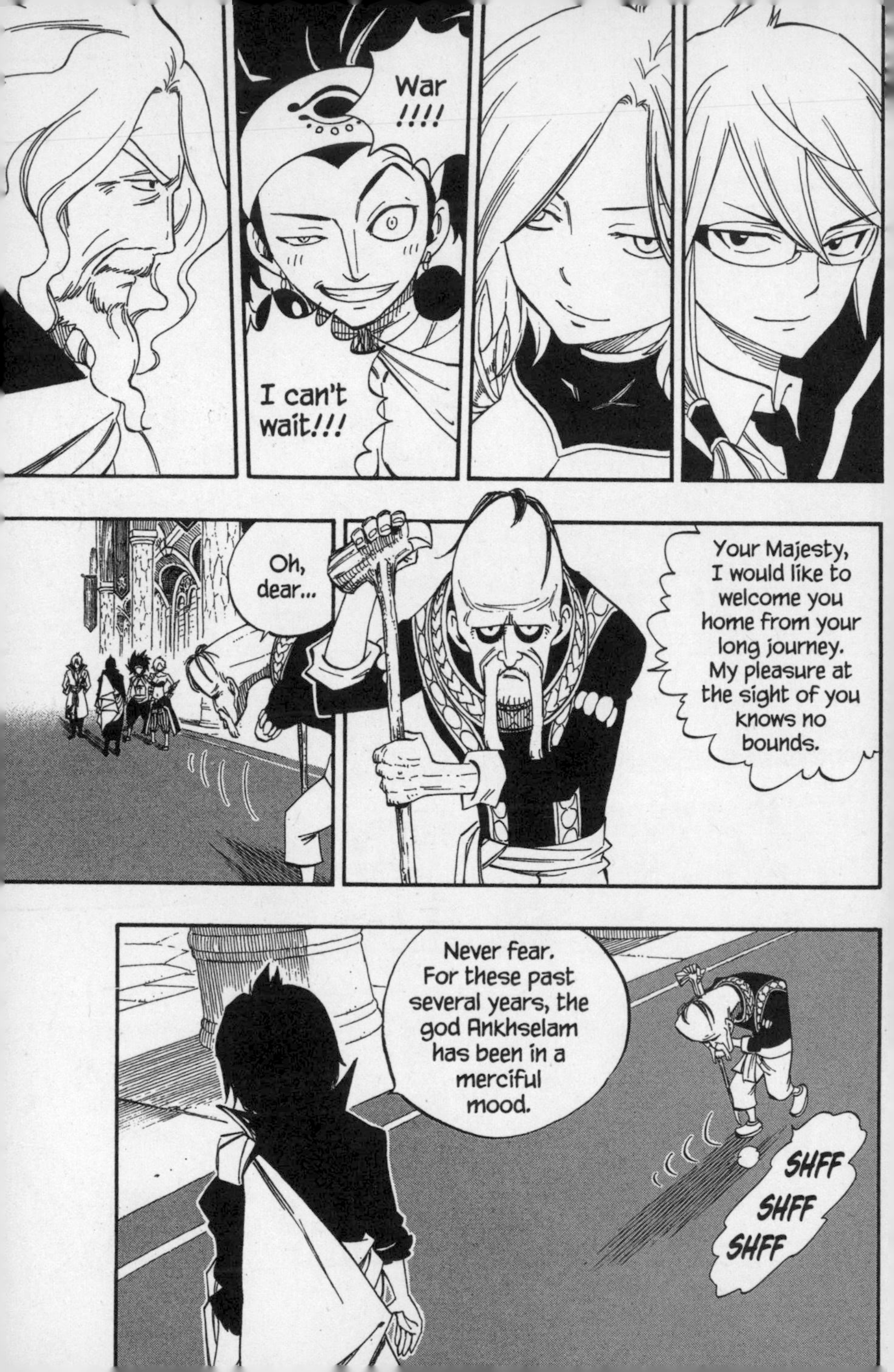
War !!!!
I can't wait!!!
Your Majesty, I would like to welcome you home from your long journey. My pleasure at the sight of you knows no bounds.
Oh, dear...
Never fear. For these past several years, the god Ankhselam has been in a merciful mood.
SHFF SHFF SHFF

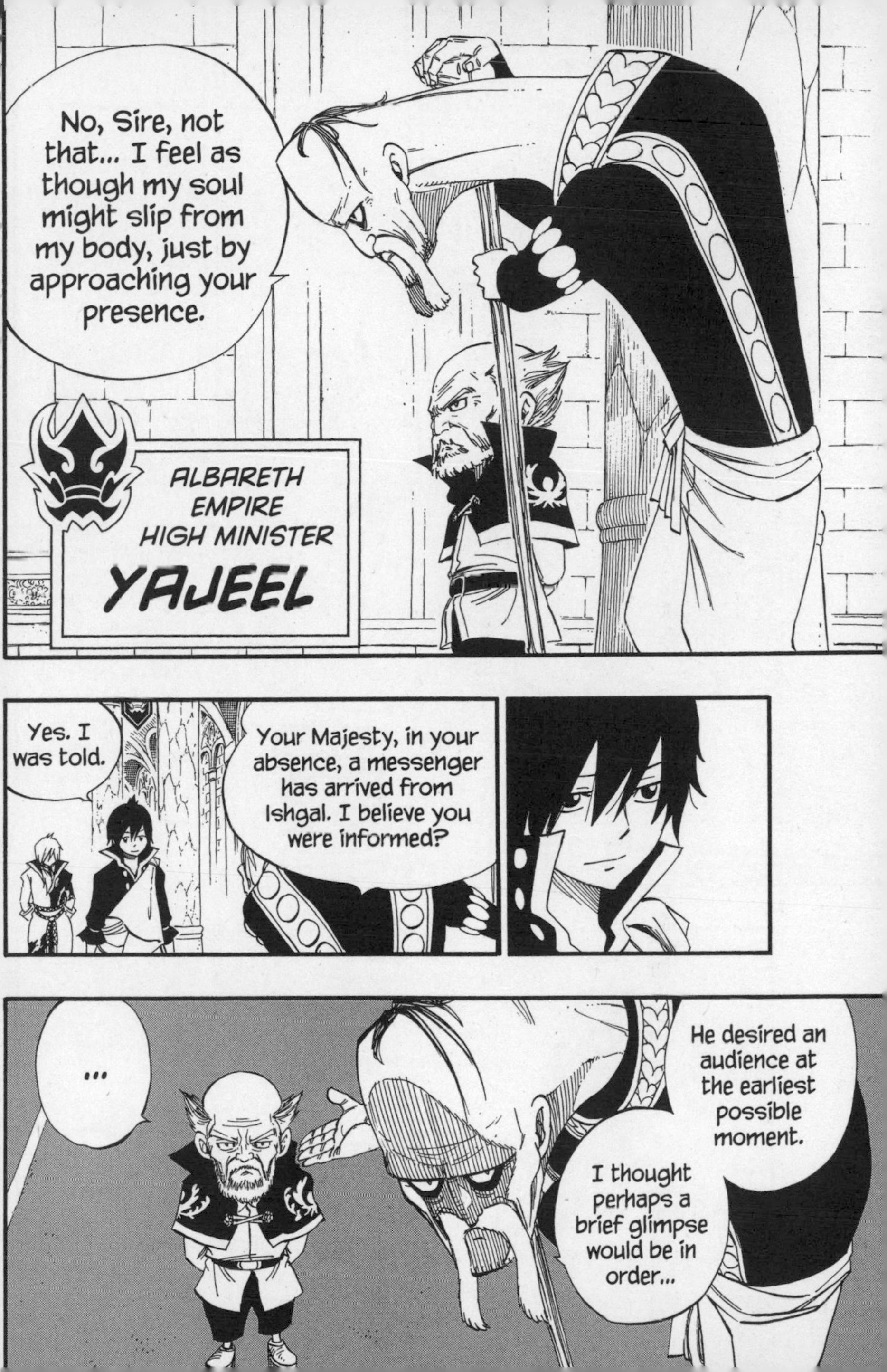
No, Sire, not that... I feel as though my soul might slip from my body, just by approaching your presence.
ALBARETH EMPIRE HIGH MINISTER
YAJEEL
Your Majesty, in your absence, a messenger has arrived from Ishgal. I believe you were informed?
Yes. I was told.
He desired an audience at the earliest possible moment.
I thought perhaps a brief glimpse would be in order...
...

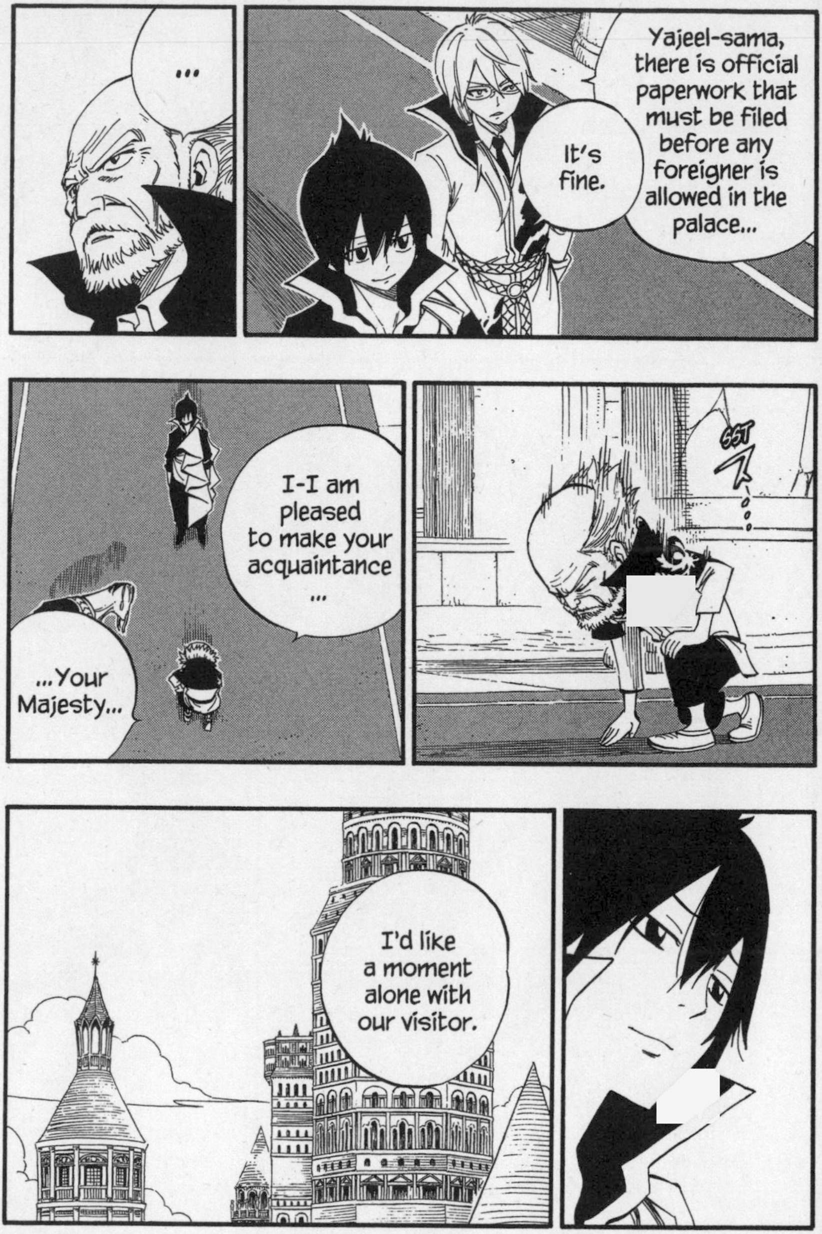
Yajeel-sama, there is official paperwork that must be filed before any foreigner is allowed in the palace...
It's fine.
...
SST
I-I am pleased to make your acquaintance ...
...Your Majesty...
I'd like a moment alone with our visitor.

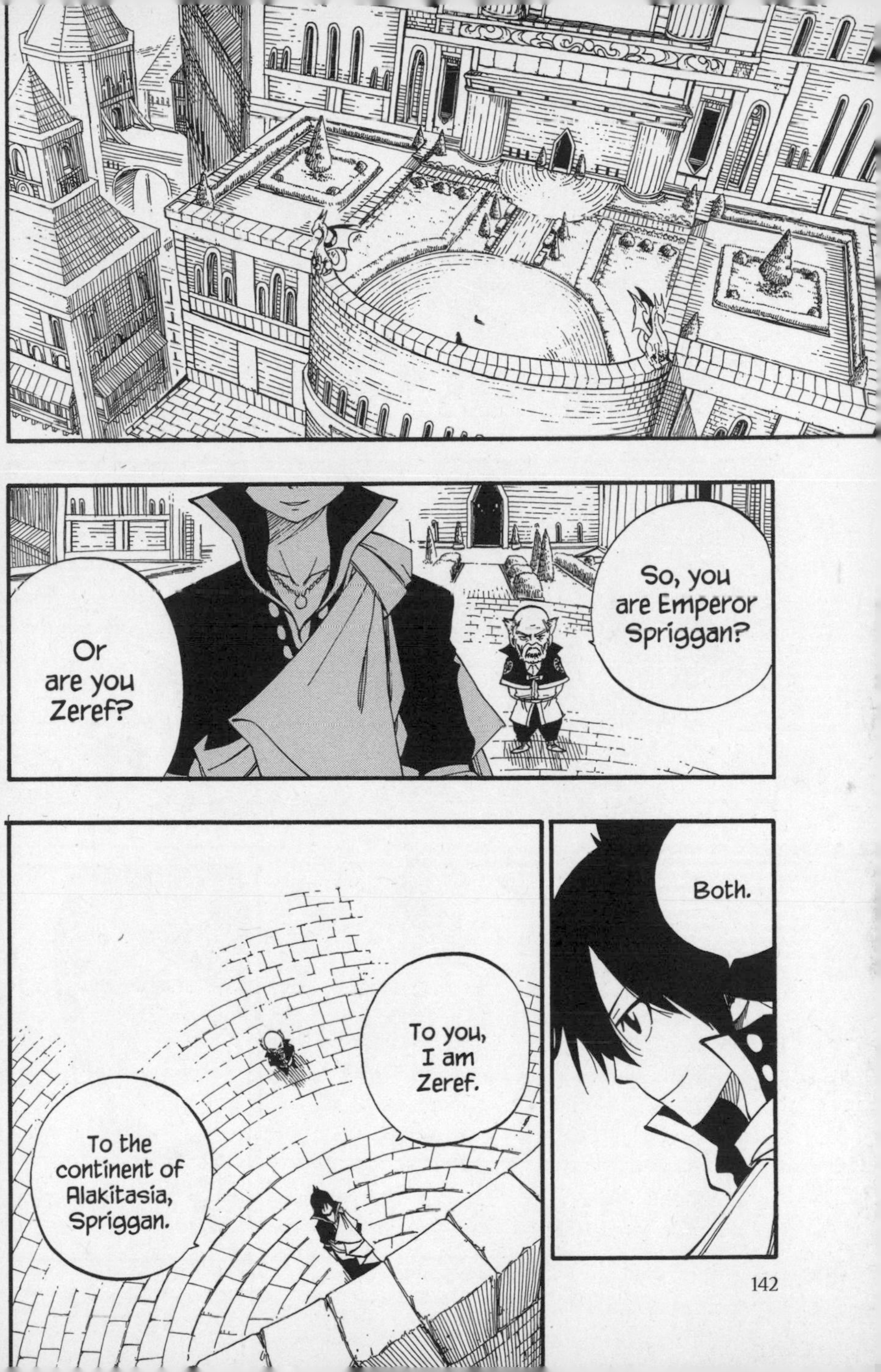
So, you are Emperor Spriggan?
Or are you Zeref?
Both.
To you, I am Zeref.
To the continent of Alakitasia, Spriggan.

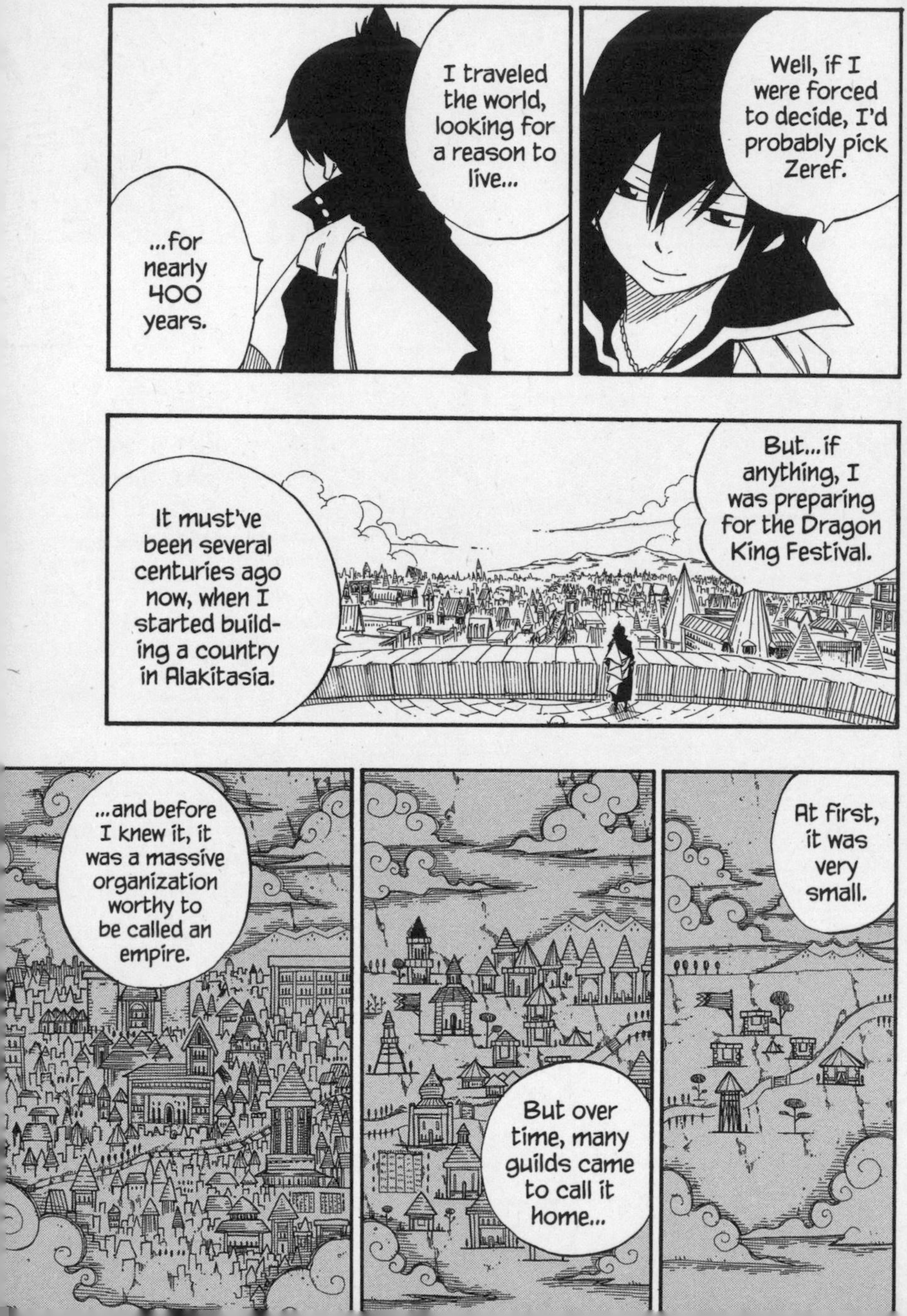
Well, if I were forced to decide, I'd probably pick Zeref.
I traveled the world, looking for a reason to live...
...for nearly 400 years.
But... if anything, I was preparing for the Dragon King Festival.
It must've been several centuries ago now, when I started building a country in Alakitasia.
At first, it was very small.
But over time, many guilds came to call it home...
...and before I knew it, it was a massive organization worthy to be called an empire.

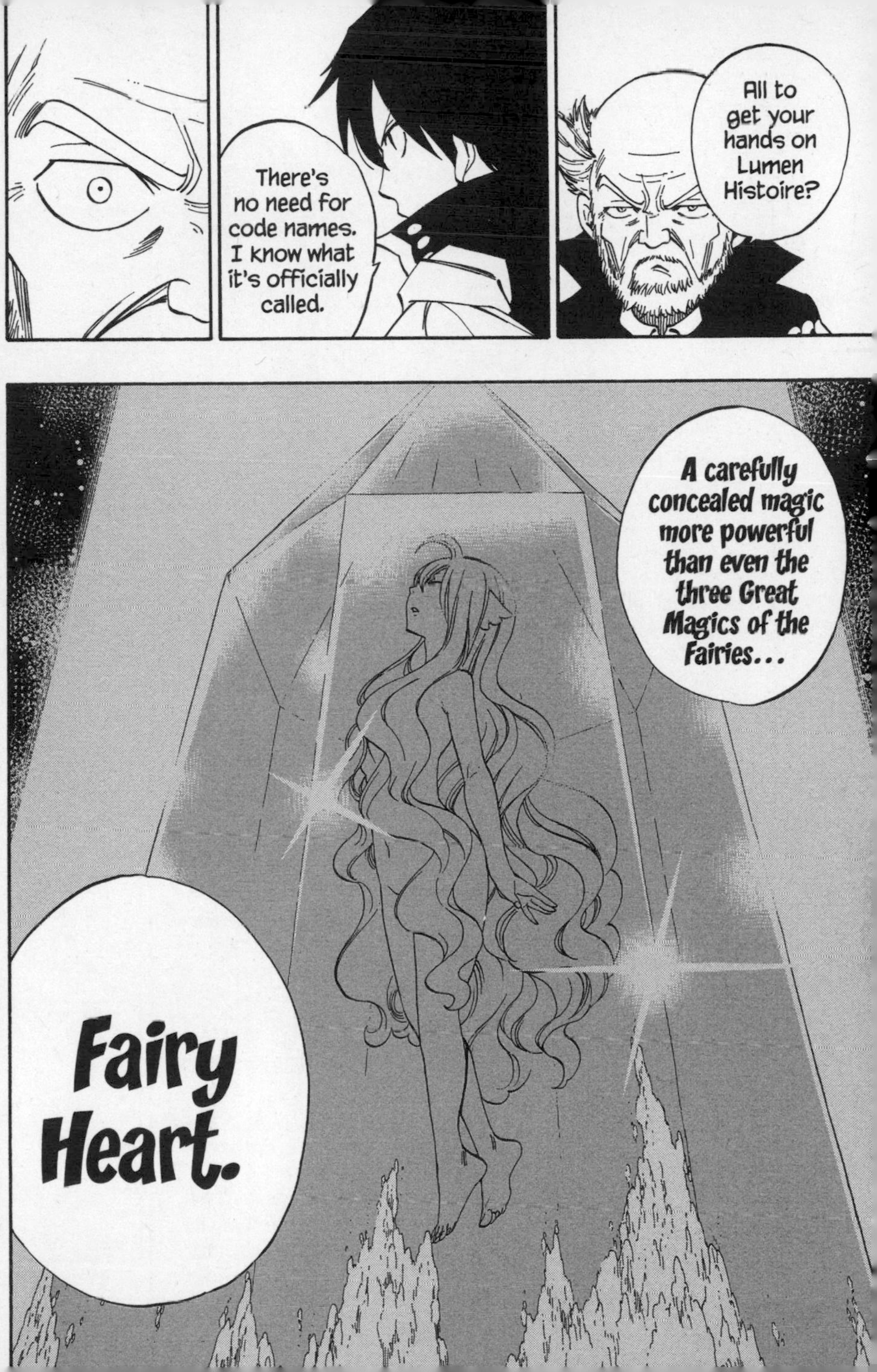
All to get your hands on Lumen Histoire?
There's no need for code names. I know what it's officially called.
A carefully concealed magic more powerful than even the three Great Magics of the Fairies...
Fairy Heart.

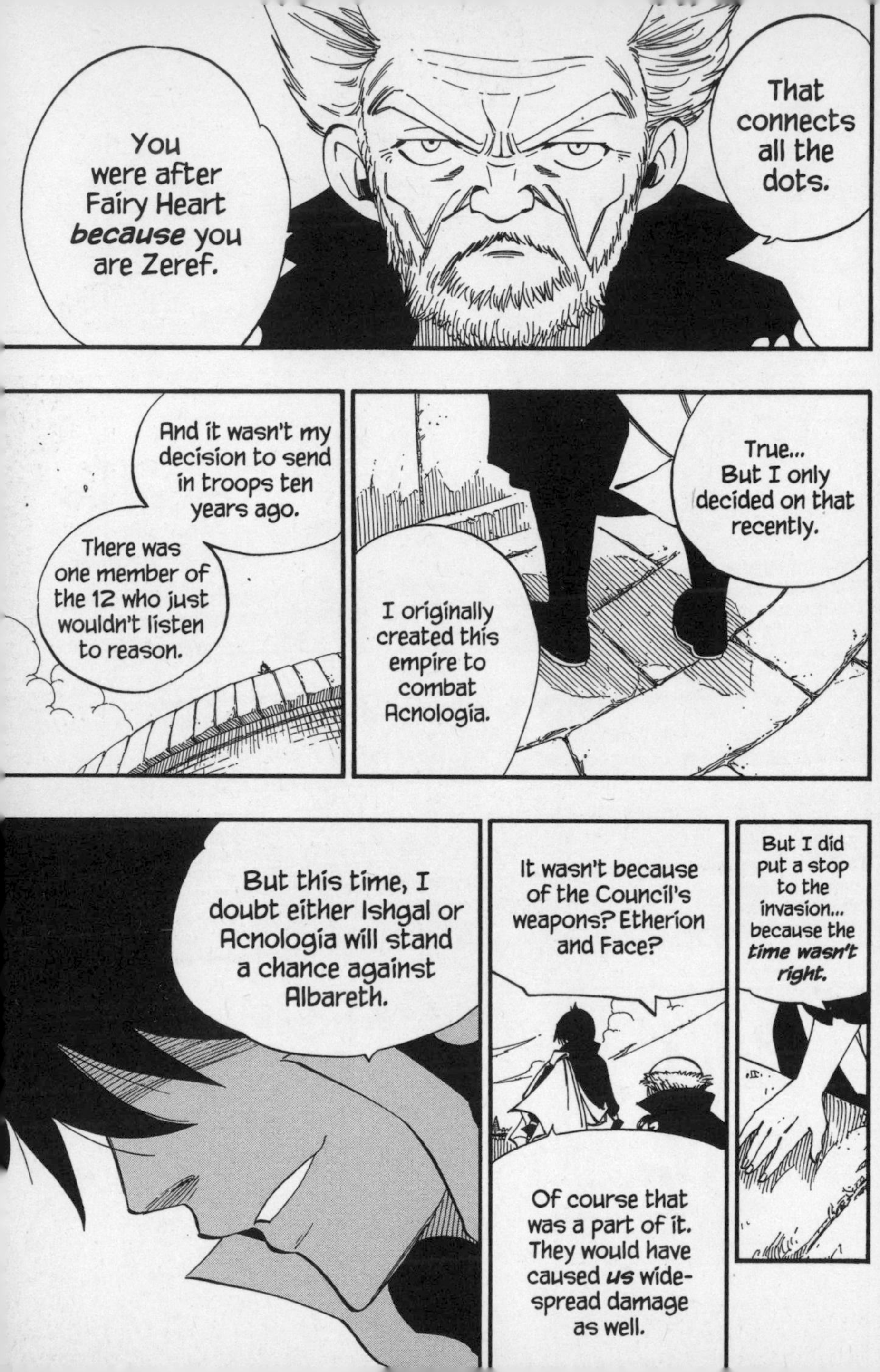
That connects all the dots.
You were after Fairy Heart *because* you are Zeref.
True... But I only decided on that recently.
I originally created this empire to combat Acnologia.
And it wasn't my decision to send in troops ten years ago.
There was one member of the 12 who just wouldn't listen to reason.
But I did put a stop to the invasion... because the *time wasn't right.*
It wasn't because of the Council's weapons? Etherion and Face?
Of course that was a part of it. They would have caused *us* wide-spread damage as well.
But this time, I doubt either Ishgal or Acnologia will stand a chance against Albareth.

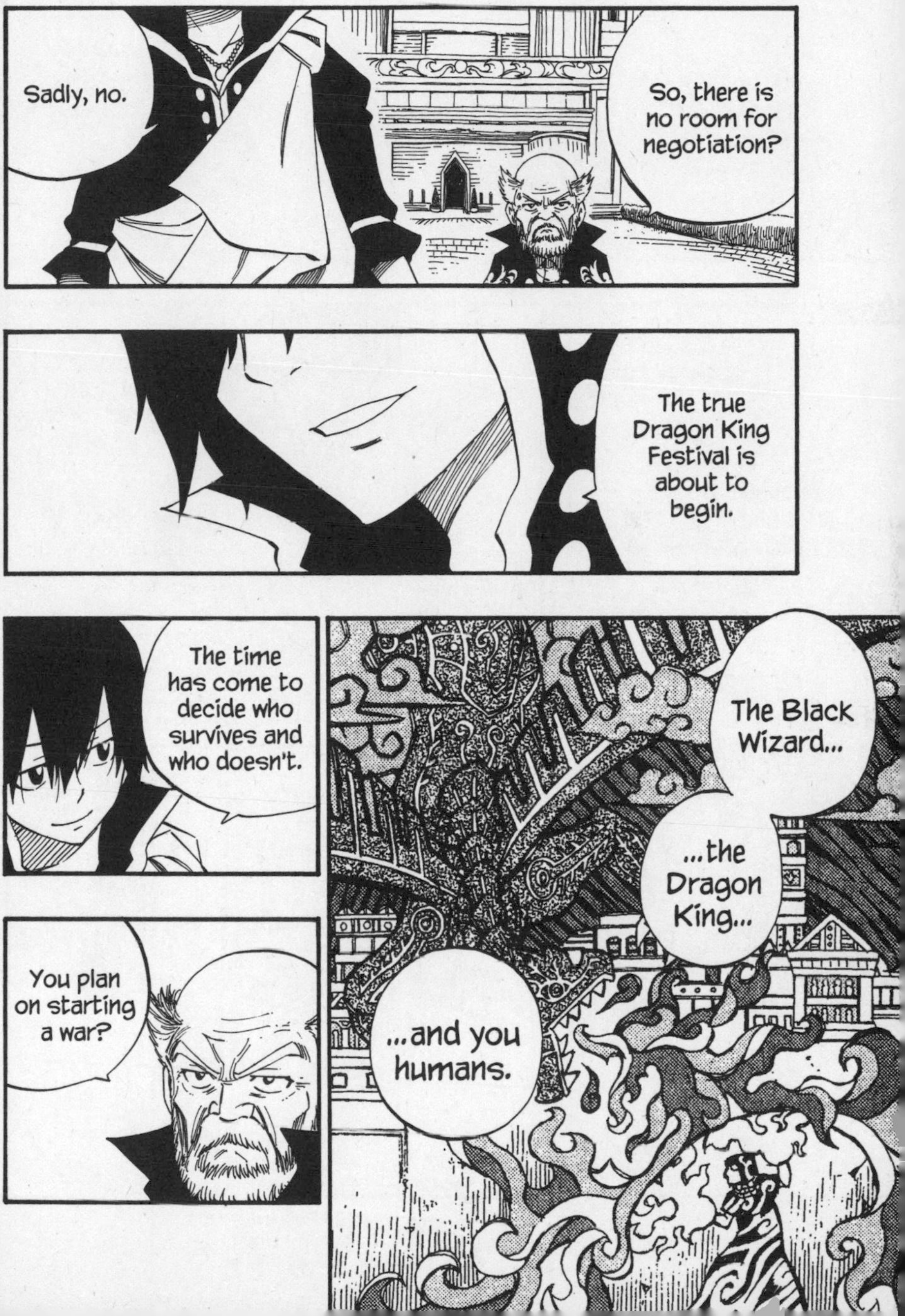
So, there is no room for negotiation?
Sadly, no.
The true Dragon King Festival is about to begin.
The Black Wizard...
...the Dragon King...
...and you humans.
The time has come to decide who survives and who doesn't.
You plan on starting a war?

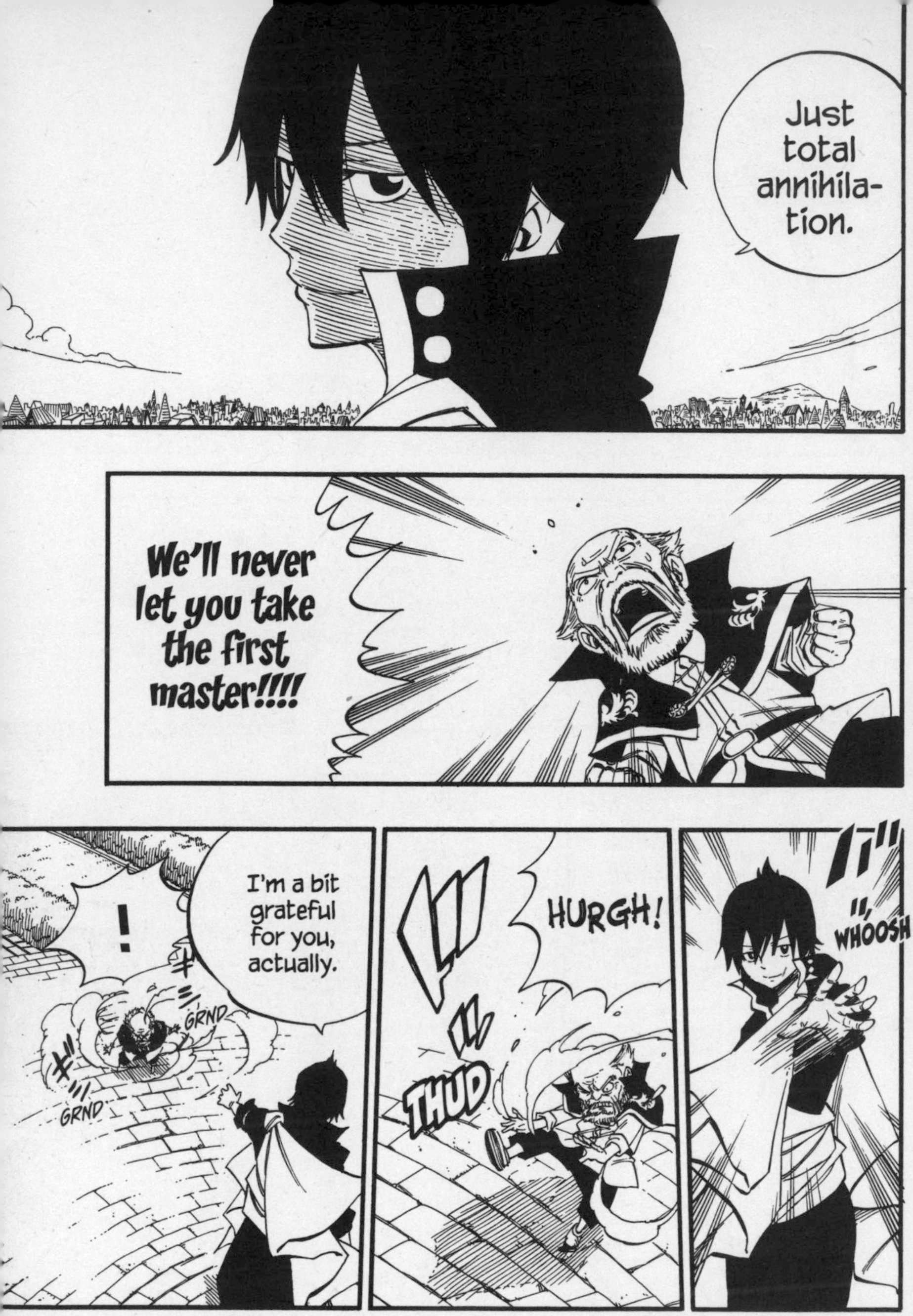

Just total annihilation.
We'll never let you take the first master!!!!
WHOOSH
HURGH!
THUD
I'm a bit grateful for you, actually.
!
GRND
GRND

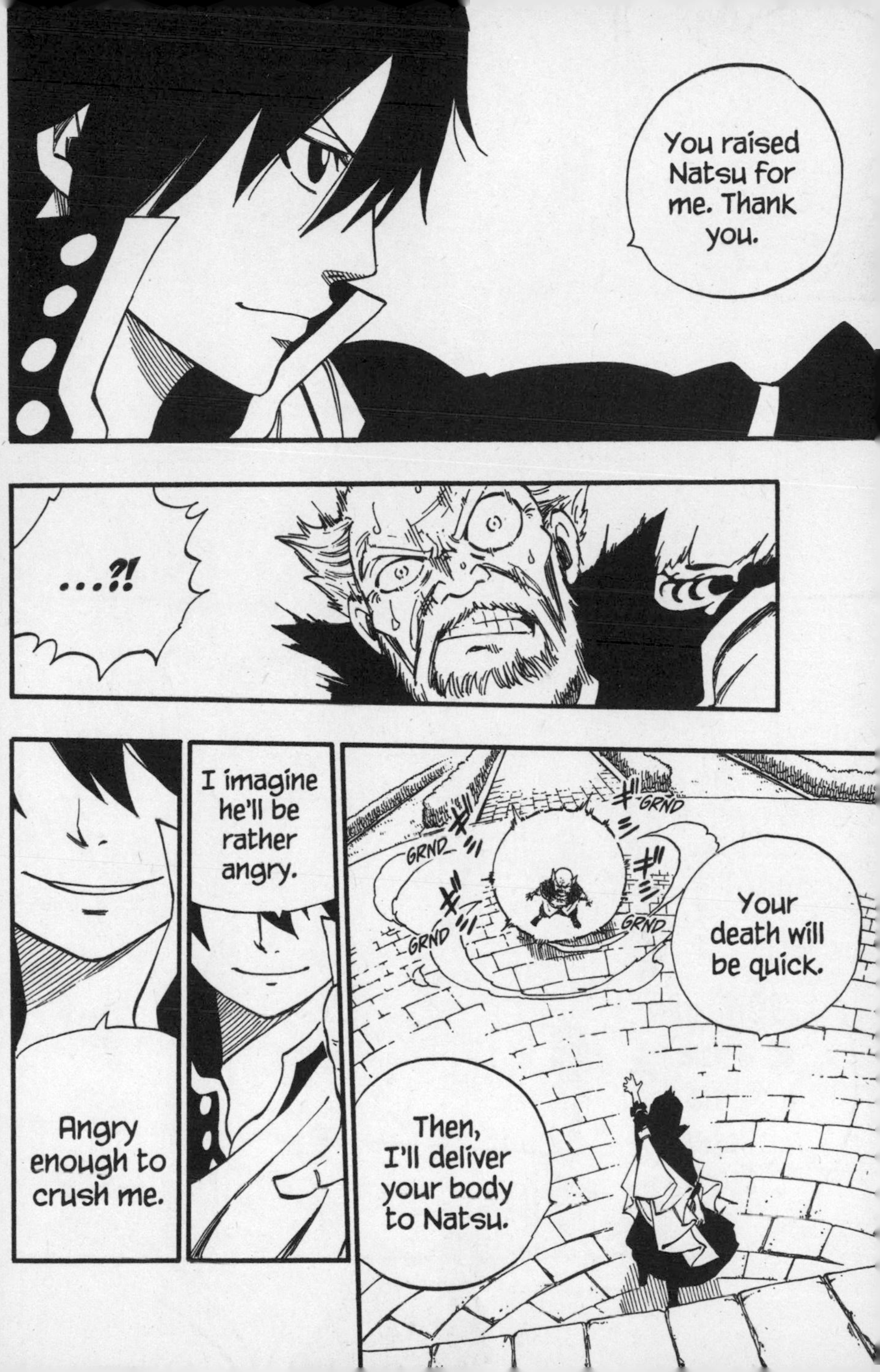
You raised Natsu for me. Thank you.
...?!
GRND
GRND
Your death will be quick.
GRND
GRND
Then, I'll deliver your body to Natsu.
I imagine he'll be rather angry.
Angry enough to crush me.

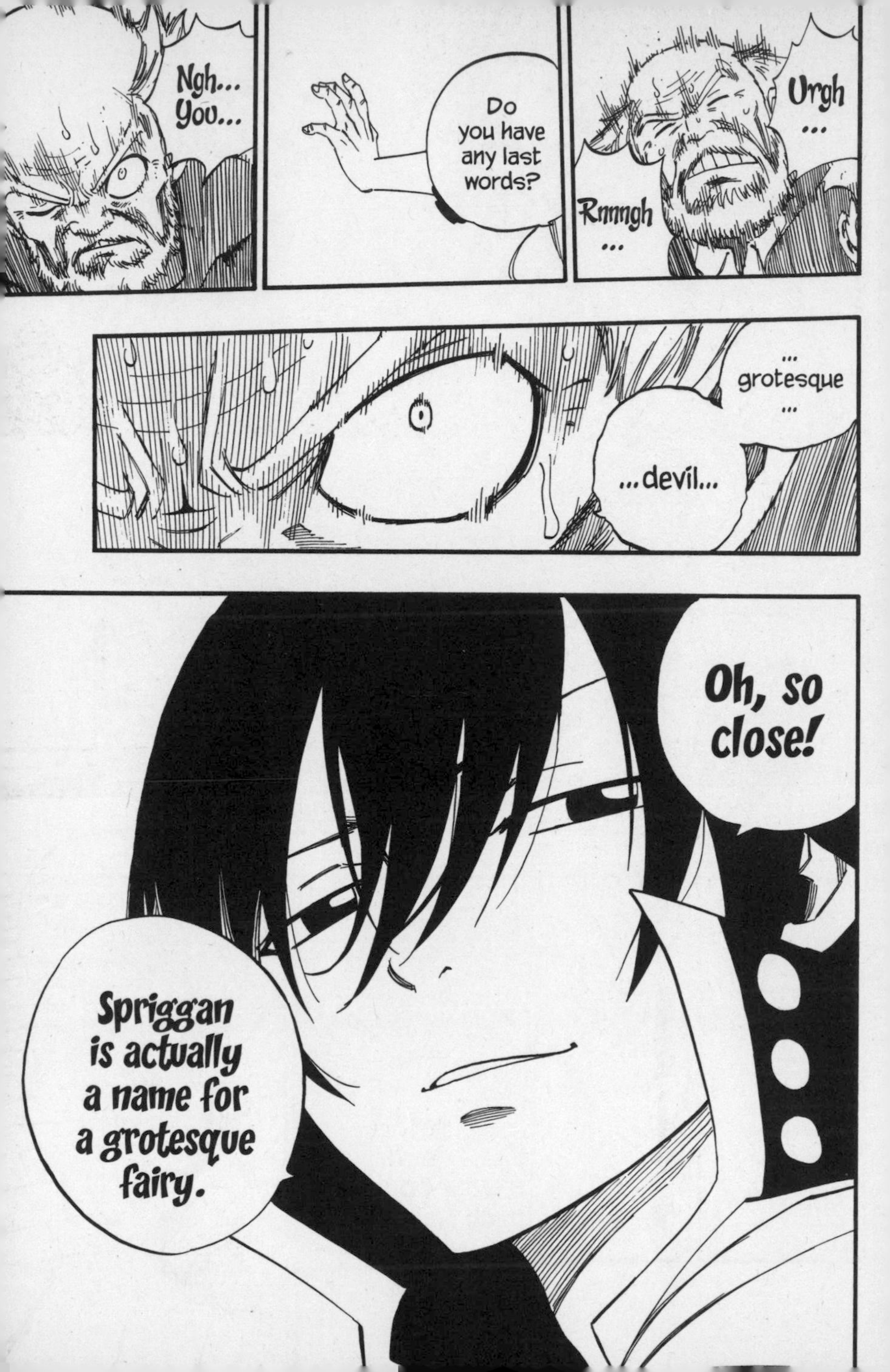
Urgh ...
Rnnngh ...
Do you have any last words?
Ngh... You...
... grotesque ...
...devil...
Oh, so close!
Spriggan is actually a name for a grotesque fairy.

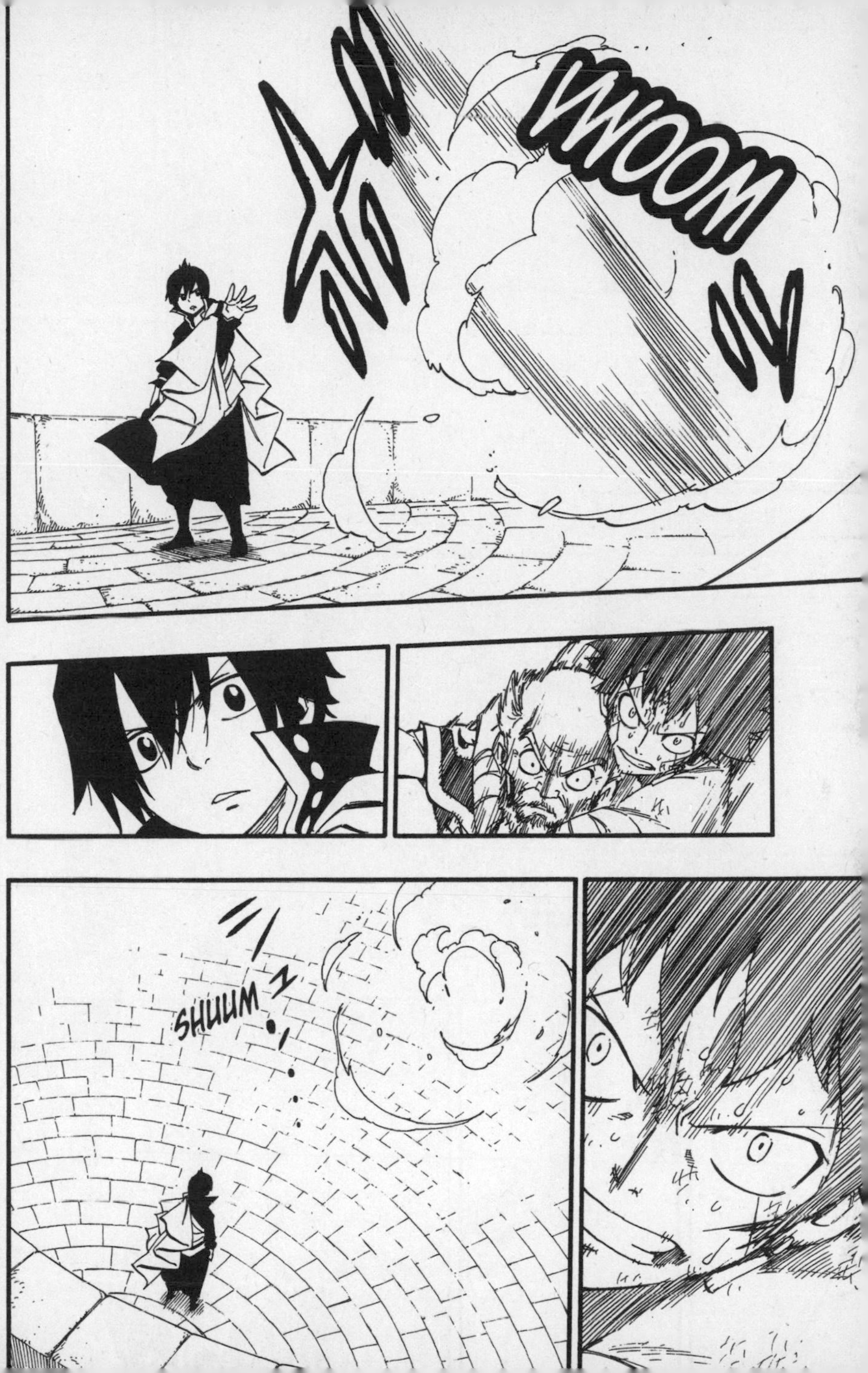
WOOM
SHUUM

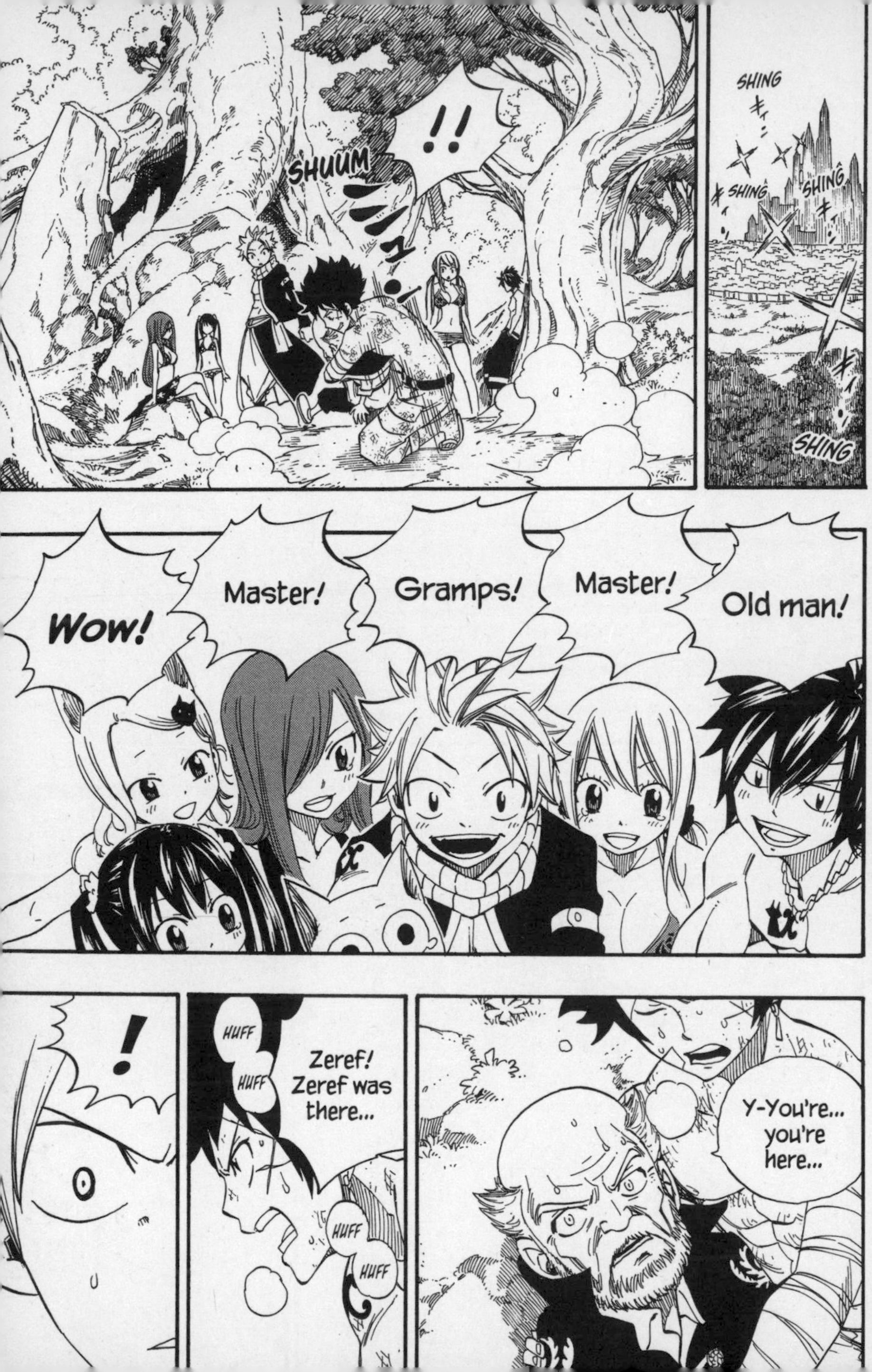
SHING
SHING
SHING
SHING
!!
SHUUM
Old man!
Master!
Gramps!
Master!
Wow!
Y-You're... you're here...
HUFF
HUFF
Zeref! Zeref was there...
HUFF
HUFF
!

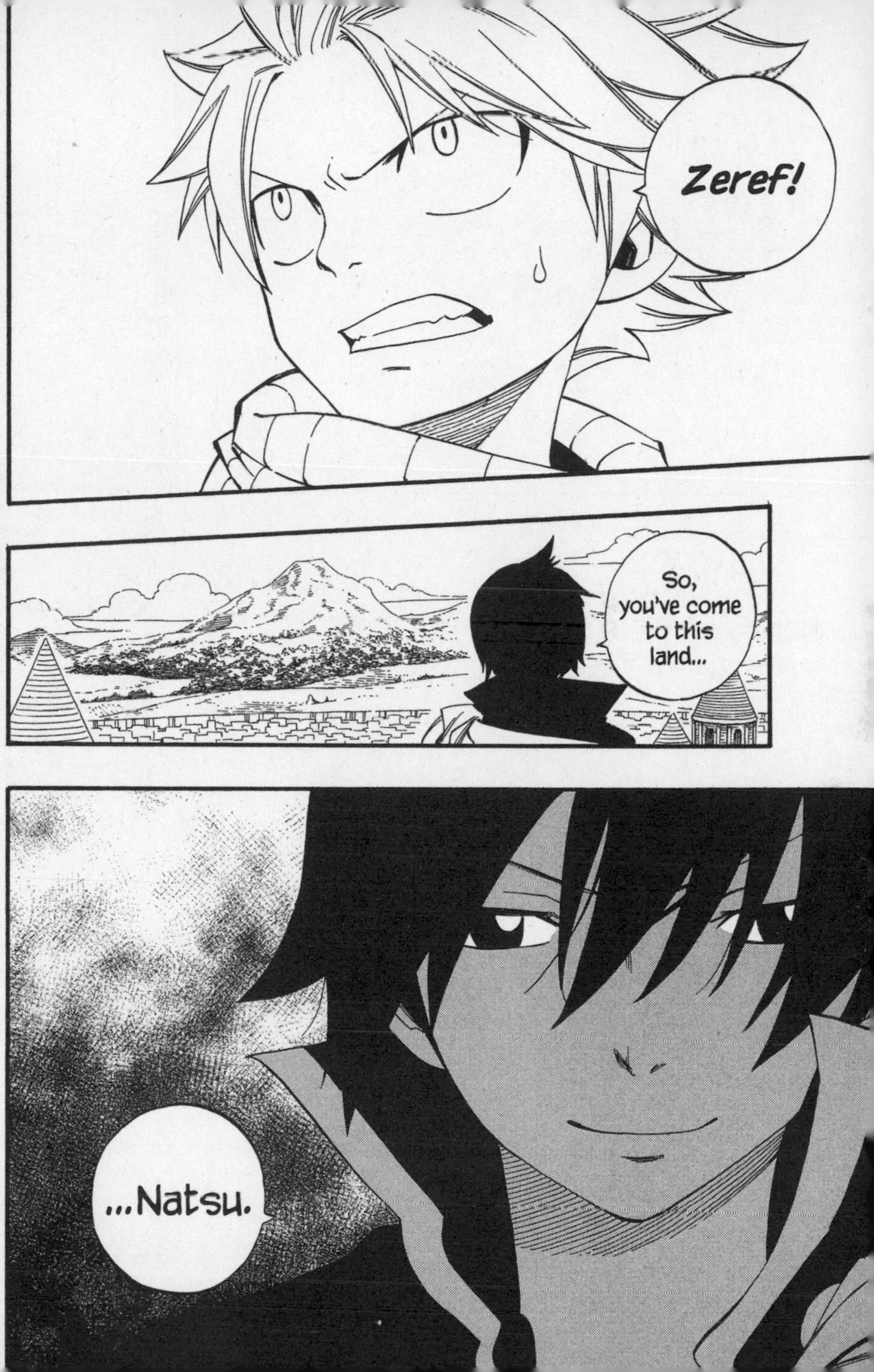
Zeref!
So, you've come to this land...
...Natsu.

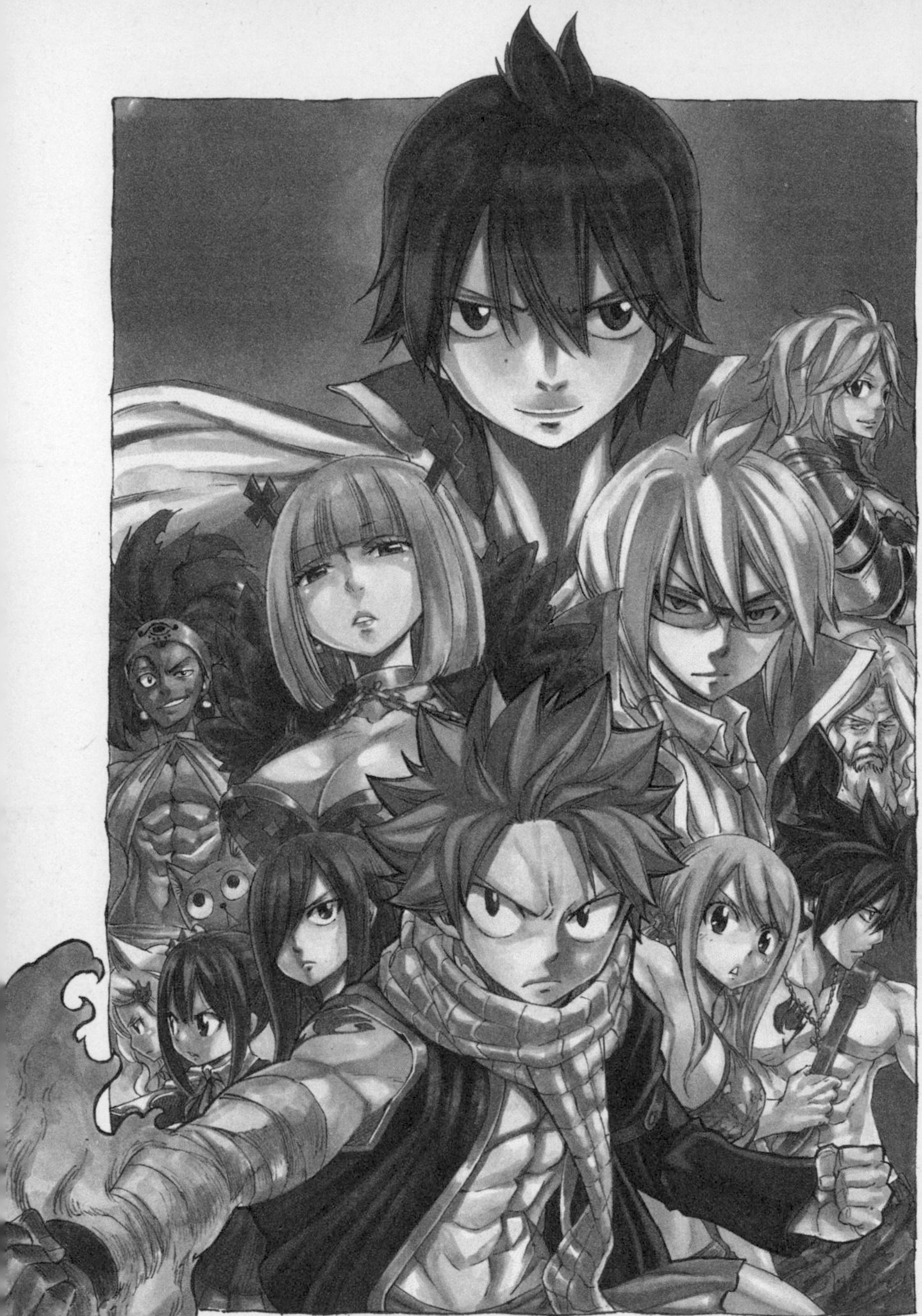

Chapter 446: The Land the Gods Abandoned

FAIRY TAIL
フェアリーテイル

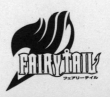

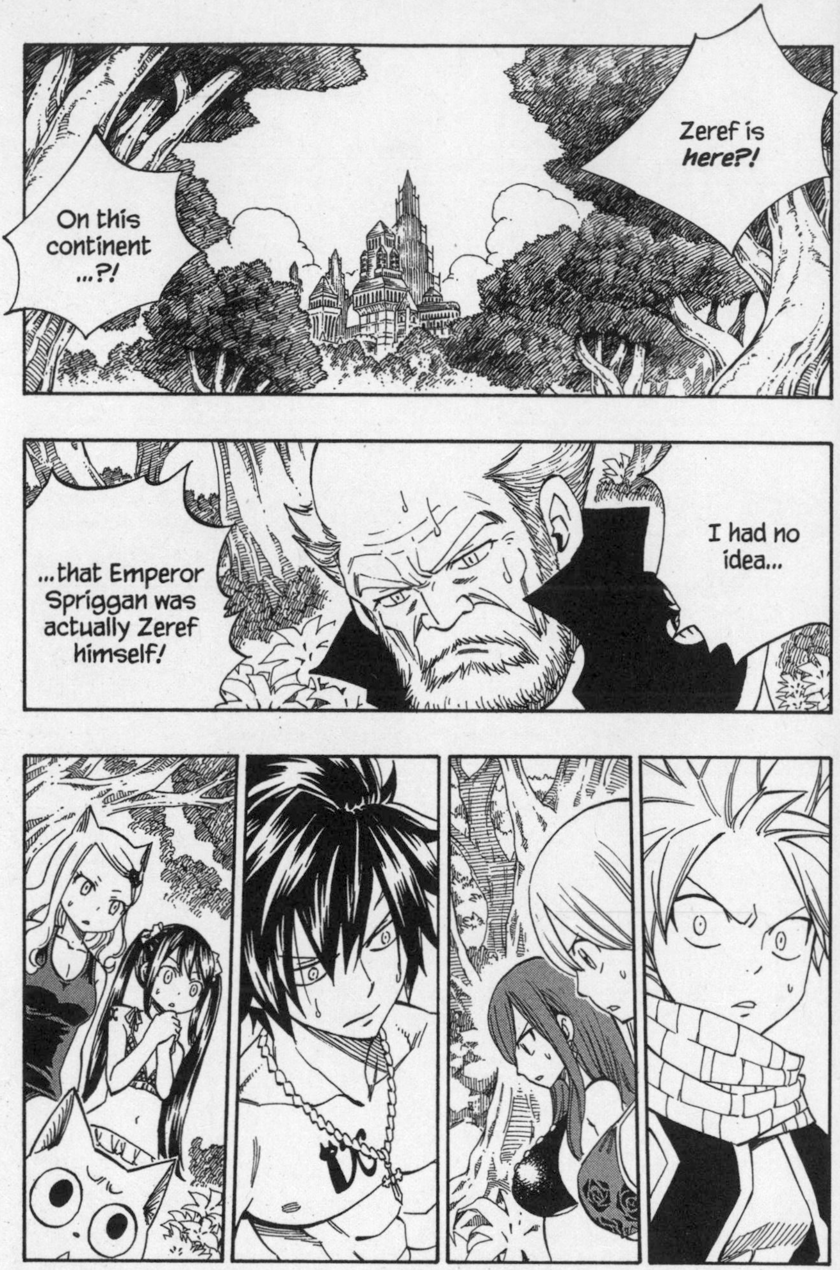
Zeref is here?!
On this continent ...?!
I had no idea...
...that Emperor Spriggan was actually Zeref himself!

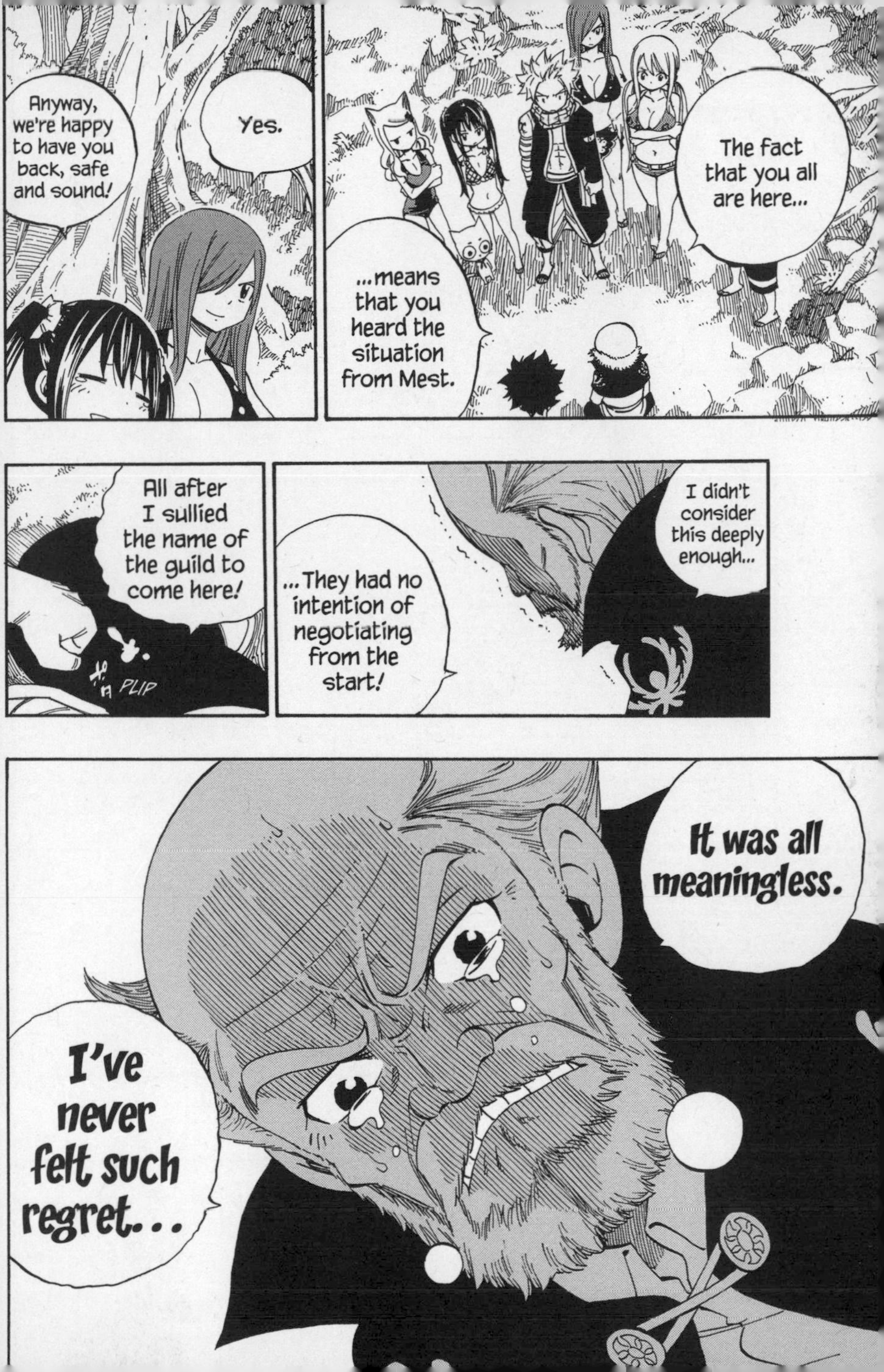
The fact that you all are here...
...means that you heard the situation from Mest.
Yes.
Anyway, we're happy to have you back, safe and sound!
I didn't consider this deeply enough...
...They had no intention of negotiating from the start!
All after I sullied the name of the guild to come here!
PLIP
It was all meaningless.
I've never felt such regret...

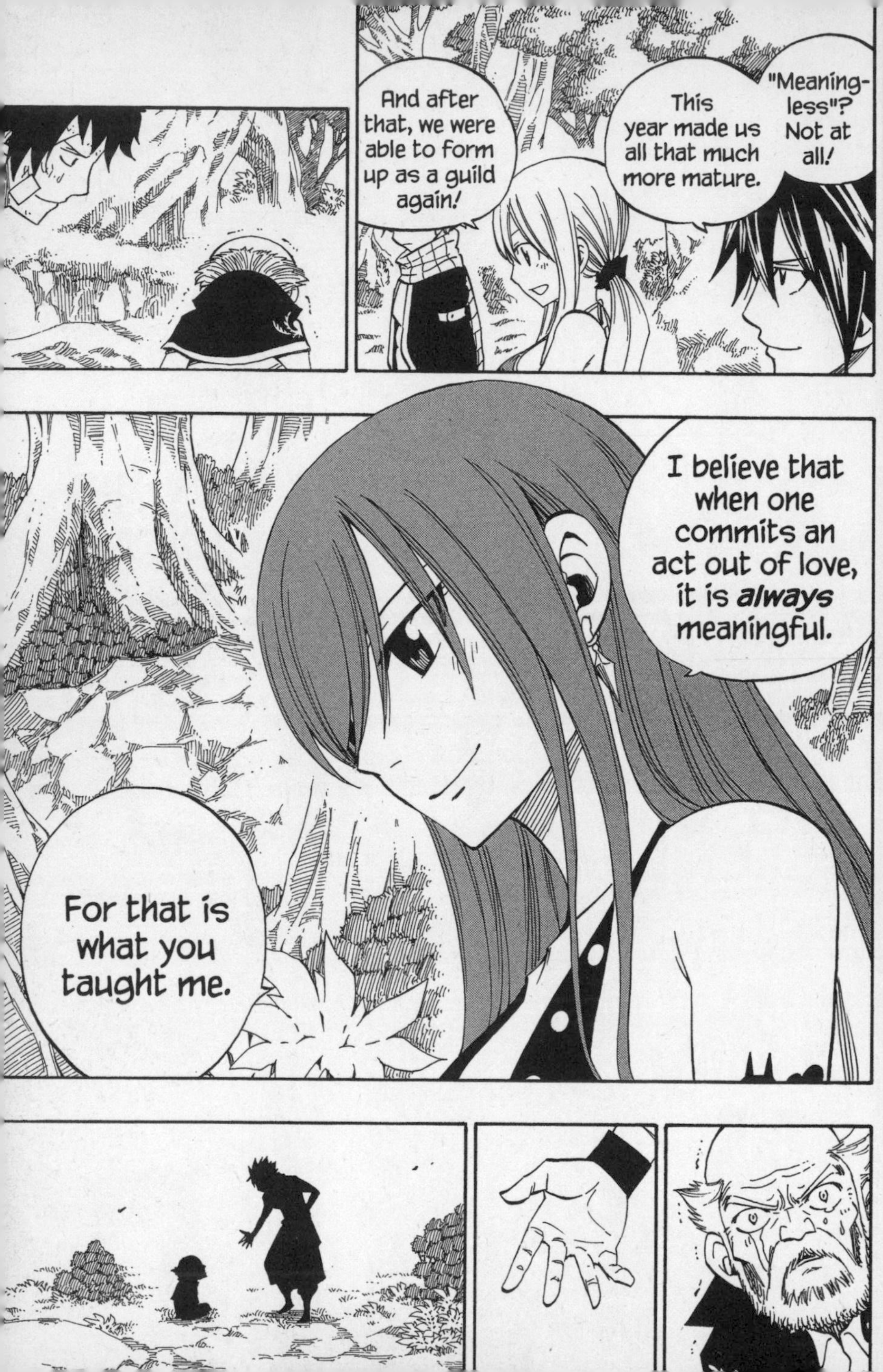
"Meaning-less"? Not at all!
This year made us all that much more mature.
And after that, we were able to form up as a guild again!
I believe that when one commits an act out of love, it is *always* meaningful.
For that is what you taught me.

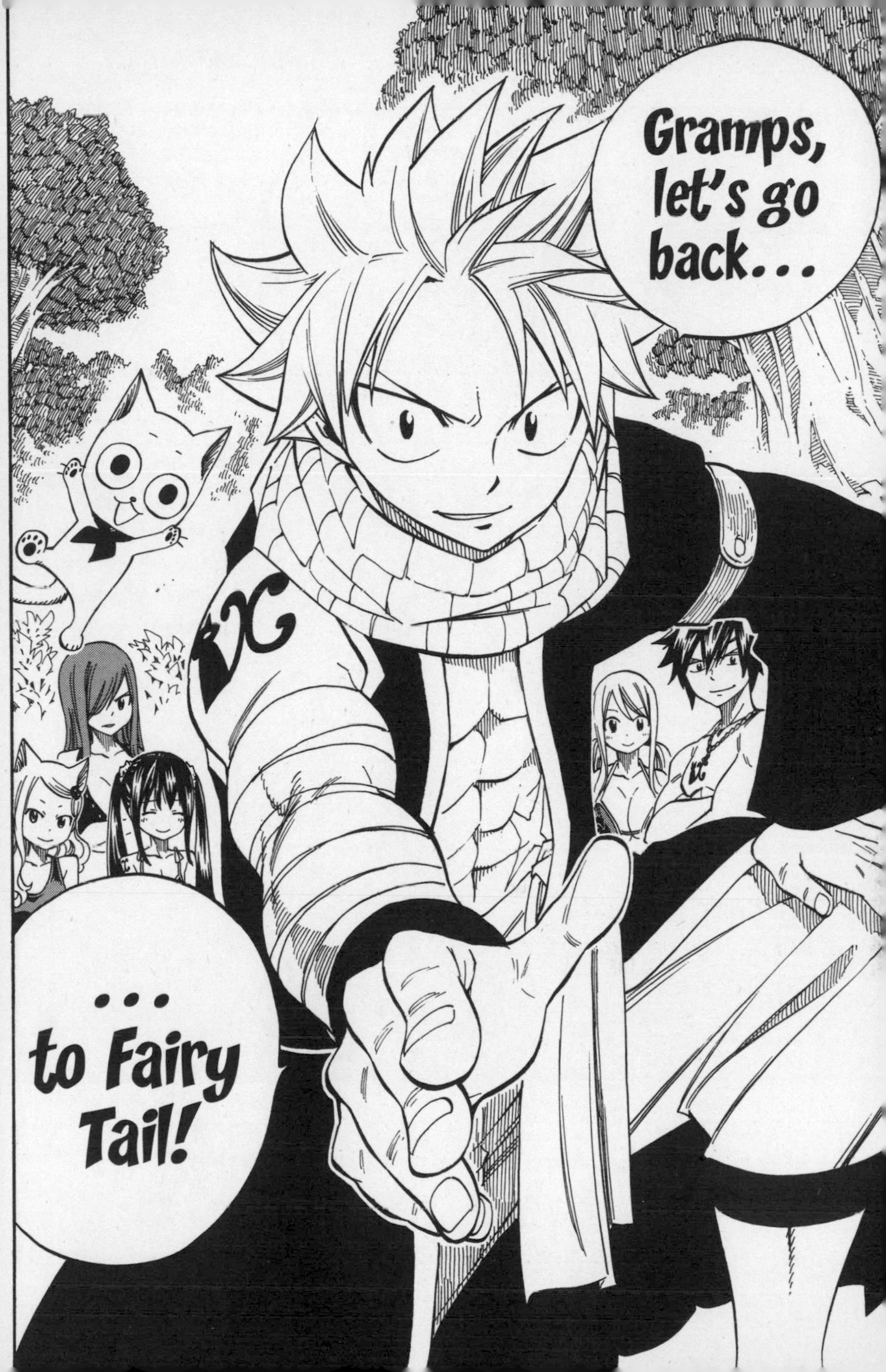
Gramps, let's go back...
... to Fairy Tail!

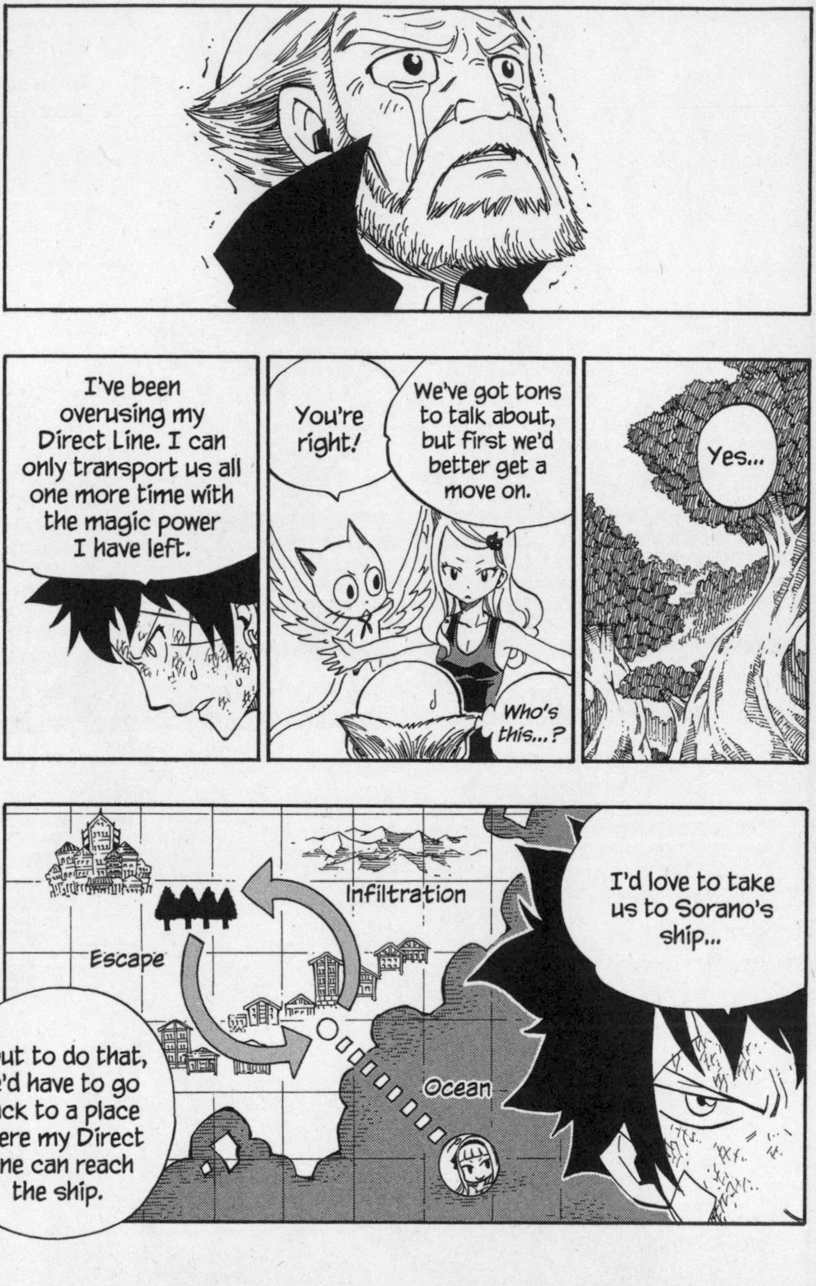
Yes...
We've got tons to talk about, but first we'd better get a move on.
You're right!
Who's this...?
I've been overusing my Direct Line. I can only transport us all one more time with the magic power I have left.
I'd love to take us to Sorano's ship...
Infiltration
Escape
Ocean
...but to do that, we'd have to go back to a place where my Direct Line can reach the ship.

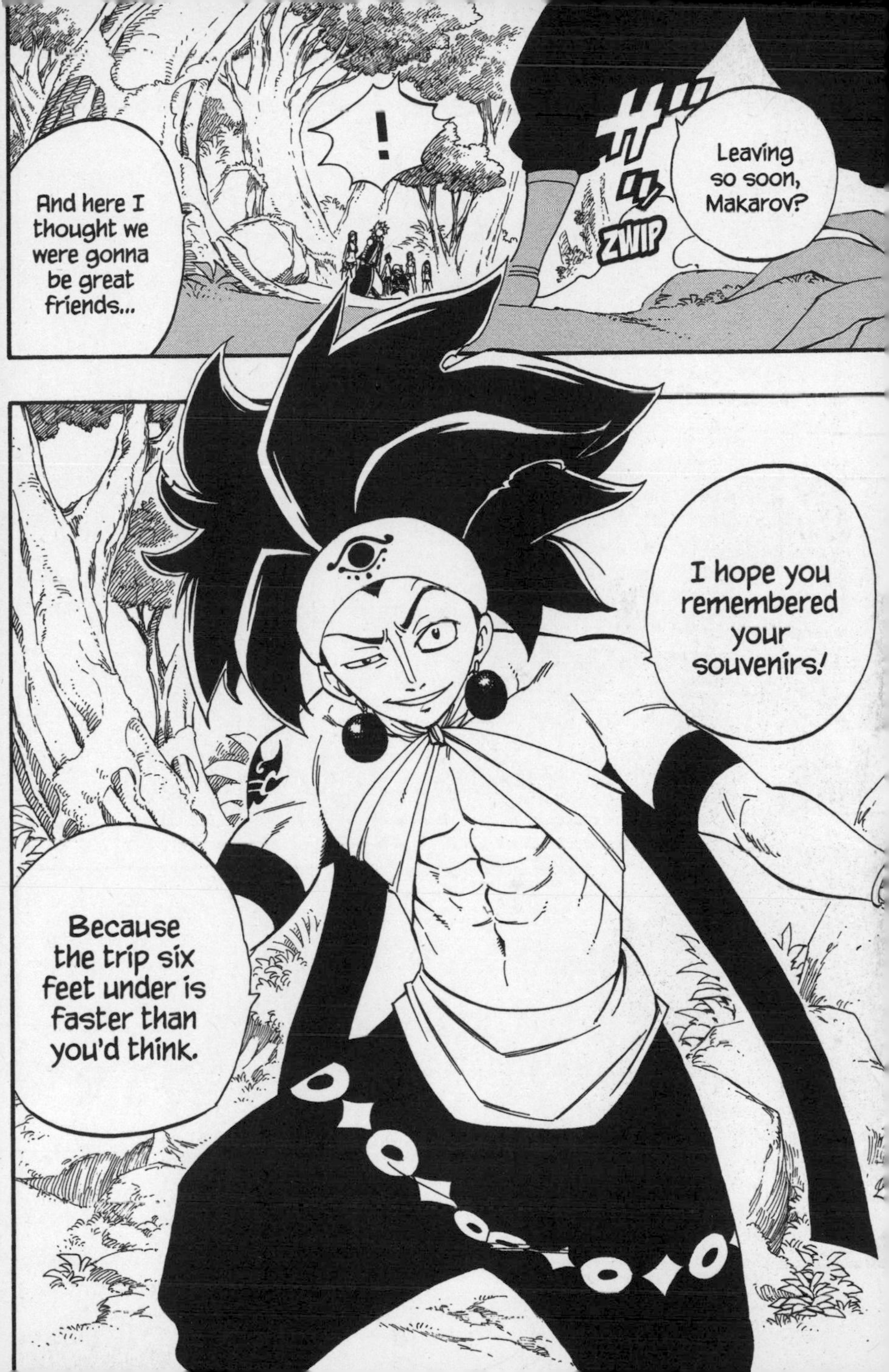
Leaving so soon, Makarov?
ZWIP
!
And here I thought we were gonna be great friends...
I hope you remembered your souvenirs!
Because the trip six feet under is faster than you'd think.

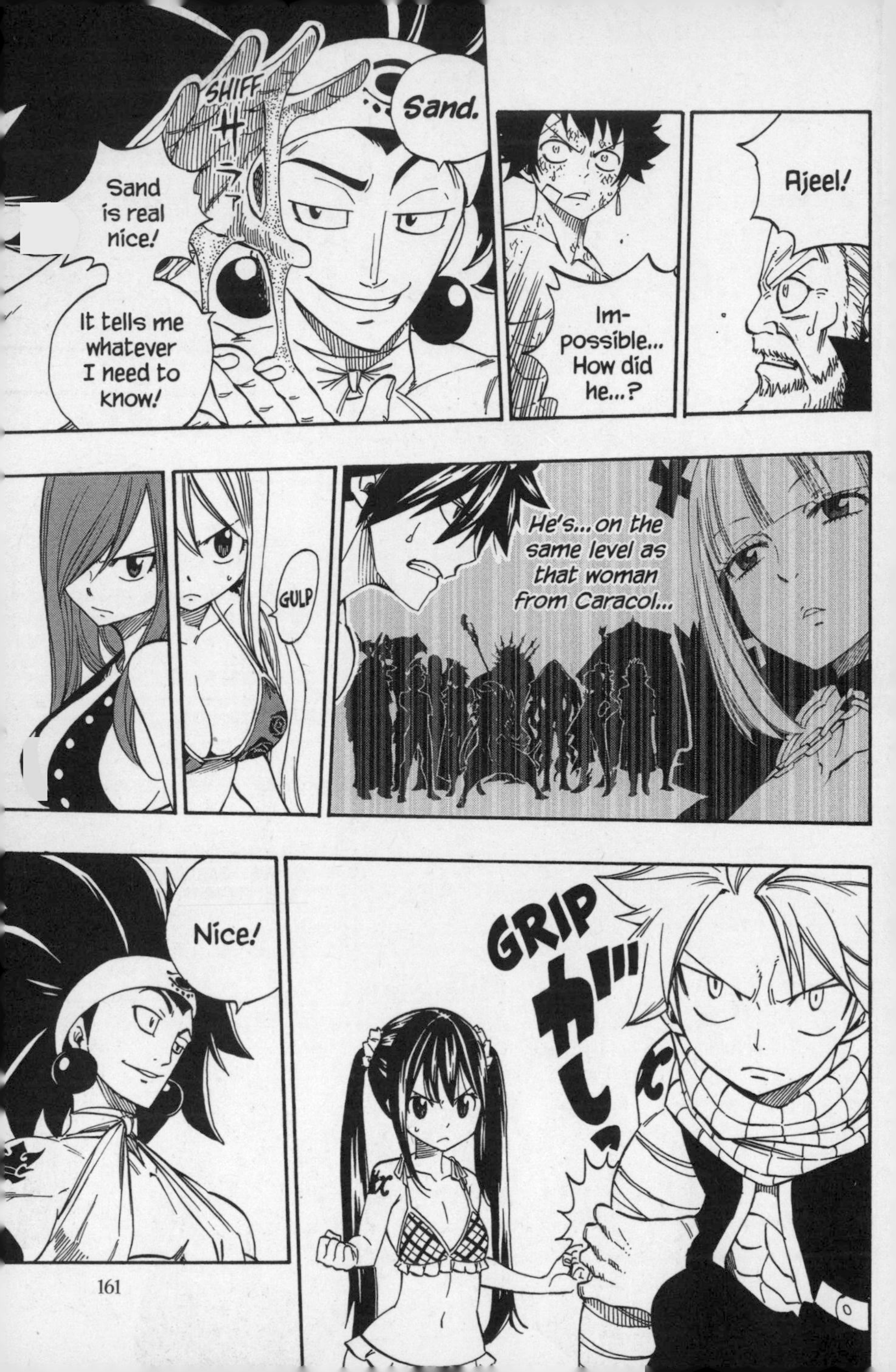
Ajeel!
Im-possible... How did he...?
Sand.
SHIFF
Sand is real nice!
It tells me whatever I need to know!
He's... on the same level as that woman from Caracol...
GULP
GRIP
Nice!

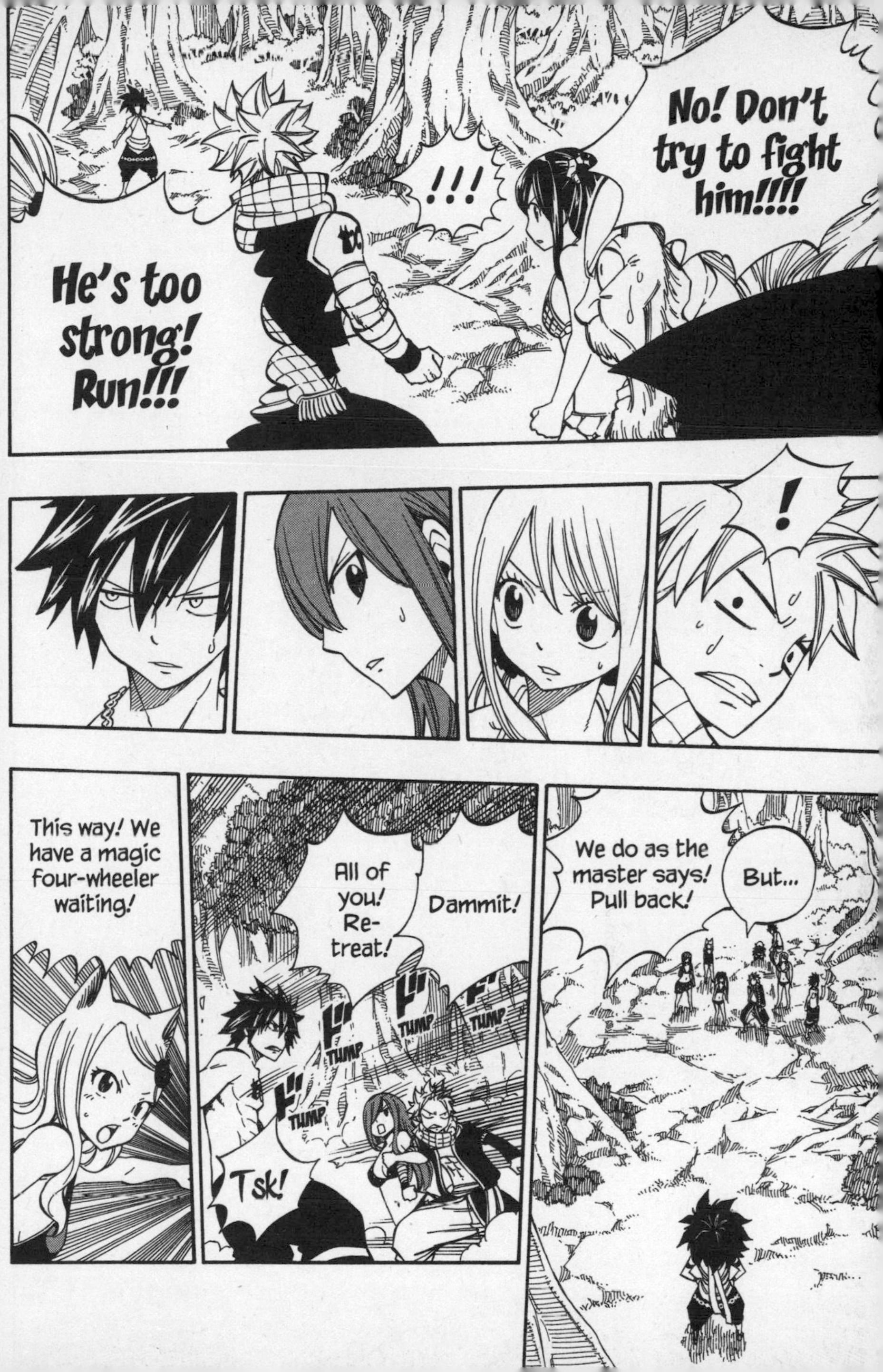
No! Don't try to fight him!!!!
!!!
He's too strong! Run!!!
!
But...
We do as the master says! Pull back!
Dammit!
All of you! Re-treat!
THUMP
THUMP
THUMP
THUMP
Tsk!
This way! We have a magic four-wheeler waiting!

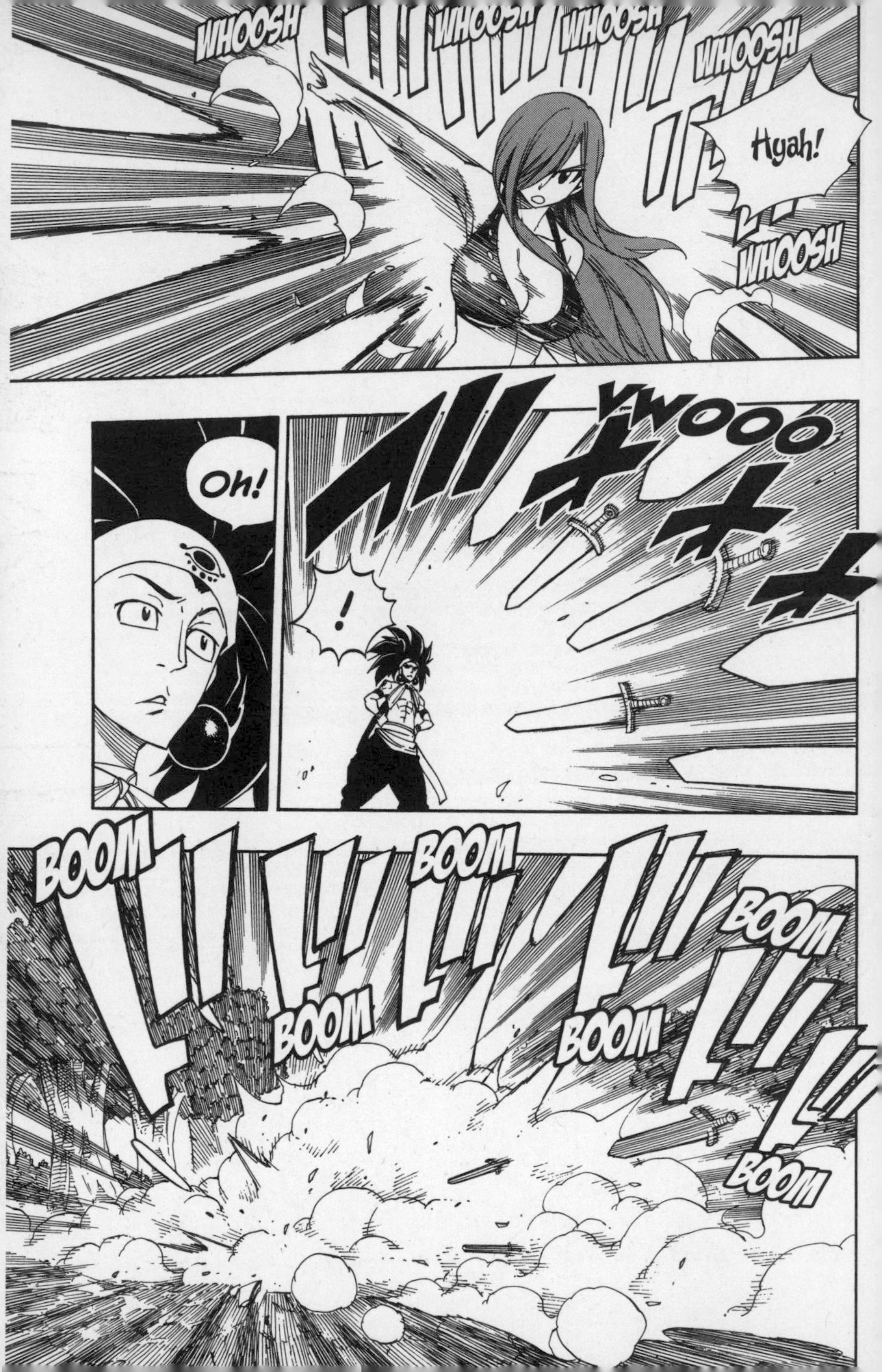
WHOOSH
Hyah!
WHOOSH
WHOOSH
WHOOSH
WHOOSH
YWOOO
!
Oh!
BOOM
BOOM
BOOM
BOOM
BOOM
BOOM

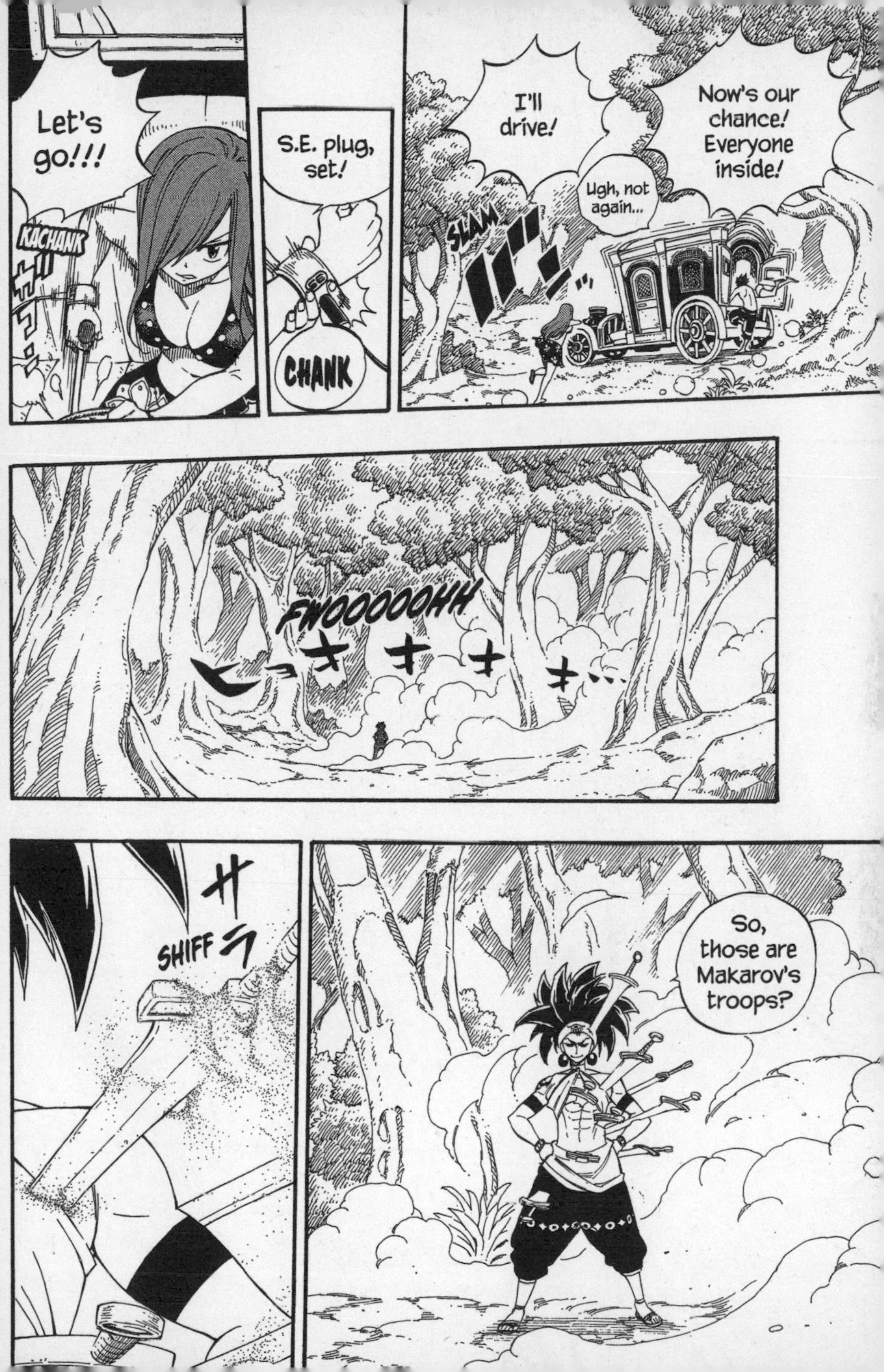
Now's our chance! Everyone inside!
I'll drive!
Ugh, not again...
SLAM
S.E. plug, set!
CHANK
Let's go!!!
KACHANK
FWOOOOOHH
So, those are Makarov's troops?
SHIFF

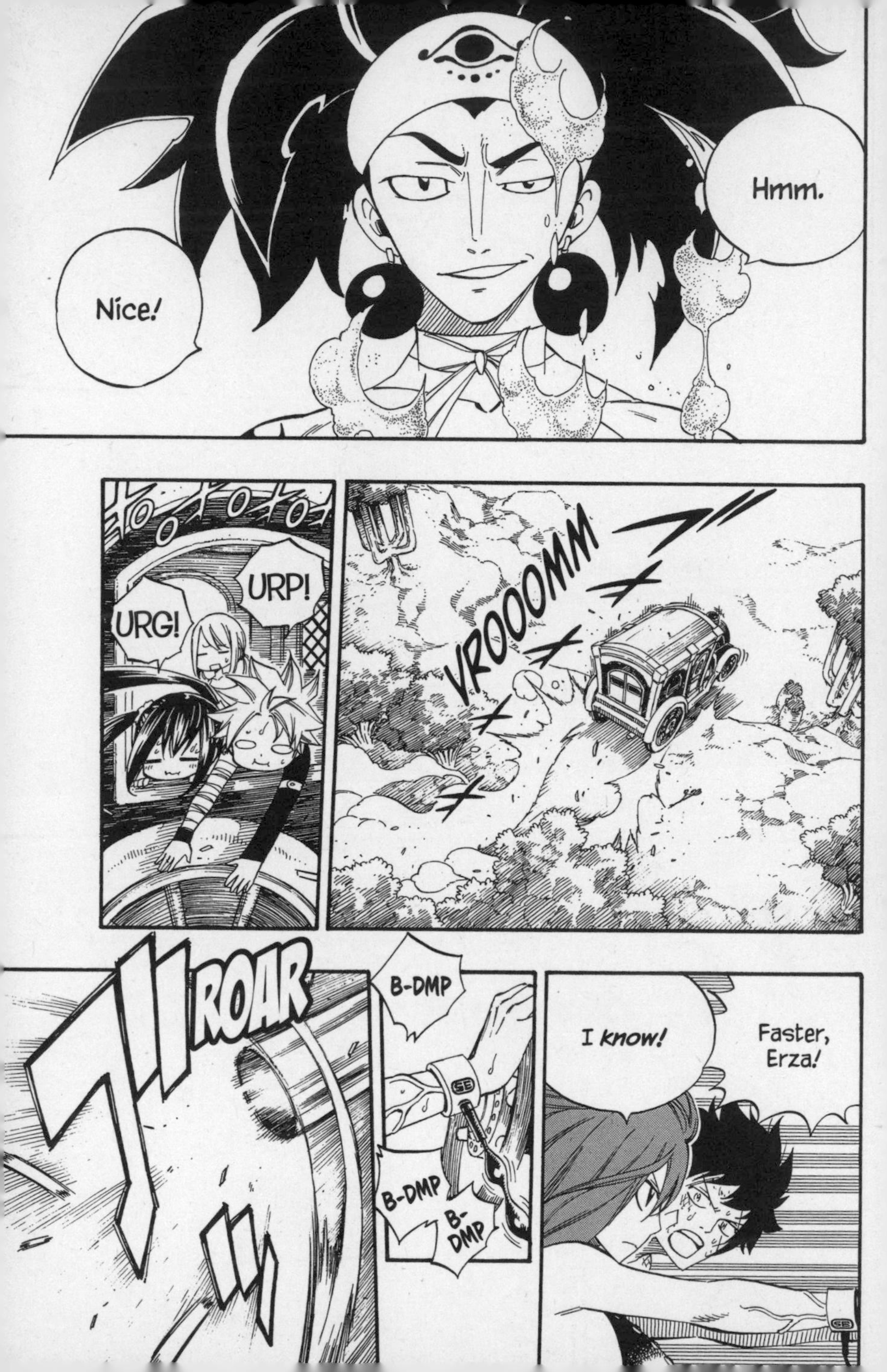
Hmm.
Nice!
VROOOMM
URP!
URG!
Faster, Erza!
I know!
B-DMP
B-DMP
B-DMP
ROAR

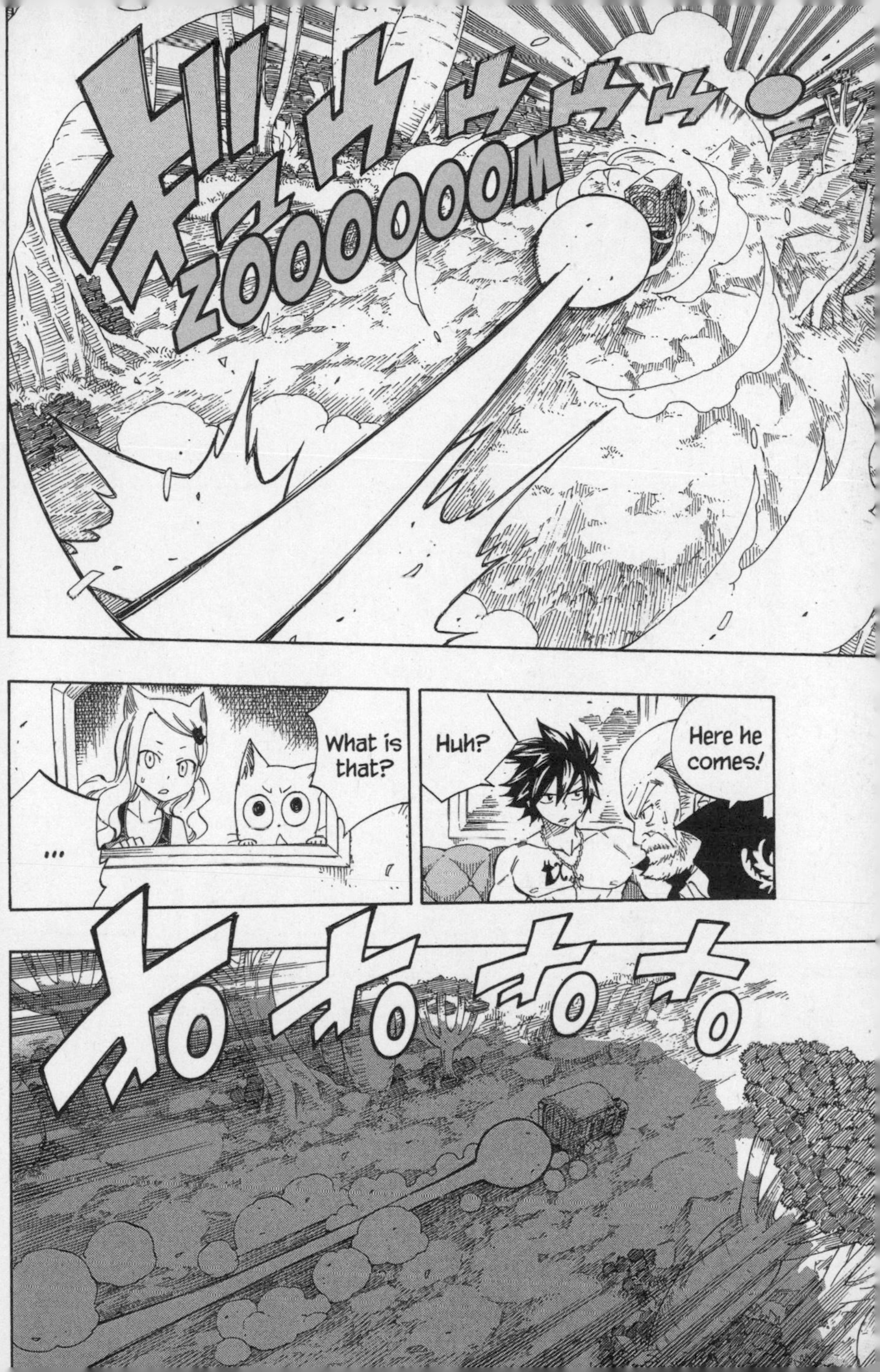
ZOOOOOOM
Here he comes!
Huh?
What is that?
...

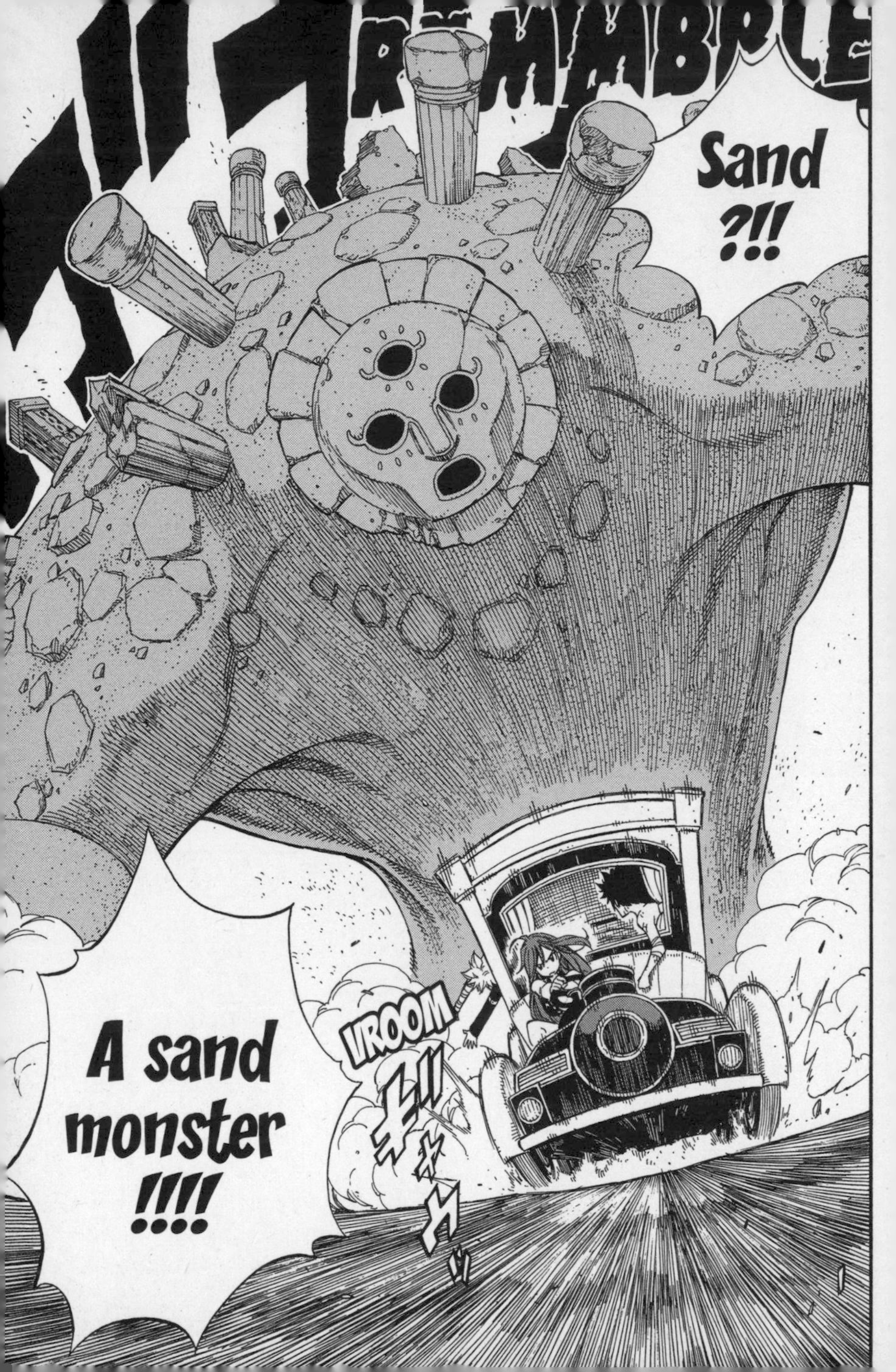
Sand ?!!
VROOM
A sand monster !!!!

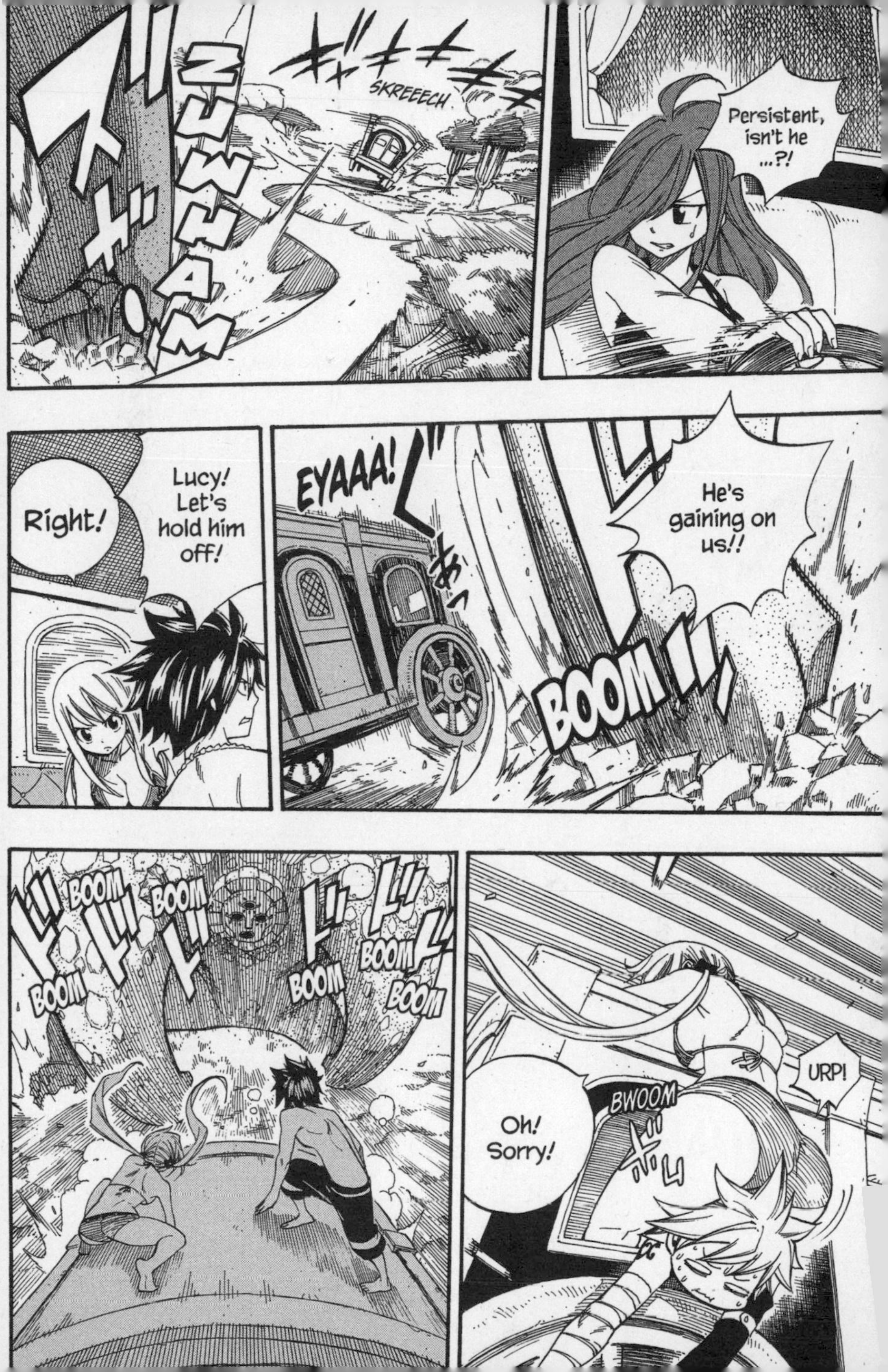
Persistent, isn't he ...?!
SKREEECH
ZUWHAM
He's gaining on us!!
EYAAA!
BOOM!!
Lucy! Let's hold him off!
Right!
URP!
BWOOM
Oh! Sorry!
BOOM
BOOM
BOOM
BOOM
BOOM
BOOM

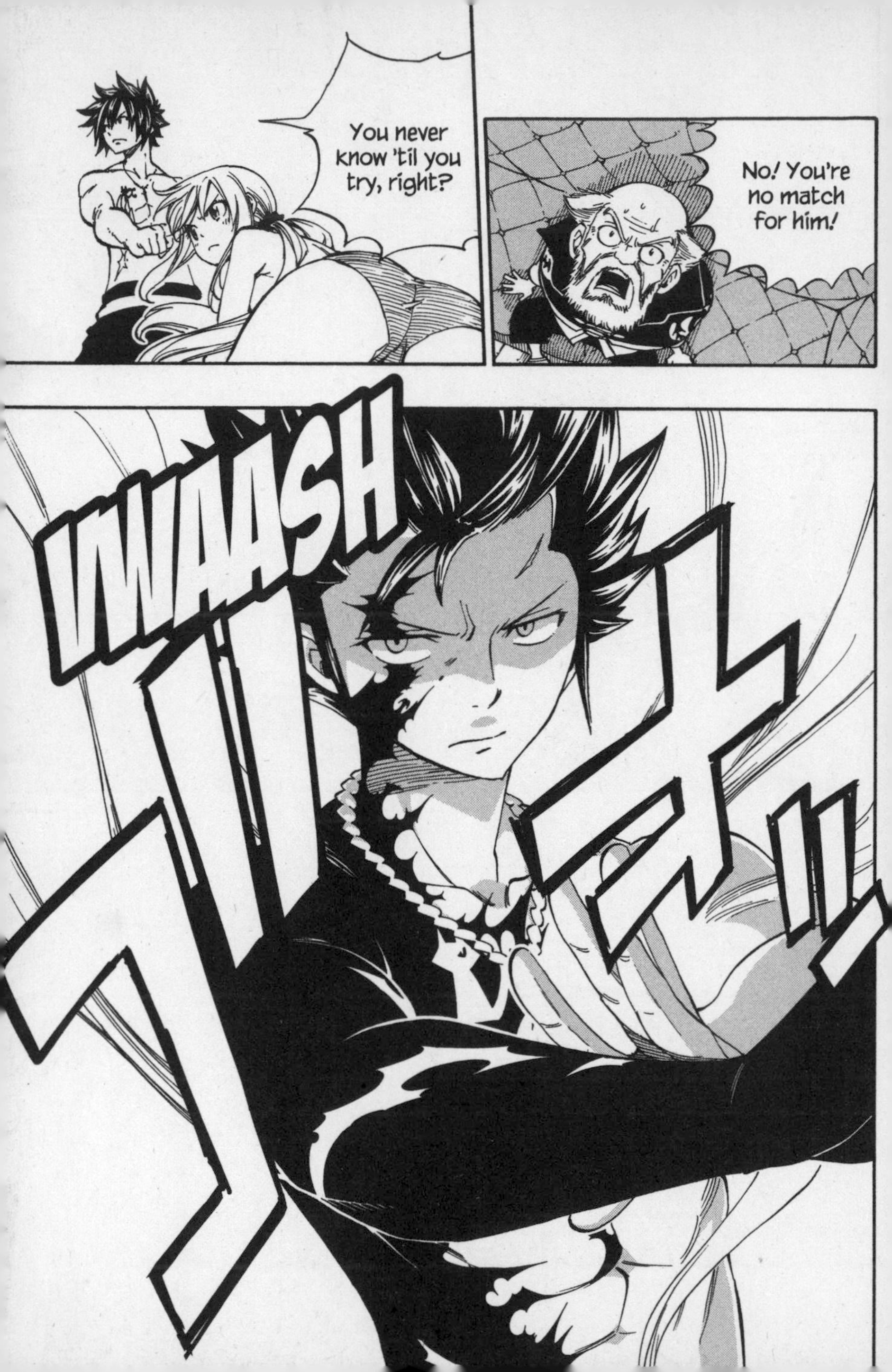
No! You're no match for him!
You never know 'til you try, right?
VWAASH

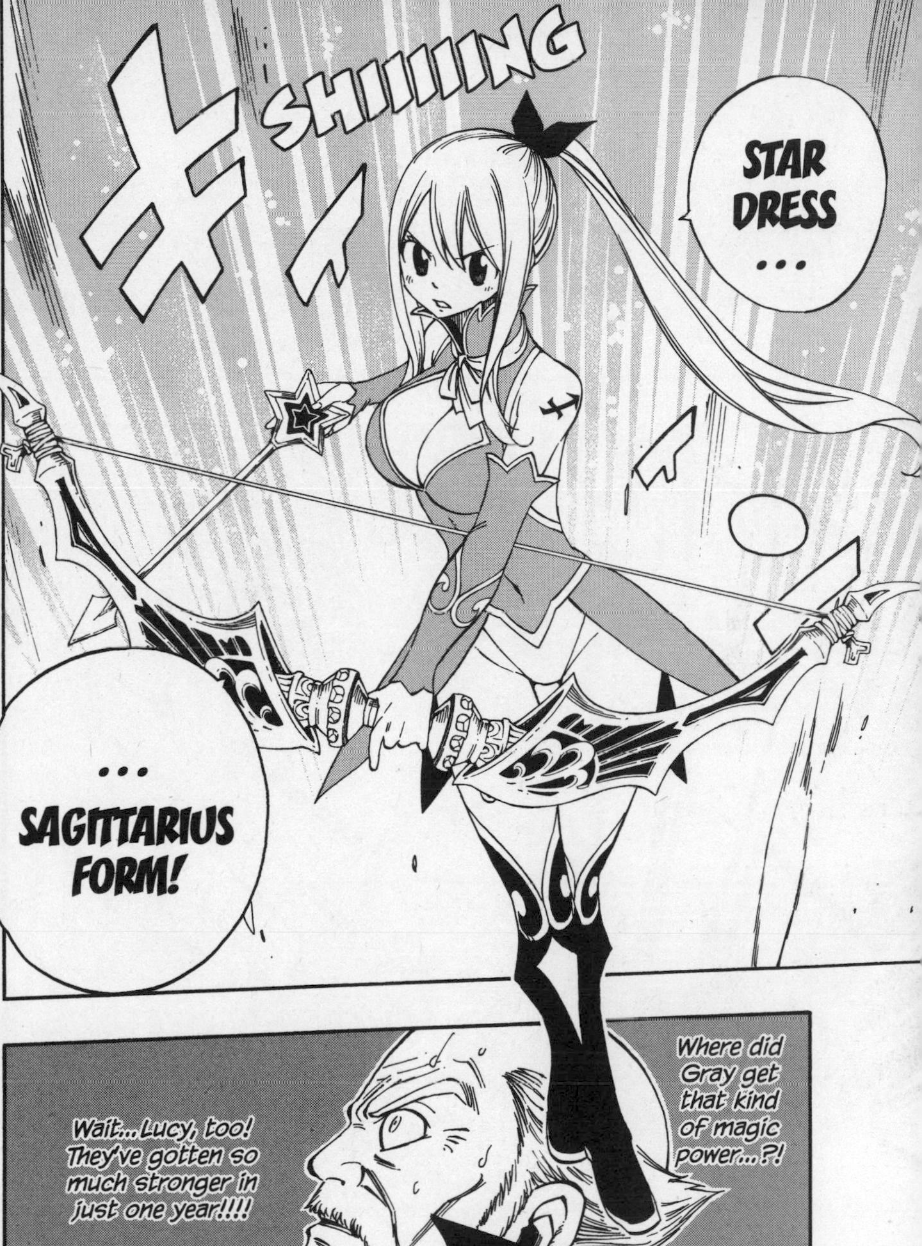
SHIIIING
STAR DRESS ...
... SAGITTARIUS FORM!
Where did Gray get that kind of magic power...?!
Wait...Lucy, too! They've gotten so much stronger in just one year!!!!

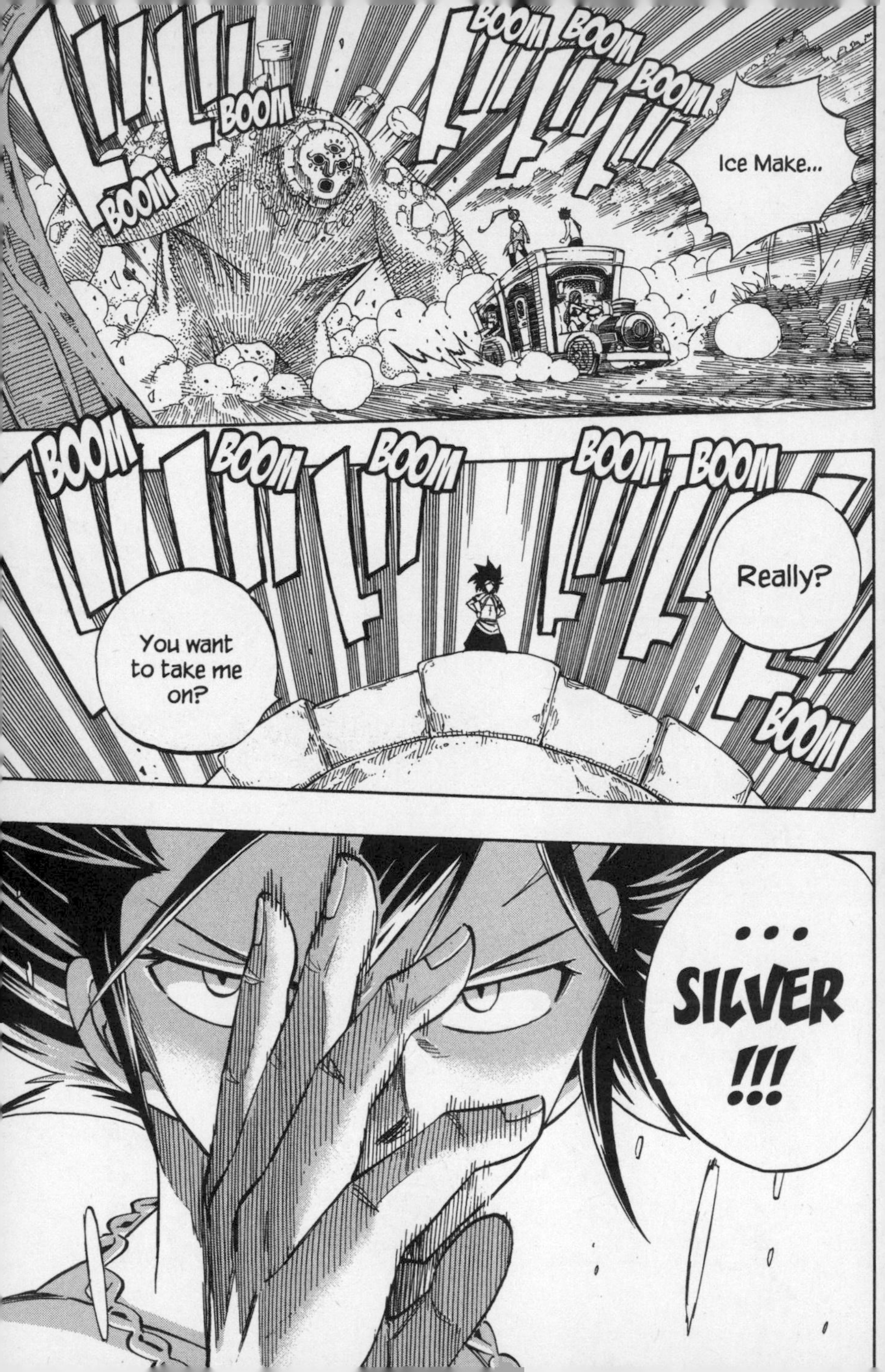
BOOM
BOOM
BOOM
Ice Make...
BOOM
BOOM
BOOM
BOOM
BOOM
BOOM
BOOM
BOOM
Really?
You want to take me on?
BOOM
BOOM
BOOM
...SILVER!!!

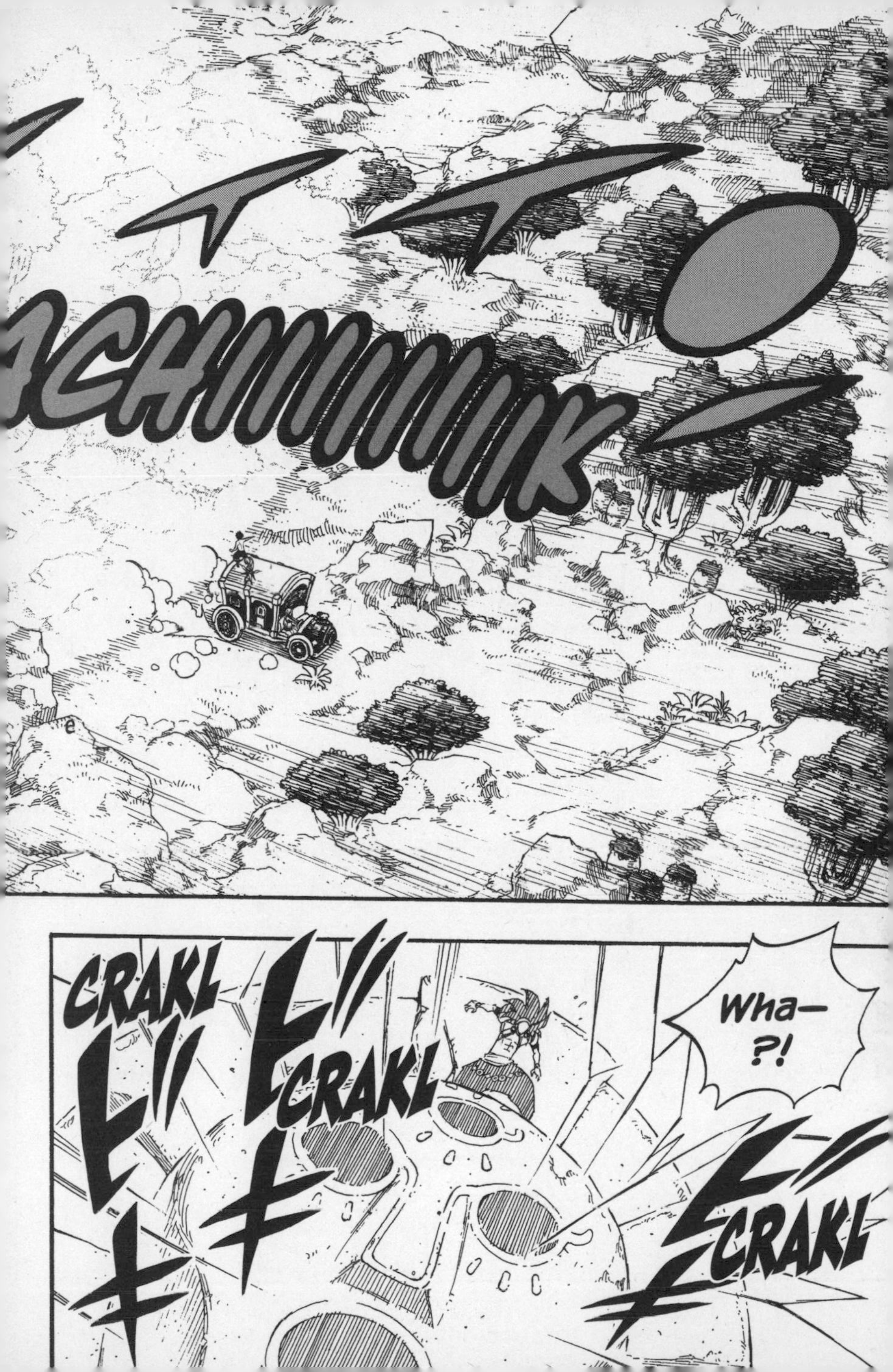
ACHIIIIIIIK
Wha—?!
CRAKL
CRAKL
CRAKL

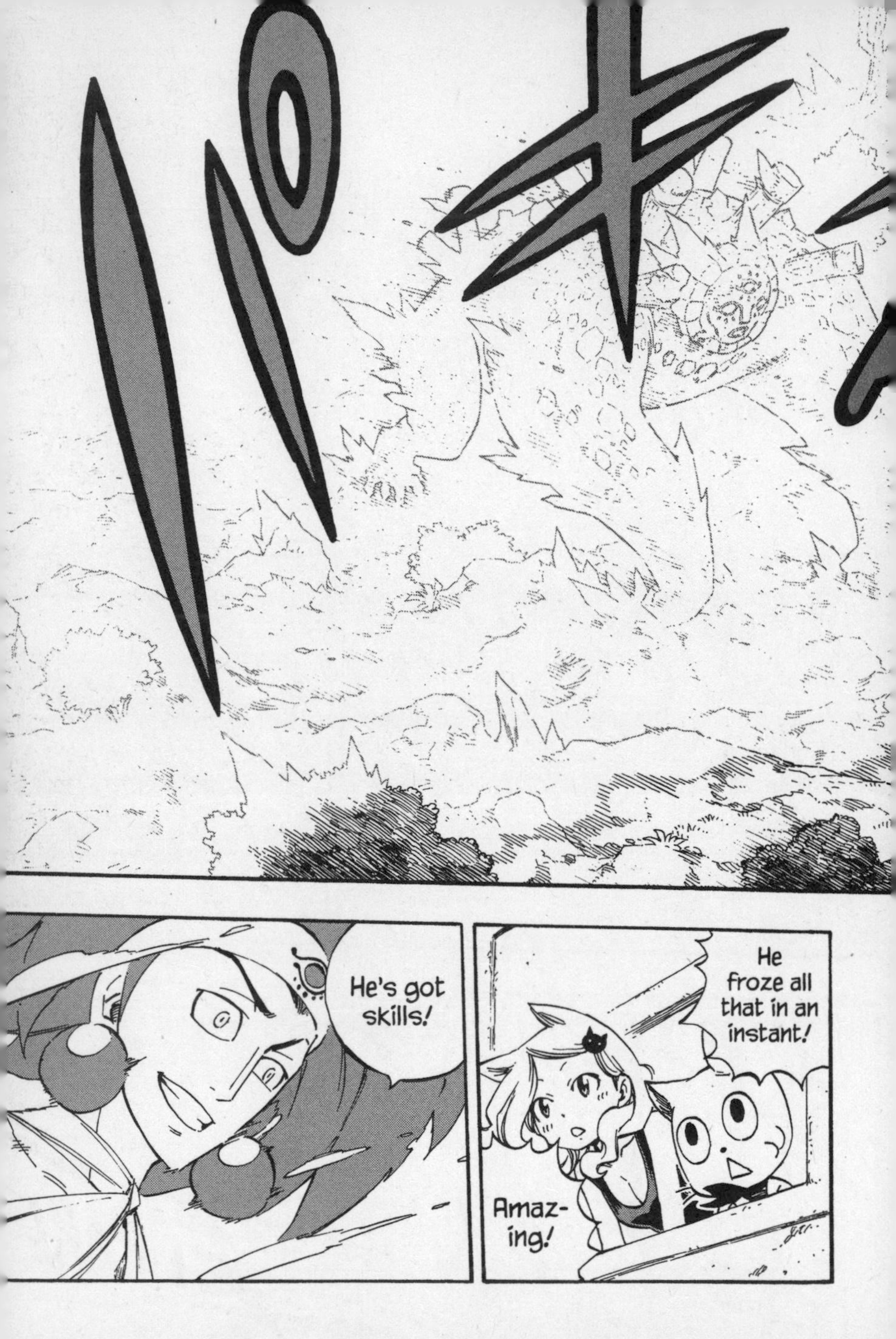
He froze all that in an instant!
Amaz-ing!
He's got skills!

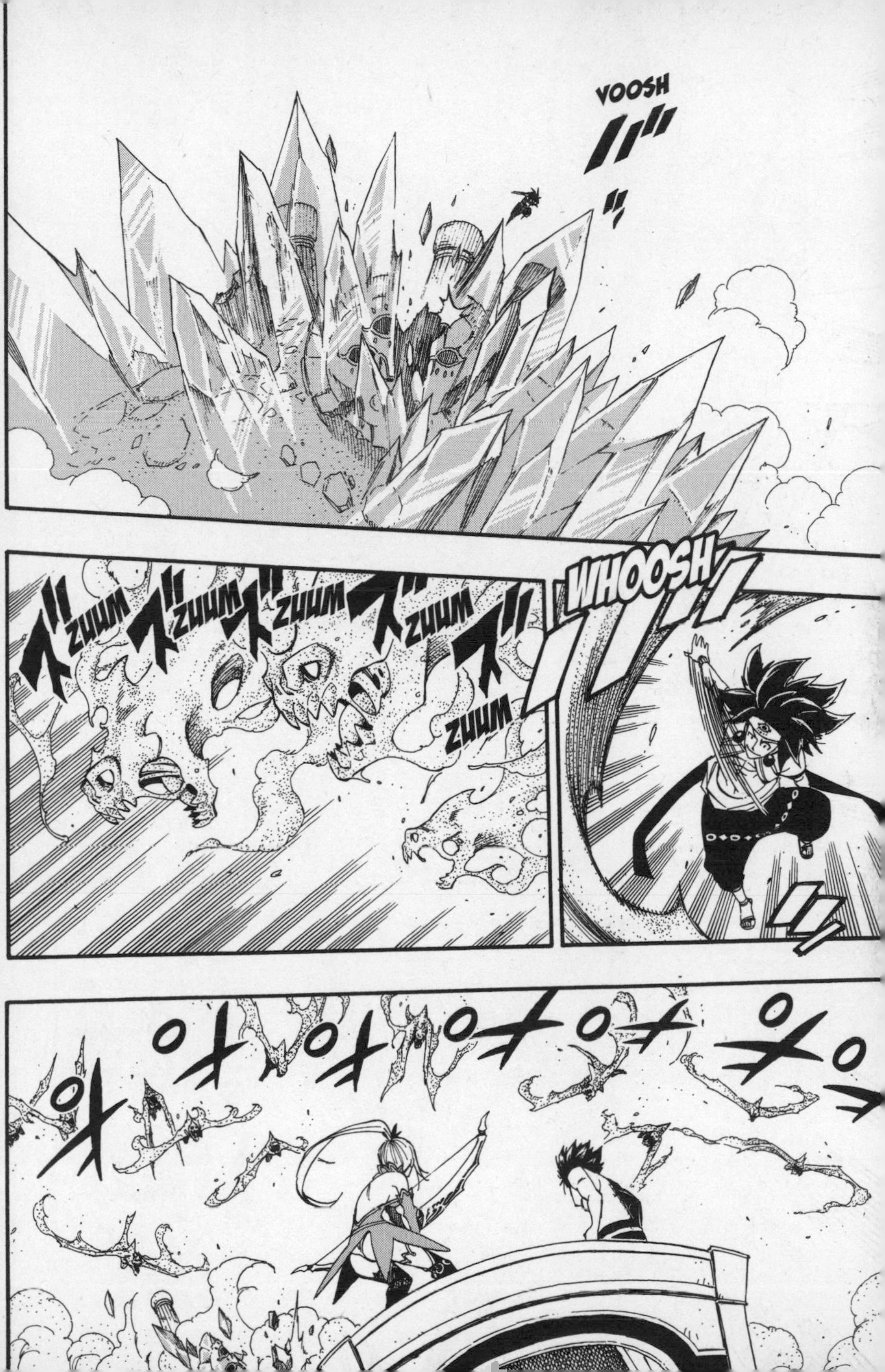
VOOSH
WHOOSH
ZUUM
ZUUM
ZUUM
ZUUM
ZUUM

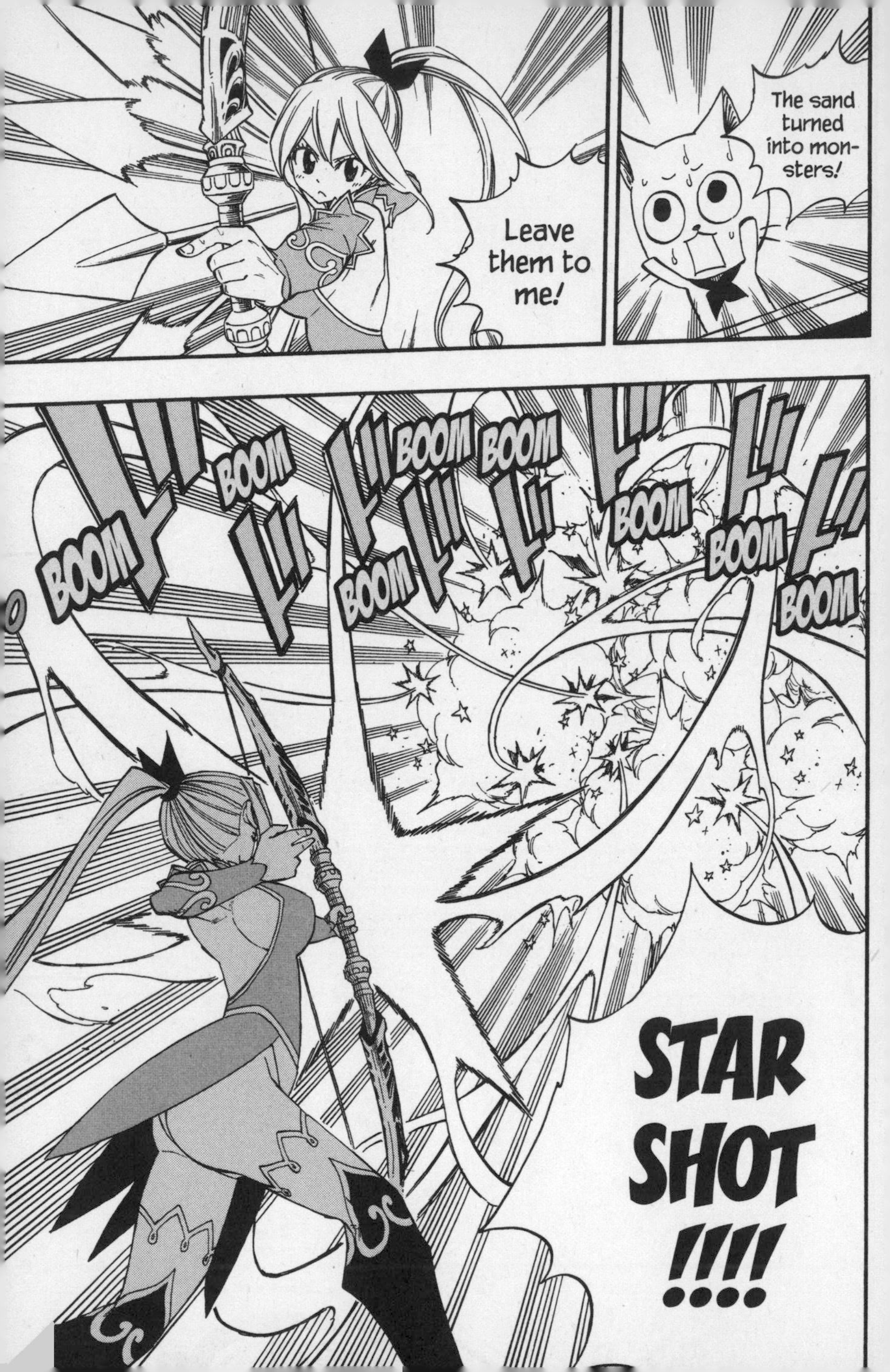

The sand turned into monsters!
Leave them to me!
BOOM
BOOM
BOOM
BOOM
BOOM
BOOM
BOOM
BOOM
BOOM
STAR SHOT!!!!

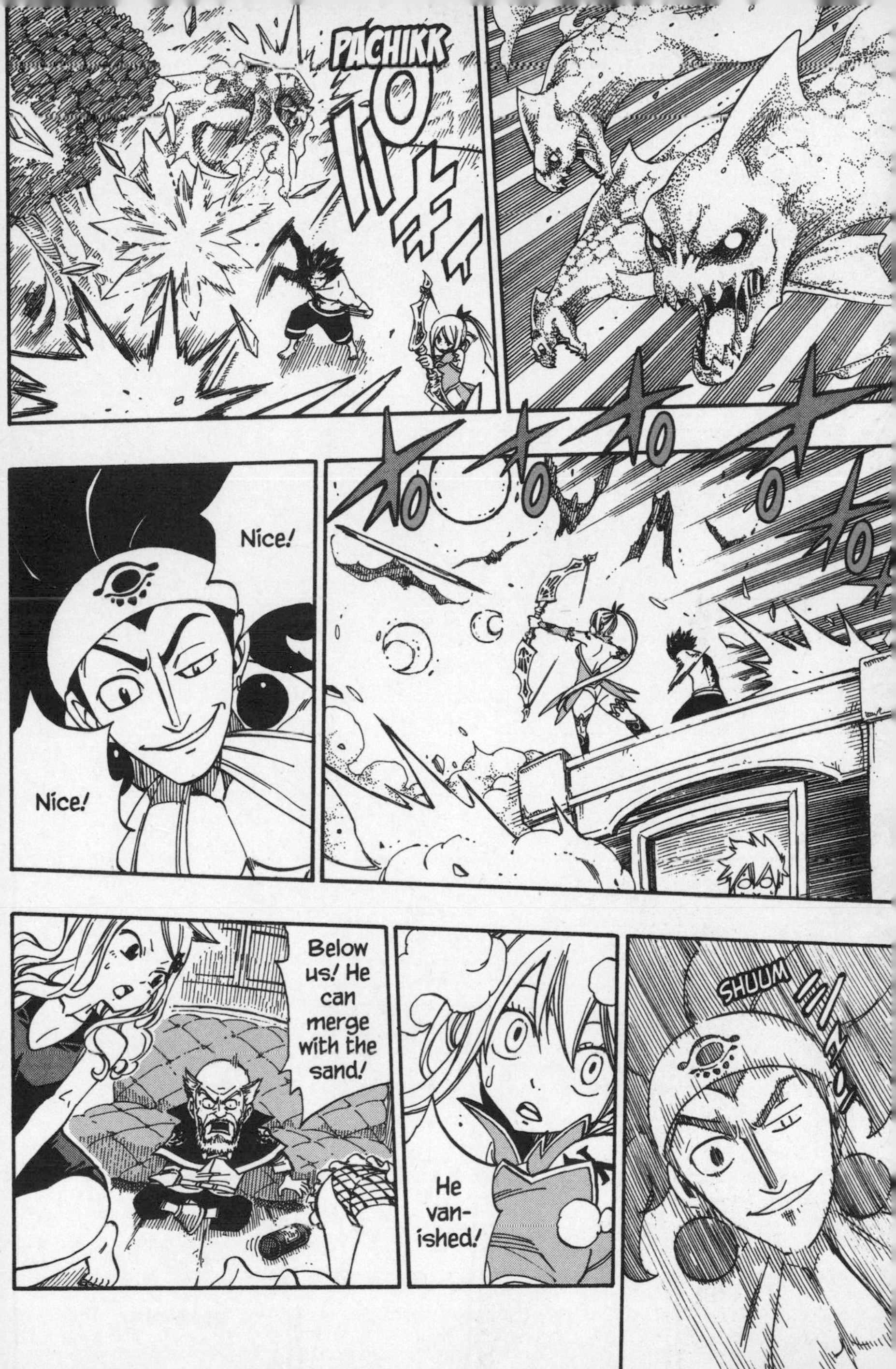
PACHIKK
Nice!
Nice!
SHUUM
He vanished!
Below us! He can merge with the sand!

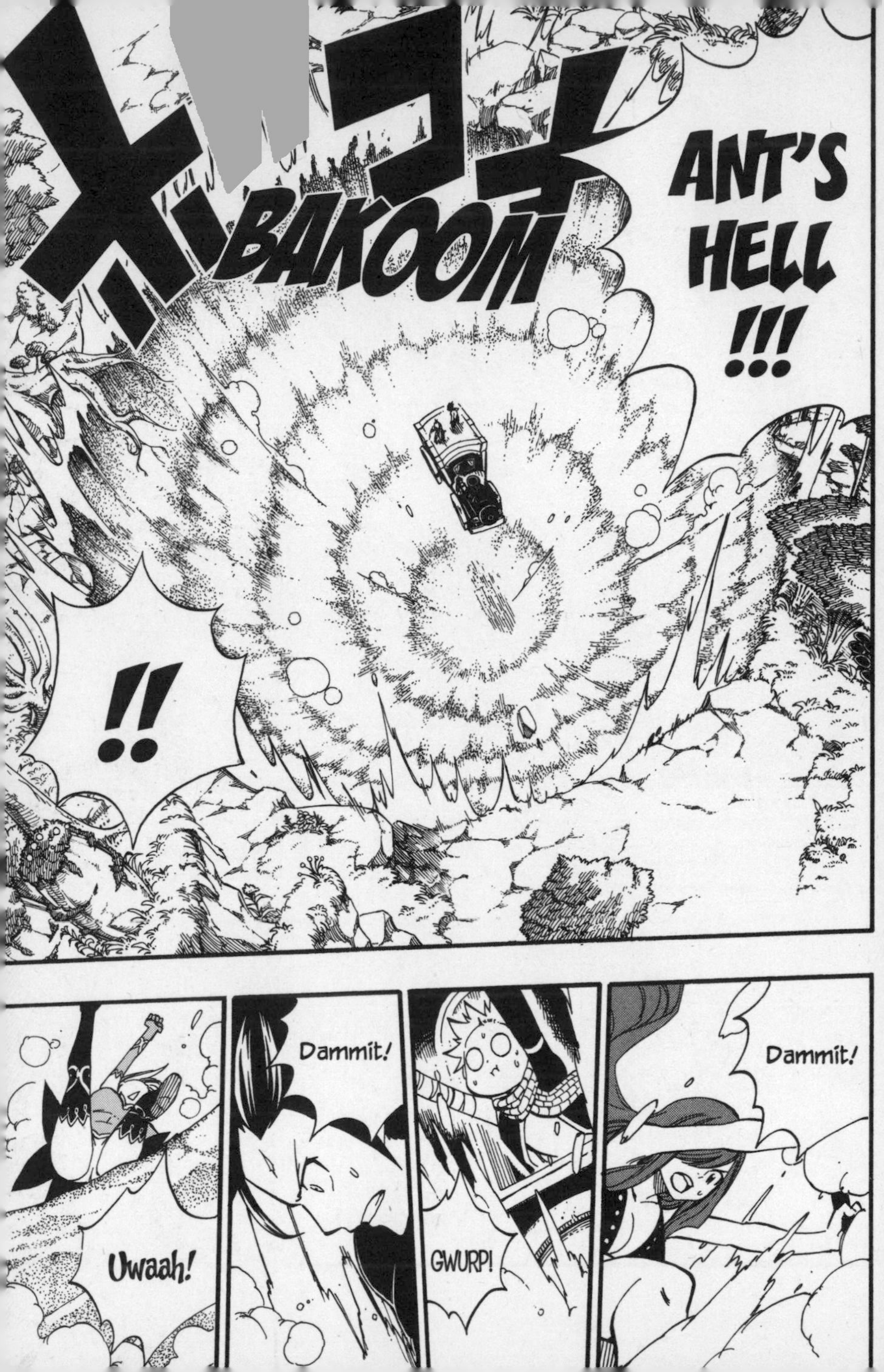
ANT'S HELL !!!
BAKOOM
!!
Dammit!
GWURP!
Dammit!
Uwaah!

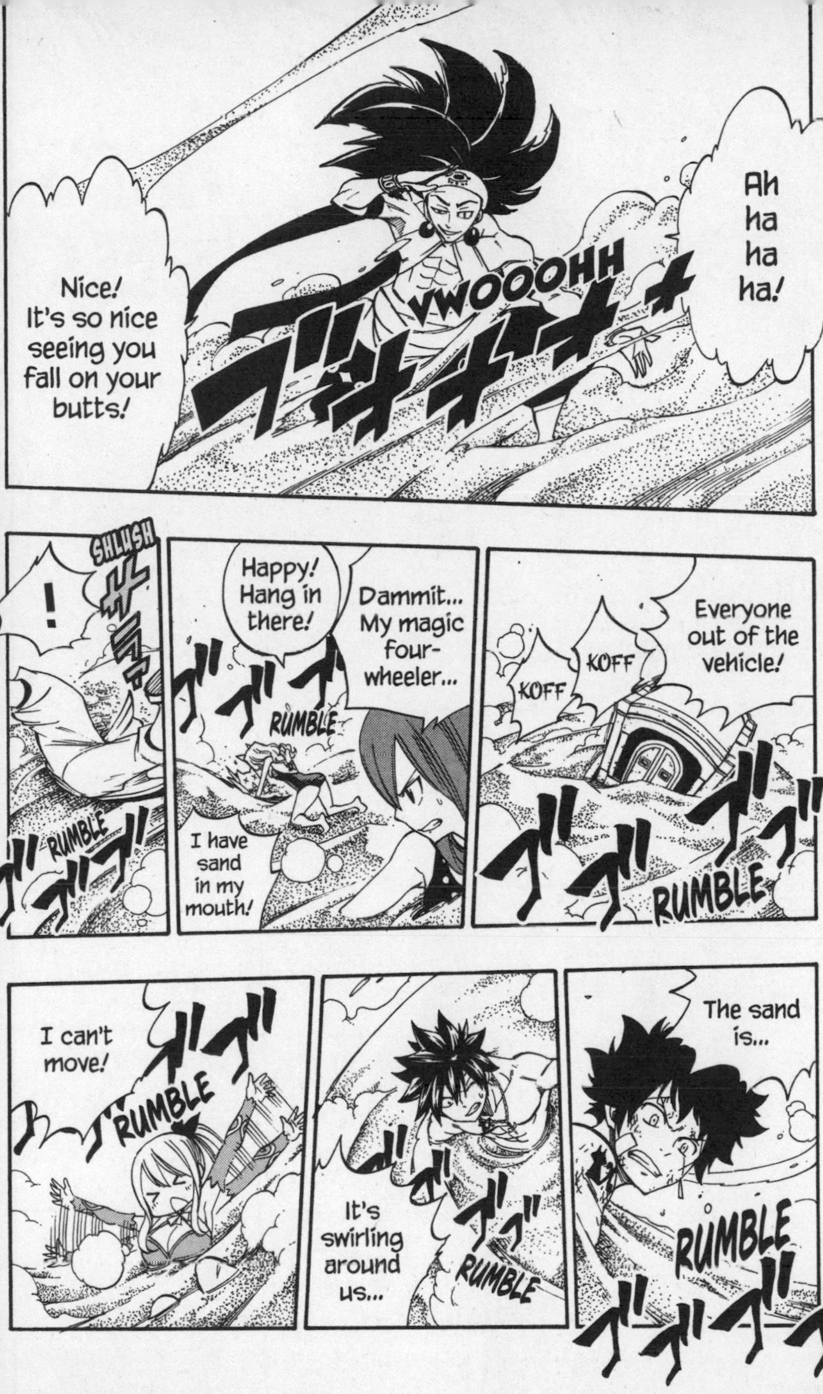
Ah ha ha ha!
VWOOOHH
Nice! It's so nice seeing you fall on your butts!
Everyone out of the vehicle!
KOFF
KOFF
RUMBLE
Dammit... My magic four-wheeler...
Happy! Hang in there!
RUMBLE
I have sand in my mouth!
SHLUSH
!
RUMBLE
The sand is...
RUMBLE
It's swirling around us...
RUMBLE
I can't move!
RUMBLE

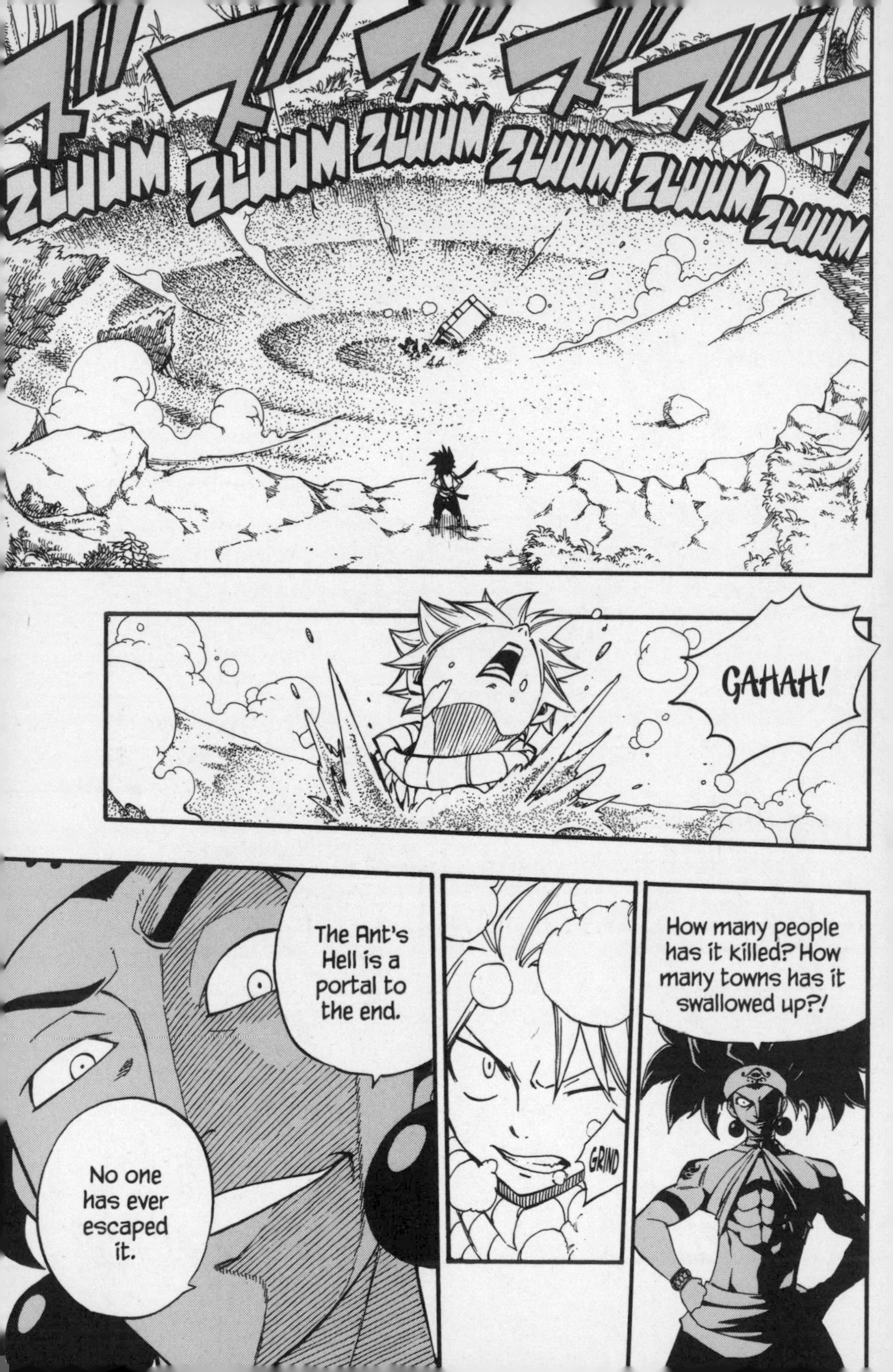
ZLUUM
ZLUUM
ZLUUM
ZLUUM
ZLUUM
ZLUUM
GAHAH!
How many people has it killed? How many towns has it swallowed up?!
GRIND
The Ant's Hell is a portal to the end.
No one has ever escaped it.

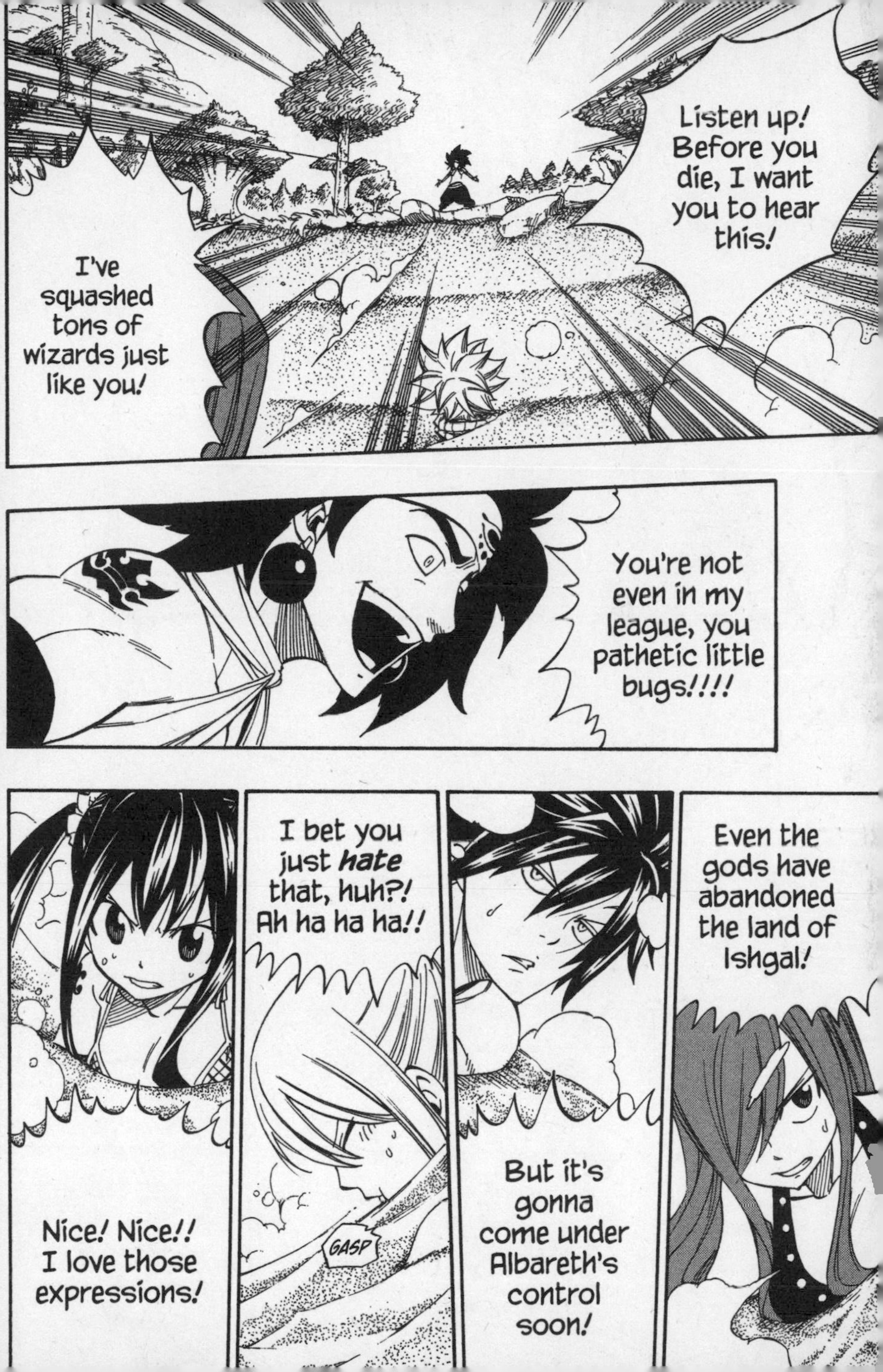
Listen up! Before you die, I want you to hear this!
I've squashed tons of wizards just like you!
You're not even in my league, you pathetic little bugs!!!!
Even the gods have abandoned the land of Ishgal!
But it's gonna come under Albareth's control soon!
I bet you just *hate* that, huh?! Ah ha ha ha!!
GASP
Nice! Nice!! I love those expressions!

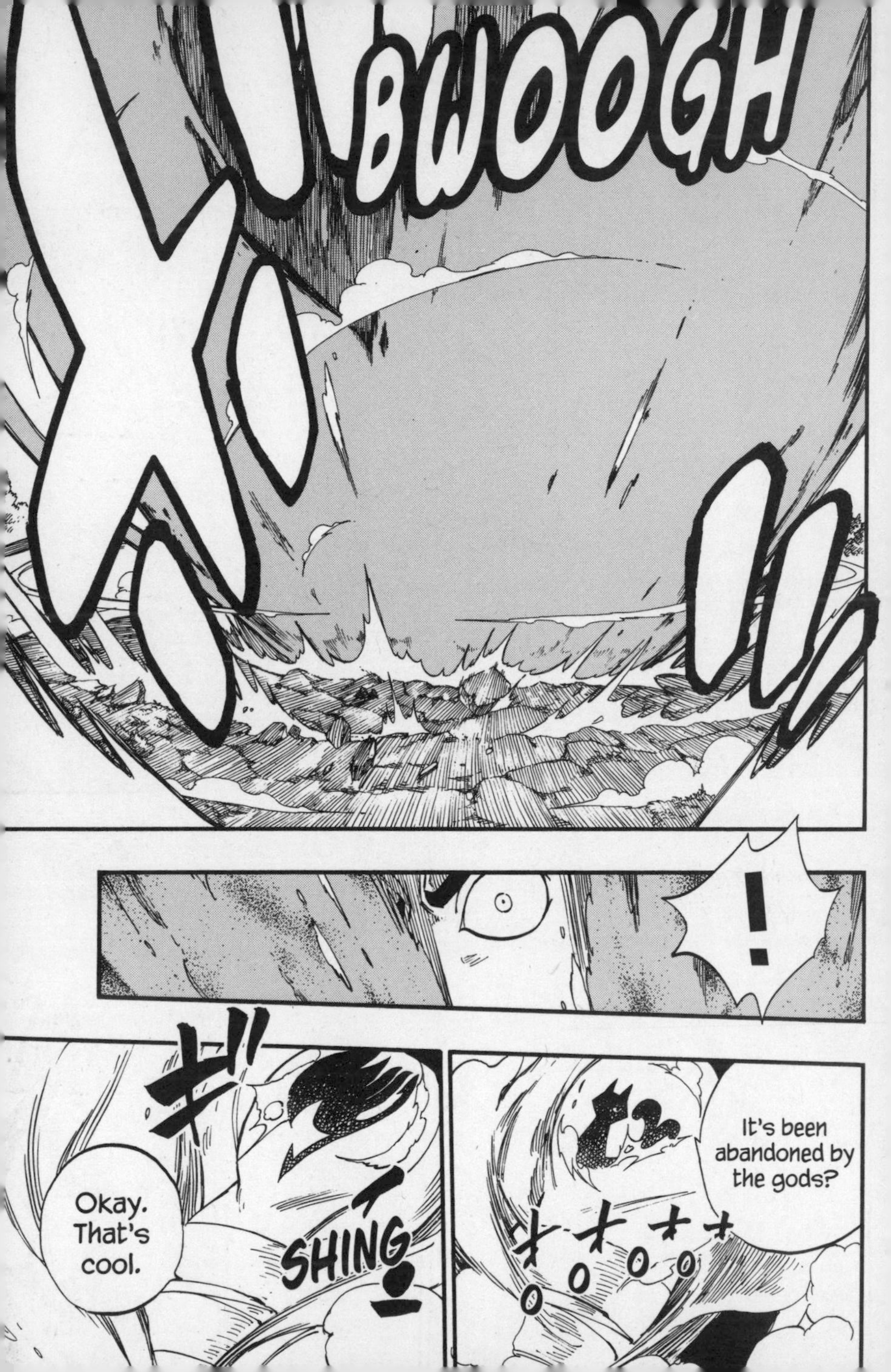
BWOOGH
!
It's been abandoned by the gods?
Okay. That's cool.
SHING

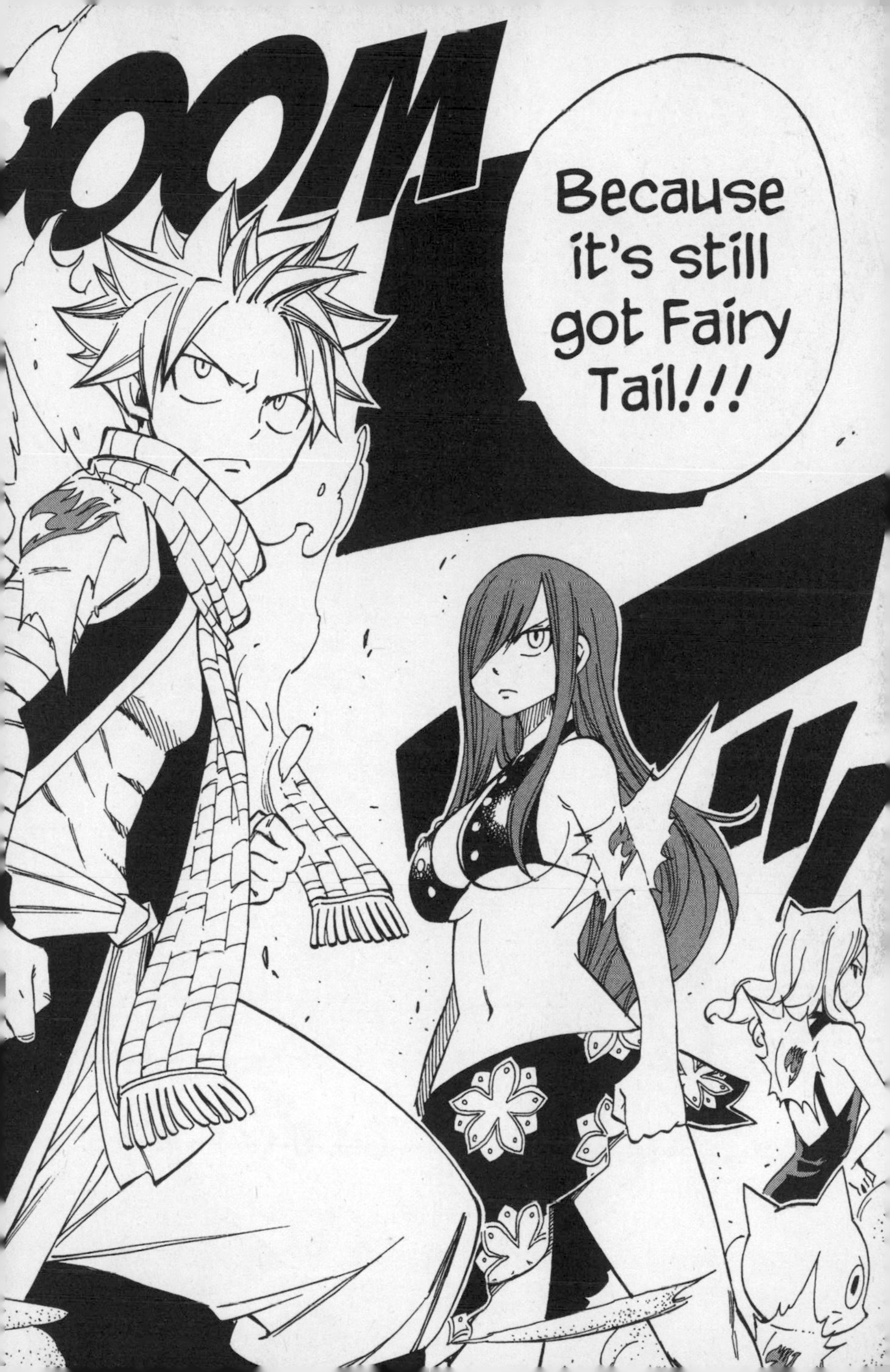
Because it's still got Fairy Tail!!!
OOM

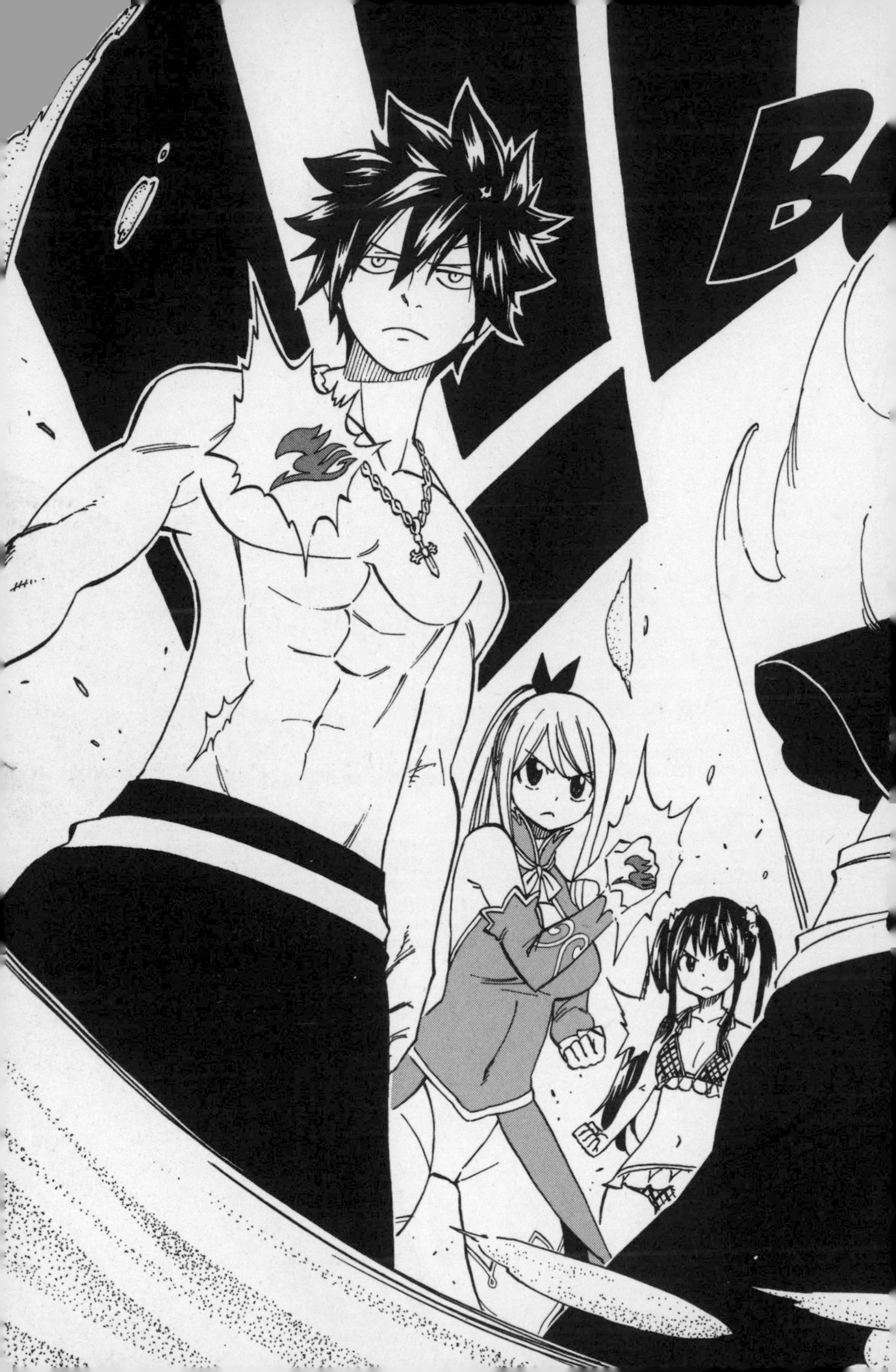

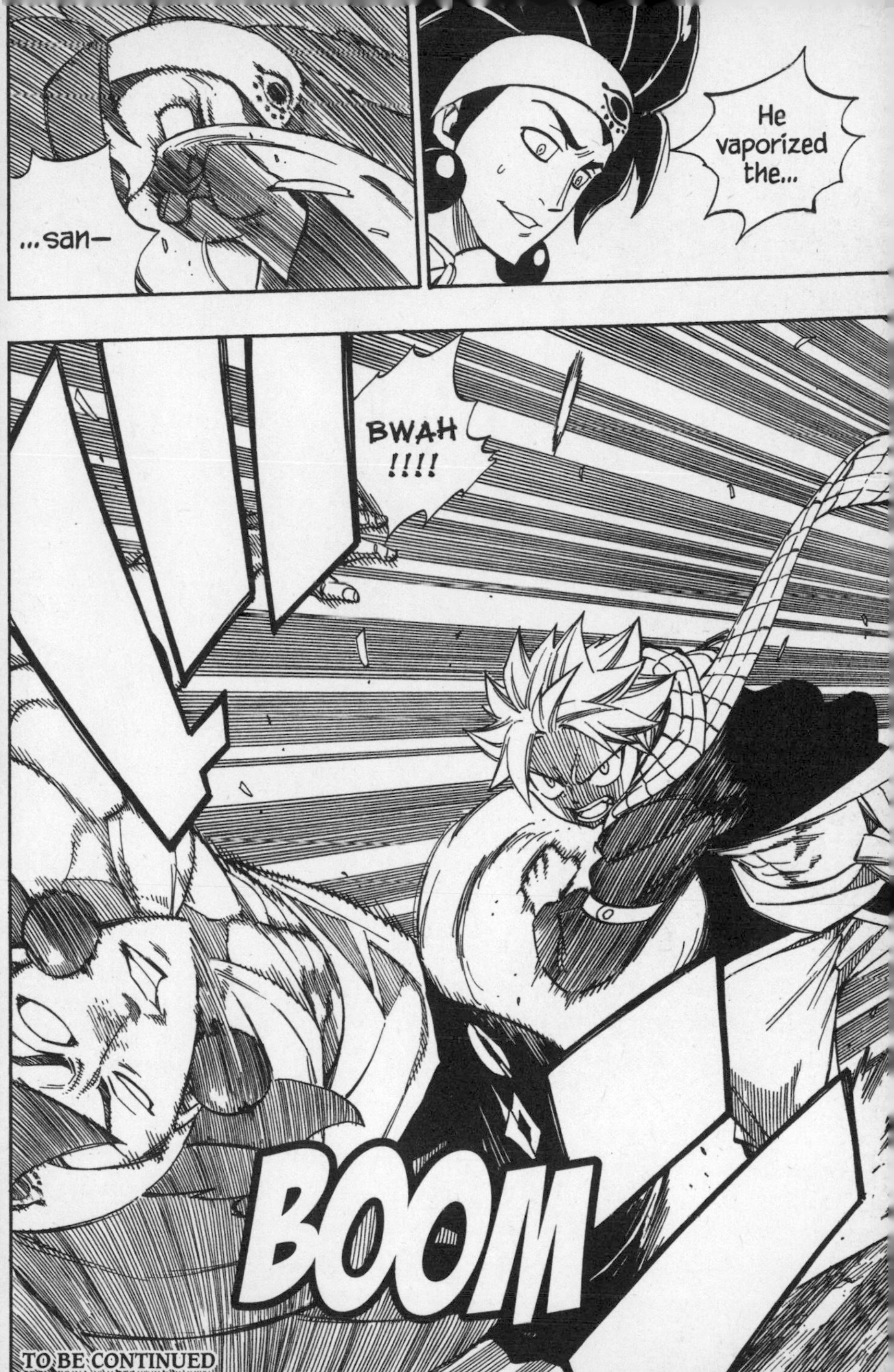
He vaporized the...
...san—
BWAH !!!!
BOOM
TO BE CONTINUED

あとがき
Afterword

Now we've broken into the Albareth Arc! This time, we're going to bring you battles with the toughest enemies we've ever seen. And maybe this will even lead to the final battle with Zeref! The enemy boss characters are also the 12 strongest characters in the history of this series!

And it's really tough to draw! Okay, we haven't seen everyone yet, but they're all so quirky! I figure one of the great pleasures of a battle manga is trying to guess who will take on who, right? And it'd make me really happy if you'd all start to imagine the possibilities!

Now, about the Spriggan 12—there was a fight over the number 12. My editor was of the opinion that five or six would do. And it's true, 12 is a lot of characters. It's hard to remember the names of all of them, and when each one has a battle, it makes you wonder just how long this arc will go on. But there's a bit of a secret reason for it, so we finally decided on leaving it at 12.

We still haven't decided on every plot twist that we'll be facing yet, but the battles are going to be on fire! So everyone, fasten your seat belts and prepare for a great ride!!

Continued from the left-hand page.

Mira: ...because at the time, Frosch's killer wasn't actually set in stone.

Lucy: Whoa! Truth bomb!

Mira: Of course, it had been given some thought, and Gray was among those under consideration.

Lucy: In other words, different people were also under consideration, huh?

Mira: Well, it felt like it was good timing to attribute it to Gray, but then some fans called us out on it.

Lucy: Still, it became a part of the story, so we gotta fix up those loose ends, right?

Mira: You're right... But I don't think this was all that inconsistent, except that maybe Gray didn't have much motivation to kill Frosch.

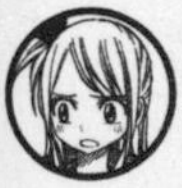
: In the future that future Rogue came from, Gray's body may have been under an evil influence, right?

Mira: Either way, I'm glad that future never came true.

So smart phones have finally appeared in the FT world, huh?

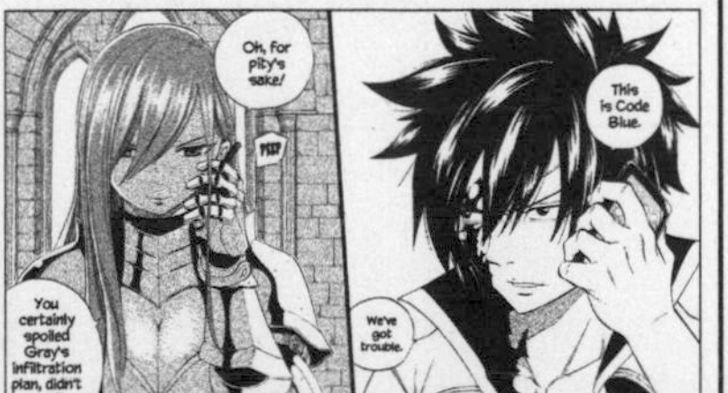
This is Code Blue.
We've got trouble.
Oh, for pity's sake!
You certainly spoiled Gray's infiltration plan, didn't you?

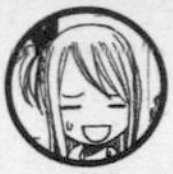
: To be more exact, it's a small-type communications lacrima.

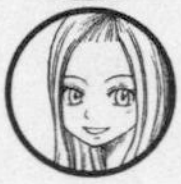
: Warren was working the whole year on it!

Lucy: And it's really convenient!

Mira: But it isn't like the cellphones where you guys live.

Lucy: First, it runs on magic power.

Mira: And the distance it can work on is pretty limited.

Lucy: Warren once said...

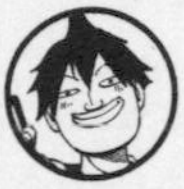
: *But I intend to make them so they can be used throughout Fiore...no, bigger! Throughout the whole continent!*

Lucy: And he was pretty worked up when he said it.

Mira: Well, it's certainly possible. But I hear he really made a lot of money off it so far.

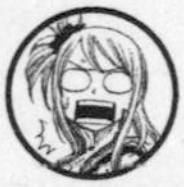
: What?!

Mira: Rumor has it, he's made enough for even his grandchildren to live in luxury!

Lucy: I can't believe he'd return to the guild after being so successful...

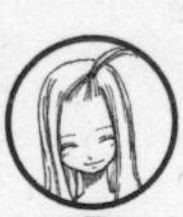
: Mmhmm! And despite it all, when he got your letter, he chose the guild over that.

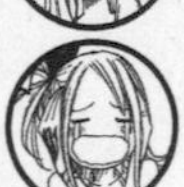
: Thank you, Warren! Thank you!

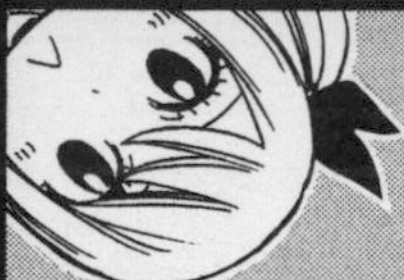

EMERGENCY REQUEST! EXPLAIN THE MYSTERIES OF F.T.!

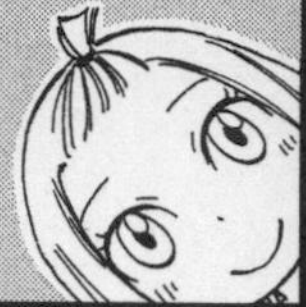

In a coffee shop in Magnolia...

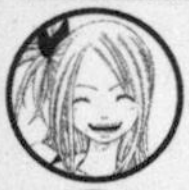

: Hi everybody! Long time no see!

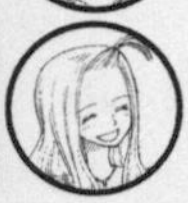

: Huh? You mean this column hasn't been canceled?

Lucy: No, we're fine. After all, this is a manga with a lot to complain about.

Mira: So, shall we get to the first question?

Was Minerva able to return to being human?

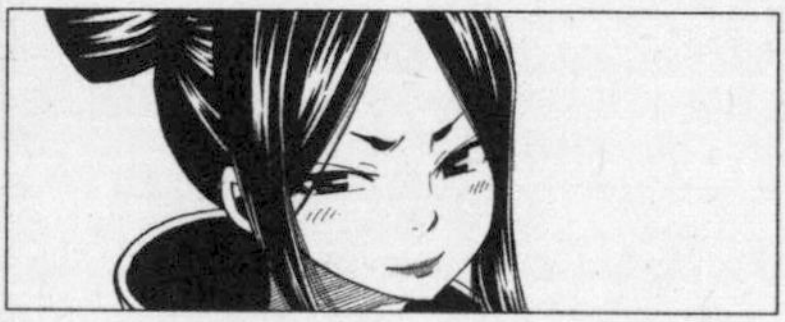

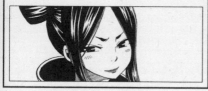

Lucy: You know, I was worried about that, too!

Mira: Well, after the battle, Porlyusica did everything she could to treat her and get her back to her original body, but...

Lucy: She *did* become a demon, didn't she?

Mira: But don't worry! You wouldn't know it just by looking at me, but I'm kind of a human-demon mix, too.

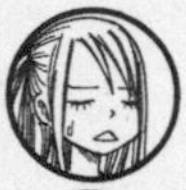

: You know, you say some really scary things in a very calm voice.

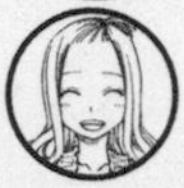

: And on to the next question!

The future Rogue said that it was Gray who killed Frosch... and he didn't. Which is good, but it brings up a new question: In the future that the future Rogue came from, why did Gray want to kill Frosch?

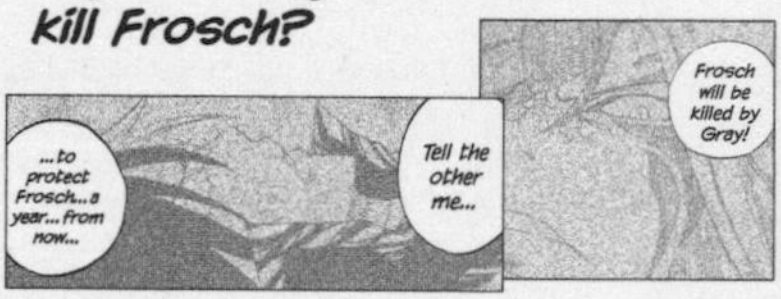
Frosch will be killed by Gray!
Tell the other me...
...to protect Frosch... a year... from now...

Lucy: ...

Mira: ...

Lucy: See! It's because the author does a lot on the fly that the situation becomes questionable.

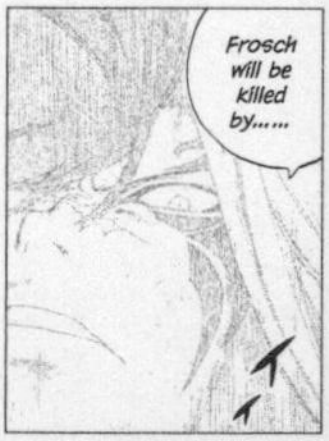
Frosch will be killed by......

Mira: I don't mean this as an excuse, but at the time, they had Rogue speaking vaguely on purpose...

Continued on the right-hand page.

TAIL d'ART

The Fairy Tail Guild is looking for illustrations! Please send in your art on a post card or at post-card size, and do it in black pen, okay? Those chosen to be published will get a signed mini poster! ♪ Make sure you write your real name and address on the back of your illustration!

Hiroshima Prefecture, Taichi Kobayashi

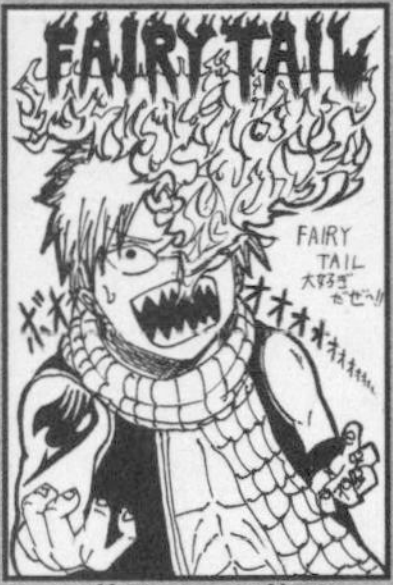
FAIRY TAIL
FAIRY TAIL

▲Ohh!! Thank you!! That love really comes through!!

Osaka, Yumika Asano

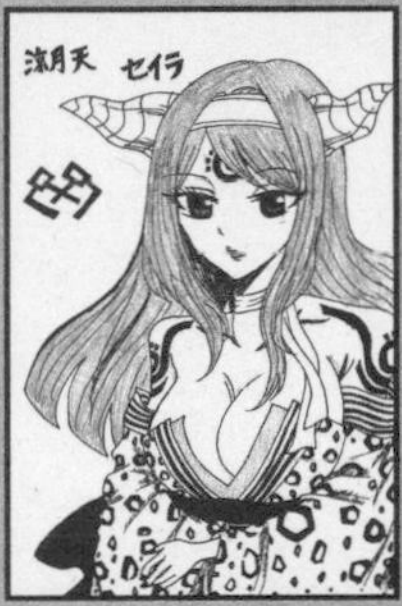
セイラ

▲Seira was both beautiful and scary during the Tartaros arc, huh? What impression did she leave on you all?

Saitama Prefecture, Saeri Nomoto

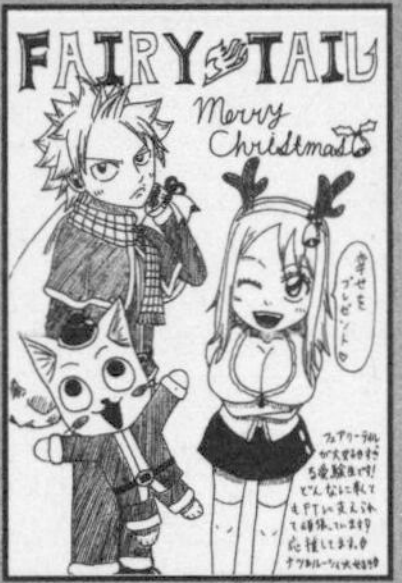
FAIRY TAIL
Merry Christmas

▲Christmas! And so cute! I think it's great that Lucy's the reindeer and not Happy!

Niigata Prefecture, Strawberry Daifuku

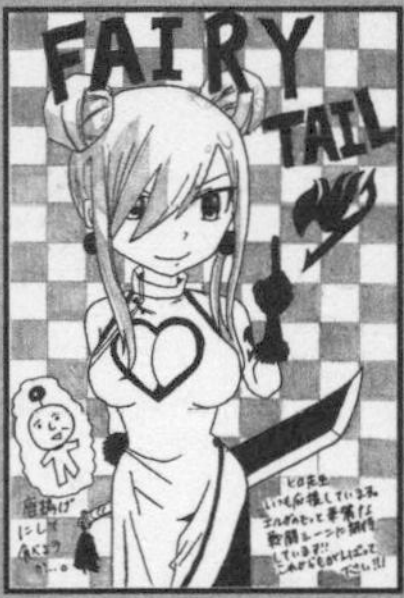
FAIRY TAIL

▲Ohh! An Erza postcard!! Erza looks really good in that get-up!

Hiroshima Prefecture, Sabu

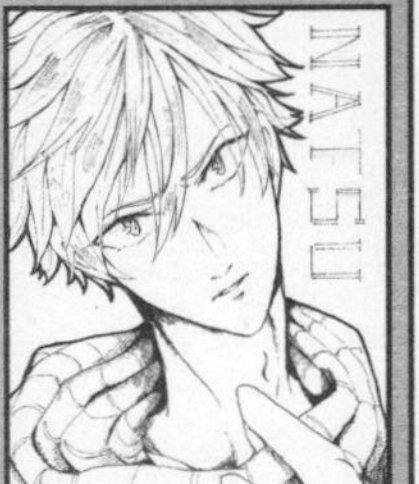
NATSU

▲An oddly adult-looking Natsu. This type is nice, too, every now and then, huh?

Tokyo, Haha

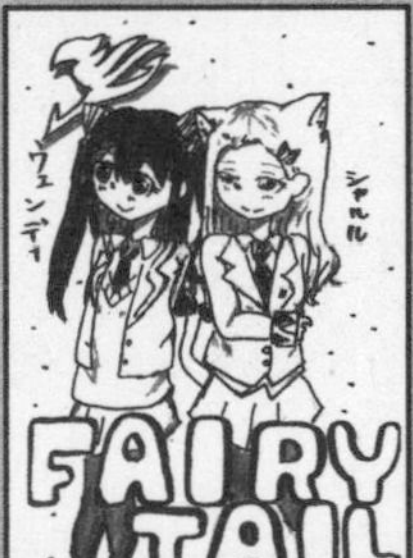
FAIRY TAIL

▲These two are always great friends. And I'm sure they'll play a big part really soon!

Tokyo, Be Alice

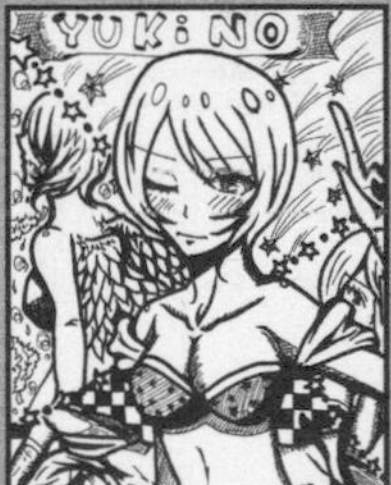
YUKiNO

▲I want her to show up again! I really like her character, too!

Send to Hiro Mashima, Kodansha Comics
451 Park Ave. South, 7th Floor New York, NY 10016

FAIRY GUILD

Saitama Prefecture, Gray

Everyone in their chibi form! I like this picture!

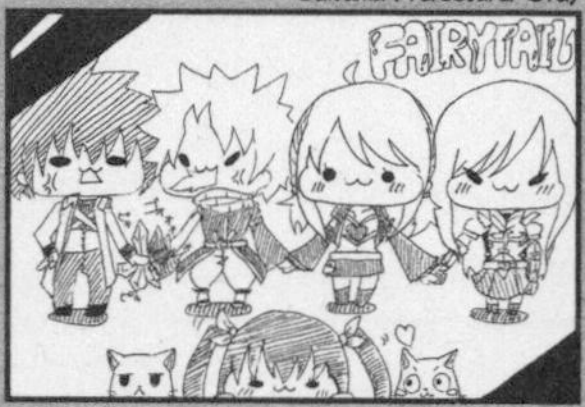
FAIRYTAIL

Chiba Prefecture, Yū Takayama

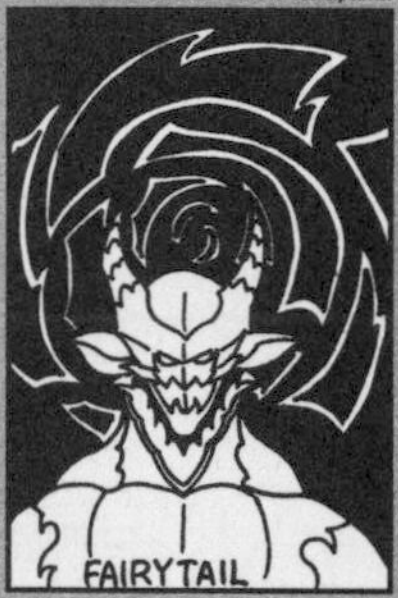
FAIRYTAIL

▲This is rare! A picture of Mard Geer in his Etherious form!

Saitama Prefecture, Ryū Shimono

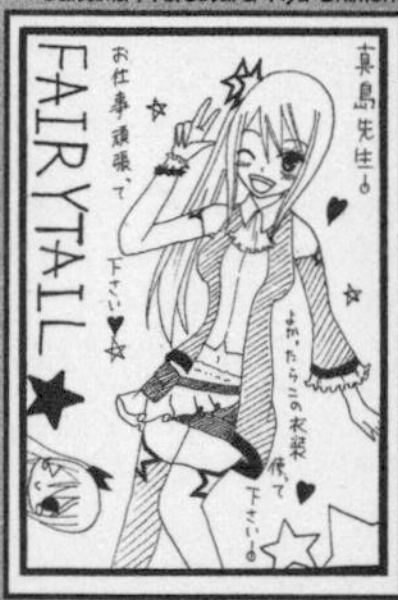
FAIRYTAIL
真島先生♪

▲The outfit's an original design! It's cute! Thanks!!

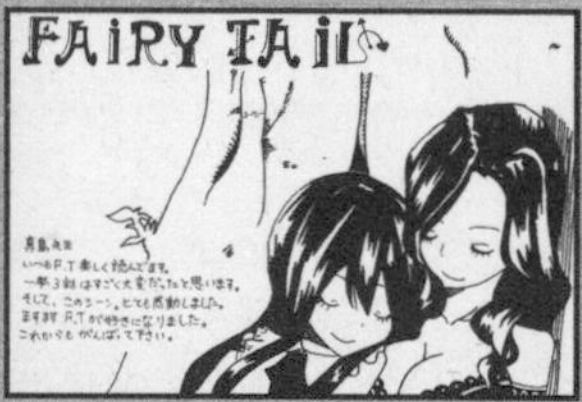
FAIRY TAIL

Saitama Prefecture, Sayaka Suzuki

They're going to include this scene in its entirety in a special DVD in Japan!

Kanagawa Prefecture, Takumi Kishi

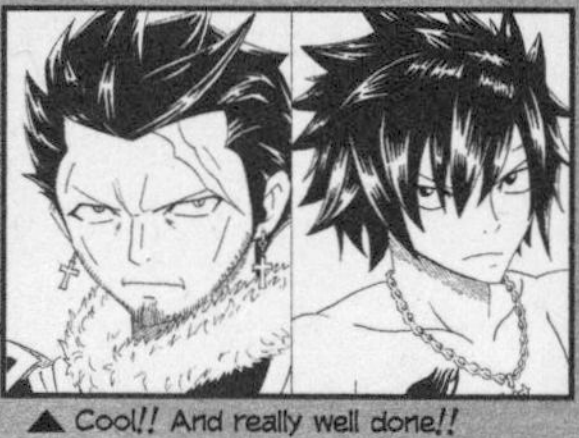

▲ Cool!! And really well done!! These two also came out great in the anime, too!

Ibaraki Prefecture, Hanae Shibata

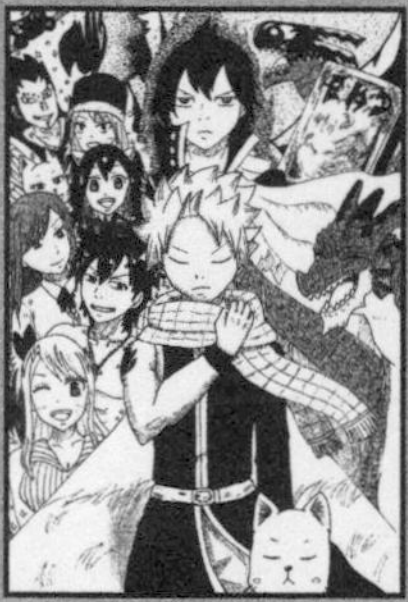

▲Look at all the characters!! Must have been a tough one to draw.

REJECTION CORNER

A beautiful Plue...or is it?! ▶

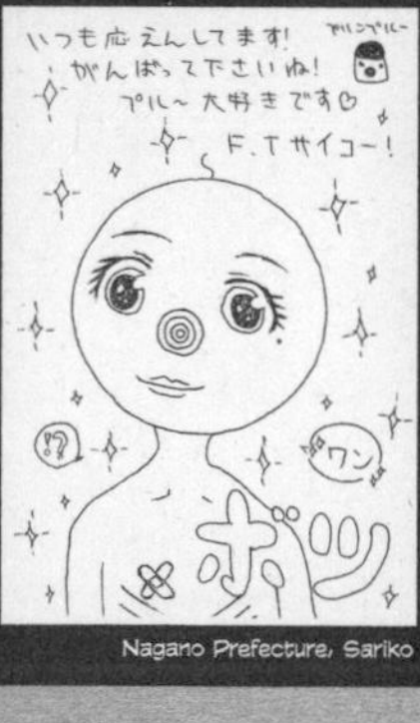
いつも応えんしてます!
がんばって下さいね!
プル~大好きです♡
F.Tサイコー!

Nagano Prefecture, Sariko

By sending in letters or postcards, you give us permission to give your name, address, postal code, and any other information you include to the author as is. Please keep that in mind.

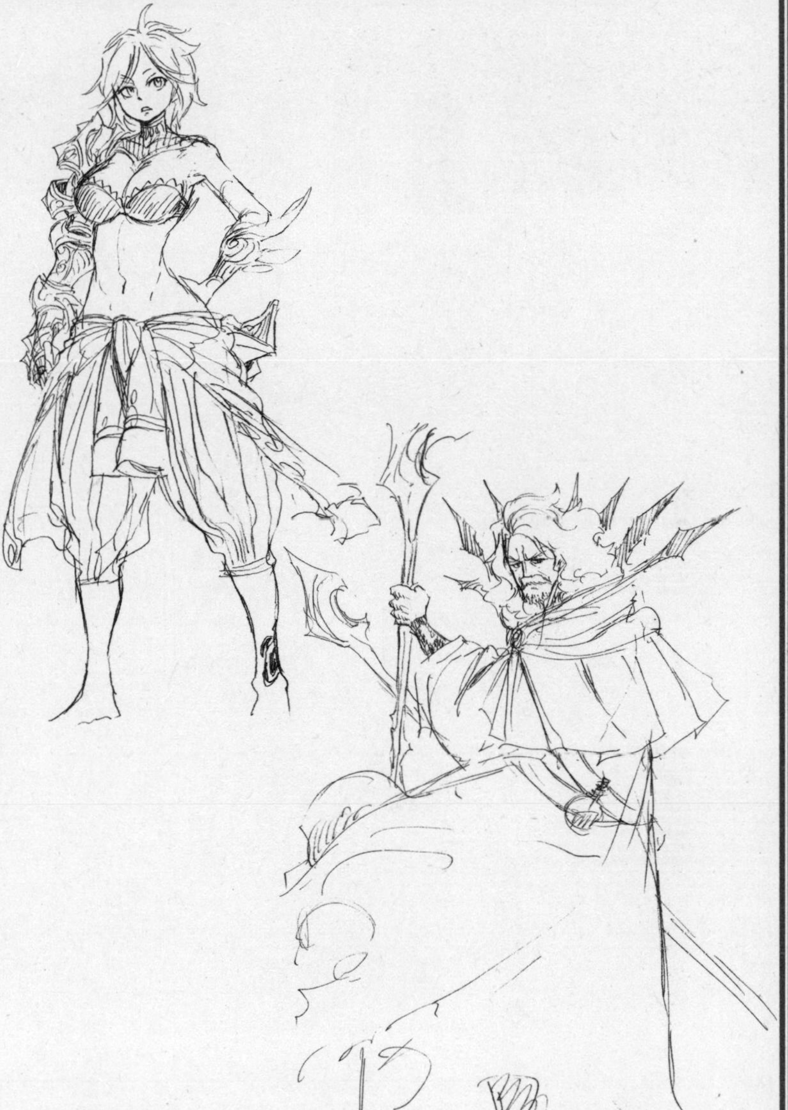

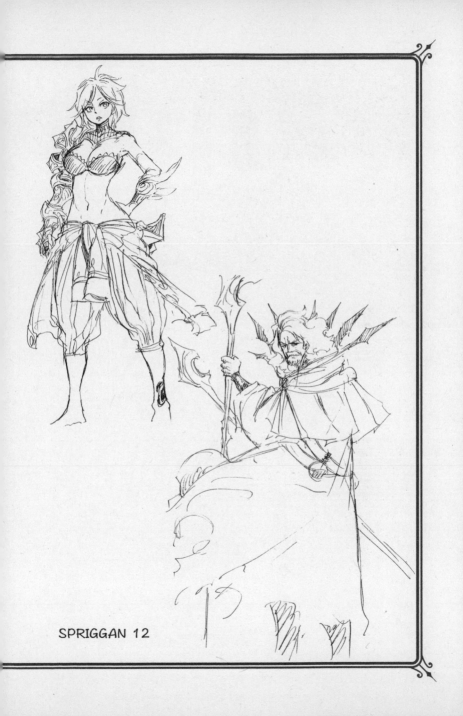

SPRIGGAN 12

FAIRY TAIL
フェアリーテイル

52

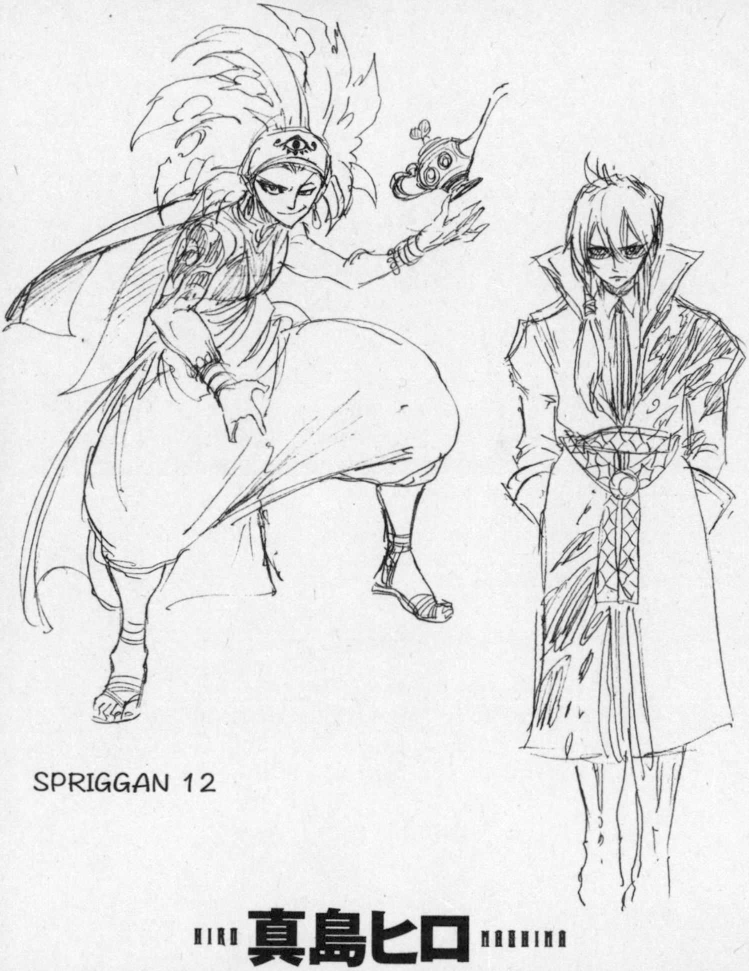

SPRIGGAN 12

HIRO 真島ヒロ MASHIMA

FROM HIRO MASHIMA

I went to a signing in Okinawa. It was in September, but it was still so hot!

There were a lot of people who came, and it was great fun! Not to mention the fact that they served really delicious food.

The problem was that I was so busy that I was stuck in the hotel coming up with storyboards during my long-awaited trip!

Original Jacket Design: Hisao Ogawa

Translation Notes:

Japanese is a tricky language for most Westerners, and translation is often more art than science. For your edification and reading pleasure, here are notes on some of the places where we could have gone in a different direction with our translation of the work, or where a Japanese cultural reference is used.

Page 41, Spriggan

The Emperor of the Albareth Empire is known as Emperor Spriggan. A spriggan is a mythical creature out of fairy lore from Cornwall in England, or, more particularly, the community of West Penwith. Spriggans are supposed to be grotesquely ugly creatures that guard treasures in old ruins and burial mounds. Of course, the emperor might have a good reason for calling himself that.

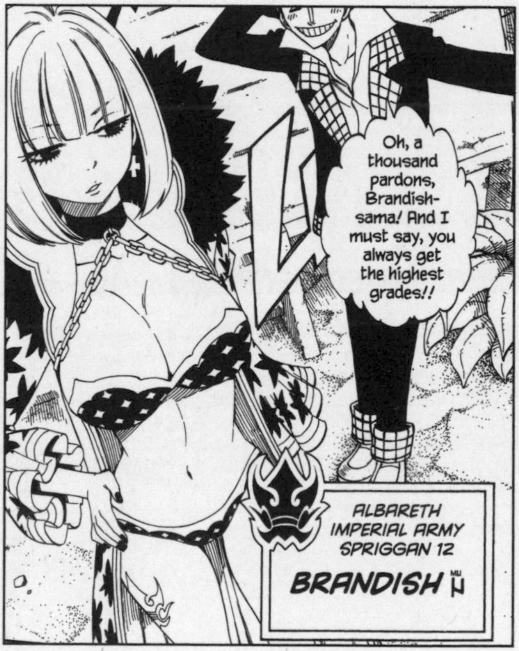
Oh, a thousand pardons, Brandish-sama! And I must say, you always get the highest grades!!
ALBARETH IMPERIAL ARMY SPRIGGAN 12
BRANDISH μ

Page 82, "μ"

The Greek letter "μ" is pronounced "myu" in Japanese. It has many different meanings, any of which may (or may not) have something to do with Brandish's character. For example, in Greek numerals, it represents the number 40, it was drawn from the Egyptian hieroglyph for water, and it is the symbol for micrometer, which is a very tiny unit of length.

Page 136, Ajeel Raml

During the translation of the weekly chapters for online publication, the translator originally spelled Ajeel's name as Ajeel Rommul, noting the similarity between Ajeel Rommul, the Desert King and the WWII German general, Erwin Rommel, the Desert Fox. However, as Ajeel started performing magic in later chapters, and the names of his attacks included Arabic words, they realized that his name was, in fact, Raml, the Arabic word for "sand." We apologize for any confusion.

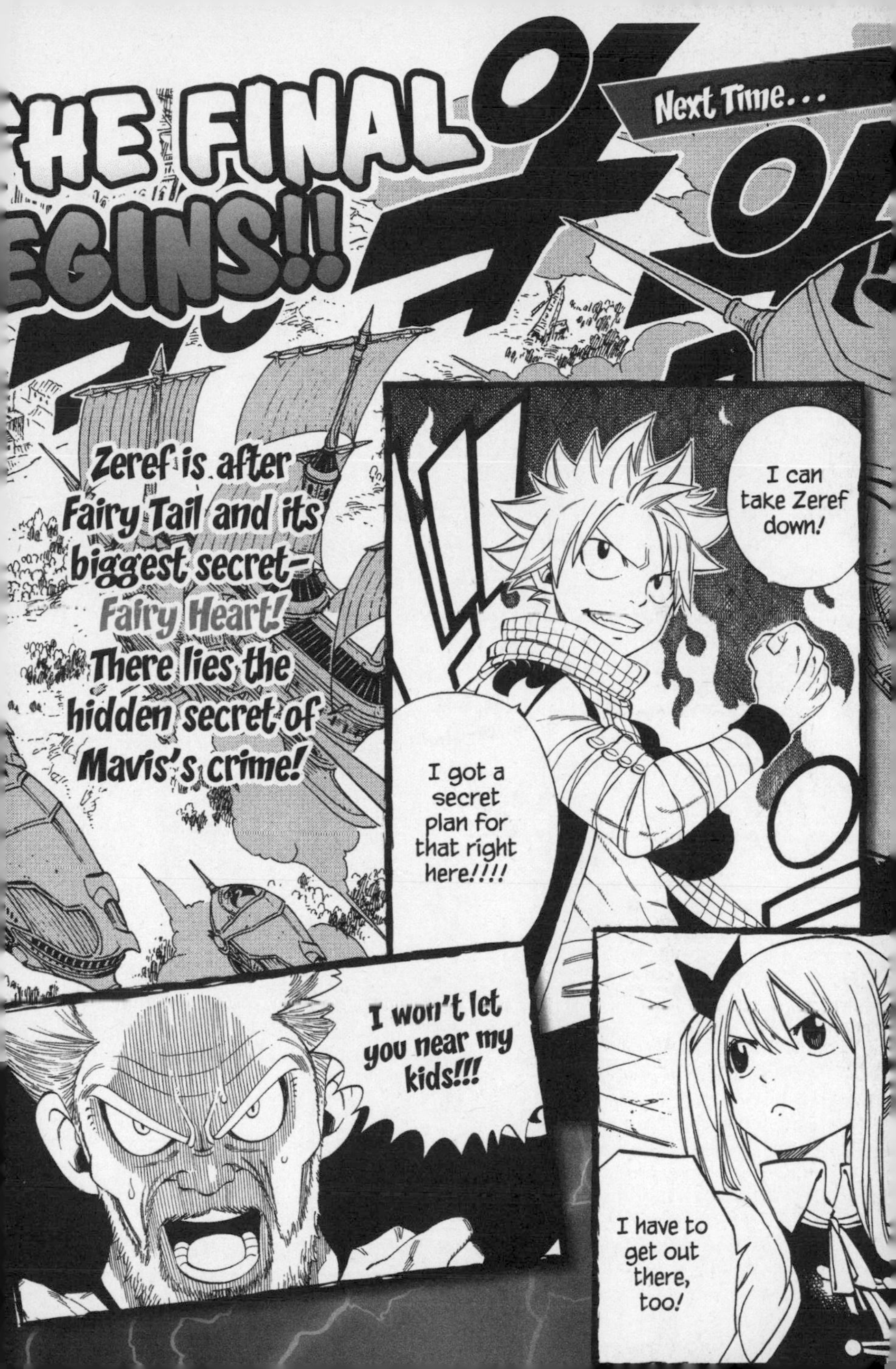
Next Time...
HE FINAL
EGINS!!
I can take Zeref down!
I got a secret plan for that right here!!!!
Zeref is after Fairy Tail and its biggest secret–Fairy Heart! There lies the hidden secret of Mavis's crime!
I have to get out there, too!
I won't let you near my kids!!!

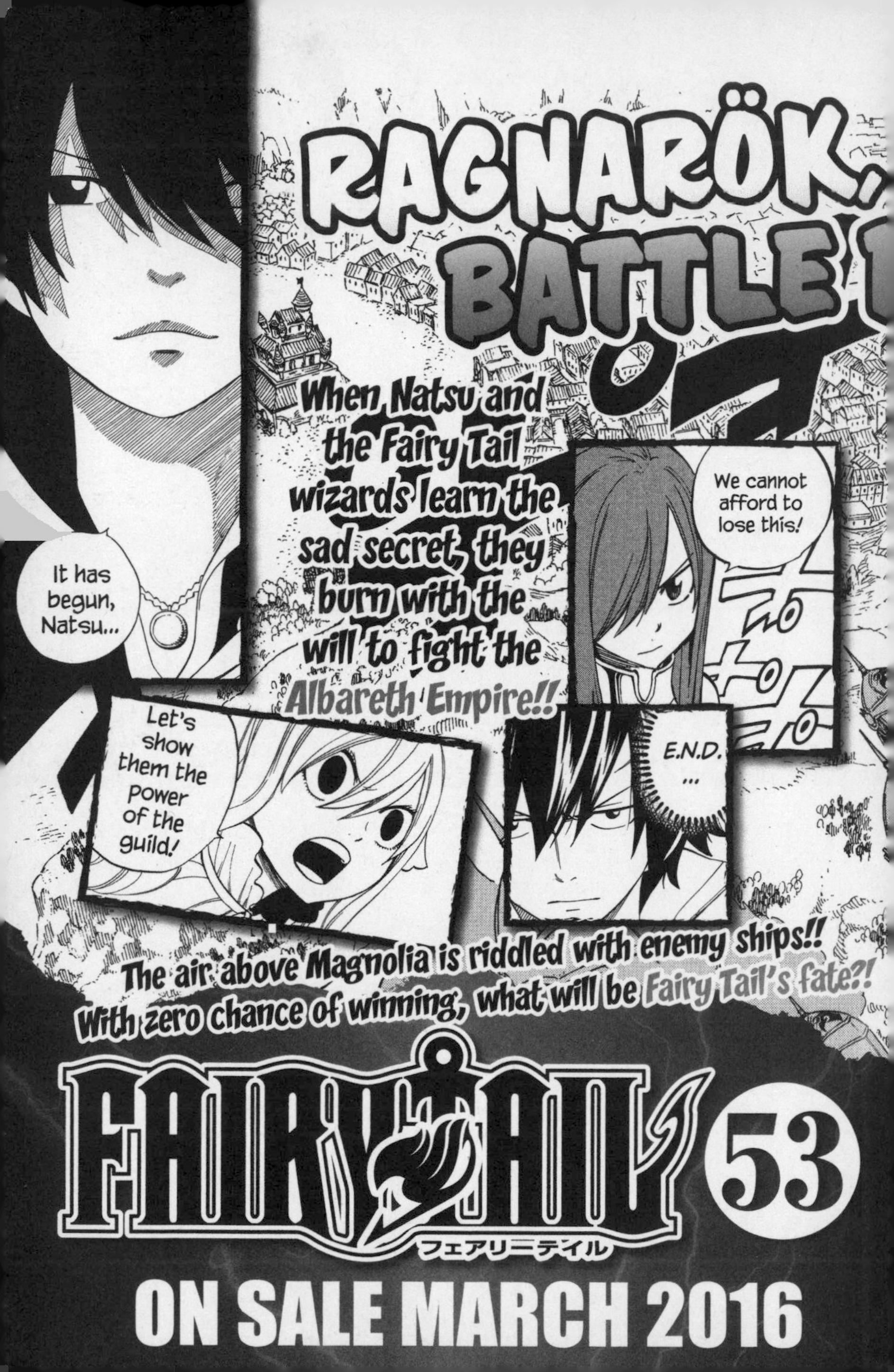
RAGNARÖK, BATTLE 1
When Natsu and the Fairy Tail wizards learn the sad secret, they burn with the will to fight the Albareth Empire!!
We cannot afford to lose this!
It has begun, Natsu...
E.N.D. ...
Let's show them the power of the guild!
The air above Magnolia is riddled with enemy ships!!
With zero chance of winning, what will be Fairy Tail's fate?!
FAIRY TAIL 53
フェアリーテイル
ON SALE MARCH 2016

FINALLY, A LOWER-COST OMNIBUS EDITION OF FAIRY TAIL! CONTAINS VOLUMES 1-5. ONLY $39.99!

-NEARLY 1,000 PAGES!
-EXTRA LARGE 7"x10.5" TRIM SIZE!
-HIGH-QUALITY PAPER!

Fairy Tail takes place in a world filled with magic. 17-year-old Lucy is a wizard-in-training who wants to join a magic guild so that she can become a full-fledged wizard. She dreams of joining the most famous guild, known as Fairy Tail. One day she meets Natsu, a boy raised by a dragon which vanished when he was young. Natsu has devoted his life to finding his dragon father. When Natsu helps Lucy out of a tricky situation, she discovers that he is a member of Fairy Tail, and our heroes' adventure together begins.

FAIRY TAIL

MASTER'S EDITION

FAIRYTAIL
BLUE MISTRAL

Wendy's Very Own Fairy Tail!

The new adventures of everyone's favorite Sky Dragon Slayer, Wendy Marvell, and her faithful friend Carla!

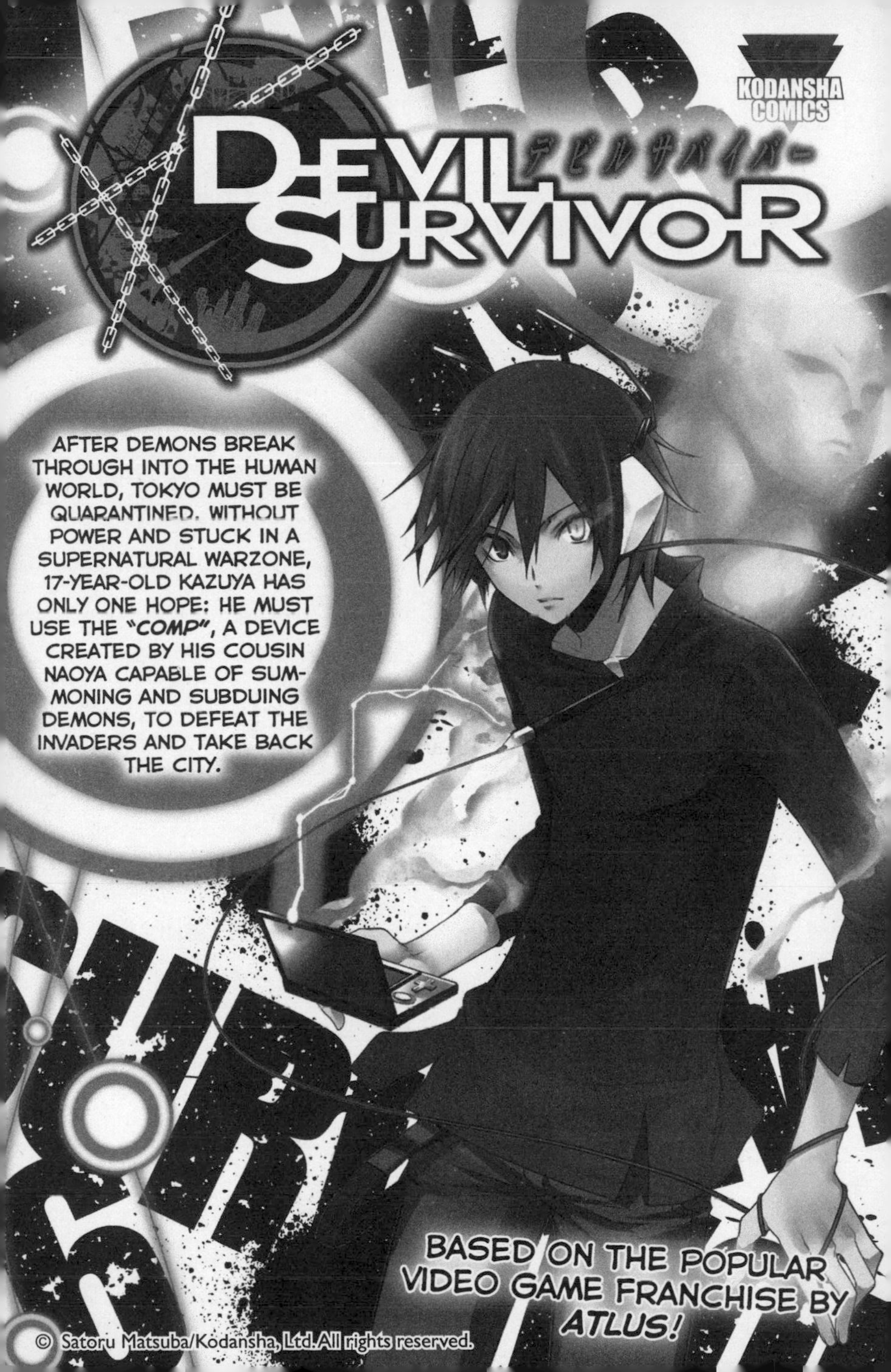
KODANSHA COMICS
DEVIL SURVIVOR
デビルサバイバー
AFTER DEMONS BREAK THROUGH INTO THE HUMAN WORLD, TOKYO MUST BE QUARANTINED. WITHOUT POWER AND STUCK IN A SUPERNATURAL WARZONE, 17-YEAR-OLD KAZUYA HAS ONLY ONE HOPE: HE MUST USE THE "COMP", A DEVICE CREATED BY HIS COUSIN NAOYA CAPABLE OF SUMMONING AND SUBDUING DEMONS, TO DEFEAT THE INVADERS AND TAKE BACK THE CITY.
BASED ON THE POPULAR VIDEO GAME FRANCHISE BY ATLUS!
© Satoru Matsuba/Kodansha, Ltd. All rights reserved.

Fairy Tail volume 52 is a work of fiction. Names, characters, places, and incidents are the products of the author's imagination or are used fictitiously. Any resemblance to actual events, locales, or persons, living or dead, is entirely coincidental.

A Kodansha Comics Trade Paperback Original.

Published in the United States by Kodansha Comics, an imprint of Kodansha USA Publishing, LLC, New York.

Publication rights for this English edition arranged through Kodansha Ltd., Tokyo.

First published in Japan in 2015 by Kodansha Ltd., Tokyo
ISBN 978-1-63236-115-8

Printed in the United States of America.

www.kodanshacomics.com

9 8 7 6 5 4 3 2

Translation: William Flanagan
Lettering: AndWorld Design
Editing: Haruko Hashimoto
Kodansha Comics edition cover design by Phil Balsman

TOMARE!

止まれ

[STOP!]

You're going the wrong way!

Manga is a completely different type of reading experience.

To start at the *beginning*, go to the *end!*

That's right! Authentic manga is read the traditional Japanese way—from right to left, exactly the *opposite* of how American books are read. It's easy to follow: Just go to the other end of the book and read each page—and each panel—from right side to left side, starting at the top right. Now you're experiencing manga as it was meant to be!